The Age of Firepower

The Age of Firepower

Military Revolution 1600–1650 and Beyond

John Pike

Pen & Sword
MILITARY

First published in Great Britain in 2025 by
Pen & Sword Military
An imprint of Pen & Sword Books Limited
Yorkshire – Philadelphia

ISBN 978 1 39908 070 5

A CIP catalogue record for this book is
available from the British Library.

Typeset by Mac Style
Printed in the UK by CPI Group (UK) Ltd, Croydon, CR0 4YY.

The Publisher's authorised representative in the EU for product safety is Authorised Rep Compliance Ltd., Ground Floor, 71 Lower Baggot Street, Dublin D02 P593, Ireland.
www.arccompliance.com

For a complete list of Pen & Sword titles please contact

PEN & SWORD BOOKS LIMITED
47 Church Street, Barnsley, South Yorkshire, S70 2AS, England
E-mail: enquiries@pen-and-sword.co.uk
Website: www.pen-and-sword.co.uk
or
PEN AND SWORD BOOKS
1950 Lawrence Road, Havertown, PA 19083, USA
E-mail: uspen-and-sword@casematepublishers.com
Website: www.penandswordbooks.com

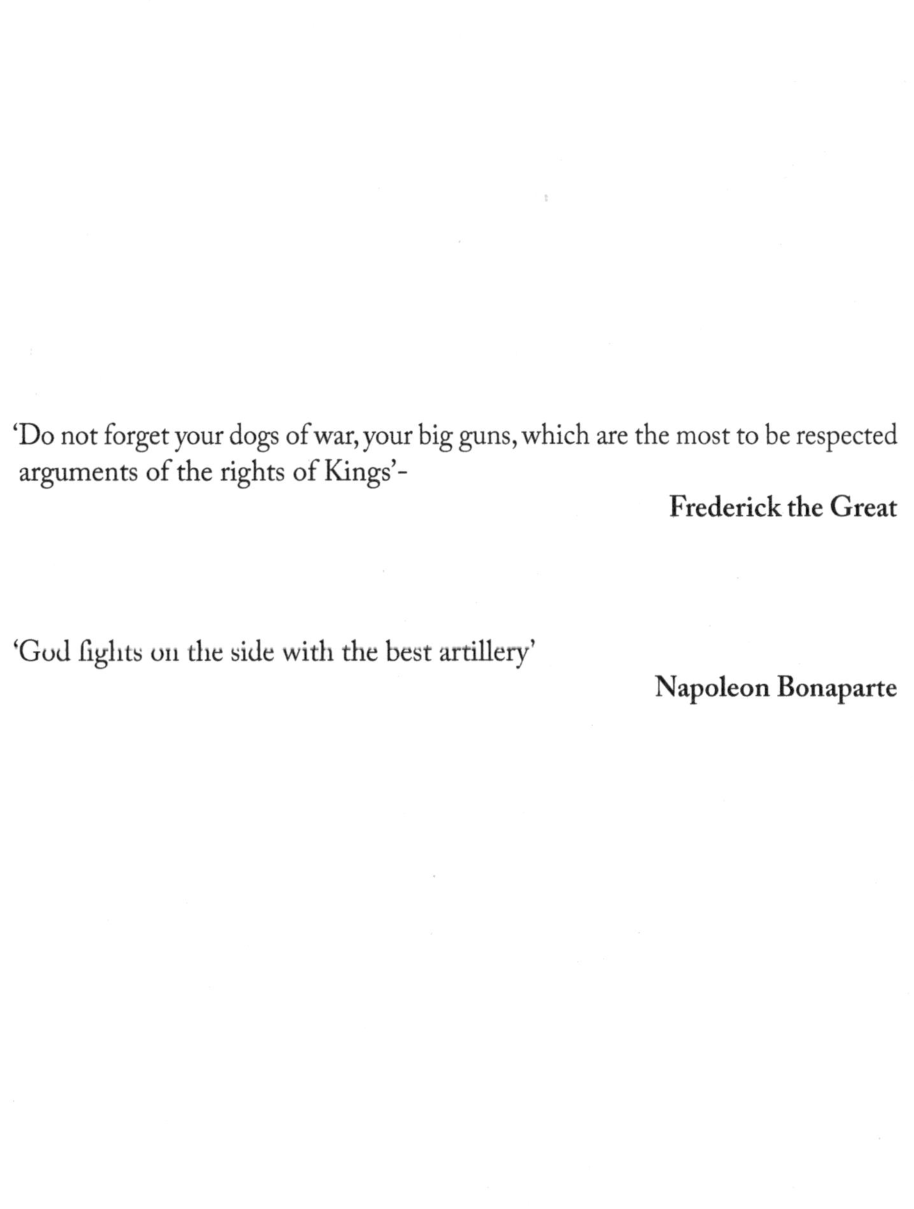

'Do not forget your dogs of war, your big guns, which are the most to be respected arguments of the rights of Kings'-

Frederick the Great

'God fights on the side with the best artillery'

Napoleon Bonaparte

Contents

Introduction

Firepower, its development and method of deployment were the keynotes of change in seventeenth-century warfare. Modern fortress defence had been introduced in the mid-sixteenth century and were to be refined thereafter, but in essence, Vauban in the second half of the seventeenth-century only furthered ideas that were already well established by the *trace Italienne* tradition developed in sixteenth-century renaissance Italy. Great lumbering cannon whose development and use were originally focused on the breaking down of fortress defence would become a truly effective mobile addition to battlefield firepower so much so that in some battles of the Thirty Years War more than half of casualties were due artillery fire.

Delivering firepower in an organized and disciplined manner became the purpose of modern state organization. The issue was well understood by some thinkers and practitioners; Maurice of Nassau, stadtholder of the Dutch Republic, with his experiments in smaller formations and higher musket to pike ratios was an early convert to the new principles. He was strongly influenced by Roman miliary thinking, the study of which was becoming a fad amongst the growing breed of military writers that sprang up in the wake of the printing and publishing revolution. Research done by military historian John Lynn reveals that 180 significant military texts were published in Europe 1599–1650. At Nieuwpoort July 1600, Maurice's Anglo-Dutch infantry using smaller 500-man units, defeated the tercio blocks of 2500 Spanish or Walloon troops. In a confused battle amongst the steep and undulating sand dunes, the Spanish infantry was wiped out as they fled across the marshes. It seems that better firepower drill from Maurice's more manoeuvrable units in the difficult terrain was a key factor in the victory, although because of the special topographical circumstances it was still not clear that the age of the tercio was over. Another important factor was Dutch artillery, positioned on top of dunes, using cannister against the condensed ranks of the tercios blocks. Maurice's well-timed use of reserves was a further factor. A few months later 21 October 1600 the Tokugawa's eastern army in the era defining battle of Sekigahara (Japan), fought against the western army, where the matchlock musket rather than the Samurai sword became the primary weapon of battle. Writing about his experience of the battle Ota Gyuichi recounted, 'Ally and foe pushed against each other. The musket fire and the shouts echoed from the heavens and shook the earth. The black smoke rose, making the day as night.'

It took Gustavus to translate and execute Maurice's ideas more widely because Maurice only fought two major battles, Nieuwpoort 1600 and Turnhout 1604. The latter was mainly a cavalry battle. However, Maurice depreciated his victory because it was against his strategy to make a risky advance into the Spanish Flanders beyond his defence lines. Maurice correctly assessed the strategic situation of his small country; if they lost a battle and their field army, they stood to lose their country. Mauritz lectured some over enthusiastic French cavaliers, 'You have gained a Battell. But let mee tell you herewithall that the state hath not gotten so much as a quart d'escu by it; and had wee lost the day, wee had lost all by it: Even all that myself and my ancestors have been these three score years a getting and preserving. And therefore Messirs, trouble me no more hereafter, with talking to mee of Battels.'[1] For the remaining forty-four years of the Spanish-Dutch war there was only one small field engagement.

Underlying this bitter comment was anger at being forced to make this risky advance beyond Dutch defence lines by the estates general. The estates of the Dutch Republic were heavily influenced by Oldenbarnevelt the Grand Pensionary; it was the beginning of the vicious feud that would arise between the two men. It ended with a coup d'etat and Johan van Oldenbarnevelt's beheading in 1619. As stadtholder responsibility for war fell on Maurice. Aversion to battle in the open field had a deep strategic underpinning from Maurice's analysis which carried through Dutch history. Fighting henceforth would be done by using firepower from behind strong defences.

Nikolaus Gabelmann: in his memorandum addressed to Emperor Matthias he wrote; 'considering shot troops, I do not think much of them as it is no great matter to fire a gun, and any peasant can do it these days. But keeping discipline and to wield the gun in such a way that he can shoot ten, while the other who attacks him fiercely fires only one, this I say is the prime art of war.'[2] He posed the question, but how does a polity get from state A to State B? from a feudal peasant society to modern state where a peasant is regimented into an effective force. The major acceleration in the use of firepower, and change to warfare, the military revolution, and its associated developments in state modernisation, occurred in the first half of the seventeenth century. It is not that firepower is the only factor in military success, however, inferiority in firepower makes the chances of victory much smaller. How much smaller depends on a complex matrix of factors, numbers, economic strength, logistics/state organization, capability of commanders, geography, experience/training, and elusive factors such as morale. There is also luck. That firepower and its delivery is the crucial factor was shown in the Azerbaijan-Armenian War 2021, when Armenia who had been winning the military contest for thirty years was defeated by drone weapons within a few days without any other factors playing a role.

By the eighteenth century the primacy of firepower was already well established. However, it was in the first half of the seventeenth-century notably under the impact of the Thirty Years War that, firepower became the dominant factor in battle, the era when military and states underwent revolutionary changes. There was no single event which brought on the change, but the battle of Breitenfeld 1631 became a marker in the history of firepower. Action is described by veteran Colonel Muschamp, 'First, giving fire unto three little field pieces that I had before me, I suffered not my muskettiers to give their volleyes till I came within pistol shot of the enemy, at which time I gave order to the first three ranks to discharge at once (their matchlock muskets), and after then the other three: which doine we fell pell mell into their rankes, knocking them downe with the stocke of the musket and our swords.'[3] Volley fire had come of age.

The fact that a smaller [after the Saxons had skedaddled in the first twenty minutes] and outflanked army could destroy the most powerful army in Europe in the open field was a most remarked on and influential event. After the battle Captain Monro, a closely engaged participant, opined on the main reason for the Swedish victory at Breitenfeld, '…next unto God, a second helpe unto this glorious victory, was the great execution made by his majesties cannon.'[4] [emphasis added] The Imperialist armies taking note of the disaster that had befallen them rapidly changed their tactical structures as well as their weapons mix to match the Swedes; notably the introduction of regimental cannon.

By 1600 there had already been a decisive shift in a soldier's weaponry from edged or pointed weapons to firearms. The onset of the Thirty Years War decisively shifted this balance still further in favour of firearms. At the start of the war General Dampierre reported to the emperor on the effect of musketry at the battle and siege of Lakompak (Lachenbach) 1620: 'The enemy being determined to attack me, I waited for them in my favourable position and did great harm to them with my musketeers. When I saw them in bewilderment, I charged them and I guess at least 1,200 of them remained on the battlefield…. myself, I think, will not have more than 30 dead'.[5]

The main point of the military action was a decisive defeat by well drilled professional army using muskets over an enemy that lacked a regular army. Not surprisingly the ratios of musketeers to pikemen increased significantly, whereas 1:1 ratios might be expected in 1600 by the early 1620s many armies were deploying ratios of 2:1. By the end of the Thirty Years War some armies notably the Swedes deployed ratios of 4:1, a 400 per cent increase in deployed firepower (for infantry alone). Cavalry were already armed with at least two wheellock pistols; except in eastern Europe and amongst the light cavalry of Cossacks, Scottish cavalry, or Hungarian hussars, use of the lance fell away.

Dragoons provided mobile firepower with the use of carbines (shortened muskets) which had greater hitting power than pistols. Increasingly the dragoon would fight dismounted with delegated horse handlers controlling the horses in the rear at the ready for a quick getaway This manner of dragoon deployment would continue and reach its apogee in the cavalry tactics deployed by Lieutenant General Nathan Bedford Forrest in the American Civil War. Not only was there a quantum shift to the use of personal firearms but good training with rapid fire and delivery by salvo could enhance firepower still further. Swedish armies would be deploying as many as sixty cannon. It was indeed a 'firepower' revolution. One hundred and eighty years later Napoleon would be deploying 600 guns at the battle of Wagram 1808 and at Leipzig the Coalition cornered Napoleon and deployed 1500 guns in the battle of the Nations.

However, this book does not just consider the technology of weapon development and tactics but considers the entire holistic development of war from economic foundations of war, logistics, uniforms, weapons, magazines, naval development-ship design, war propaganda and war law. Emerging from this welter of iterative change brought on by war and the existential need for political entities to survive was the formation of modern states; albeit the pace of change and nature of the change was very varied but in essence, whatever the varietal mix, the concept of state and nation state began to be developed. A key inflection point in the change from feudal society, the Thirty Years War set in train the transformation of a collection of dynastic polities to a state-based order of nation states with identifiable and fixed national boundaries. Under the impact of Protestantism and the dynamic of existential war, European polities were freeing themselves of the shibboleths of the mediaeval period including the concept of a universal Europe centred kingdom under God. With the aid of economic development, and trade, cannon, and naval architecture, European polities would project European power globally from the barrel of a shipborne cannon.

Change drove a transformation in the size of armies in turn transforming war strategy and war objectives. Economic objectives not just territorial aggrandisement became a primary focus for grand strategy. Long-range penetration and independent corps ranging across a vast battlefront became the norm. Olivarez poring over his great table maps and chess pieces of war, was a master of grand strategy and Machiavellian diplomacy, operated a huge military machine across a vast canvass.

There was indeed a military revolution, but it was just a smaller part of a much wider societal, economic, and political change, a move from cabinet war, from part time chivalric war to professionalism, to total war and global war where the stakes were survival not merely swapping of a few castles leading to a dynastic marriage. There were serious consequences for those polities which did not change their military systems. As JFC Fuller observed, 'Feudalism had not only outgrown its usefulness but also its ideals. Beaten as the armoured knight now was in the field, all that was lacking to accomplish his final doom was a weapon which would batter down his castle'[6] Developments in war were not just about technical and tactical matters, they were symbiotically linked to social and economic change; change was about much more than a few lumbering and primitive cannon brought up to the curtain walls of a castle to replace catapults and trebuchet in making breaches. Modern war required sophisticated modern administration because of the increasing cost, complexity, and technical sophistication of its weapons. Whereas a warrior in the fifteenth century, when called to arms, might just rescue his halberd from the barn from amongst his farm implements, find his rusting breastplate in the loft, and put on his moth-eaten quilted jacket before trudging off to war, the early modern soldiers had to be uniformly armed and equipped with an array of weapons, including firearms, powder, and accoutrements. Each cavalry needed a pair of expensive and complex wheellock pistols and or a wheellock carbine.

In early modern war, kings would be shot down not just captured and held for ransom as at the battle of Poitiers when Roi Jean II was captured. In one of the last examples of chivalrous warfare Prince Rupert was captured rather than killed in the battle of Vlotho 1638 because his finely engraved armour denoted a valuable prize of a person of rank. When finally corralled after dispatching an Imperialist soldier, Captain Lippe raised the visor of the young prince exclaiming, 'Sacre met, you're a young 'un'.'[7].

Much of the focus for the developments in war described in the book rests on the Thirty Years War 1618–48 as well as its antecedents; early seventeenth-century warfare was the crucible in which the modern world was formed. The military revolution in the first half of the seventeenth century would have momentous consequences for the states that did or did not modernize their military-state nexus because the existential requirement in early modern Europe was for a highly organized professional standing army and navy. The point of the military revolution was just this; for the state to maximise the delivery of firepower on the battlefield or at a chosen point on the high seas and coasts of the world, the whole society and its institutions had to be transformed. Whoever did this most effectively won, survived, prospered in territorial conquest, or conquered empires. Those polities which did not transform enough would be destroyed and taken over or fall into decline. Such capability needed the holistic reform of the state to mobilise all the resources of a state or proto-state in the most efficient way across the whole matrix of state affairs; tax system, conscription, military production capacity, and education as well as propaganda to motivate and rally a population. A proto-state needed education to train gunners in the mathematics of trajectory, engineers for the construction of forts, siege lines and bridges, good transport links to deploy quickly, for administrators, for staff officer and for civilians charged with procurement. Skilled staff was needed and investment for arsenals and arms/munitions manufacture, government contract support for dockyards and naval shipbuilding and the establishment of magazines. This understanding of the role of government developed explosively under the impact of existential war in the first half of the seventeenth-century. It was exemplified by the outstanding military successes of two of the smallest nations in Europe during the Thirty Years War, the Dutch Republic with a population of 1.5m and Sweden with a population of 1.7 including Finland and Livonia. They led the way but Bavarian army organization under the capable duke Maximillian also proved the value of strong administrative control and organization by a small state. Larger and populous proto-states and states had to adapt to survive and to catch up; to use their resources better, to organize better and if they could not win qualitatively to at least organize their massive superiority in manpower and resources. In the Thirty Years War there was not just an arms race but a race to modernize the state to enable the delivery of battlefield firepower.

The essential point of this modernization was the disciplined delivery of battlefield firepower with as large an army as could effectively be deployed and supplied. Once the foundations of modernization had been established, then increasing the size of armies would be the next focus of the modernizing state.

We might not like it, but delivery of firepower is still the primary role of states in the twenty-first century; with the stalemate of the Cold War, and the benefit of the US nuclear and conventional arms umbrella some states have become lethargic, lazy, and complacent. Nuclear weapons are the ultimate in firepower delivery and it requires massive investment, but conventional firepower is also critical because the use of nuclear weapons is only really a weapon of last resort because of the threat of mutual and apocalyptic destruction. Even battlefield nukes, which have never been used, are a risk too far as we see from Russia's reluctance to use them in the Ukraine even when in helter-skelter retreat. What has ultimately saved Ukraine for now, is the superior deployment of firepower weapons that combine the matrix of flexibility, firepower, and deadly accuracy such as the Javelin and the NLAW followed by the HIMARS and MLRV: (Modern NATO rocket systems) On the other side the sclerotic Russian army had fallen behind in their technology and organization such that their superficially superior army and access to vastly greater resources in money and manpower availed them nothing. It is to be seen whether Russian can modernize fast enough, both in state organization and in technology/industrial capability to counter the firepower and resourcefulness of the NATO-supplied Ukrainians.

What was forgotten by the west and NATO, however, was the need for rapid increase in munitions, now so complicated that increases in production can take years. The states of the west forgot that weapon systems without munitions are useless and that in a war of attrition munitions production is vital. The lessons of the UK's shell crises of 1914–15 are once again coming home to roost. Supplying from existing stocks was only a time limited solution. States have therefore failed in their primary existential duty; the efficient and effective delivery of battlefield firepower.

The other deficit in the west is the will to win to understand the existential need to fight for their freedoms and not to rely on outside help. Mired in years of appeasement and financial degradation through their energy policies and the financial undermining of the German Social Democratic Party as well as Merkel's CDU by the Russian state, has sapped the strength of Germany's elites. The west's torpor and sheer cowardice is undermining the moral and morale in western Europe in the face of malignant aggression. Unfortunately, this rottenness in political ethos has eaten deeply into Europe's most powerful important nation; Germany. As by far the richest country in Europe, Germany's failure to take a fair share of defence burdens and to lead by example is undermining credible western defence to be effective. State delivery of battlefield firepower also needs moral backbone and leadership, something utterly lacking in modern Germany in recent times. While there are historic reasons for this policy of sloth and decadence, pleas in mitigation will hardly cut much ice in the court of history if it were to lead to the defeat of democratic Ukraine and the enslavement of fifty million people and the exodus of millions.

Chapter I
Infantry

The Infantry fight in early modern Europe

At the start of the Thirty Years War infantry tactics were in flux. Tilly used the traditional Spanish tercio system of solid blocks of infantry about 2,000 strong with a 1:2 ratio of pikemen to musketeers. This ratio had rapidly changed to 1:2 ratio by 1630s due to the proven effectiveness of firepower. This 'hedgehog' formation provided excellent all round defence against cavalry as well as the offensive capability of the Greek phalanx, where an ordered and disciplined advance would sweep away less well drilled forces, 'shoulder to shoulder, like moving castles, their long pikes levelled in front while the rear ranks of musketeers volleyed in security.'[1] Tercio columns would tend to have ranks thirty deep and with the back ranks completely unable to manoeuvre or fight; the sheer mass of these units would carry the day usually by breaking the opponents 'will to combat'. Musketeers would mill around on the fringes in loose formation under the shelter and protection of the long pikes, or as formed units called 'sleaves' with some Spanish units organised to counter-march and reload by rank and fire by salvo. In Japan arquebus numbers were about ten per cent of an army but the ratio of spear men (the equivalent of pikes) rose to about parity in the early seventeenth century.

As in other areas of life, the Thirty Years War would become the inflection point in military equipment between the mediaeval époque and the early modern era. Pikemen were heavily armoured at the start of the war with a full set of breast and back plate, tasset (to cover the groin) and *gorget*, (around the throat); by the end of the war, use of armour was beginning to fade as shown by Swedish armoury inventories. Infantry may have started the war wearing breastplates and helmets, but this practice decreased as the war progressed and was accelerated by the increase in musket ratio. Helmets and armour were also used less throughout the course of the war. Firepower and the need for battlefield mobility was trumping armour so armour fell increasingly out of favour. Moreover, the increasing range and marches of continental wide warfare meant that infantrymen refused to carry more weight than was necessary; armour was clobber that could easily and readily be discarded so it was hardly worth the expense of supplying it. Musketeers already had to carry a heavy musket load were not inclined to wear armour; they wore floppy wide brimmed hats not helmets. In 1619 Edward Davies at the start of the Thirty Years War noted with the cynical disdain of a veteran that 'by the time they have marched twelve English miles, they are more apt to rest than readie to fight,' (Charles Ffoulkes *Armour and Weapons* p.81). If breastplates were worn and available, they would be worn by men placed in the front ranks. As the war progressed on long marches men would be tempted to cut down on their equipment and this was literal in the case of unwieldy long pikes which would often be shortened from the standard length. Monro complained of this slovenly practice which showed up on parade with a ragged assembly of pikes in different lengths 'as often seen on marches, being very uncomely to see a squadron of pikes not all of one length.'

The Protestant champion Maurice of Nassau had developed alternative ideas based on smaller infantry formations of 600 troops in a more linear formation with a troop depth of eight columns and a firepower ratio reversed to 1:2 pikeman/musketeer. The emphasis was shifting to mobility and firepower. And 600 men represented an optimal balance between the linear and firepower balance; it was the optimal size mainly because in linear form it was the extent to which officers or NCO could shout and thereby control a formation. Apart from shouted orders, the alternative method of unit command was by drumbeat. Different drumbeats, which could be heard above the din of battle, were battlefield commands or manoeuvres e.g., retreat, advance, rally to the drum, close up etc. At Breitenfeld, Munro recalled that the Scots were rallied after a successful charge when 'we were in a dark cloud (of gunpowder smoke) whereupon having a drummer by me I caused him to beat the Scots march till it cleared up which recollected our friends to us.'[2]

In the smoke of battle a unit's flag could also been seen at about 30 metres. [Erected at the centre of the formation with troops standing one metre apart in ranks of eight implies a span to the wing of the unit of about 30–35 metres on each side] The system had been tested at the battle of Nieuwpoort 1600 in the Dutch War of Liberation where the Spanish had suffered nearly 4,000 casualties dead to less than a hundred for the Dutch. After this Dutch success, Protestant states in the Thirty Years War, perhaps more impressed and culturally attuned to with modern or reformist ideas, had taken up the new tactics with alacrity. However, at the start of the Thirty Years War it did not help them much in the face of veteran tercios. The 'veteran factor' was more important than the tactical disposition factor. Following Gustavus's visit to Holland in 1620, the Swedish army followed Maurice of Nassau's precepts but took them further by forming up in ranks six files deep, sometimes with a pike: shot ratio extending to 1:3.[3] Gustavus introduced complex drills, for counter-marching musketeers through the ranks to fire and reload-three files at a time, so that constant fire (volleys by rank followed by counter-march) or high impact salvoes could be maintained. Inspiration for their new approach to discipline and drill in small units came from 'what they had learnt about the Roman legions from Caesar's 'Gallic wars'.... from the seventeenth-century onwards, it is Roman practices–drill, discipline, uniformity of dress-and Roman military ideas of intellectual leadership, ...loyalty to unit-which are dominant in the European soldier's world.'[4] The influential treatise of Duc de Rohan's on military theory, called Le Parfait Capitaine; a discourse on Caesar's Gallic Wars commentaries 1631, carried on the Maurice's retrospective Roman theme to inform on the best modern practices. Fire discipline, maximisation of firepower, salvoes and impact at short range was central to Gustavus's system. 'Don't fire until you see the white of their eyes'[5] is attributed to Gustavus; it certainly represented his tactical precepts. Also required was a wider understanding of military organization as a function of a highly organized state; miliary theorist General JFC Fuller noted that:

> '...in the technique and tactics of Gustavus we find a notable advance in armament and firepower...Gustavus saw that the day of the national army was dawning and that the dominant weapon was the musket[6]'.

State modernisation in Sweden and other polities, including the introduction of conscription, was intimately connected to musket drill and formations. Modernisation came out of the barrel of a musket. Other polities followed suit.

These developments were adopted quickly by Wallenstein who preferred to draw up his men in ranks of eight. Regiment sizes were 1,000. While the Protestant forces early in the war were disposed to follow the concepts of their Protestant champion Maurice of Nassau the contest between the different tactical formations had been little tested. As Parrott points out, most Dutch warfare revolved around sieges and not pitched battle, so Maurice's tactics were relatively untested in set piece battles, except for Nieuwpoort 1600: a battle that featured special topographical features (steep dunes) favouring smaller units. In addition, the smaller formations with counter-marching and linear concepts required a high degree of training and standardisation of equipment, which the inexperienced Protestant forces in Germany and Bohemia did not have. Though modern unit sizes of about 600 were nimbler in the field compared to the lumbering tercios, such innovatory formations required high levels of training and unit morale in order to face a mass attack by tercios. Copying the Imperialists, the Swedes would later combine regiments into brigades to counter the larger Imperialist units. The manoeuvres described above was soldiering at its best and in many cases basic formations and drills must have broken down under fire especially with units composed of green troops, who may well have tended to bunch and lose fire discipline or run. Effective salvo fire required complexity, and complexity needed a core of veterans to lead the way.

Veterans were essential to prevent the mass of inexperienced troops running away on first contact with the enemy as Protestant green units did at White Mountain 1620 and the Saxons at Breitenfeld 1631. Units that had been well established as social units for a long time tended not to run. Scottish units in the war fought gallantly together because of the social bonds of clan. Veteran officer Monro wrote proudly of his Mac-key regiment. Crack tercios were close knit and insular communities, which fought to the last man or retreated as disciplined units, as they did at Rocroi. Crack regiments in the Swedish and Imperial armies likewise. At Lützen, the Swedish yellow regiment led by General Brahe, was slaughtered. Scots mercenary Watts, another witness, noted laconically, 'These two brigades were the flower of the army: old soldiers of 7 or 8 years' service.... but it had been so long since they had beene last beaten, that they had by this time forgotten how to runne away..."[7].' Weimarian units formed a prodigious social élan; they were often referred to as Bernadines after their leader Berhard of Saxe-Weimar. French units were often full of family retainers, servants and peasants belonging to the aristocrat in command of the Regiment. Social links and the habit of battle formed the basis of elite veteran units.

Count Grammont at Alerheim 1645 speaking in the third person recorded that;

> 'found himself surrounded on all sides, and with four horsemen who were going to kill him, arguing together over who would do so. His [Grammont's] captain of the guard killed one, and Hemon aide de camp killed another, which gave him a little respite. He survived by good fortune: a captain of La Pierre Regiment named Sponheim, heard him named Marechal de Grammont and rallied two or three officers from his friends, who diverted the company [enemy], pulled him from the entanglement and saved his life. The captain of his guards died there, the lieutenant was injured and taken prisoner with him, the cornette and the quartermaster were killed, and all the company of his guards, who were a hundred maîtres, with the exception of twelve who were also taken: four aides de camps were killed, three of his pages, and all his servants who followed him were also killed at his side. Such is the result of affection for a much-loved master.'[8] The point of difference here was that unit élan was built more on regional and feudal cohesion rather than more artificially constructed cohesion, i.e. uniforms and rigorous drill. As the war progressed French units showed outstanding courage and élan under fire and against formidable defences; at Freiberg 1644, Imperialist General von Mercy noted of the French infantry attack uphill onto fearsome field fortifications and masked cannon 'In truth only the French that are able to undertake such things..."[9] (Mercy's letter to Baron de Sirot)

Richelieu's regiments were also based on regions; this was not just administratively convenient but reflected the ancient regime's decentralized aristocrat led social structure. It was also a fundamental requirement in a country with dozens of a mutually incomprehensible languages and dialects, some Latin based, others Celtic in origin or German. Middle French developed since the fourteenth century, applied to much of the north but even then, there were Picard, Breton, Alsatian, and Walloon languages, In the south languages included Basque, Limousin (Dordogne, Haute Vienne, Correze), and Périgueux-Languedocien and Corsican etc. In the campaigning off-season, Henri Campion recounted how he would go recruiting for the Normandie regiment in his native region where his father had estates. Speaking the local dialect and tapping into his local connections and the prestige of his name, he would more readily recruit suitable men than an officer alien to the region. Feudal loyalties still ran strongly in early seventeenth-century France.

Formation of regiments developed rapidly in the early seventeenth-century as proto-states sought to imposed great regimentation and consistency in their operations by developing a core of skills and knowledge and pride from soldiers who were readily available for service to the state directly rather through the arcane and indirect mechanisms of feudal patronage; rather than allow the peasant soldiers simply to return to their aristocratic latifundia gathering them in each year which would be a laborious process and inefficient process producing variable quality and unpredictable numbers. Richelieu and Louis XIII tried to counteract the centrifugal forces of French feudalism by tightly controlling the appointment of officers, both senior and junior.

Soldiers fought more for the esteem of their friends than for their cause. Twentieth-century analyst and researcher on the psychological and social phenomena of unit morale, General S.L.A Marshall noted that 'When a soldier is ...known to the men around him, he ....has reason to fear losing the one thing he is likely to value more highly than life-his reputation as a man among other men.'[10] Phrased in a different way is a universal and timeless characteristic of warfare which was attested to for example by Colonel Langlais after the battle of Dien Bien Phu 'We were not fighting to defend our homes, we were not fighting to chase a foreigner from our land, we were not even fighting to keep Indochina for France. Then why? The honour of the profession of arms, and that is all.' Monro also had a strong sense of professional honour; but there was comradeship also, his memoires of the Thirty Years War clearly show the tender regard he had for those comrades that were known to him and deep regret when they died in battle or by disease. 'Yet one rare spark being a resolute fix souldier with a musket dyed here of the pest, as he was stoute so he was merry, and sociable without offence, such another was his cozen, Kiernies grand-child who died of the burning fever, being alive without feare before his enemy, and of merry and quick disposition.'[11]. Imperialist General Montecuccoli suggested that soldiers fought for their honour in the eyes of their wives in the encampment behind.[12] Mercenary soldiers fought for their profession and their kinsmen as much as for money; they were especially effective if their troops had a unifying social, ethnic, and cultural connection: the Scots with their clans and Swiss mercenaries with their valleys, deployed units with high morale, fighting spirit, and disciplined cohesion.

Salvoes, first introduced in seventeenth-century Japan, were notably exploited by Shogun Nobunaga in sixteenth-century Japan at the battle of Nagashino where his musketeers behind bamboo field defence mowed down the renowned Takeda clan cavalry. Developed further by Maurice of Orange from 1594 and then Gustavus in the 1620s in Europe, their purpose was to produce high impact shock to break the morale of the enemy. Describing an engagement in 1601 in the Balkans during the 'Long War', veteran Ottoman officer Abdülkadir wrote, 'The infantry of the infidels… fired grapeshot (saçma) and bullets as if they were rain' (Yılmazer 2003, p. 315). Salvo or continuous firing was complex and required constant training to make the troops efficient in the techniques of counter-marching back through the files to reload in regular time. Disciplined firing by rank meant a continuous rate of fire to deter attack by an enemy formation, which might otherwise take advantage of a reloading time gap to press home a charge against defenceless musketeers, wiping them out before they could reload. In the absence of pikemen or when the 'pike: musket' ratio was low, firing by the rank was essential when in close proximity to the enemy: 'Musketeers employed a system called counter-march. The man in front would fire, then go to the rear of the formation to reload, while the next man would step forward and fire in turn.... By the time the last man in the file had fired, the first had finished reloading and was ready to fire again.'[13] For optimum efficiency balanced against risk, in computing the right ratio commanders had consider a complex matrix of factors including the quality and experience of the troops, their weapons, their training, the support available from cannon or cavalry, and the capability of the enemy.

Salvoes were highly effective; at Nördlingen the defeated Swedish General Horn was to complain that the Imperialists ducked behind their defences whenever a salvo was being loosed.

Musket drill, in theory, comprised ninety-nine positions directed by 163 orders to speed the reloading process. Books on musket or pike drill were readily available. However, it very doubtful that the manual was rigorously followed. Seventeenth-century printed plates reveal soldiers clad with calf-length breeches, stockings, and a jerkin. Floppy wide brimmed felt hats with a feather are worn rakishly. Bandoliers dangling with pouches of pre-measured powder are draped around the body and powder horns and satchels for shot hang from a belt. The heavy musket or arquebus was rested on a forked 'rest,' a stick pushed into the ground. The carrying of powder in bandoliers was dangerous because, when they take fire, they commonly wound and kill he who wears them and those near him'[14] After pouring in the powder and ramming down the ball, the third stage in the loading process was the priming of the piece at the firing breach with the separately carried powder flagon or horn, which contained finer grained powder. It has been suggested that Gustavus, introduced the all-in-one ball and powder cartridge shortly before his death in 1632 but recent evidence suggests that the new cartridge system was little used at Lützen. Cartridges improved loading efficiency and stopped the ball rolling out of the barrel if the musket barrel was depressed. Lastly the heavy musket would be rested on a forked rest and crudely aimed with the burning match cord being touched to the powder trail the firing pan by a crude trigger mechanism or directly by hand. The weapon would usually be pointed at the enemy formation rather than individually aimed as such.

Poorly trained troops might require three minutes to load while the best trained could reload in less than one minute. The system would only be as robust as its weakest member. Rolling volley firing was the only effective way of preventing being overrun by cavalry when pike ratios were reduced. Rate of fire determined the number of ranks. If a commander such as Gustavus was confident in the training of his men he could afford to deploy in fewer ranks. The better trained the troops, the more effective the delivery of firepower and the greater steadfastness against cavalry. The lessons of musket and rifle fired weapons by salvo has been constant through early modern times up to the US Civil War and beyond. Most troops in the heat of battle aim too high and most shots passed over the heads of the enemy. Trained troops will tend to shoot low. However this was an additional problem in early modern armies because the infantry, as a contemporary noted, 'seldom put any paper, tow or grass, to ram the bullet in; whereby if they fire above breast high, the bullet passes over the head of the enemy; and if they aim low, the bullet drops out ere the musket is fired; and tis this that I attribute the little execution I have seen musketeers do in time of fight, though they fired at great battalions [= large tercio target!], and those also reasonable near.'[15] [bracket and emphasis added] However, well drilled veteran troops in the Swedish army achieved much better results according to veterans such as Monro.

However, there must be some scepticism as to the extent of sophistication in drill and training. Due to rapid depletion of troop numbers in every campaigning year, by desertion and illness, even before battle was joined, army commanders relied on a small core of veterans with 'occasional troops' or captured enemy added whenever possible. An efficient regiment might need just one in five veterans at the start of the war though by the end the smaller more professional armies had up to fifty per cent veterans. Bavaria did not over expand its field army which remain at a constant level both in quantity (circa 20,000) and quality until nearly the war's end. Geometric precision, standardized unit size and design of formations seen in Dutch manuals and faithfully copied in history books are mainly pure fantasy, but battle formation prior to engagement was taken very seriously by commanders. Infantry regimental sizes varied considerably as we can see from the recorded orders of battle, for example at Nördlingen the variance in the Swedish army ranged from 200–500 men and brigades from 1200–2000, in the Spanish army 750–1800, Imperial army 500–1,000. Contemporary prints give overwhelming evidence of highly structured unit deployment, but the uniform size of units is improbable however there would probably have been some amalgamations to try to make the blocks of troops more even. This happened extensively in the French army where units would dwindle to very small sizes with an overabundance of officers. This led to constant amalgamations and waste when experienced officers found themselves unemployed.

Order of battle and deployment was minutely planned so at least the start of a battle would have shape even if it descended into brutal chaos thereafter. Being able to deploy solid blocks of second line reserves was essential also in the counter-attack or in rallying broken first lines. Initial false steps, misalignment or the wrong distance between units could be disastrous. Examples of this were the exploitation by General Torstensson of deployment mistakes made by the Imperialist left at second Breitenfeld 1642, and Conde exploited the gaps in the French left's first echelon at Rocroi 1643. At Górzno (Poland) 1629 confusion in the deployment on the Polish left allowed Wrangel to seize the initiative and win the battle. Turenne was nearly defeated at Alerheim (second Nördlingen) 1645 because the reserve Hessian third echelon of cavalry on the French left was too far distant.

When battle was joined, then covered by the fog of gunpowder smoke, formation discipline quickly broke down especially among poorly trained or green troops, which was typical of Protestant armies in the first phase of the war. Even the best-drilled troops could lose formation in the fog and confusion as Monro's testimony in respect of Breitenfeld 1631 above indicates. However, it was the ability of veterans to reform, line up and rally that was crucial. Generals would tend to choose the system of formation and drill according to the capability and experience of their raw material, the soldiers. It was also important not to change formation style without proper training. Veteran of the German wars, Sir James Turner noted; 'any new form wherewith your men are not acquainted, you shall not fail to put them in some confusion…'[16] However, the importance of hiring and retaining veterans was well understood at the time and Parrott emphasises the virtual neurosis on this point exhibited by Richelieu and his ministers. Richelieu opined that 'It is near impossible to successfully enter wars with French alone. Foreigners are necessary to maintain the army corps, and although the French cavalry fights well, we cannot do without the foreign cavalry ...'[17]

It accounts for the high premium put by Richelieu on coaxing Saxe-Weimar's veteran army to join the French. The fact that the shady freebooter Count Mansfeld was continually rehired by successive Protestant states despite his track record of failure is explained by the desperate shortage of experience as well as his ability to recruit. Retention of veterans and the maintenance of experienced entrepreneur colonels throughout the war was a prime aim of governments and military commanders. One of the main reasons for the change in military concepts towards year-round military employment in early modern warfare, and the provision of winter quarters, was the desire to maintain veteran cores in the best regiments. They could quickly be expanded in the spring to a full measure like white wine added to cassis. The main point of veterans was their ability just to stand under fire rather than flee. Veterans experienced with the horror and terror of battle, enjoying camaraderie, good morale, and unit élan, were more likely to stand, hold their unit shape, hold their fire to await the command, and keep firing until the other side broke and fled.

Early in the French participation of the war, the 1636 siege of Dôle, capital of Franche-Comté, the problem of experience was telling, as one officer admitted on reflection some years later, 'the French did not have the experience which they acquired afterwards. It was enough for a man to have served in Holland to be listened to as a great oracle. The kind of officer who was then acclaimed as a great general would now be hardly fit to command a company.'[18] The siege was duly abandoned, a decision made easier by the Spanish-Imperialist invasion of the Champagne.

A leavening of experience veterans was essential for victory. At Breitenfeld the élan and mass of the all-conquering tercios would face disciplined small unit firepower from the six file ranks of the well drilled Swedish army. The question was, what would happen when both armies were composed of veterans, but each deploying different tactical styles, met in combat? At Breitenfeld the Saxons were beautifully uniformed soldiers, well turned out and drilled, but they contained very few veterans; they broke and fled at first contact with the dreaded tercio so exposing the left flank of a severely outnumbered Swedish army. This would normally lead to retreat and defeat in short order. In the smartest drill manoeuvre of the war, Gustavus's veteran and reserves taken from the centre and left, wheeled into position in perfect order with a refused flank to the oncoming tercios whose slow-moving drill wasted time to fall upon the Swedish open flank. Then the Swedes opened fire. Gustavus's stunning victory against Spanish-trained German and Bavarian veterans in tercios was well noted, then copied.

Likewise at Marston Moore 1644, Sir James Turner with the covenanter army which had allied to Parliament, had noted before the battle that the Scots troops were 'lustie, well clothed, and well monnied, but raw, untrained and undisciplined; their officers for the most part young and inexperienced.'[19] In the battle they were mostly dispersed early on and fled with the Earl of Manchester, Parliament's commander.

Musketeers were sometimes deployed in loose formation in front of the main battle lines, as a screen to disrupt the enemy advance and draw their fire when it could do least damage. Not surprisingly, the French called it them *'enfants perdu' or 'forlorn hope'* which was the term used by Cromwell and civil war soldiers. The Spanish had first deployed this method. Loose formations would also be adopted for special mission, ambushes, and storming parties. Napoleon's armies would employ large screens of light troops before the main body.

Loading drills and formations would be much more rough and ready in practice. In the heat of battle the idea that troops pirouetted through ninety-nine firing steps is plainly ludicrous. Military trainers who would takeover in a later époque reckoned on four years training for full musket drill and formation proficiency whereas cavalry could be trained in one.[20] Though the Thirty Years War started the trend towards the highly trained and minutely drilled forces in serried ranks, capable of changing into various formation shapes and frontages upon command, that would be common in the next century, it was still very early days for the mechanical drill and in-step marching systems which would characterize eighteenth-century warfare, and the glory days of Frederick's Prussian Grenadiers, or Wolf's redcoats. Nevertheless, unit discipline could be maintained due to the peer pressure of veteran troops. There were many different systems of drill, which varied from army to army and even regiment to regiment, depending on the calibre and experience of the men. 'Drill', any old soldier will tell you, is the basis of military discipline, confidence, and unit élan, as an army needs men who will follow orders with automatic and complete obedience. Soldiers need to fear disgrace, savage punishment, and shame more than death.

Elite tercio formations swept away *'green'* Protestant formations until they met an army of equally toughened professionals. Regimental formations (italics) drilled; salvo firing was well practiced, and as was)manoeuvre in formation., However inexperienced armies, and perhaps experienced ones too, may quickly have taken on the characteristic of a dense rabble after battle was joined. Officers had at their disposal a plethora of military manuals, many of them inspired by proven Dutch military practice, and the victory over the Spanish at Nieuwpoort in 1600 where western units used volley fire for the first time as well as cannon firing cannister munitions; (the Japanese beat them to it and the Song dynasty with crossbows ca. 1044 CE)[21]. The emphasis was on the efficient delivery of firepower. The better armies were drilled, and unit formation was important for the simple reason *that* 'A well drilled unit, by making every motion count, could increase the amount of lead projected at the enemy per minute of battle.'[22] There are many descriptions from the Thirty Years War of the devastating effect of volley fire; in 1636 at the siege of Turin junior officer de Campion described how he charged with the regiment. Volley fire is even more effective when delivered from the safety of entrenchments. '...we attacked an enemy held redoubt from two sides...' He charged with the regiment only to be met by a "furious volley" from 500 Spanish musketeers, which felled many including his commander du Repare and a lieutenant Serisi...we climbed up the sides of the redoubt despite the efforts of the enemy, and after having come to grips with them, they asked for quarter because of our overwhelming numbers. Their commander surrendered to me personally'.[23] After the battle the Imperialists and Bavarians would quickly copy Gustavus's methods.

Drill also had a socialising effect in bonding disparate individual groups of men into units with morale. If attacks were joined in a melee, a sort of brutal scrum ensued, but fire fights at close range were the norm until someone gave way: unit on unit, moral was almost always the deciding factor. Drill was important even in the midst of battle because casualties created dangerous gaps in the formation which might be exploited by the enemy to penetrate and destroy the formation cohesion which might easily lead to flight and disintegration. Monro recalls ordering his men to close up or fill the gaps left by the dead and injured.

The number of ranks deployed depended on the rate of fire of the different kinds of weapon and the level of training of the troops and on the ratio of protecting pikes. Different systems operated depending on whether the formation was attacking, retreating or static. Tercio were much less firepower efficient with the musketeers milling about around the protection of the pikes; with files of twenty-five men the fire efficiency was reduced by forty per cent compared to linear formations[24] However, there was no immediate adoption of 'modern' linear tactics. For the first two-thirds of the war units were placed in chequerboard blocks, with second line blocks covering gaps between brigades in the first line: the Swedish system. There was sometimes a third echelon in reserve. The real test of the relative merits of the various tactics was the first battle of Breitenfeld when two experienced armies of veterans met each other on a flat field of battle outside Leipzig: a perfect 'test' experiment in relative efficiency. After Breitenfeld Wallenstein deployed Imperialists regiments along similar lines, such that Monro said of his army; 'the enemy's army was ordered like ours.' Along a front of about 120–150 metres a regiment had central pike block front of 57, 7 deep but fronted by three rows of musketeers, while on the wings of the block were 'sleeves' of musketeers twenty-two by ten deep. Not quite as firepower efficient as Gustavus's formation it was still a vast improvement on tercio formation. De Rohan in 1635 described the infantryman's equipment as being 'the pot, the cuirasse, and the doublet; and for the offence the sword, the pike and musket, which are by and large the arms of the Greeks and romans…which is a proper arm to resist cavalry, with many pikes together in a solid corps…'[25]

The Swedes had a particular fear of the Polish cavalry. With bitter experience of defeat at their hands, the Swedes and other nations would play tactical chess whenever faced with superior enemy cavalry. This explains the chess board appearance of unit formations on many battle prints of the period, where musketeer units were interspersed with cavalry. Munro recounts how at first Breitenfeld Gustavus, 'appointed platoons of musketeers by fifties, which were commanded by sufficient officers to attend on several regiments of horse'[26] (Known thereafter as 'commanded musketeers') The extra firepower was meant to disrupt the enemy's cavalry charge. It was fear, which was the biggest danger for infantry in the face of cavalry; if cohesion was maintained enough to service rolling salvoes, they could survive but if they panicked and ran then slaughter would be the result. Military historian John Keegan comments on the 'illuminating truth about the nature of battle: that soldiers die in the largest numbers when they run, because it is when they turn their backs on the enemy that they are least able to defend themselves.'[27] It was a point well noted in Napoleon's VI Maxim '…retreats cost always more men and material than the most bloody engagement. It was important to have veterans in the ranks to prevent panic and flight, i.e. to hold on long enough to allow the enemy to be the first to flee. There are many numerical examples to illustrate this;

Turnhout 1597 -Dutch v Spanish	62 dead and wounded	2,000 +700 prisoners
White Mountain (Prague) 1620 Imperialists/Bavarians v Bohemians	650	2,800
Höchst 1622 Imperialists/Bavarians v Protestant army	100	2,000
Stadtlohn 1623 Imperialists/Bavarians v Protestant army	1,000	6,000 +4,000
Lutter 1626 Imperialist/Bavarian army v Danish army	700	3,000 +2,500
Breitenfeld 1631 Swedish v Imperialist/Bavarian	5,550	7,600 +14,000 (of whom some dead)

*Figures for early modern battles are necessarily rough estimates

Battlefield fortification and entrenchment

Another development that was a direct result of increasing firepower was battlefield entrenchment. The practice of battlefield fortification was well established and natural development from the contravallation fieldworks thrown up by the Dutch and Spanish when besieging cities during the Eighty Years War 1568–1648. Entrenchment was being used on the battlefield from the start of the Thirty Years War, almost always thrown up by the weaker or outnumbered side which intended to fight on the defensive. The greater the disparity the more the entrenchment and fortification. The retreating Bohemian army threw up field defences at Raknovic Nov 1620 on the retreat to Prague as they were being hunted down by the Tilly and Burqcoy's Bavarian Imperial army, making a fortified line too strong for the Imperialist Bavarian army to risk an attack. A few days later at White Mountain they threw up field works again with six redoubts put up across their front; however, the works were not complete for a shortage of spades; the result, rout of an inexperienced army. Spades became a standard piece of equipment for Imperialist armies. Wallenstein would have them supplied to his troops from his foundries at his Friedland estates in huge numbers. Even by the start of the war German soldiers were well known for their digging habit; Transylvanian Prince Bethlen Gábor warned his commanders at a war council in 1619 to be fast in their movements and attacks, 'avoid any delay with the Germans, for with time they burrow themselves into trenches, and it takes great effort to get them out of there.'[28] In 1621, the huge Ottoman army attacked the vastly outnumbered Polish army whose battle line encompassed two large redoubts. After weeks of attacks at the battle of Chocim (Khotyn) 1621 on the Moldavian border the Turks retreated.

Perhaps about half of all major battles in the Thirty Years War involved fieldworks. They included the battles at Dessau Bridge where Mansfeld failed in his attacks; for several years the Poles failed to break in on Gustavus entrenchments at Montauer spitze near Danzig; at Werben on a bend in the Elbe, Tilly's army failed in its attacks on Gustauv's fortified trench lines in 1630. Gustavus would flank and overrun the Bavarian fortified lines at the battle of the river Lech 1632; while drenching the Bavarian lines and redoubts with his powerful batteries he ordered a double envelopment of the enemy left flank by secret river crossings. But at the Alte Veste battle outside Nuremburg 1631, with Wallenstein's army strongly entrenched on a hill line, Gustavus's veteran army made a full furious attack but was bloodily repulsed; there were no possibilities for outflanking and his powerful artillery shooting uphill made little impact on the enemy lines. Although Torstensson's division made a lodgement in the Imperialist lines, his troops had suffered too heavily and lacked reserves or support from the other beaten regiments. Imperialists holding adjacent position could lay down enough fire to prevent reinforcement. It was a problem that would become familiar to generals attacking on the heavily fortified trench systems of the Western front in the First World War or the entrenched lines of Lee's confederates at Spotsylvania, Cold Harbour, and Petersburg in Aug 1864–March 1865. Wallenstein was a master of entrenchment, preferring to weaken the attacker against his defences before launching a devastating counter-attack; this nearly succeeded at Lützen though Gustavus held second line reserves for just such an eventuality. Wallenstein's method was widely copied by other Imperialist generals: it became the standard operating procedure for Imperialist armies including the capable Franz Mercy who used the method at Freiburg 1644 and Alerheim 1965, both times resulting in devastating losses for French infantry. Uniquely at Wimpfen 1622 the Margrave of Baden established a convex fortified line of specially produced gun-wagons which caused great loss to the Imperialist and Spanish force until they were overrun on the flanks.

At Lützen, Wallenstein was surprised by Gustavus brilliantly conceived rapid advance. Wallenstein, had enough time to throw up some entrenchment around a shallow ditch running along a road. Monro reported that Wallenstein gave 'out orders they should incontinent make the moat or ditch they had before their front deeper than it was first made, and to lodge musketeers within it, which they might have before them, equal to any breastwork or parapet for their better safety.'[29] These field works extended the length of the road for about 1.5 kilometres but little was achieved in deepening the works, probably because the order was given quite late in the day: soldiers wanted to eat and sleep. The aim was to weaken the Swedish attack, break up their formations in the crossing of the ditch, and then hit them with counter-attacks. In the event the digging was too shallow to be effective as it turned out; the Swedes had no problem in rolling over the ditches with infantry and cavalry. However, there is contradictory evidence on the amount of fight in and around the shallow ditches. Wallenstein's main battery at the windmills was strongly entrenched on a shallow hill line.

At first Nördlingen 1634 the Spanish threw up defensive works on the key Albuch hill and defeated the Swedes whose attacks were thrown back with heavy losses; Imperialist general Franz von Mercy adopted entrenchment tactics when heavily outnumbered at Freiburg 1644 and Alerheim 1645. At Freiburg Condé's army was decimated as it made assault after assault on Mercy's successive lines of abattis fronted entrenchments punctuated by cannon encasements protected by earth filled wicker gabions at the five-day battle of Freiburg 1644; only Turenne's suggestion of a wide flanking advance manoeuvred Mercy into retreat. At Alerheim the French infantry were once again slaughtered before Mercy's entrenchments; the Imperialists would have won but for Mercy's death from a random cannon ball. Charles Duke of Lorraine threw up two defensive redoubts at the battle of Poligny in 1636 but the one on the left flank was outflanked and stormed in an attack led by the young Duc d'Enghien [Condé]; the battle was drawn but the French held the field. Strong defencive works guarded the whole French army at Honnecourt 1642, but barrages of plunging shot from de Melo's cannons from high ground, softened up the enemy who were dislodged and utterly crushed by superior Spanish forces. Using typical tactics bequeathed by Wallenstein, Count Hatzfeld, the Imperialist commander at Jankov 1645, prepared entrenched positions on a hill line only to have them made redundant by Torstensson's deft outflanking advance on Chapel Hill.

Henri Campion, a lieutenant in the French army, describes as a participant the Prince of Condé, [the elder] attack on the Spanish fortified lines at Salces in Spanish Roussillon 1639;

> 'As soon as we were at the bottom of the hill, the Spaniards began to fire and we walk up to them on level ground as if in a room. They killed some of our soldiers during this walk, which we performed, as the whole army saw..., as calmly as if it was an exercise, respecting the distances of rows of files, finally in a way, which marked the resolution of the whole body, though still a lot were falling. When we were in the middle of the plain, almost within reach of the guns, the enemy fired all their guns loaded with grapeshot, and made at the same time a volley of the first rank of their musketeers. ... The disorder did not prevent our advance to the entrenchments. Reaching the gap, we were taken by fire from all the lines, which were now only concerned with us [the other regiments having fled]. From this salvo, Tucs, Poilens, Jourdon, all captains, were lying dead on the edge of the ditch along with du Parc, major, a lieutenant and two ensigns, ...
>
> The remaining officers and soldiers threw themselves into the ditch, where they had more cover from the fire of the Spaniards. Marshal Schomberg, who felt pity at seeing such determined men die in vain, sent a galloping aide with an order that they should retire. Espaneller rallied as best he could with his remaining fit troops, and brought off some of the officers dead and wounded. I was carried away by four soldiers in the company where I was a lieutenant.'[30]

The description could be taken from the first day of the Somme or the union attack on Lee's entrenched lines at Fredericksburg or Cold Harbour. This is the effect of firepower, where the instinct of any soldier in any age is to get behind cover, lie down, or run away.

At Kallo, before Breda 1637, the Dutch army were caught in the open, something they always tried to avoid; they hurriedly threw up entrenchments but were overwhelmed nonetheless before they could embark on barges. At Wittstock the Imperialists and Saxons made up a defensive barrier of wagons.

In 1645 at Jankov in Bohemia, General Hertzfeld entrenched his line to block Torstensson's Swedish army marching to relieve Olomouc. It was strong defensive position with perfect fields of overlooking a mild gradient which would have broken his army, but Torstensson neatly outflanked the entire position before the Imperialist knew what was happening. Surprised, put off-balance, and with their plans in chaos, the Imperialist army was annihilated. Gustavus's and Torstensson's tactics were the timeless essentials of infantry fighting; reconnaissance, followed by decisive action to seize the initiative, to maintain momentum in advances and provide covering fire or distractions. At the Lech, Gustavus's bold river crossing was supported by flanking cannon fire from the adjacent bends in the river. Strike where the enemy is weakest-the indirect method applied to tactics. They are the same tactics described time and again in Erwin Rommel's book *Infantry Attacks* 1937. Duke Leopold set up a fine defensive at Lens in 1648 which Condé declined to attack, but using Parthian tactics he withdrew and tempted the Imperialist to attack his rearguard and 'retreating' army; when that army turned around in good order the Imperialists who had rushed own from their defences were smashed.

Mercy the Bavarian commander, led on the French army to break themselves on his defences abattis implanted fortifications, but even he was astonished that it would be attempted with so much élan, we were entrenched in places that I believed approachable only by birds. We had covered the entire mountain with tree trunks that we pushed down the slope; we were fortified in different places and covered by a number of forts.' (Mercy's letter to Baron de Sirot) There were 4,000 French casualties against 1,000 for the Bavarians.

Entrenchment combined with fast improving firepower from musketeers and cannon often won against frontal attacks, although they could be outflanked as eventually they were at Freiburg and Jankov. It was the lesson of firepower. A lesson to be repeated time and again in history as the ordinary infantryman paid in blood for the lessons of, Cold Harbour, Gettysburg, St Privat, Ypres, Verdun, Gallipoli, the Somme, and Kursk. Even if the enemy was pushed out of their redoubt defences by attrition and brute force, the losses would be staggering as Marlborough discovered at Malplaquet before his flanking movement won the day. However, where defensive field positions could be outflanked or defeated on the wings as at Alerheim 1644, the attacker would generally win. Frontal attacks are sometimes necessary, but they often involve significant and disproportionate losses in troops. Sometimes direct attacks are unavoidable but in the Thirty Years War there was usually room for flanking attacks. But sometimes geographically strong and/or fortified lines must be stormed in well-organized battles of attrition as at El-Alamein, 1942. At Zaporizhzhia 2023 there is no practical flanking movement and the necessary superiority in men and materials was not there; so stalemate ensued.

Entrenchment was only very rarely used in the English Civil War. In one of the exceptions, General Sir William Waller with 4,000 troops, he exploited a stone wall to shield his outnumbered army. Facing by 6,300 troops under Sir Ralph Hopton. Ironically, the two men had been comrades in the Bohemian army before White Mountain 1620 and were knighted for their service to Queen Elizabeth of Bohemia as she fled from Prague in her coach after the battle. Perhaps remembering the successful entrenchment of the Bohemian army at Raknovic 1620, Waller entrenched on Lansdowne hill 1643. After resisting fierce attacks, he withdrew to a wall further back up the hill. He held out all the day and killed 300 royalists for the loss of sixty men. At night he retreated. It is not clear why there was so little entrenchment in the civil war but there was parity in numbers for most battles. Some generals and the Dutch in general understood the psychological boost of fighting behind cover; but it hampered manoeuvre and made outright victory more difficult. Wallenstein's defence-counter-offence method of battle became into ingrained in Imperialist armies who always reckoned on the aggressive spirit in Swedish and French armies. On the royalist side Prince Rupert always reckoned on attacking while the Parliamentarians did likewise, increasingly look to Cromwell's cavalry to win the battle.

In the 'Year of Corbie' 1636 the combined Habsburg armies launched an invasion deep into France but were eventually forced into retreat as the French rallied their 'nation' to arms. The Cardinal Infante did not want to risk anymore, so against the entreaties of Von Werth, Gallas led the Imperialists into retreat through Burgundy, but his army disintegrated through failures in logistics. Gallas had to be rescued from a pursuing French army by the combined forces of Werth, von Gronsfeld, and the Duke of Lorraine, who combined on the 18 October 1636 at a defensive entrenchment at Rambervillers, on the edge of Lorraine, which according to Hagendorf 'lay along an entire mile of path on a beautiful mountain a quarter-mile from the enemy. We had thirty-two entrenchments. Self-contained redoubts/sconce strong point). There was a sap (connecting trench) going all the way around from one entrenchment to another. There were in total 136 large and small cannon there. The troops numbered 60,000.'[31] Extending for miles it was the largest concentration of the war. Pursuing French armies caught up but were not tempted to do battle against such strong works, besides it was time to think about going into winter quarters. Nor could such huge assembly of troops last for more than a few weeks before exhausting all possibility of supply from within a practicable radius of about 30–50 kilometres. Gallas marched his troops back into winter quarters.

Chapter II
Cavalry

Cavalry fight and the impact of the pistol

At the start of the Thirty Years War infantry was regarded as the dominant force on the battlefield mainly due to the reputation of the Spanish tercio which was a massive phalanx of long pikes with musketeers in attendance, that had come to the fore in the sixteenth century. Swiss pike-armed infantry had also a well-established reputation over several centuries of mercenary professionalism. They had superseded knightly lance holding cavalry around the second half of the fifteenth century, taking over where the English archer left off in the previous century but this time with skilled and disciplined *Landsknechts*. Only in Poland and other regimes on the eastern steppes did infantry remain as 'despised auxiliaries.'[1] The problem for cavalry was succinctly put by Miklos Zrinyi, an experienced Hungarian commander who served under Bethlen Gábor, in his book 'A Valiant Commander' 1650; 'when you encounter a foot soldier digging himself in just a little, how do you attack him with a horse? If he only has a pike and is in formation, like a hedgehog, how do you hurt him? Even if you charge, you cannot drive your horse against such terribly dense crowd, because it will terrify them…'The use of battlefield entrenchment became a feature of the war, and the problem of pikes was well understood. However, by the 1640s there had been a turnaround. 'It is the cavalry which wins battles,'[2] declared Marshal Turenne in mid-century. The reason is simple. If cavalry defeated their opponents on the wings, they could outflank and isolate the enemy's infantry, who could then be surrounded and dispatched at leisure by a concentration of firepower. Alternatively, the mere fact of being outflanked would induce such panic in infantry units that they would fall back or flee in disorder. This is the psychology of the soldier in all wars unless imbued with strict training and confidence as was done by General Slim in Burma, or Wellington at Waterloo. With formation lost infantry could easily be broken up into small and vulnerable packets or cut down individually. What changed this balance was the increasingly disciplined control of cavalry for use in second phase action following the defeat of enemy cavalry.

Following the general abandonment of the lance in the latter part of the sixteenth century it took some time for cavalry tactics to be optimised. As they were being developed the infantry tercio, which was favoured due to its ability to counter cavalry flanking attacks, became extinct when its vulnerability to well deployed firepower became obvious. Ironically the development of linear infantry tactics that optimised firepower, only accentuated the importance of the cavalry arm because of linear weakness to flanking attack as well as the lack of attacking power in linear formations. It was difficult for equally matched troops firing in line to punch a decisive hole in the line of the enemy because it was relatively thin, unlike the great imposing mass of a tercio which might burst through the enemy like bulldozer against a thin wall.

Cavalry tactics were also forced to adapt to the new lessons of firearms and firepower. At the start of the conflict when the dominant weapon of attack remained the hedgehog formations, i.e., phalanxes of tercio, cavalry were to play a supporting role by a manoeuvre known as the caracole: firing then peeling off to the rear by rank, harquebusiers rode up repeatedly to the massed ranks the enemy prior to charging them down when the tercios' formation broke up. Envisioned as a system for attacking tercio, this tactic was almost discredited by the time of the Thirty Years War, because it was ineffective especially against arquebus units who fired large calibre bullets from high-powered firearms sitting on rests. Caracole was only used in desperation when a charge *en masse* had failed, for example by Pappenheim at first Breitenfeld, when his heavy cavalry was defeated by musketeer units interspersed amongst Swedish cavalry units. The weaknesses of the caracole system were already well understood by 1618 and its use by the Bohemian army's cavalry was heavily criticised by Bohemian general Christian von Anhalt in his analysis of the White Mountain debacle in 1620. The caracole tactic was the outcome of a technological development called the wheellock pistol, which had completely displaced the mediaeval and early renaissance lancer; however, pistols were only effective at point-blank range in cavalry melee. A melee presupposed a cavalry charge in shock formation mode; i.e. no wheeling away to discharge at a distance. At White Mountain Anhalt's son's regiment defeated an enemy tercio by his 'shock charge' but he was unsupported: eventually Anhalt junior was overwhelmed by sheer numbers. Christian Anhalt complained that Thurn's cavalry unit, on the left wing, made one caracole attack then fled.

At the battle of Nieuwpoort 1600, a Spanish caracole attack on Anglo-Dutch cavalry was charged down by lancers after a volley from some command musketeers.[3] In defence of the caracole, there are reports of the battle of Turnhout 1597 which have it that the English cavalry under de Vere slaughtered the Spanish infantry with caracole fire from pistols and carbines. However, the sources are from 1792 in volume three of the history of Philip II by Robert Watson, so are probably highly unreliable and 'patriotic'. Having been abandoned by the Spanish cavalry the Spanish infantry broke and were duly cut down in large numbers. We know that the pistols could hardly have penetrated infantry armour though carbines would have been deadlier. Point-blank shooting in the face of long pikes would hardly be possible, though in chasing fleeing infantry there would have been the opportunity, perhaps against infantry who had discarded their breast plates but most likely the sword would have been the weapon of choice. Cavalry became a deadly weapon in the pursuit of enemy infantry; the effect was brutally described by Cromwell: 'God made them as stubble to our swords'[4]

The problem with the caracole was that heavier hitting, longer range and more accurate, arquebus or muskets would easily outmatch cavalry pistols, a point noted by General Fairfax when his right wing was defeated at Marston Moor 1644 'I drew up a body of 400 Horse. But because the intervals of [their] Horse, in this wing only, were lined with musketeers; which did us much hurt with their shot…;' besides, according to early modern military writer La Noue, 'the Pistoll worketh almost no effect, unlesse it bee discharged within three paces.' (1644) Recent research on the penetration power of early seventeenth-century pistols by the Austrian army have proved this conclusively. Eye witness Munro made the same point about Pappenheim's caracoling cavalry who were roughly handled at Breitenfeld 1631 by Swedish cavalry units interspersed with musketeer companies. Munro's analysis at Breitenfeld notes, that 'the fourth helpe to this victory, was the plottons of musketiers, his majesty had very wisely ordained to attend the horsemen, being a great safety for them, and a great prejudice for the enemy, the musket balls carrying and piercing farther than the Pistolet:'[5] With higher ratios of musketeers to pikemen, the prospects for 'pistolet' carrying, caracoling cavalry became even dimmer. The wheellock pistol was a puny weapon except at point-blank range and even then it worked best when pressed under the breastplate of the enemy or aimed at his face.

Professor Wilson's claim that caracole tactics continued to be effective in the Thirty Years War must be questioned in the face of numbers of contemporary commentaries on the severe limitations of the pistol.[6] The evidence is that improved musket design and higher musket ratios killed the caracole as an effective tactic. We have one eye witness description [Anhalt 1620 White Mountain] who lamented that, 'most of our cavalry did not engage properly. The proper way…was to reject the bad habit of caracoling when facing the enemy… this custom of charging without properly engaging [i.e., wheeling away having discharged firearms] is to be avoided like the plague.'[7] An interesting sidelight on changing cavalry tactics: the *caracole* was already out of favour with anyone familiar with modern military thinking. Lack of training in tactics, reflects again on the quality of military leadership including Anhalt's.

Another participant's evidence of a caracole charge comes from the memoires of Comte de Bussy-Rabutin who commanded a light cavalry squadron in the retinue of Prince Condé at the siege of Mardyke [the Coast of Flanders] in

1646. He used the tactic against a command battalion of Spanish musketeers who had launched a sally against the French trenches. Encouraged by Condé, de Bussy led a charge. It proved to be near suicidal; de Bussy-Rabutin recalls 'we fired pistols at ten paces from the enemy.... Finally of forty troopers launched at the enemy, only twenty mounts returned....it was proof of musket power'[8]. de Bussy-Rabutin suffered five men killed from his company plus several distinguished volunteer aristocrats, and many wounded: his unit effectiveness had been depleted by 50 per cent in just one charge There was no question of launching another charge. At ten paces the pistol volley, unless there was a lucky shot, aimed from a moving horse and in the heat of battle would have done minimal damage. Count Grammont discovered the inadequacy of the caracole as a tactic when he was swept away while performing the manoeuvre as a way of rallying his cavalry for another charge. speaking in the third person 'Comte de Guiche [Grammont] was himself hit three times...[then] he found himself enveloped and swept along by an enemy squadron when he performed his caracole to regroup and charge'.

According to Austrian army testing with live weapons and armour of the same thickness as used by early modern troopers, there is conclusive evidence that at twelve paces a bullet could penetrate armour but due to the loss of kinetic energy it would only cause bruising; and maybe not even that if a thick buff coat was worn underneath.[9]

Armour including the helmet provided could provide significant protection to the wearer even from powerful musket bullets; at Alerheim Count Grammont, on his own account 'during a lively skirmish he received a musket shot in the middle of his helmet, by which he was so concussed that he fell on the neck of his horse as if dead: but he came to himself a little time after, and as the shot had not pierced him, he suffered only serious bruising...'[10] Likewise General Turenne in the same battle, as he was charging... 'the enemy had at two extremes of the wing, gave fire, and the cannon had time to give three or four discharges, the first with ball, and the last with cartridge-shot (grapeshot), with which Mr Turenne's horse was wounded, and he himself received a shot in his cuirass...'[11]

Monro described the effect of musket fire on Pappenheim's Imperial cavalry at Breitenfeld 1631; they were 'cruelly plagued by our plottons (platoons) and musketiers; you may imagine how soone he would be discouraged after charging twice in this manner and repulsed.'[12] Because of the range and hitting power of the matchlock musket on a rest, Pappenheim had to resort to ineffective caracole tactics. His cavalry wing was heavily defeated, and he ended up wounded and semi-conscious under a pile of bodies.

It has been suggested that the caracole was very effective at Lützen but archaeological evidence of a mass grave where forty cadavers were found suggests something else. Recent archaeological evidence taken from a grave site testifying the extraordinary percentage of deaths caused by pistol shots to the head, must lead to speculation as to the cavalry riding them down and shooting pistols into their heads at close range. More remarkable if some of them were wearing helmets. Of forty-seven cadavers discovered on the site of the Blue Regiment's last stand, forty-four per cent had died from pistol shots to the head. The evidence from the calibre of the balls found in the excavated skulls is that they were from pistols. Alternatively, and possibly more likely given the inaccuracy of pistols even at short range, some of the surrounded troops surrendered having been overrun and were executed on the battlefield by Piccolomini's cavalry who were plentifully equipped with wheellock pistols; a practical measure given it was the middle of a battle shrouded in fog. A less likely possibility is that the Imperialists used caracole tactics, which would have involved firing making head shots from a distance as if an absurd John Wayne in a western movie. Austrian army tests at Gratz showed that wheellocks were accurate in perfect conditions but we can reasonably assume that they were not so accurate when fired from a moving horse during a furious battle.

The epicentre of the battle of Wittstock at the foot of the Scharfenburg is now marked because of a rare discovery at a European battle site in 2007 of a mass grave of 130 bodies packed in the sandy earth, stripped of everything except undergarments, the skeletons and skulls reveal hideous wounds. Skeletal heads were found, jaws are gaping open, still with the pitiful death screams of agony and despair, bones showing signs of extreme trauma; skulls were smashed by musket balls and bones marked by sword cuts and shrapnel damage[13]; [possibly from fused exploding-cannon balls but more likely from canon-fired grapeshot or hand thrown grenades] Even without scientific analysis it is obvious that the dead were from the victor's side. Who would bother to bury thousands of enemy? they would be stripped and left for wolves, wild boar, and packs of dogs, which emerged from the forests at night.

Based on the levels of strontium in the tooth enamel, research has pinpointed the geographic origins of the remains. The grave holds the bones of Scots, Swedes and Germans from the Danube Basin. Franz Schopper, director of the Brandenburg Monument Preservation Office, has noted that: 'The strontium content of the teeth provides a unique geographic marker, indicating where each of these soldiers originates. It is linked to known levels in the drinking water in areas across Europe in the seventeenth century. We believe there are Scots among them.' which ties in with what we know of the Swedish army units deployed. At least three soldier from the 140 sample also showed signs of advanced syphilis; a soldier's curse, there was no cure for venereal disease in the 1600s and it was widespread among soldiers.[14] Wittstock hosts one of the better battlefield museums in Germany, with an excellent exhibit, lecture and research centre.

By 1646, as a matter of mere logic, the caracole as a sustainable and effective tactic was dead. The evidence of combatants is decisive on this point. As weapons changed so did saddles. Lances and jousting require high protective pommels with calves set in place between retaining pads on the side of the saddle. Hips were locked into wrap-around cantles[15]: The idea was to provide a strong platform to give and take the shock of lance contact. In the seventeenth century, the focus on sword and pistol, as well as the importance of the *melee*, meant that riders needed more flexibility to swivel with sword or pistol to hand; stirrups were slightly shorter and forwards, better for the *'rising trot'*, without which a *trot* becomes unbearably uncomfortable, and to accentuate the push forwards as the rider lunged with the point of sword at the opponent. A lunging pointed sword was general more deadly than a wild slash. The sword had a primary function in a shock attack, but pistols were often used in the melee at point-blank range; sometimes they were fired by salvo proceeding a charge, as Monro explains '...our horsemen with a resolution, abiding unloosing a Pistoll, till the enemy had discharged first, and then at a neere distance our musketiers meeting them with a salve; then our horsemen discharged their pistols, then charged through them with swords.'[16]

The wheellock pistol invented in the early sixteenth century, reputedly on the designs of Leonardo da Vinci, had revolutionised cavalry warfare because it gave the mounted arm a reliable system of firepower, which was adaptable to horse warfare.

A cavalryman just needed to draw the weapon from its holster and pull the trigger. Standard equipment would be two holstered pistols on either side of the pommel, but troopers wise to the utility of the weapon and the sheer impossibility of reloading in the middle of a *melee* might sometimes carry up to six pistols, tucked into their riding boots and in holsters at the back of the saddle. It made sense since the value of the cavalryman was, in large part, the multiple of his mobile firepower. Similarly, and for the exact same reasons irregular Confederate cavalrymen in the American Civil War, such as Quantrell's Missourians, Mosby's raiders in the Shenandoah or Nathan-Forrest's Mississippian cavalry, hardly bothering with the sword, would often carry two braces of six shot army or navy *Colts* or nine shot *LeMats,* plus a carbine. At the battle of Omdurman in the Sudan, subaltern of the Queen's Own Hussars, Winston Churchill packed his privately purchased ten-shot Mauser [with a distinctively boxy magazine] that became his mainstay and lifesaver during the last large scale British cavalry charge in history against the vast jihadi horde of the Mardi's army. He is worth quoting, Churchill's experience of close cavalry fighting would have been little different from a seventeenth-century cavalryman 'The Dervishes appeared to be ten feet deep at the thickest, a great grey mass gleaming with steel, filling the dry watercourse. Straight before me a man threw himself on the ground… simultaneously I saw the gleaming of his sword as he drew back for a hamstringing cut. I had room and time enough to turn my pony out of his reach and leaning over on the off side I fired two shots into him at about three yards. As I straightened myself in the saddle I saw before me another figure with uplifted sword. I raised my pistol and fired; so close were we that the pistol actually struck him…. [another dervish appeared] he staggered toward me, raising his spear. I shot him at less than a yard. He fell on the sand and lay there dead…. I found I had fired the whole magazine of my Mauser pistol so I put in a new clip of cartridges before thinking of anything else.'[17] Some of his sword-wielding colleagues were less fortunate as they were skewered by long spears. Firepower at point-blank: a pistol could be the difference between life and death.

The idea of a caracole as being the standard early modern cavalry tactic is probably somewhat caricatured because there is plenty of evidence that by 1618 the heavy cuirassier, 'which' according to Poyntz 'are horsemen armed cape a pied from head to foot'[18] were used in much the same way as the Polish cavalry, as a shock or impact force. The overlapping flexible plates of the armoured cuirassier, *'cap a pied'* made them look like *'lobsters,'* which is the nickname given to them in the English Civil War 1643–46, where Sir Arthur Hazelrig's regiment would distinguish itself in several crucial battles, at Lansdowne 1643 and Cheriton 1644. The equipment of these units with full or calf-length armour and arm armour made them ideal as shock troops; after Breitenfeld they were handled as such by the impetuous and valiant Pappenheim and famously by Piccolomini's use of his 'black devils' at the battle of Lützen where they slaughtered the yellow and blue brigades, the latter having no pikemen and the former rather few.

Logistically complex and expensive, a carry-over from the mediaeval days of knights, full cuirassiers were still effective but increasingly an anachronism in an age when firepower and manoeuvrability were becoming more important. For the same reasons the visored helmet gave way to the open-faced helmet with nose guards similar to cricket's modern test batsman, because all round visibility in the *melee* became more important. Although excellent as shock troops in optimum conditions, they were no longer value for money due to the excessive cost of high-quality light weight armour and its plated complexity.

The steadfastness of the Swedish cavalry and infantry under attack by such heavy units at Breitenfeld 1631, was testament to the Swedish drill and discipline, particularly as they were less well armoured and poorly mounted: In due course the Swedes acquired better chargers, and the tactics changed accordingly. They wore a simple breast plate, painted black to avoid rusting, and open-faced helmet with nose or face guards, and a buff coat of varying quality depending on rank;

what would be called a *harquebusier.* Even from close range a bullet penetrating the breastplate would not penetrate the thick buff coat. Fully armoured cuirassiers, *cap a pied* 'lobsters,' declined, except for senior officers, and a simple breastplate and backplate became the standard by the war's end for reasons of practicality, weight, standardization, and cost.

The distinction between the more heavily armoured *cuirassier* and the *harquebusier* decreased over the course of the war so that by the end they were indistinguishable. By 1643, Montecuccoli, an Imperialist cavalry general, described Cuirassiers thus: 'Cuirassier should be equipped with breast and back harness, storm hat [i.e., Helmet] together with two pistols and a sword. This is the way that the Swedish cuirassiers are armed.'[19] As with the infantry the increased range of campaigns and need for speed and impact meant that unnecessary and expensive armour was discarded. If the core of the body was protected that would suffice. However the lack of a thigh protecting 'cuisse' would lead to Sir Philip's death at the battle of Zutphen 1586, so the reduction of armour was still a trade off with consequences as Gustavus Adolphus would discover at Lützen 1632.

Another innovation was the combined ball-powder cartridge introduced by Gustavus. This made loading on horseback much easier. It also saved embarrassment. When the pistol was pointed downwards from the horse against an infantry target, it would prevent the ball dribbling out of the end of the barrel before firing. Standardisation of charge also prevented mishaps such as exploding barrels. This system was probably introduced first in the cavalry arm to aid the reloading of weapons on horseback as well to better enable the trooper to shoot downwards at the enemy from close range. Turenne opined towards the end of his life that 'Horsemen should always have the charges of their pistols in patrons (boxes), the powder made up compactly in paper and the ball tied to it with a piece of packthread.'[20]

Regiments of dragoons, or mounted infantry, were also raised during the Thirty Years War. Not dissimilar to cavalry, they often fought as cavalry but the outstanding difference in equipment was a musket or arquebus, or carbine [a shortened musket or wheellock] which would enable them to fight as mobile foot-. Unarmoured 'Dragonniers' as Monro referred to them were often used in a rearguard role to delay a pursing enemy. Rather than pistols, they were armed with heavier hitting carbines. Christian IV of Denmark deployed them in this role unsuccessfully as his army fled for safety before Lutter 1626. Another use for dragoons was for guarding baggage trains or for covering retreats and slowing down the enemy's advance when an army was trying to buy time to get away clean. Tilly recounted how he dealt with a rearguard of dragoons from the Danish army before the battle of Lutter. After the battle of Lutter, General Tilly in a post battle reported to Maximilian of Bavaria; 'The next day the 26th, the enemy set fire to several villages to cover their retreat. But not withstanding that, my advance guard clawed at them, and having cut to pieces some 600 retreating musketeers and dragoons, they were forced to turn and face us with their whole army. In the night the enemy continued their retreat, and I followed at day break, on the 27th'[21] General Fairfax placed Captain Oakey's 100 dismounted dragoons behind a flanking hedge on his left wing at the battle of Naseby 1645 to fire on Rupert's cavalry as they charged past. Dragoons were essentially mobile infantry; ready for a quick getaway, horse handlers would hold the reins of up to four to six mounts while others fought. Imperialists used dragoons similarly; It was reported in the independent Dutch newspaper *Tijdjingen uyt versescheyde Quartieren* (news from various quarters) published by Broer Jansz's on 11 June, that 'The Bavarian army, consisting of 200 companies and some dragoons, has reached the bridge at Regensburg; whether they will dare to turn to face the Swedes, time will tell.' Monro recounts an action during his regiment's campaign around Lake Konstanz ', the enemy followed them still, till they were repulsed by our dragoniers.'

Swedish cavalry operating in Germany were trained to deliver a condensed and heavy impact by riding knee-to-knee. Gustavus developed a cavalry arm in Germany, which relied on the discipline and momentum of a charge to disperse the enemy with a shock effect. This was also Cromwell's method; a reader of military manuals he would certainly have been aware of Gustavus's tactical changes. Cavalry attacks were generally not made at the gallop although some commanders such as Pappenheim, Werth or Prince Rupert did have a penchant for the glorious *'Hollywood'* style of charge. If a galloping charge were made too soon the horses would be blown. If control were lost in a headlong pursuit, or dash for plunder in the enemy baggage train, then the tactical advantage won in the fight could either be lost or only half realised. Amongst many examples Rupert's charge at Naseby was wasted in this way as was Werth's at Alerheim. If a charge was delivered at the gallop rather than the trot or canter, it would be difficult to reign in the supercharged adrenalin rush of both horses and men. Although a high impact charge at the gallop could smash the enemy, such a tactic if wrongly applied made second phase cavalry deployment difficult or impossible because the horses would either be blown or dispersed or succumb to the adrenalin rush of the chase. Likewise, their riders who would be tempted to go after soft targets or looting in the enemy's baggage train.

Winceby and Gainsborough July/Oct 1643 proved the point. Of particular significance in these examples was the tactical control of the two-echelon attack to keep the cavalry in hand for second phase tactical deployment on the enemy flanks after defeating the enemy's cavalry, rather than let them disperse in a grand charge, which would only blow the horses. The problem was highlighted at the start of the war at Edgehill 1642 when according to the official by the

Duke of York (later James II), 'the same errour was committed by the second rank of each wing, for instead of staying by their foot, or charging the enemy's foot, they also followed the chace of the routed horse…with such eagerness that notwithstanding all the endeavours which were used by Prince Rupert, they were not to be rallied…' Sir Richard Bulstrode who participated in the charge admitted 'our great erroring leaving our foot naked who were rudely handled by the enemy's horse and foot together, in our absence, who fell principally upon the King's royal regiment of foot guards, who lost eleven of thirteen colours, the King's standard bearer Sir Edmund Varney killed…' Learning ability and drill were lacking in the royalist army so it was repeated by other battles including Naseby. The ideal cavalry attack and the controlled use of cavalry is described by Parliamentary Colonel Somerville about the battle of Marston Moor, 1644 'having routed the prince's wing (Rupert), these two commanders of the horse upon that wing, Leslie and Cromwell wisely restrained the great bodies of their horse from pursuing these broken troops, but wheeling to the left (right) hand, falls upon the naked flanks of the Prince's main battalion of foot, carrying them down with great violence…'[22]

Swords were drawn and pistols discharged at close quarters during the melee at point-blank range, which is how Gustavus was killed at Lützen, shot point-blank in the back as was his attacker. Other leading cavalry commanders, including Prince Rupert and Oliver Cromwell, would adopt this method.[23] Some Imperialist commanders chose to fire a pistol salvo before closing, as demonstrated at the battle of Lens 1648. This was a variety of the caracole tactic, and it seems to have been ineffective probably because the pistols were fired at *close* range rather than the optimum point-blank range in the melee. Given the motion of horses and the stress of battle, pistols were inaccurate weapons at anything but point-blank range. Swedish cavalryman, constitutional theorist, polemicist, and military theorist, Bogislaw von Chemnitz noted that, 'only the first or at most the first two ranks when near enough to see the whites of the enemy's eyes were to give fire, then reach for their swords; the last rank [of four] was to attack without shooting but with swords drawn, and to keep both pistols in reserve for the *melee*.'[24] This became the Swedish/German method that was slowly taken by the French under the influence of Saxe-Weimar's allied cavalry. They preferred the sword that was still an important weapon. Cromwell is said to have been influenced by Cruso, John. *Militarie instructions for the cavallrie: or Rules and directions for the service of horse*: Cambridge: the printers to the University of Cambridge, 1632. The text was only the revised 1644. This edition showed that modern cavalry practitioners had moved on past the antiquated caracole tactics to recommend "charging through" in the Swedish style.. So his tactical ideas probably arose by informal channels and/or by his own methods. Caracole tactics were not used in the civil war.

Fighting in the *melee* was brutal and chaotic. In one English Civil War cavalry action Prince Rupert was nearly killed when 'three sturdy roundheads at once assaulted him; one fell by his own sword (Rupert's), a second was pistolled by one of his own gentlemen, and a third, laying his hand on the prince's collar, had it chopped off by O'Neal; his own troop now struggled up to him, with Sir Richard Crane, and set him free, with only one shot through the gauntlet.'[25] In this reeling madness the mystery of it is how and why one side decided to spur their horses to the rear? As if swept up by some telepathic force this moment always arrived: then one side or the other would be victorious unless there were reserve echelons. Cavalryman in the cardinal's regiment, Vicomte de Montbas, writing after the battle of Rocroi described how an enemy trooper gave me such a stroke of the sword that he made my helmet fall off.'[26] Despite the rough and tumble, casualties were generally far fewer than amongst the great blocks of infantry subjected to mass artillery and musket salvoes, unless subjected to cannon and musket fire. Being armoured was a great help, it would prevent most pistol shots unless the pistol was pressed against an unprotected part. More importantly the cavalryman could escape with speed, whereas the victorious enemy cavalry would hack the fleeing infantryman down. As noted in the section on infantry, it was in retreat that the bulk of casualties were sustained in early modern battles.

The adjacent battlefield to the burning town of Lützen 1632 was the scene for the most famous cavalry skirmish of the Thirty Years War. Lützen had been deliberately set on fire by Wallenstein in order to deny its use to the enemy. It caused 'much inconvenience,' complained Colonel Fleetwood, an English officer in the Swedish army, 'the wind bloweing the smoak just upon us.'[27] With the flame of the town glowing through the gloom, the stinging smoke, orange flashes in the gloom, followed by the crash of musketry and cannon, mingled with the cries of the dying me and horses, the atmosphere must have struck the senses like a scene from hell itself: and 'one could barely see another at four paces.[28] Black armoured Imperialist cuirassiers emerged through the smoggy gloom at Lützen and rode at a wounded Gustavus and his bodyguards who had become lost after Gustavus had ridden forward in the mist to take charge of his right wing at a decisive point in the battle. As one of them, 'got hold of the king's bridle an enemy came up behind the king and fired a shot into the king's back.'[29]...recorded Colonel Dalbier. A minor aristocrat called Moritz von Falkenberg had identified the king and fired a pistol into his back at point-blank range, which shot dismounted him. Falkenberg was shot dead in his turn by a blast from a pistol pressed under the lip of his breastplate armour by one of Luneburg's troopers. Such was the chaos of a cavalry melee. Gustavus would be finished off by a headshot and a thrust by a cruciform Croat rapier thrust through the chest. (A fact attested by the cruciform penetration mark in Gustavus's buff coat which is on display in the Liverkammer Museum in Stockholm). Sometimes a cavalry skirmish would mix the mediaeval with the modern. Sir Richard Bulstrode described a cavalry action in which he participated during the battle of Edgehill 1642, having smashed the Parliamentary left wing with Rupert's command he chased he enemy until confronted by a fresh Parliamentary unit whereupon he was pursued in his turn, 'In this pursuit, I was wounded in the head by a person who turned upon me, and struck me with his pole-axe, and was seconding his blow then Sir Thomas Byron being near, shot him dead with his pistol…'[30].

Musketeers were only deployed together with cavalry when the commander, fearing that the enemy cavalry was superior, decided to fight a defensive cavalry battle. If a mixed formation were used for an attack, the infantry would become separated, being unable to keep up if their accompanying cavalry moved to the attack at a canter or a gallop. The slow trot was optimal in these circumstances if there was any movement at all. If the musketeers became detached from the cavalry, they would be vulnerable and were on occasions massacred by enemy cavalry when caught out in the open. 'God made them as stubble to our swords'[31] boasted cavalryman Cromwell, after cutting down the broken royalist enemy infantry at the battle of Marston Moor 1644. When an enemy fled or broke formation the cavalry had their chance to do maximum damage.

The ideal, as perfected by the great commanders of the war was to develop an effective second phase battle by deploying reserve echelons on the flanks or rear of the enemy infantry: this could only be done by keeping horse formations intact and well in hand. The great victories of the époque were won by disciplined tactical deployments. Such tight handling of the echelons allowed the crucial turning and battle-winning movement against the enemy infantry's flank or rear, once the cavalry battle had been won. Typically, one echelon would pursue the enemy while the second echelon would crash into the vulnerable flank of the enemy's infantry. Such tightly controlled encircling or tactical turning movements won the decisive victories at second Breitenfeld, Rocroi, Lech, Naseby, and Dunbar. Notable failures due to undisciplined charges were conducted by Werth at Alerheim and by Prince Rupert also at Naseby. Master of the tactical control of cavalry were Torstensson, Turenne and Cromwell, the horse breeder from Cambridge. A stern disciplinarian and trainer of cavalry Cromwell was a natural soldier; he held his troop of sixty together during the Parliamentary defeat at Edgehill, then as a member of the Eastern Association he won important cavalry engagements at Winceby and Gainsborough July/Oct 1643.Of particular significance in these examples was the tactical control of the two-echelon attack to keep the cavalry in hand for second phase tactical deployment on the enemy flanks after defeating the enemy's cavalry, rather than let them disperse in a grand charge, which would only blow the horses.

By the middle of the war the ratio of infantry to cavalry was 2:1. Richelieu's contract with Saxe-Weimar in 1635, specified exactly this ratio. However, by the war's end the ratios were often more than 1:1. The reason for the change is clear; the recasting of the cavalry in a shock and battle-winning attack rather than the ineffectual 'caracole' tactic. Cavalry was the decisive attacking arm of battle, so commanders wanted more.

From the mid-1630s cavalry started to be used in an independent strategic role. Cavalry flying columns were sent on expeditions deep into enemy territory to cut communications, spread fear, intercept supplies, create diversions, capture cities by surprise, or even force a country to sue for peace, for example Bavaria in 1647. At a tactical level Imperialist generals Gallas and Werth started this trend during the Imperialist-Spanish invasion of France in 1636. It was a method which Torstensson, Königsmarck and Turenne also adopted very effectively in the 1640s. It foreshadowed modern deep penetration philosophies for cavalry and armour, including von Manstein's '*Sedan*' plan, operationally turned into the '*blitzkrieg*' by Guderian and Rommel, following the precepts of English tank theorists Major General Fuller and Captain Basil Liddell Hart. An excellent use of cavalry in a wide geographic context, the method was extensively used by both sides in Boer war and in the American Civil War, most notably and effectively by the great Tennessean cavalry general, Nathan Bedford Forrest on the western front, where he helped to delay and frustrate union offensives on many occasions. Forest used his cavalry as dragoons with horse handlers, keeping to the rear while the troopers used carbines to fight. In effect they were mobile infantry. This method was widely used in the American Civil War. Independent cavalry columns in the Thirty Years War tore up the supply trains and communications of the enemy. In 1644, Torstensson sent Königsmarck on a deep penetration raid which cut off supplies to Gallas's stranded army near Magdeburg. The Imperial army disintegrated – a mere few thousand escaped from a total of 15,000. Königsmarck went on to capture the major cities of bishopric territories of Bremen and Verden.

Armour, at least a breast plate was essential to encourage cavalry to stand and fight. Against pistols, unarmoured cavalry would be extremely vulnerable to their pistol armed opponents. In his second mobilization in 1633 Wallenstein lacked the funding that was available in his first mobilization on account of the fall in his credit standing; (following his banker de Witte's bankruptcy). He had neither the funds nor the time to equip all his cavalry regiments with armour. On account of this fact one regiment which fled suffered seventeen post battle sentences of death under court martial, with Wallenstein describing 'how evilly Colonel Hagen behaved at the recent battle near Lützen in that he and all his men ran away in a disgraceful manner… therefore the wickedness must be repaid….'[32]. A notorious event, this seemed unfair because after the battle

Wallenstein noted in a letter to General Aldringen that 'in the battle of Lützen the difference between armoured and unarmoured cavalry could be observed clearly; the former fought, the latter took flight. Therefore, over the winter, all colonels should equip their cavalry with cuirasses.'[33] It was at this time that the arquebusier cavalry regiment financed by Vaclav Lobkovští, converted into a cuirassier regiment.[34] Unarmoured cavalry were no better than dragoons but missing the carbine.

Infantry or cavalry? The tactical advantages of the different arms depended on the battle circumstances, especially the availability of open flanks, and the nature of the terrain. If the ground was broken or full of hedges as at the battles of Newbury 1643/1644, then cavalry had only limited use. In hilly or forested country, infantry also had the advantage; Xenophon remarked on his long march and flight from the Persians across Asia Minor, 'the Greeks were pleased to see the hills, as was natural enough as the enemy's force was of cavalry.'[35] The same rules applied in early modern warfare and similar principles apply in tank warfare.

Croat and Hungarian/Transylvanian light cavalry 1618–48 and the role of light cavalry

Light cavalry was to become an important element of warfare in the Thirty Years War. A colourful racial group that was recruited into the European fray by the Imperialist army thanks to their connections in Eastern Europe and the Balkans where the Habsburgs ruled parts of Hungary and Croatia. Light cavalry were an important component of the permanent forces guarding the 'military frontier' against the Ottomans and their Transylvanian satrapy. Not particularly disciplined or reliable in set piece battle they nonetheless had a valuable role in scouting, raiding, ambushing enemy convoys, and foraging for supplies. On occasions they made contributions in set piece battle by raiding the enemy baggage train so diverting and disrupting enemy attack; for example, at he battles of Lützen and Jankov. They were also useful in the pursuit and hacking down of retreating infantry, who would be denied the chance to rally or reform into coherent units. These units were an essential part of Wallenstein's method of war as a result of his early experience in the Long War 1593–1606 in the Carpathians and later in fighting the Transylvanians or Vlach irregulars in the Thirty Years War. Following the 1634 campaign in which the Croat cavalry had been so effective, Wallenstein doubled the number of Croat regiments. It was clearly a deliberate plan and revealing of a strategy which would concentrate on logistical starvation of Swedish armies. By 1636, Croat cavalry built up to a peak of nineteen regiments.

Subsequently declining, mainly due to financial difficulties, to ten three years later and five by the war's end. Bavaria also recruited a unit. Recruitment came from all over Croatia, in 1636 for example the Imperialist army deployed 1,500 Croat light cavalry recruited in Fuili and Dalmatia. Although Croats were the core racial component, the Croat regiments recruited from all over eastern Europe including experienced hajdúk horsemen from Hungary and cossacks from the Polish steppes (cossacks). 'The tenth part of them are not of that country; for they are a miscellany of all nations, without God, without religion; for they have only the outsides of men, and scarce that too.'[36].

The value of light cavalry was impressed on Wallenstein in the western Carpathians when serving under General Basta and at Göding 1623. He must already have been aware light cavalry effectiveness. In 1621 Imperial commander count Bucquoy, the victor over the Bohemians at the White Mountain 1620, tried to capture Neuhäusel (Érsekúvjár) in Carpathian Hungary (to the East of Pressburg-Bratislava) but was ambushed, killed, and beheaded by Gábor's hussars as he led a foraging expedition. In 1623, Wallenstein's Moravia-raised units combined with other Imperialist troops to form a corps of troops under General Antonio von Caraffa to advance on the fortress of Pressburg (Bratislava). Finding themselves faced by the Transylvanian horde of Hungarian horsemen, hussars, Szeklers and hajdúk mercenaries, Caraffa's Imperialist army was starved of resources; when their siege failed, they were forced to retreat, harried all the while by light horsemen. Eventually trapped and encircled at Göding in eastern Moravia they circled their wagons and entrenched their laager. It was a familiar tactic in wars on the Hungarian steppe, as it would be on the South African veldt in the face of Zulu attack, and reminiscent of old cowboy and Indian films set in the great plains of the Dakotas when settlers' wagon trains were faced by indigenous light cavalry. Wallenstein, as second in command to Caraffa, had been influential in equipping the force with sufficient cannon, which the 30,000 Hungarian horsemen were loath to attack. Despite access to a foundry and copper, Gábor was weak in artillery which was anyway some 600 kilometres distant from his capital at Alba Julia. Gábor, facing supply problems himself, decided to accept favourable peace terms under the Treaty of Nickelsburg.

The story is instructive of light cavalry capability but also highlights the importance of mixed arms in warfare. As a one-dimensional cavalry army, the Transylvanians had limited military value, being only able to field a modern army if Gábor's overlord, the sultan, allowed him to used his Buda based janissaries. Gustavus did not possess light cavalry and suffered for the want of it, but not for the lack of trying to secure the services of Prince György I Rákóczi's Transylvanian cavalry in 1629–30.

Croat cavalry was recruited extensively by the Imperialists after 1623 and formed a regular part of the Imperialist army and system of war. Wallenstein organised the first Croat cavalry regiments in 1625 under Hector Ludwig Isolani, a colourful Cypriot nobleman, who would become one of Wallenstein's favourites and general of all Croat cavalry. The motivation for the light cavalry was not regular pay but regular booty and plunder, which was attuned with their foraging and scouting role as they travelled far in front, or at the flanks of the main lines of march. A contemporary citizen recorded the typical behaviour of a Croat troop by whom he had been waylaid and… 'to whom I had to give a pair of knitted socks, two loaves of white bread, my purse along with my seal, my children's coral necklaces and twelve florins in cash, as I wanted to save my life.'

Distinctive in their floppy red berets, the Croats usually wore the national colour red, intermixed with green and blue. Wearing a short, often fur lined tunic, with baggy trousers to the knees and a long red cape, they were unmistakable. A further sartorial distinction was a long neckerchief of wool or silk, which served for protection from dust or sweat while preventing chaffing at the neck. The scarf took on the name 'Croat' or 'crabat' and the word would morph into kravate(e) in English and French. Croat light cavalry, armed with pistols, harquebuses, and swords, did not wear armour; uniquely they carried the cruciform-sectioned *Panzerschreck* sword.

Transylvania's Hungarian army

The backbone of the army was its light cavalry; imbued with the DNA of their Mongol forebears the plains hussars were natural horsemen. Horse and cattle breeding was the business of Hungarians who lived on the steppes of the Province; they exported huge numbers of cattle to western Europe. On their small ranches and *latifundia* the Hungarians wallowed in the cult of the horse; like the south American gaucho or the plains Indian they were only 'men' when mounted; the horse and rider moved as one. Dressed in their colourful array their preening machismo and egotism drove them forward to raid their enemies, hitting fast, looting, pillaging and killing. These men proud and independent were not tuned to the idea of formations or ranks or formal military discipline. Loosely grouped in regiments of 500 they were likely officered by the ranking feudal magnate from their district. Many of the cavalry raised were former cattle drovers who had been emancipated by Prince Bokcsai in 1602–4; they were called hajdú.

There was little standardization in costume, weaponry or armour, if any. Hungarian cavalry were a mixture of more heavily armoured hussar units and lighter units of hajdú cavalry–essentailly a local militia settled on land in return for military service. They were expected 'to keep good horses, lances and other well maintained equipment ready for war'.[37] Hajdú cavalry wore knee length dolman, mainly red in colour, pewter buttoned with classic hussar cross bars might be topped by a light chain mail topcoat. A round felt cap dressed with feathers would adorn the head. Some wealthier hussars in 'heavier units' might sport a breastplate or a cuirassier's helmet imported from Germany. Lightly armoured a hussar might well deploy a Turkish style arm protector called a 'Vambrace' which could parry and defend slashing strokes against vulnerable forearm. A long red cloak sometimes fur lined was commonly worn. They wore long length leather boot to just below the knee. The main weapons of the hussar were a curved slashing sabre and a short lance; alternatively, a Turkish style long broadsword might be deployed. Firearms were possessed by some; usually a short carbine or sometimes pistols in pairs either side of the saddle though these were probably owned by the wealthier horsemen and nobility. A particular vernacular weapon of choice was the battle axe or war hammer with a sharp curved spike which could be driven into the skull of a victim. However, it was the lance that was the prime weapon in battle, although this required stocks of lances for replenishment in battle because the lances snapped off upon impact. Describing the battle of Zólyom 1621 in a letter to Bethlen Gábor, István Eghri noted '...and they could not spare two hundred lances-all of the weapons were broken, and they had to resort to swords.'[38]

The tactics of the Hungarian trooper were those of mobility and surprise ambush. When charging they would gallop in several lines from all directions so as to panic and confuse the enemy who would usually flee in terror and expose themselves to being hacked down as they fled. Imperialist commander Basta recorded that a hussar charge 'It is like a summer shower; when it rains it pours but is soon over'.[39] Hussars were expert at picking off unguarded wagon trains or small enemy detachments.

However if infantry were well trained it was the hussars who might come off worse; a contemporary recorded the events of the battle of Goroszlo 1601, 'Basta [the Imperial commander] sent more and more units which stood their ground against the lancers charge; finally when his own army appeared, and the lancers were gone, the soldiers could not withstand the fire, so the bridge was taken...'[40]

However, the Hungarian hussars had great warlike qualities and instincts for battle. As the Bohemian army retreated to Prague in October 1620 Frederick of Bohemia recorded in a letter to his wife on 22 October that 'Yesterday the Hungarians defeated sixty horsemen and gained a good number of fine horses; today they have taken a number of wagons with provisions which were being taken to them. Thus every day we have prisoners...'[41] This was the warfare at which the Hungarians excelled. They foraged and captured enemy food stocks and robbed and burnt their way across large swathes of country side making defence virtually impossible. The free spirit of steppe horseman might be a romantic notion, but the reality was quite different, 'the hajdús attacked them and cut them down including their children and whores. Only a few managed to flee into Varad.'[42]

What they could not do or do well was stand in battle as Count Anhalt recorded bitterly of the battle of the White Mountain 'so I confirm that when I withdrew, of all our Hungarians, only a hundred were left'.[43]

Against organized ranks of enemy heavy cavalry the individuality and ill-discipline of the hussars would take over; but in any case it would be suicidal to take on well armoured heavy cavalry in tight formation. There were other severe limitations to the operation capability of Transylvanian hussars. They would not fight on foot and operate as dragoons which might have been a logical extension to their operational effectiveness. However, this would mean giving the reins of their mount to another man; no self-respecting hussar would willingly dismount from his horse, the very thing that meant the most to him in life, nor trust some else to guard the horse. It was anathema.

A further well noted operational constraint to hussars was their refusal to take static positions as guards to wagon trains or infantry. Such slow moving and fixed positioning was a sheer horror for the freewheeling cavaliers of the steppe. Hungarian cavalry whether in the Imperial or Transylvanian army would often refuse such duties, 'the cavalry did not want to obey the command; some refused to march with carts…and some even opposed the slow march itself-I other words they wanted to do as they pleased. They said that would not be guardians of foot soldiers forever….saying that being last in line would result in getting a bad quarter'.[44] As ever the main day to day concern of a soldiers was good food and comfortable quarters. Even more impossible was asking hussar troopers to dig trenches and engage in the hard graft of siege warfare. Gábor remarked on this 'allergy'.[45]

The logistical system of the Transylvania was weak. A mobile light cavalry army did not need it. Troopers would bring their own horses and weapons. For long raids into enemy territory they would have taken one or two spare horses with them in the manner of the tartars; these spare horse would enable them to avoid the mortal danger of being left behind on foot in case their horse fell sick or was killed. Unencumbered by artillery or wagon trains the hussars could move quickly and load their plunder onto the spare horses. Gábor himself was loath to engage in the details of modern logistics; nor did he have a modern administration or tax system to deal with such matters. Gábor said of himself, that he 'liked to go into battle, and I heard him say, if only someone took care of the accounts, recruitment, and provisioning-apart from that he was happy to manage battles including all difficulties and would never want to stay at home in peace'.[46]

Further cavalry auxiliairies were bought in as mercenaries. Gábor hired 4,000 fearsome Tartars in 1623. Tartars were light cavalry; they did not wear armour and were mostly armed with swords lances and bows and arrows; the same as their forebears. They were a terror force empolyed as light cavalry skirmishers, raiders, scouts. Other light horse were hired in from Transylvania's allied Romanian [vlach] *voivode* in Wallachia. The so-called 'red cavalry' or Curteani were armed with bows and arrows. They acted as advance guards and for reconnaissance. Each of the voivode sent about a 1,000 cavalry in 1623 and 1626. They would be sent again in 1644 Prince Rákóczi advised 'we have enough heavy troops but are in great need of light ones.'

For the Hungarian troopers whether hussars or hajdús, a free-spirited life on the hoof roaming and plundering the enemy lands in fine summer weather was the very essence of freedom, happiness and cultural affirmation. the DNA of Genghis Khan and the Mongol hordes ran in their blood. Sleeping rough under the stars and riding freely was the dream of his ancestors; as one of Bethlen Gábor's aristocratic lieutenants, Miklos Zrinyi, put it in his epitaph 'May a casket or the wide blue yonder be my shroud if honour is with me in my last hour. May I be devoured by the raven or the wolf, always the sky above, and the ground below'[47]

Chapter III
Pistols and Gunmaking

Guns and collections became a great fascination for the wealthy aristocracy of Europe. There were large collections in all the great houses and in the places of princes. Firearms especially pistols were collectors' items and frequently given as gifts: (as they still are, note the recent exchange of gun gifts between Putin and Kim Jong Un Castro gave Salvador Allende a golden gun and he died fighting with it in the Presidential Palace in Santiago); they were a matter of fascination for many men very much as expensive watches are today, names such as Patek Philippe, Vacheron Constantin, Audemars Piguet, Hublot, Rolex and Omega. Ironically, the mechanism for the most sought-after weapons, i.e. 'clockwork', was the same; wheellocks operated with complex mechanism which synchronised the striking of the cock; the cock gripping a piece of iron pyrites, against steel plate and with the opening of the priming pan; sparks produced the detonating flash into the loaded barrel so exploding the course grained gunpower charge which had been rammed in ahead of the wadding and the bullet. As we have noted above this type of weapon was developed originally in Germany, although recent scholarship suggests that Italy in the fifteenth century might be the real birthplace.[1] Like a watch with a mechanical movement, high-quality precision engineering was required for wheellocks to prevent the ingress of dirt damp or fine grain priming powder; so great was the precision that the gap between the wheel and the lock should be no more than 0.04mm to 0.08mm.[2] This precise engineering and the spring set clockwork mechanism meant much higher costs of production.

When wheellock pistols came commonly into use the tradition weapon, the lance, was soon abandoned; lances were only retained by Polish Hungarian, Tartar, and Ottoman cavalry. As contemporary military writer de La Noue explained in the 1580s, 'Squadron of lancers give a gallant charge, but….it is a miracle if anyone is killed with a spear….it may wound a horse…. however, the perfect reiter only discharges his pistols upon entering the mele, firing from close, they wound by aiming at the face or the unprotected thigh…. a squadron of pistoliers properly trained would beat a squadron of lancers.' *De la Noue*. Lancers would return in the Napoleonic era and were still used in First World War Tassigny. De Tassigny, who had just sabred three of the enemy was, plugged with a lance by a German Ulan; it took the full strength of a comrade to pull the deeply embedded lance out of his chest. He survived to become the general who led the French army's invasion of Germany at the end of Second World War and supreme commander in French Indochina in 1950–51.

Wheellock pistols started to be used by cavalry increasingly from the 1540s; by 1600 it was the standard weapon though 'caracoling' was the standard tactic; a very inadequate tactic as Sir Philip Sydney would discover when killed using it.

Wheellocks were most commonly used as cavalry weapons in pairs on either side of a saddle, individual pieces were made for rich collectors of the aristocracy. Such cavalry pistol would invariably have a ball butt to make easy the act of grabbing the pistols and drawing it from the leather holster. Some handles were strait but increasingly they were bent. As long form muskets and the shorter carbines, these weapons in wheellock form would be used by guards of powder wagons and the artillery, the reason being that the alternative and common weapon of the early modern period was the matchlock which otherwise would have involved trapsing around with a lighted match cord in the vicinity of gunpowder barrels. Matchlocks were at least thirty per cent cheaper to make than the wheellocks; moreover, with a simple mechanism they were easy to maintain and replace whereas the more delicate wheellock was prone to jamming and malfunction through the ingress of grit and dirt or from hard wear and tear.

Some Swedish troops were armed with firearms incorporating snaphance mechanisms. This became the common form of lock for firearms as the war progressed; an early form of flintlock which only came in towards the end of the war, the snaphances lock mechanism and cock was separate from the action of the steel against which the cock would strike. The steel would be set manually, and this acted as a safety system because it would be the last action before firing. Advanced snaphances would have the operation of opening the priming pan synchronized with the trigger and lock mechanism, rather than done manually.

Gunmaking was an artisan craft with very diversified places of production. However, there were some major traditional centres of gunmaking such as Nuremberg, Augsburg, Suhl [Thuringia] and Teschen [Silesia]. Dresden, Cologne, Essen,[3] and Munich also were centres for production. Sweden became a major producer given their access to iron ore. Similarly, the Steyr arms works in Styria Austria was located on the iron road near to the Erzberg mines. Another nearby centre was Ferlach where the industry was encouraged by Baron von Dietrichstein. The Rhine land also developed as a major centre during the Thirty Years War based on pre-existing centres of production; gun producers at Essen were located near iron ore deposits. The Ruhr would later become synonymous with heavy industry and weapon production in the German empire. When Suhl was destroyed after the Swedish defeat at Nordlinghen 1634, many producers there moved to Salzburg in Austria.[4] In France; Paris, St Etienne, Metz, Sedan, and Grenoble became major centres. The Dutch Republic had many centres for excellence in Amsterdam, Bruges, Tournai, and Ghent. There was a Royal Armoury at Innsbruck; in Greenwich the Royal Armoury produced weapons and in Copenhagen Christian IV set up an arsenal to cover all military and naval production. In Spain Madrid was a centre of gun production and in Italy Brescia. In Poland each of the great families would have gunmakers on their own estates or they imported from Silesia or from Holland. With such a weak elective monarchy there was no royal armourer or arsenal, only stabling for thousands of horses in a country destined to underweight the importance of firepower. There was considerable specialisation and interchange of parts for assembly, with various minor centres of production being mere assemblers of component parts. Some places specialized in the clockwork or snaphance or matchlock mechanisms; others produced the barrel, others the stock.

Finishing and decoration for the fine pistols produced for the aristocracy were conducted in family workshops. The names of the families with passed down artisanal skills became brand name selling points for collectors, just as luxury watchmakers today. These Pistols were highly decorated with carved stag or cow horn inlay or mother of pearl or tortoise shell. Damascened silver and gold adorned the barrels and locks or engraved brass panels. Barrels might also be blued. The ball butt could be made of enriched gilt bronze. Stocks might be made of walnut or ebonized wood. Famous gunmaker names included the Markwarts of Spain, who had emigrated from Augsburg around 1530. In a treatise on gunmaking in 1644 Spanish gunmaker Martinez de Espinar informed his readers that, the most famous gunmakers were a Master Simon the elder and Master Pedro his brother, 'They were brought from Spain to Germany by the Emperor Charles V as the best he found there and they worked for King Philip II and King Philip III...Master Simon had four sons all in the trade.'[5]

Other great names were the Sadelers of Antwerp and Munich, or in France Piere Monlong, Martin and Boular, and Isaac Cordier. In Bohemia there was the Keiner family of Eger. Pierre Bergier of Grenoble made the clock mechanism and the gun. In Germany there was the Klett family of Suhl, five of whom emigrated to Salzburg when Suhl was destroyed in 1634.[6] They then supplied the Habsburg court. All the great families of Europe had gun collections; the largest and most famous belonged to gun obsessed Louis XIII. His collection which still exists has a catalogue of 337 exquisite pieces. The immensely wealthy Raziwill family had a huge collection which was dispersed from their castle in Courland (USSR and Latvia) at the end of the Second World War and there were many great collections in Saxony; in the seventeenth-century guns were made at the armoury in Mitau in Courland. Wheellock guns made at Teschen in Silesia were known as Tschinkes because of their distinctive mechanism. Given their geographic position, these weapons were widely exported to Poland, Bohemia, Hungary as well as Germany. From the nest of artisans around Brescia in Italy, the barrel maker family of Cominazzo stands out, 'his barrels were esteemed in all Europe and still are for their surety,' noted a Madrid gunmaker in 1795.[7] They all produced exquisite collectors' pieces; but fashions changed during the Thirty Years War from about 1625. Decorations became less and more austere and guns more practical in design; they might actually be used!

How many firearms needed to be produced? If we just take Germany at the war's peak in 1632, there were about 350,000 troops under arms between Sweden, the Imperialists, Catholic League, Hesse, and Bavaria. Many of these were in garrison. Perhaps there were 60,000 cavalry all told, who needed two or three firearms each, pistols, and carbines. We can calculate an active arms stock of perhaps 400,000. Assuming that reserves of weapons are steady, we could estimate reasonably that twenty per cent would have to be replaced each year due to damage, wear and tear or loss; then we have a necessary production rate of 80,000 firearms per year. This entails not just the production of barrels, but complex mechanisms and stocks and time for assembly; a major industry indeed in early seventeenth-century Europe.

For requirements across Europe as a whole, we could easily double and triple that number to 200,000–300,000 p.a with a replacement need of perhaps 50,0000 p,a. When the British civil wars started in 1642, adding perhaps another 150 to 200,000 men needing to be armed, with a firearm replacement need of perhaps 30,000 p.a. Overall stocks of weapons would have been much higher than the needs of permanent garrisons and armies because each town and city would multiply its defensive capabilities by perhaps four times in a siege and most of these militia would be musketeers tasked with defending the walls. If we take the Dutch example, the sum complement of Dutch garrisons was about 30,000 1626–8, (their standing army was about 20,000) but we know that at the time of the Spanish attack on their eastern frontier provinces in 1629 during the siege of 's-Hertogenbosch, the Dutch raised a total of 125,000 for militia. This implies a need for at least an additional 100,000 firearms in stock implying a total stock of at least 150,000 and probably more because not all militia were called upon. If we add the needs of the standing army and garrisons and militia on standby across Europe, we must reckon on a stock of firearm weapons in early seventeenth-century Europe of well over million if the needs of navies were included. High replacement rates would only apply to active field armies, but with new start up demand as the war spread and intensified there must have been some peak years when new demand and replacement demand required production of some 200,000–300,000 firearms across Europe. This excludes demand to equip colonial fortresses, militias, private estates, and merchant vessels across the globe as well as export markets.

Chapter IV
Artillery

The role of artillery

Cannon, 'the last reasoning of Kings' noted Cardinal Richelieu; his words came to be inscribed on artillery pieces. So important had cannon become that by the war's end the Treaty of Westphalia included a clause on the return of 'cannon found at the taking of places, and which are still in being.' Article CXIV [IPM]. Gustavus Adolphus was an early exponent of artillery use, believing that it was an essential component of modern aggressive warfare. Lennart Torstensson was his protégé and first general of artillery in a move towards functional specialty in different aspects of military operations. (Gustavus would later set up the first engineering corps). Gustavus understood that 'lightness' was a key ingredient for balancing mobility with firepower. In advice passed to the Czar of Russia in 1631 in respect of the planned attack on Poland, Gustavus advised that the Czar needed to equip himself with 'many cannon and other armaments, the cannon being neither too heavy or bulky'[1][emphasis added] The Swedes tended to have more standardisation in their gun sizes, with the field artillery batteries being composed of 24lb [siege guns], 12, 9, and 6 lb. guns made of brass (a copper derivative much lighter than iron) with shortened barrels which might reduce the metal weight by up to twenty-five per cent and lighter gun carriages and limbers; from the early forties the new limber designs were supervised by Torstensson.

'Artillery developed as a means by which an enemy could be hit at longer ranges or with greater weight of fire than infantry or cavalry…could achieve.'[2] Before every early modern battle brightly painted cannon, often reflecting the house colours of their country or their dynastic master, were lined up in front of each army. Habsburg cannon for example, were painted black on the wooden elements, while the metal parts were picked out in red or yellow, e.g. the barrel, wheel rims, metal bindings on the transom or carriage, axels, and carriage's female towing connector for the limber.[3] Spanish-Italian guns were red and yellow: blue and yellow for Sweden: as if they were the colours of rival soccer supporters.

Normally deployed just to the front of infantry formations, cannons were on occasions sited on elevated ground behind the front line. It was important to be on higher ground because of the danger of blue-on-blue incidents as at Werben

1631 when Monro had to instruct the artillery to move to higher ground. At the start of the Thirty Years War in Germany, artillery was a lumbering profusion of cumbersome long-barrelled field and siege pieces in a multitude of calibres, which made provision of ammunition difficult. Guns were for sieges and their use in battle but an afterthought. After all most military operations were geared to the capture of places with less emphasis on field battles. Fired at the start of the battle, almost as a symbolic act, cannon then tended to be forgotten about when the armies locked into a scrum of pikes. Pointless Imperialist opening salvoes at White Mountain were typical of many battles in the early modern period, especially when the guns were being fired uphill which was often the case because defenders normally positioned themselves on heights or higher ground. Cannon were static lumps left on the battlefield and without purpose once the armies had locked in combat. They did not move with the action. Nevertheless, cannon had a significant impact in various fifteenth and sixteenth-century battles including Fornovo 1495, Ravenna 1512, Marignano 1515, Pinkie 1547 and Mohacs 1526.[4]

Cannoneers, at first civilian amateurs, developed as a separate branch of the military and the value of cannon was reflected in the increased shame in losing them which was testament to their cost, their status as siege equipment, the terror inspired and symbolic significance as to modernity. Education, especially an understanding of mathematics for range and trajectory, as well as fortress design for optimisation of killing zones and arcs of fire, was recognised as a fundamental requirement for a professional gunner. This explains the fact that the educational skills of Jesuit priests were often exploited during the conflict. For example during the defence of Dôle when under attack by the French in 1635. A leading missionary in China, Jesuit father Adam Schall even wrote a widely disseminated treatise on gunnery, which developed further the knowledge that originated from by Italian experts, Urfano and Collado. Reflecting their importance, post battle reports increasingly focused on cannons won or lost as well as casualties.

In China the illustrated *Treatise on Western Gunnery* was published in in 1624–5; a book co-produced by famous scientist and mathematician, Father Johan Adam Schall von Bell, and Yang Huo Thu Sho.[5] This was followed in the 1640 by another book, *The Essentials of Gunnery*. Fathers Adam Schall and Rho became living legends in China after the siege of Macau 1621 when their extraordinary accuracy [and divine trajectory] resulted in the defeat of the attacking Dutch army, as a result of a direct hit on the enemy's powder wagon and the sinking of a Dutch warship by plunging fire. This military capability more than anything else elevated Jesuit prestige at the Ming court and gave Jesuit missions a privileged status, enabling the expansion of converts from 13,000 in 1617 to 250,000 by 1650. It is the reason why the Catholic church has such a large following in China today. At the time the Ming dynasty was involved in its last desperate phase of defending itself against the Manchu threat. Ming military thinking was much influenced by western thinking; prints dating from 1649 depict Ming soldiers firing by volley[6].

Crude but effective aiming devices had been around from the 1500s. Something known as a 'gunner's quadrant use an L-shaped device of 2 x 60cm with a plumbline of brass to measure the angle of fall. This measurement was then combined with the gunner's staff of 240cm to measure distance, again by a process of triangulation and ratio calculation. Such careful aiming was probably more important in sieges rather than in the heat of battle as large culverin sized 18 or 24lb guns looked to batter away at a single point on the enemy's fortification in order to secure a breach.

The Swedish army put an enormous effort into providing maximum firepower, regarding artillery as an arm of the military, to be separately controlled and developed. The Imperialists were to follow suit, but they never attained the professionalism of the dedicated Swedish artillery corps, nor were they so well supplied with excellent bronze cannon, which were produced in Sweden from their high-quality copper ore. Gustavus also introduced the cannon into a tactical support role at the regimental level, in addition to field guns in battery, with two 3- to 6-pounder guns per 500–600-man regiment; a very modern concept, it was a development well ahead of its time, foreshadowing close mobile infantry support by the light machine gun, light anti-tank guns, bazooka, RPG or light mortars, of modern times.

Firing grapeshot at optimal short point-blank range of up to 250 metres[7] or roundshot at 700 metres, small regimental guns represented a substantial increase in firepower at the lower tactical level. The Swedes had used the famous leather guns in their campaigns against the Poles: these were particularly light, being made from layers of leather bound with copper strips, but they were replaced by solid copper guns before the German campaign. Eight leather guns were captured by the Poles at the battle of Honigfeld 1628 when they were used to accompany Gustavus's cavalry foray from his base at Marienburg fortress. As the capture of places became less important Swedish artillery under Gustavus was redirected more flexibility as a battlefield asset. Torstensson introduced the 9-pounder as the standard Swedish field gun in the Swedish artillery regiment. No longer deployed haphazardly across the front they were positioned and clumped in batteries at key points to concentrate fire either on the main enemy threat or to support the main attacks on the enemy. If possible, they were placed on higher ground because plunging shot was more devastating because the ball would run further and faster as long as the ground was not sodden. Gustavus's emphasis on gunnery and firepower, also evident in his tactical infantry deployments and in higher musket ratios which were complemented by an increase in guns per thousand men from the standard 1:1,000 ratio to 6:1,000.[8] This was indeed a multiple of revolutionary proportions.

The theoretical rate of fire for the regimental gun was twenty to thirty shots per hour (six-, nine-, and twelve-pounders) compared to ten to twelve for the heavier field and siege artillery. This could mean that four to six rounds could be fired in the 11.5 minutes it would take for a standard infantry attack from 760 metres to reach the guns: for cavalry it would be approximately two to three respectively.[9] We must suppose that the choice of the smaller gun as the standard for field artillery was due to the higher rate of fire. For Swedish artillery using all-in-one cartridges of either grape or single balls, rates of fire were very significantly higher, up to three rounds every minute. Standard field artillery placed in battery, some 25 metres apart would mainly be 12-, 9-, and 6-pounders. With heavy weight of shot, 24lb cannon were good for sieges, but relatively less effective against infantry because of the slower rate of fire although Wallenstein would choose this size of cannon as the mainstay of his heavy batteries in the Alte Veste and Saxony/Lützen campaign in 1632. As the war progressed standardisation of cannon's weight of shot, ammunition types and calibre improved significantly. Not surprisingly given his philosophy of mobility and firepower, in contrast to Wallenstein, Gustavus preferred the 9-pounders as the mainstay of his artillery.

Clearly the development of powerful rapid firing field artillery and close support pieces represented the death knell for the massed ranks of the tercio system which, because of their depth, would be torn apart by concentrated artillery fire, arranged in battery to set up crossfire zones on advancing enemy units. Tercios were also slow moving so the time taken to close in on the enemy would enable well trained gunners even more opportunity to cause damage. According to Monro the use of cannon against the tercios was the main reason for the Swedish victory at Breitenfeld, '…next unto God, a second helpe unto this glorious victory, was the great execution made by his majesties cannon.'[10] Tilly, the losing general, agreed. Files of thirty or a dense square mass of 1,000–2,000 men presented too good a target. Even for troops in line, artillery fire could be devastating: at first Breitenfeld, 'our arrays of horse and foot stood firm like a wall,' recorded Munro 'the cannon now and then making great breaches amongst us, which was diligently looked unto, on all hands, by the diligence of officers in filling up the void parts,…'[11] [Emphasis added] In the English Civil War there is a graphic description from the First battle of Newbury where Captain Gwynne witnessed the decapitation of a whole file of six soldiers by a single shot. Interestingly this was a rare mention of the effectiveness of artillery in the English Civil War. In Germany, Monro recounted how at Ingolstadt on 19 April 1632, 'by one shot I lost twelve men of my own companie'[12] apart from Breitenfeld, the devastating effects of cannon fire are *often* reported in the Thirty Years War, for example at the battle of Alerheim, where masked batteries destroyed Condé's infantry. Special mentions to the role of artillery were given at Freiburg 1644, Lützen 1632, Jankov 1645, and to Spanish cannon fire at Arvin 1635 and Honnecourt 1642.

Artillery munitions

'Ammunition is artillery's true weapon'[13] noted Major General J.B.A. Baily of the royal artillery; different types of ammunition were required for various battle phases. Solid shot was the means of battering a breach in the enemy fortification, which was the essential preliminary to calling for surrender under the articles and traditional usages of war or to the storm which would follow upon refusal. Used at longer ranges in an open field battle, solid shot cannon balls killed and maimed by scything through ranks of densely packed soldiers, either directly or by skipping along the ground. Therefore, dry ground or frozen ground made cannon fire much more effective, like a deadly game of skittles. Positioning of guns on top of a hill was therefore not necessarily effective: if the ground were sodden, the ball would tend to plough harmlessly into the earth, in which case only a direct shot would be effective. Heavy rain was an important (and possibly decisive) element in Napoleon's failure at Waterloo. A hit by solid cannon shot anywhere on the body was invariably fatal either instantly by dismemberment of the body, or by degrees in excruciating agony if an extremity was hit or removed; 'Sir, God hath taken away your eldest son by a cannon shot. It brake his leg. We were necessitated to have it cut off, whereof he died.' reported Cromwell laconically to the man's father.[14] But others survived such *clippings*, such as Scottish Colonel Hepburn who lost a leg outside Mainz. When a companion of Munro's had his shoulder removed by a cannon ball, his survival was regarded as a miracle. General Tilly was not so lucky at Lech where a 'falconet' ball, from a small regimental piece, smashed his leg: it led to his death several days later, but he *was* over seventy so the chances for surviving such an injury, and amputation for this type of wound were limited. General Mercy was unlucky to be hit by a cannon ball at Alerheim 1645, where the French deployed few cannons; this occurred just at the moment when he anticipated a great victory delivered from his masked cannon spewing grape shop on French frontal attacks. In his analysis of the battle, Napoleon I criticized the lack of cannon to the French support the infantry attack. Another method of long-range killing was by explosive balls filled with gunpowder and lit with a fuse to detonate after firing. Short-barrelled mortars were usually the delivery method for fused munitions. Given the complexities of manufacture and the inherent dangers in early fused munitions, explosive filled balls were seldom used except in sieges, although the method is recorded in use by the Chinese and Venetians in the early fifteenth century, and was in regular use by the end of the sixteenth century. A rare description of such a munitions' utility during an attack on Salces, on the Spanish coast, is given by Campion whose regiment led the attack: (probably a 'petard' fired by a short-barrelled mortar) 'One of their shells fell into the middle of our battalion and the shot, together with the explosion, took out six rows or thirty six men (so the file was here of six men).'[15] Another mortar shell singed the Great Condé in the trench lines at Mardyke in Flanders. The Spanish army were early innovators in exploding shells; they were often fired from mortars and made of clay or cast iron; when the Spanish army invaded France in 1636, their use of exploding shells shocked the French whose fortress towns of La Capelle and Le Catelet fell in short order.[16] A contemporary print of the siege of Magdeburg 1631 shows the city being bombarded with exploding shells fired by Tilly's Spanish-trained Imperial Bavarian army.

For killing at close range, usually in a defensive mode, cannoneers used grapeshot, consisting of metal balls or small stones if metal balls were short. Cartridges were introduced by Sweden halfway through the war; the shot were clustered and bound on to an explosive cartridge [an all-in-one package of powder, wadding and shot] or canister [a round metal or wood contained for shot only] filled with varying material, small musket balls normally, but also wood, scrap metal, or even small stones. All-in-one cartridges were a Gustavian innovation; revolutionary in concept they were the forerunner of the artillery shell. Powder packed in standardised cloth-bound charges removed the need for the powder shovel and required only one ramming action, and one sponging action, so increasing the rate of fire. Looking like a long, large corkscrew, 'the worm' (which looks like an oversized corkscrew) was still needed remove the detritus of the discharge. Swedish rates of fire using cartridges were said to be up to three rounds a minute, faster even than the more complex loading of muskets, and much better than anything achieved by the enemy.[17] In contrast there was the slower method used by other armies, canister was loaded after wadding, wicker and cloth had been rammed down the barrel behind the gunpowder charge. This required three ramming actions, one ladling action for the loose powder, and two sponging actions as well as a 'worm' action. A collateral effect of the introduction of cartridges was that the number of cannoneers per gun could be halved.

When emitted from the barrel, the balls from a grape canister would spread out like a shotgun blast, causing the sort of casualty rate that might be expected from machine guns. A single cannon blast of grapeshot could kill and wound as many as sixty to eighty soldiers.[18] Optimal point-blank ranges are defined as up to 250-340-460 metres for 2-6-12 pounders respectively.[19] Sweden's General

Wrangel attested to the terrible effectiveness of grapeshot at second Breitenfeld 1642.[20] At the battle of Avin 1635 Spanish cannon fire using grapeshot was particularly effective according to French officer Pusegur, 'our infantry always advancing, came very close to their entrenchments. They fired two shots of cannon charged with grapeshot, with which they killed thirty or forty men of the battalion; and wounded as many.'[21]

A lethal munition innovation at medium to short range was chain shot, for attack or defence, whereby chain-linked solid cannon balls whirled through the air like aerial scythes causing horrific injury to soldiers or horses in packed formations. Similar in concept were the crossbar shot, the jointed crossbar shot, and the expanding crossbar shot.[22] Just twenty-eight-years-old, the young and gifted Swedish General Lilliehöök was killed by such a munition at 2nd Breitenfeld, as was Pappenheim at Lützen, when the side of his body was sliced off: he took a while to die.

Artillery development in the war was revolutionary in its impact on military tactics.

Rates of fire and casualties

Using Swedish artillery rates of fire for the Thirty Years War with cartridge ammunition by analogy to the Napoleonic period [because the technology was essentially the same and had made comparatively little advance since the end of the Thirty Years War], casualty rates from one gun on advancing infantry and cavalry would be as for the table below. The only significant technological difference was the method of elevation adjustment using a winding screw rather than quoins [different sized wedges].

Cavalry **Advance five minutes approx. 960m**	960–480 metres round shot And 480–240 round shot 240–0 **grapeshot**	4 killed 2 wounded 6 killed 4 wounded 9 killed 23 wounded total 19 killed 29 wounded Total-casualties-48-excl horses
Infantry **Advance 11.5 min approx. 960m**	960–720m round shot 720–480m round shot 480–240m round shot 240–0m **grapeshot**	4 killed 4 wounded 8 killed 2 wounded 16 killed 10 wounded 32 killed 90 wounded Total: 60 killed 106 wounded Total casualties: 166

C.E Franklin, British Napoleonic Artillery, 1988, p.34/5 [as researched by Muller]

Casualty rates increased in a non-linear progression at close ranges as the effects of grapeshot fired by canister and cartridge took hold below 250 metres. Rates of fire in the battle were often deliberately slowed by the need to conserve munitions or by sloth in bringing up reserves.

Casualty rates from cannon fire could be very high during the Thirty Years War, especially considering that armies in Germany often employed 15–20 field guns excluding dozens of regimental 3 pounders. If every field gun caused 166 casualties as the armies closed and assuming that regimental pieces caused half that number, then given a standard army quota of 15 field guns and thirty regimental pieces – three per infantry regiment, [assuming conservatively an average of a hundred casualties per field gun and fifty casualties per regimental gun, total casualties in open field battle might be 3,000 from cannon fire alone against the attacking side These figures above assume a battle between opposing armies of 20,000.] Battles where each side attacked in turn or where guns were turned round, as at Lützen, saw the highest casualty rates from cannon. Frontal attacks against cannon in fixed and fortified field positions resulted in much higher casualty rates. Masking of guns in prepared positions behind earthworks and gabions not only allowed careful preparation of the field of fire and ranging but also protected the gunners, so allowing them to operate with more concentration and less fear. Guns would not be put out of action so easily through loss of gunners.

Casualty figures and optimum rates of fire given above are for *optimal* conditions or when the cannoneers are protected: i.e. when the cannons are dug into earthworks, masked by gabion, or fired through enclosed fortress portals. However, conditions were rarely optimal, nor enemy commanders, except Condé, so obliging as to feed their troops into the mouth of guns spewing grapeshot from fixed positions. So, except at Freiburg and Alerheim, where total casualties from cannon probably exceeded fifty per cent the casualties caused by cannon were probably around thirty per cent but might be much lower depending on condition and topography; At White Mountain 1620, cannon casualties were probably less than five per cent. It seems likely that casualty numbers from cannon increased exponentially through the war as cannon professionalism improved as training increased, numbers increased, and tactical deployment improved. Levels of casualties inflicted by artillery were a matrix of factors *including* the following, the nature of the battlefield collision [set piece or encounter type], troop deployments, munition availability, the terrain, the weather, visibility, the number of guns, the tactics employed by the generals, the extent of field entrenchment, the length of the battle, and the proficiency of the gunners. Following Sweden's lead the Imperialist also appointed Hatzfeld as Imperial general of artillery. It is no coincidence that this was a route to high command because both Torstensson and Hatzfeld became commanders in chief.

It is estimated that from 1750–1850 century 50 per cent of casualties were due to cannon fire[23], so given the similarity in equipment, handling, and tactics from the middle of the Thirty Years War, i.e., from about 1630, we could by analogy estimate a rate of thirty to fifty per cent (taking into account a sharp increase in quantity and quality since the early seventeenth-century), depending on variables listed above. Supporting evidence for high casualties caused by cannon fire comes from comparisons to the English Civil War: lack of effective artillery meant that the percentage battle casualties in the Civil War were much lower than for battles in Germany. Important English Civil War battles had total casualty ranges from six to twelve per cent of combatants compared to fifteen to thirty per cent in an analogous sample of German battles. Such a large difference in battles employing the same weapons and tactics points to ineffective use of artillery and this is notable because the Civil War did not start till 1642 when the artillery arm was already well advanced on the continent. The fact that English armies did not use battlefield entrenchment in the open field as a tactic is also significant: if cannon had been effective, English armies would surely have entrenched.

The artillery trains

Lennart Torstensson was the leading exponent of gunnery in the Thirty Years War. As artillery general his guns won the battle of Breitenfeld and his rapid deployment of a defensive gun line at Wittstock 1636 to cover the right flank was the key factor in allowing enough time for the decisive envelopment and outmanoeuvre of the Imperialist left flank, which so threw the Imperialist formations and battle plan into chaos. Torstensson's return from Sweden in 1641, accompanied by a new limber equipped artillery train, was a significant event in the war. After the first phase of battle of Jankov 1645, Torstensson was able to advance his guns with such speed over several miles to prevent the Imperialist retreat and force a decisive second phase of battle. He went on to become the greatest general of his day, the first exponent of mobile artillery deployment. Whereas by the mid-1630s nearly a hundred per cent of infantry and cavalry units in the Swedish army in Germany was composed of Germans, Scots or sundry other foreigner, the Swedish artillery was an exception in remaining manned by Swedes or Finns. The artillery regiment remains to this day as an honoured part of the Swedish army. It is the measure of the importance attached to the arm by Swedish generals and leaders and was reflected in Swedish success in battle.

Because variables, such as quality of powder or the age and quality of the gun were so critical, gunnery at the start of the war was still as much an art as a science. But the Swedes certainly built on the increasing directional shift towards science, which had been gathering pace through the sixteenth century especially with Italian led innovation in gunnery and fortress construction. Swedish improvements had less to do with science and theory, but more with practical incremental improvements or design innovations in equipment, munitions, logistics, gun-handling, and training. Excellence in foundry techniques, production standardisation, and the high purity of Swedish copper were also factors in making sure that Torstensson's Swedes excelled. Significant too were the improvements in metallurgy made by Swedish smelters using their depth of experience over centuries and leavened by foreign expertise. (Research currently being conducted at Oxford University will soon throw more historical light on developments in early modern Swedish metallurgy) The reductions in weight of cannon were not just helped using bronze but also by the refinement and experimentation in improving the strength to throwing power ratio (range) between gun barrel weight and quantity of powder. Increased rates of fire, of power, range, mobility, and accuracy resulted in a significant increase in deployed battlefield firepower.

Wagoneers and teamsters, who remained as civilians during this époque, went far to the rear when the shooting started. However, Torstensson's ability to move guns quickly, necessarily involved the militarisation of these personnel so that they stood in nearby attendance and ready to move when ordered. Wallenstein's Imperial army and others quickly copied Swedish innovations, although the Swedes maintained their edge in quality of equipment, numbers, and training. However, Swedish guns were predominantly of bronze whereas Imperialists, with limited access to copper, would mainly have heavier iron guns.

Limbers with horses in harnesses were not universally used and many armies would simply drag their guns around using large horse teams as if pulling a plough. Reducing gun barrel size and metal weight also had an important knock-on effect in reducing the weight of wood and metal needed for the transom, trail carriages and limber: the wheeled limber attachment via a pintle to the gun carriage effectively made the combined gun-limber into a four wheeled vehicle, which made the unit easier to handle over roads and open ground because of greater weight distribution. Simple limbers were used early on but better design including larger wheels helped to increase efficiency and speed; e.g. less bulky, the development of the split trail carriage and the use of lighter woods for some parts all helped reduce weight. Woodcut prints of cannon show that the length of gun barrel decreased by about thirty-fifty per cent over the course of the war. However, wheel size, though not weight or wheel width, would have remained constant with the diameter increasing from fifty per cent of the barrel length, a norm in 1618, to about seventy-five to a hundred per cent, as barrels became shorter. Weight reduction was essential for speed and mobility especially over open fields, let alone muddy roads. By 1648, a field gun and limber would have been as much as thirty per cent lighter than at the start of the war: this explains Torstensson's rapid cross-country deployment of field guns at Jankov 1645.

Clumsy long-barrelled leviathans dragged round by huge horse teams, as depicted at the early period of the war, were replaced by the war's end with muzzle-loaded cannon pulled by limber attached horse teams that were not too dissimilar to those deployed at Waterloo, Gettysburg, *Königgrätz* [by the Austrians] or Mons 200 to 300 hundred years or more later.

Torstensson's guns were produced in Swedish factories from the metal that was mined and smelted in southern Sweden. Cannon involved huge logistical expense, with a single 24lb gun in Tilly's train requiring twenty to twenty-three heavy horses. Twelve-pounders required at least fifteen horses. Each gun would also need a train of up to ten wagons for cannon balls and powder, with as many as ten horses per wagon. After all, a cannon, even an excellent one, is useless without ammunition as the Ukrainians are discovering today with their shell crisis. despite having far superior delivery systems, it counts for nothing without adequate shell or rocket supply. Swedish logistical capability was an essential ingredient to the effective use of artillery because apart from sheer numbers and positioning, effectiveness 'depends on the logistical system's ability to provide the right type of ammunition at the right time and place on the battlefield.'[24] Spanish general Francisco de Melo campaigning with twenty-four cannons required 800 wagons just for the guns and 2,000 mules or horses. Serving the guns were 245 cannoneers, about ten men per piece, but less in Swedish artillery units due to the use of cartridges. The regimental pieces used by the Swedish army needed one or two horses each or three to four men, if of the smallest calibre, and the number of these pieces at two per regiment might be as many as forty for an army. The logistical effort necessary for a gun train was massive: all testament to the increasing importance of artillery in the battle order.

Turenne made the commonsense remark that guns that were brought up by horse were less effective than those planted in defensive positions. The casualty figures from the battles of Freiburg and Alerheim prove the point.

Artillery effectiveness in Thirty Year War battles

The number of cannons brought to battle by the Swedes tended to be higher than their opponents because of the use of light regimental guns. However, the Swedes also deployed more field guns; all of this is hardly surprising as Sweden was the world's largest producer of high-quality cannon. At first Breitenfeld 1632 Gustavus's army deployed sixty-six guns to the Imperialist twenty-six. The battle of Wittstock saw the Swedes deploy two times more guns than the Imperialists, approximately sixty versus thirty. At second Breitenfeld in 1642 the Swedes took seventy-six guns into battle compared with forty-six for the Imperialists. Note that these numbers include the small regimental pieces, so the advantage in field guns was lower, notably at Breitenfeld before the Imperialists copied the regimental gun concept. Efficiency in rate of fire and the quality of the equipment were the main Swedish advantages. The most spectacular 'modern' use of artillery occurred at the battle of Lech 1632. Tilly's Imperialist army was entrenched in redoubts behind a strong river line barring Gustavus's advance into the Danubian plain and Ingolstadt and Munich beyond. Bringing up seventy guns against twenty for the Bavarians, Torstensson's cannon pinned down the Bavarian army in their entrenchments, as well as providing covering defensive fire for Gustavus's double bridging manoeuvre of Gustavus, to prevent and brake up Imperialist counter attacks against the bridgehead.

At Lützen Wallenstein deployed thirty-eight guns in entrenched defensive positions, especially at the key windmill position on his right, while the Swedish artillery in the absence of Torstensson (captured at Alte Veste) was less effective than usual. The use of guns enabled Wallenstein to hold back the Swedish army while Wallenstein's guns decimated the Swedish right in an attritional battle, which was only won by the sheer heroics of Saxe-Weimar. However, the death of Gustavus and the losses inflicted by the Imperialist guns prevented any follow up to this Pyrrhic victory. Sweden's captured Imperialist gun battery in the centre-left of the Imperialist line was used to good effect to check the Imperialist counter-stroke. The efficacy of cannon had already been noted by Kynphausen's adjutant at Lützen in 1632, where both sides suffered thirty per cent losses; he wrote 'It was the cannon in particular that caused the great damage to both sides…'[25] Staggering losses Lützen were probably accounted for by cannon fire, which may have claimed as much as fifty per cent of all battle casualties. At Alerheim in 1645 the French infantry suffering eighty per cent-casualty rates was all but wiped out after making frontal attacks on masked cannon positioned in the churchyard, where cannon probably accounted for well over fifty per cent of French battle losses.

The battle of Freiburg was similarly bloody as French troops made headlong charges against strongly entrenched cannon protected by redoubts and rows of *chevrise de feux*. Having significantly outnumbered the Imperialist on day one of the battle, the French army was significantly outnumbered by the end of day two. At Wittenweiher (Wittenweier) in 1638, the crucial point in the battle was the turning of the captured Imperialist guns on their erstwhile owners to defeat a dangerous counter-attack. Napoleon, the master cannoneer, commenting two hundred years later the battle of Alerheim, said that the French attack unsupported by artillery was hopeless. Earlier in the war artillery had been of little consequence, with Tilly deploying just twelve guns at the White Mountain in 1620, against ten for the Bohemian army. Their impact on that battle was negligible: probably accounting for no more than five per cent of casualties, because of the small numbers deployed and their inefficient use. However, although the battle was lost by the Protestants, defensive gun lines of mobile falconet size pieces [3lb] at Wimpfen in 1622 seem to have caused heavy Spanish casualties.

Encounter or ambush battles like Rheinfelden in 1638, Mergentheim 1645, and Tuttlingen in 1643 would have seen far fewer casualties from cannon because there was too little time to bring up or deploy all the guns effectively or at all. Although there were relatively few guns in play at Rocroi, heavy tercio losses at the close of the battle included many caused by cannon fire at close range. At the battle of Avin in 1635, French commanders noted the effectiveness of well positioned Spanish cannon in a set piece battle, 'their artillery which was posted very advantageously for them, started at the same time such fire and such noise that many of the troops on the left wing were completely shaken.'[26] France, deficient in manufacturing capability, deploying few guns in battle, suffered in consequence heavy infantry casualties.

The Imperialists used cannon as an essential part of their defensive field work positions at the battles of Dessau Bridge, Lech, Wittstock, Alerheim, Freiburg and Jankov. Gustavus used field works lined with cannon extensively in Poland at Mewe and in Germany at Werben and Nuremburg, where over 300 were deployed. The fieldworks would often include cannon protected by gabions; [masked batteries with the gunners protected by sand filled wicker baskets, or earth banks]. Fortresses shaped as horns or stars would look to funnel infantry attacks into batteries' arcs of fire; killing zones for grapeshot spewed from cannon.

In the English Civil Wars, the lack of a major impact for canon is remarkable; numbers were far fewer and there was a lack of expertise. However, there were a few occasions where artillery was mentioned and where cannon was deemed as effective. A Newbury, a whole file of men was decapitated by one shot. At Hopton Heath in 1643 a witness described how, 'at this tyme alsoe wee drew up our cannon which was one very good piece and did great execution for the first shot killed six of their men and hurt four and the next made a lane through them that they had little mind to close againe'[27] .

At Lostwithiel the effectiveness of guns firing plunging shot was shown when the king captured Beacon hill; immediately he 'caused a square work to be there raised, and a battery raised upon which some cannon pieces were planted, that shot into their quarters, and did them great hurt, though their cannon [firing up hill] though they returned twenty shot for one, did little or no harm,' [According to Clarendon's memoires] Height in the gun position was a key factor in its effectiveness; at Honnecourt the Spanish guns mounted on a hill overlooking the French positions disturbed the French defenders considerably with their plunging shot and this helped Spanish troops to score a signal victory even though the French were seemingly well protected behind a wall. Conversely Gustavus's massed guns at Alte Veste had little impact because they were firing uphill, a problem that General Lee would encounter at Gettysburg when he massed his 100-gun battery to open fire uphill at the centre of the federal line.

Chapter V

Muskets and Grenades

'Gustavus saw that the day of the national army was dawning and that the dominant weapon was he musket'

JFC Fuller[1]

The arquebuses came in different sizes and weights; because of their heaviness, 4–7kg, and length, about 1.3 metres; a rest pushed into the ground supported them. They were loaded using standardised pre-filled powder pouches that were carried in bandoliers. The weapon had a bore of 15–20mm, a range [inaccurate] of 150–200m, as well as considerable stopping power, including the ability to penetrate armour at 50–75 metres. Muskets were heavier still at 10 kg, and definitely needed a rest. At the start of his wars against Poland, Gustavus chose to arm his troops with the heavier calibre matchlock weapon which had a larger hitting power suited to taking down Poland's famous cavalry horses. It was also simpler and cheaper to produce and maintain but match cord had to be imported. Later in the war some units on all sides began to be equipped with smaller, lighter muskets without rests. These were called caliver, had a smaller bore 15.9mm and a shorter length. The stopping power was less, with less armour penetration, but in the latter years of the war soldiers carried less armour. In 1632 it was noted by Sebastian Dehner, a German chronicler that in Rothenburg '6th May…a company of Swedish infantry arrived, among them were musketeers armed with the new very light muskets without forks.'[2] However, use of the rest still predominated till the war's end. As horses were not armoured a shot could at least put down a horse or send it careering to the rear. Spanish tercio troops may not have adopted linear tactics but nonetheless they adjusted their ratios of muskets to pike as the war progressed.

As for the musket itself the old-fashioned musket/arquebus or matchlock type with the constantly burning match was increasing replaced by the 'snaphance' adopted by the Swedes. The *'snaphance'* type had a firing mechanism akin to the later flintlock; they were developed by autarkic necessity and produced in Sweden because of deficient domestic raw materials to produce match cord; [made from hemp which was grown in Russia]. Enjoying the technical capacity to make more complex mechanisms due to the downstream industrial benefits from their metal industries, the Swedes could manufacture on an industrial scale what was technologically a far superior weapon.

For close personal defence the musketeer might also carry a short sword but he would often use his musket as a club in close combat. Wheellocks with complex clockwork mechanisms had a more stable type of firing mechanism and were issued to cavalry or troops guarding powder wagons, because burning cords would be too dangerous. Both sides employed mounted infantry regiments, dragoons: the difference from cuirassiers was the carrying of a carbine or musket and the lack of armour.

Match cord for arquebus or musket was a dangerous and complex firing method. A permanently burning match cord was something hazardous, when musketeers carried powder bag bandoliers and powder horns. De Gehn's drill of 1607 describes thirty-three firing steps.[3] Even if not all of these were followed in practice it is likely that firing was slower than for a snaphance which required as little as ten steps. A higher rate of fire would give a great advantage to infantry because it would effectively increase the battlefield value of the infantry unit relative to an enemy using matchlocks; i.e., a unit firing twice as fast as another would need only half the number of men for firepower parity. Swedish innovation with all-in-one cartridges reduced ramming and cleaning actions to just two, so the rate of fire increased by an estimated fifty per cent.[4] And some historians such as Chandler have argued that the rate of fire was doubled. This could also explain the early adoption by the Swedes of much higher musket/pike ratios than other armies, of 3 or 4:1, because a higher rate of fire could better deter cavalry attacks on musketeers who would otherwise be more vulnerable. Firing in rolling volleys by rank, with the front rank counter-marching through the files to the back to reload, Swedish infantry could reckon on the enemy not being able to charge them during a 'loading gap'. However, this took great discipline and tight formation which would be under threat in the heat of battle where smoke obscured the battlefield.

When the elite Yellow and Blue regiments of the Swedish army were obliterated at Lützen we may speculate that there was a breakdown in fire discipline and formation. Fed into the battle piecemeal it is possible that in the fog and smoke that their order was broken, and/or they were taken in the flank by heavy Imperialist cavalry or that their ranks were broken up by heavy artillery fire. Fire discipline did not save them; weak in numbers of pikemen to fend off cavalry it seems likely that they were surrounded and ridden down. Eyewitnesses noted the 'mounds' of yellow cassock clothed bodies. The Yellow regiment according to *Oberstleutnant* Giulio Diodati, was 'in a moment reduced to a mound of corpses'[5], having been engulfed by three Imperialist regiments. Count Brahe the upcoming Swedish general was killed with them. Scots mercenary Watts, another witness, noted laconically, 'These two brigades were the flower of the army: old soldiers of 7 or 8 years' service.... but it had been so long since they had beene last beaten, that they had by this time forgotten how to runne away…'[6]

Archaeological evidence as to the extraordinary percentage of deaths caused by pistol shots to the head must lead to speculation as to the cavalry riding them down and shooting pistols at close range. Of forty cadavers discovered in the site of the Yellow Regiment's last stand, twenty-seven had died from pistol shots in the head. Alternatively, and possibly more likely given the inaccuracy of pistols even at short range especially in battle conditions, the surrounded troops surrendered and were executed on the battlefield: a practical measure given the impossibility of securing prisoners on this smoke and fog enshrouded battlefield in the middle of a battle. [see later section on battlefield archaeology] The alternative idea that has been posited is that the killings, with pin point accurate headshots, were the result of successful caracole tactics by Piccolomini's cuirassier. Cuirassiers were impact troops, and given that the yellow and Blue Brigades at Lützen deployed few or no pikemen (in the case of the blue brigade), there would be no need to caracole even if that was an effective tactic which we know it was not. (See above section on cavalry)

The French army which seems to have used matchlock weapons retained an official 1:1 ratio until the war's end although it is likely that they moved to a 60:40 or 2:1 ratio under the influence of other armies: There are only displays of match-cord type muskets rather than snaphances at the French Army Museum of Les Invalides. The French also had specialist musketeer units, which might also skew the numbers. Emphasis on maximum efficiency and firepower was logical for a small nation like Sweden with a small population: in contrast to France.

The other main weapon was the pike of about 5.3 metres [or 15ft in length according to Markham's '*Soldier's Accidence*'] but very often cut down in size by a metre. Traditional pike lengths were 18ft but his reduced during the war to a less unwieldy 12–16ft.[7] Pikes should be 'well headed with steel and armed with plates downward at least four feet.'[8] This was to prevent the head being lopped off by sword or axe and the pike rendered useless. The pike should be aimed slightly upwards at the throat and face of the opposition. It was phalanx warfare not unlike the methods of the ancient Greek Hoplite, with the same tendency for formations to veer to the right as the left-hand man closed up on the right-hand man for protection. Gustavus insisted on pikemen having a full set of body armour and helmets, especially in the front rank, but after his death, by the end of the 30s, the full set was discarded in favour of lighter buff coats and a cloth cap or felt hat: Less protected but more comfortable. As long as *someone* in the company had a metal helmet the unit could at least have a pot to stew rabbits in. Buff coats varied in quality and thickness, but a good one could absorb a weakly powered or dropping bullet or blunt a sword strike. Armoured pikemen would normally be placed in the front rank but the wearing of armour declined during the war for reasons of cost and sheer weight. Pikemen might also carry a short sword, dagger, or axe for close fighting, especially useful in trench warfare during sieges or attacks on redoubts. Pikemen enjoyed lower prestige than a musketeer who were paid a small premium of about fifteen per cent[9], seven reichsthaler per month. However, despite inferior status as the age of firepower took hold, veteran Colonel Monro asserted that 'Pikemen being resolute men shall ever be my choyce in giving an execution as …in retiring honourably and with disadvantage from an enemy, especially against horsemen… when musketeers doe disabandon of greediness to make booty, the worthy pikeman standing firm with his officers, guarding them and their colours'

In practice battles did not often come to push of pike: psychological timidity tended to stop infantrymen from rushing on into a wall of musket fire. Often infantry would stand their ground and blaze away at each other; such a psychology was also noted in the American Civil War. As in modern wars, few really liked the idea of hand-to-hand combat unless the enemy was helpless, i.e., on the ground, wounded or with his back turned. 'It is true,' noted veteran Sir James Turner, 'the business very oft comes not to push of pike.'[10]Rather the formations would stand and deliver fire until one side broke. [Such observations of battle behaviour of infantry in line were the same in the eighteenth and nineteenth centuries] They would rush in to massacre a fleeing enemy when the opposing formation showed signs of morale collapse. Sometimes this moment would be occasioned by heavy losses, by being outflanked by the enemy or by a false rumour. Or it could be the loss of a charismatic unit officer; 'he [the officer of the opposing unit] being slaine' recounted Scots veteran Colonel Muschamp, 'wee might perceive their pikes and colours to topple downe, to tumble and fall crosse one another; whereupon all his men beginning to flee, wee had the pursuit of them until the night parted us.'.[11]

The importance of veterans lay in the requirement for the spread of the knowledge of musket drills and linear formation manoeuvre, as well as for the necessary discipline and moral cohesion based on 500–600-man regiments.

It is not surprising therefore that the highly experienced Spanish Walloon and Neapolitan tercios of Tilly's Bavarian/Catholic League/Imperial army were able to smash the Protestant forces at the White Mountain and subsequently at Wimpfen, Höchst, Fleurus, Stadtlohn and Lutter. The key to victory was not so much tactics or strategy on the battlefield but the dominance of experienced battle-hardened veterans of the Spanish military system over inexperienced Protestant levies, who were often little better than militia, and mercenary captains. With a disciplined mass of pikemen in elite Spanish or Imperial tercio bearing down on them it is not surprising the thinner ranks of green troops would cut and run. '…from documentary evidence …large masses of soldiers do not smash into each other, either because one gives way at the critical moment, or because the attackers during the advance to combat lose their faint hearts and arrive at a point of contact very much inferior in numbers to the mass they are attacking. In either case, the side which turns and runs does not do so because it has been physically shaken but because its nerve has given.'[12] Where the armies did smash into each other the fighting was particularly brutal with attendant heavy casualties; such instances were experienced at second Breitenfeld. Blocks of infantry locked horns; as they advanced according to Swedish General Wrangel the troops 'suffered great loss from the grape and cartridges of the enemy…' [23 October 1642] After the opposing infantry closed the fight became 'a very hard action and we fought long pike to pike.'[13]

Performance of early modern firearms

Test firings of authentic early modern small arms conducted in 1988–1989 by the staff of the Landeszeughaus (Provincial Armoury) in Graz, Austria, a division of the Provincial Museum Administration produced extensive data on the ballistic characteristics (muzzle velocity, accuracy of fire, bullet penetration) of firearms. Bullets lost most of their kinetic energy in the first 30 to 50 metres of flight which were both inaccurate and inefficient in that they lost much of their kinetic energy within 30–50 metres. bullet holes made in paper with targets set at 100 metres (30 metres for pistols) composed of rectangular target measuring 167 cm x 30 cm (5 010 cm^2) was used to simulate the frontal area of a standing enemy soldier and armour plate was used and soap as a substitute for human flesh. Authentic width steel plate was used to replicate seventeenth-century armour. The results showed that at 9 metres a pistol ball could penetrate but it would cause just bruising because of the dramatic loss in kinetic energy. At 8.5 metres against an original cold pressed breastplate of 3mm with a spherical bullet from a pistol penetrated the armour but not the two layers of linen behind it with no penetration of the sandbag behind. A 31/27grm bullet from a matchlock would penetrate with a cavity of 530cm^3/369cm^3 at 9munarmoured but dropping for 27grm to 115cm^3 at 100m.

As for accuracy, due to the magnus effect the accuracy of long a barrel matchlocks was very poor with only a sixty per cent hit rate on a screen target of 30m x 2.13m at 75m range and forty per cent for 150 m. It is unlikely that long ranges would be relevant and its seems that a salvo might only let loose at 30–50m which shows that Gustavus was well aware of the accuracy and hitting power characteristics of the muskets and matchlocks of the day even for pistols firing at shorter ranges the hit rate was as high eighty-five to ninety-nine per cent which shows why 'it was not infantry but pistol armed cavalry who put an end to the classic lance armed heavy cavalry'.[14] However, this cannot be the only reason because lancers would make a strong comeback with European armies in the Napoleonic era; perhaps when the novelty and overrated effectiveness of pistols had worn off. Another point about the conclusion on pistols is that they were fired from fixed positions at very close ranges (9m) so the accuracy test from fixed positions rather than galloping horses skews the results. The marked difference between the two weapons is simply a matter of distant because the 'magnum effect' accentuated any aerodynamic distortion like a hook or slice shot in golf or a swinging ball in cricket. Distance magnified the effect. There is no solace in these number for supporters of the efficacy of 'caracole' tactic thesis not least because of the very poor penetration effect even on unprotected targets, where the result was likely to be sub lethal even at 9m. The other point to note about matchlocks is that the heavier bullet weapon chosen by Gustavus had a significantly and proportionately greater 'cavity wound' impact than the snaphance's lighter bullet. According to the data, fifteen per cent increase in weight fired by a long-barrelled firearm led to a forty-three per cent increase in the cavity wound created. which was most particularly chosen to shoot down horses, very few of whom would have armour protection on their breasts, except for the chargers of senior officers anxious to protect their expensive mount. It seems very likely given his professionalism that Gustavus was well aware of the difference and chose the weapon with the most hitting power to bring down horses. Accuracy would be far less significant if salvo power was released at short ranges 30–50m because it would give less opportunity for 'magnus' effect distortion. Ballistic tests on Japanese arquebuses of the late sixteenth century have produced similar results with very effective penetration of wood or metal (replicating Japanese armour) at 30 metres but reducing sharply at 50 metres. Accuracy, which was excellent at 30 metres, with a hundred per cent hits from skilled marksmen, reduced to twenty per cent at 50 metres, due to the 'magnum' effect. (Turnbull sourcebook p.137)

A trained ashigaru gunner could reload in fifteen seconds so ranks of three could put six bullets in the air in thirty seconds. Expert bowmen were also on hand to fill any gaps left in firepower potential. It is unlikely that an average soldier would fire every fifteen seconds and be able to keep up this rate of fire for a sustained period. Thirty to forty-five seconds might be more realistic. Samurai musketeers were armed with the best weapons, and they were trained as snipers to hit the highest value targets.

In the early seventeenth century there was a switch to European style breast plates something that saved the life of Naruse Yoshimasa during an attack on Osaka castle in 1614, 'It struck Yoshimasa on the left side and he fell from his horse...because he was wearing western armour it did not penetrate his body' (Naruse Kaizu). The shot was fired from a specially powerful and large calibre 'bird gun' musket. Yoshimasa's armour with a large dent is still in possession of his ancestors.

Master swordsmiths and armourers, the Japanese were perfectionists, so the weapons produced and copied from the Portuguese were improved on and were very fine pieces, both relatively light and accurate. Unlike western muskets, the Japanese did not use rests.

Musketeer were accompanied for protection by ashigaru with long spearmen whose function replicated that of pikemen. Musket ratios were smaller than in Europe with only 10 per cent of armies being composed of musketeers in the 1570s; it seems likely that this ratio increased considerably by the times of Sekigahara 1600.

Grenades, 'fireworks', and mortars

Gunpowder filled grenades and mortar shells came to be widely used in the early seventeenth-century, particularly in sieges or in around the confined spaces of the trench systems, saps, and redoubts around besieged places. These weapons came to the fore in the early seventeenth century, though they had been invented by the Chinese centuries before as we know from Chinese prints and literature.

'The shells (pào) are made of cast iron, as large as a bowl and shaped like a ball. Inside they contain half a pound of 'divine fire' (shén huǒ, gunpowder). They are sent flying towards the enemy camp from an eruptor (mu pào), and when they get there a sound like a thunder-clap is heard, and flashes of light appear. If ten of these shells are fired successfully into the enemy camp, the whole place will be set ablaze…'

Such mortar projectiles were commonly used in sieges; fired from mortars. Contemporary prints of the siege of Magdeburg and 1631 and the siege of Bautzen 1620 (Lusatia). (John George of Saxony captured the city when he took over the province Lusatia as part of his Faustian bargain with the emperor, to participate in the crushing of the Protestant Kingdom of Bohemia). Henri de Campion's memoires gives evidence as to the use of the effectiveness of exploding shells during French attempts to storm the lines of circumvallation at Salces on the Spanish Mediterranean coast. There is also forensic evidence from the skeletons uncovered at the Wittstock battlefield of injuries caused by shrapnel from exploding shells or grenades.

Fights and raids around the trenches were vicious affairs where the raiders would often arm themselves in a manner more suitable for hand-to-hand combat, with wheellock pistols, carbines, halberds, half-pike, axes, swords, clubs, and knives: All less unwieldy than full length pikes or arquebuses requiring a rest, which were weapons suitable for formal battle rather than hand to hand combat in confined spaces. Just as in the First World War hand grenades (grenadoes or fireworks) became a favoured weapon by the defenders in early sieges, being enabled to drop the 'grenadoes' into the dead ground beneath walls. For attackers 'greandoes' were for clearing trenches or storming redoubts.

Street fighting was not very common in the Thirty Years War because garrisons surrendered or fled once the walls had been breached. But there were exceptions, for example at the town of Saverne in 1636 where the French stormed the walls. In one counter-attack 500 men alone, from one French regiment, were lost to a fierce counter-attack by the defenders; Count Grammont in his memoires, attested to the effectiveness of grenades describing how 'from the top of the wall it rained an infinite number of grenades and musket shots, all the officers and a majority of the soldiers were killed or wounded, we had to abandon our gains…'.

Soon after in the latter half of the seventeenth and early eighteenth centuries the term 'grenadier' would join the lexicon of specialist soldiers and their units. In memoires of the time, they are often referred to as 'fireworks'. They are referred to in many memoires and clearly played an important in war at the tactical level; we hear of their use especially in trench warfare and siege warfare, at Stralsund, Frankfurt an der Oder, and Mardyck. At the siege of Leicester in 1645, they were used extensively, and their use was credited with the capture of several key hornworks.[15] It is possible that Prince Rupert, using his German experience, was particularly aware of the effectiveness of this weapon and may have heard of their use by royalists at the siege of Newcastle.

Just as in the First World War, Second World War, and at the battle of Dien Bien Phu hand grenades (grenadoes or fireworks) became a favoured or even primary weapon used by soldiers in close quarter combat in sieges, in defence of trench lines, strongpoints or by attackers for clearing trenches. Monro notes their use at the siege of Frankfurt an der Oder, and Mme de Montpensier describes the Great Condé's injury when he was nearly 'killed by a grenade which exploded near him whilst standing in the trenches…his face was burned by it.'[16]. At the siege of Newcastle in 1644, Scots officer Lithgow noted that 'we suffered more from hand grenades than from pikes, muskets and Herculean clubs.'[17] as they scrambled up rubble at the narrow entrance to the breach. After throwing grenades over the wall to drive back the defenders, they pulled it down using halberds and partisans. Fiennes's cavalry tried to counter-attack, but their horses flinched when faced with 'fire-pikes', pikes to which 'fireworks' were attached.

The effectiveness of grenades was also attested to by Monro who said of the defence of a ravelin at Stralsund 1629, that 'our soldiers valiantly and bravely defenced the ravelin with pikes and fireworks'.[18] This is an interesting comment because muskets are not mentioned and the reason most likely was the time taken to load them, after the first discharge, in the face of an onward rushing enemy. At Ingolstadt 1632 the Swedish Monro described the attempt to take an outlying sconce giving access to the bridge before the town was decisively beaten off 'with musket and with fire-workes (grenades)…leaving three hundred men killed about the Skonce...'[19]. Recently, seventeenth-century ceramic hand grenades were found in Ingolstadt's keep.

There is not one example of a modern fortress being stormed in the period 1600–1650 without first being mined. When new fortresses were built mining works would be pre-dug into the rear of the counterscarp and into the area underneath the glacis as listening posts or a means for countermining and counterscarp; as trip wires for enemy mining. Other engineers called 'petardier' or 'veurerker' specialised in grenades, mines, or explosive shells.

Not surprisingly Gustavus was in the forefront of developments in exploding shells and grenades, and organizational reform to promote this weapon. In 1629 Gustavus reorganised the artillery train into a separate regiment: this was in recognition of the vital element of Gustavus's concept of war that this arm of battle had become. No longer an incidental part of an army to give some morale boosting 'boom and bang' (or 'shock and awe 'in modern US parlance), in the opening phase of battle, it was to become a rigorously professional and significant arm of war. *'Firepower'* the coming concept of war, was thoroughly understood by Gustavus long before other commanders. In 1629 the various specialised companies of artillery built up since 1623 were formed into one regiment then put under the command of twenty-seven-year-old Torstensson, who was given the title 'Grand Master of Artillery'. He was the first colonel of the regiment that was still part of the Swedish army in 2012. The four companies in the new regiment included a *'fireworks'* company for siege work including bombs, grenades and petards, a type of mine fired from mortars. Sweden's arms industry also produced cast iron grenades and mortar bombs.

Chapter VI
Logistics

The horses

The supply of horses became a major issue of logistics in the Thirty Years War. Not only were thousands of horses needed as cavalry mounts but also as workhorses to pull supply wagon convoys and artillery pieces. A single wagon would require up to eight horses. So, a convoy of 1,500 wagons such as the one resupplying the French army at Arras might need about 9,000 horses. An artillery train of fifteen guns needed as many as 1,000 horses, though this was an improvement on earlier times when in 1554 a diverse fifty-gun Spanish train needed not just 1,014 horses for the guns but about 4,500 horses for the 575 accompanying wagons and another 473 for the guard[1]. Given the usages of war the turnover in horses would have been high and not just from battle losses which could be horrific. At Lützen 4,000 cavalry corpses of horses littered the field[2]; second Breitenfeld 1642 saw 3,571 horses killed on the Imperialist side alone. At the closing of the war in 1648 in the empire, there were a combined total of 63,195 cavalry and dragoons, [excluding the Spanish], implying at least the same number of horses in reserve, plus foals, one- to two-year-olds, and breeding stock. This implies a need for perhaps five times the cavalry mount figures, perhaps 300,000 dedicated or in the pipeline for military purposes. This compares to 150,000 military horses, excluding reserves and horses in the pipeline, in the Ottoman empire at the end of the sixteenth-century.[3]

A staggering number of work horses were required to feed the military machines of both sides. Maurice of Nassau's 24,000-man army in 1602 required 3,000 wagons. James Turner, a contemporary soldier, calculated that, 'a modest army of 5,000 horse and 9,000 feet would require 1,800 wagons not counting those of artillery.'[4] If we reckon that roughly half the troops were in garrison, then assuming that each corps of 10,000 men needed 2,000 wagons[5], and that each side in Germany deployed two *field* armies of 20,000, then 8,000 wagons would be required in addition to those for each of four artillery trains. If we assume that each wagon averages six horses, then total numbers of draft horses on active service may have been about 48,000 *excluding reserves* of at least double the number and the needs of the camp followers who might number the same or double those of the army being followed. The needs of the camp followers/sutlers etc. might require another 20–50,000 draft horses. Hauling cannon may have required another 1,000 horses in each artillery train of fifteen field guns making a total for the front-line armies of 52,000 work horses excluding reserves and camp follower needs. For example, in General de Melo's campaigns twenty-four cannons required 800 wagons just for the guns plus 2,000 mules. A single twenty-four-pounder siege gun needed at least twenty work horses. Muddy road conditions would require even more pulling power. These numbers exclude requirements for horses in the war economy's logistical chain, e.g. supply convoys small and large, up to 2,000 wagons. So, it would not be unreasonable to double the number to account for these sundry needs to over 100,000 draft horses excluding those in breeding, training, transit and in reserve. Further there were more than two armies operating in Germany at any one time. Perhaps a total stock of 300,000–400,000 draft horses for hauling wagon trains and towing barges was needed for military purposes in Germany alone: excluding larger numbers for agricultural and civilian needs. Replenishment needs must have been very high given the workloads.

Total cavalry mount needs plus total draft horse needs may have been about 300,000. If we assume that military needs represented twenty per cent of total needs in Germany during the Thirty Years War, it is perfectly possible that total horse population, cavalry plus draft horses plus farm horses in Germany was approximately1,500,000–2,000,000. This figure is analogous to and can be checked against the figure produced by Braudel for horses' population in France in the mid-eighteenth century when France had a population of twenty-five million (compared to twenty million for Germany in 1620) and a horse population estimated at 1,780,000 without the exigencies of civil wars. If there was an average ten-year life [assuming shorter lifespans in war and lack of veterinary skills in the seventeenth-century], annual livestock yield to maintain populations may have been as high as 200,000 and more perhaps in war conditions and with war demands. The spike in wartime demand must have been hard to keep up with. Cavalry mounts had to be of higher quality than ordinary farm horses; they needed height strength and endurance to survive the rigours of long marches irregular feed and constant outdoor life. Landing in Stettin in 1630, the Swedes brought their horses with them; a hardy Asiatic breed they hardly measured up to the magnificent German or Polish cavalry chargers. It took several years to replace them with German hoses. The Swedish cavalry, reported Salvius before Breitenfeld, were mounted on small nags in comparison to the massive German chargers; 'Our Swedish and Finnish nags looked puny next to their great German chargers.'[6] [Salvius 1631 Arkiv II]. Riding wild ponies of Mongolian stock from the northeastern Baltic, standing just eleven to fourteen hands high they would be contending with Friesians, Polish trans-don 'Turks' or Lipizzaner hybrids of fifteen to seventeen hands.[7]

There are no figures for livestock imports into Germany during the period of the Thirty Years War when war needs of the multiple armies would have been quite huge, not just in sum but in replacement requirements because death rates and casualties were higher in wartime through the excessive workloads, poor diet, and battle casualties. The main livestock countries available to export were Poland and Transylvania; and it was high quality. Bloodstock export was banned though some smuggling probably occurred in border areas; given the weak central government controls in both countries we should assume that there was considerable smuggling of bloodstock driven by good prices and high demand. The great wheat barons would hardly take notice of central government strictures on exports. Cossack cavalry hired in increasing numbers through the war brought their own mounts and probably extras. It would be surprising if they did not establish a conduit for the trade. We know that Transylvanian cattle exports ran at about 200,000 pa annum[8]; it would be surprising if the same channels were not used for horse smuggling across fluid borders. Domestic bloodstock breeding must have increased dramatically but apart from the aforementioned countries it is likely that there were imports also from the Dutch republic, Groningen, from Denmark's Jutland, from Italy and probably from the Bey of Buda.

A horse is only capable of ten days loaded work before it needs to be rested otherwise rapid impairment sets in. Recovery time can take weeks.[9] Horses are also edible items so hungry infantry would steal horses to eat them, something alluded to by Hagendorf's memoires. Swabian priest Father Meyer from the parish of Unteregg in the Benedictine lordship of Ottobeuren recorded how on 4 June 1634 'a cavalryman beat a horse to death with a hammer because it could go no further. (the animal) was butchered and eaten by the parishioners…'[10]

Logistical requirements for fodder were huge. Transportation was a problem because if green fodder were carried by wagon, the carthorse would consume their own load within three days.[11] A passive grazing horse consumes three per cent of its body weight per day and active service could easily double or triple this amount. Horses cannot live by grass alone so about twelve pounds of grain day would have been a standard requirement in addition to fodder: twenty-five pounds of hay. Grain could be substituted for four pecks of oats.[12] This is not to mention *passive* water needs of eight to ten gallons per day. So, grain supplies to the army became a large and larger component of supply needs throughout the war[13]. As we shall see army level strategy towards the end of the war was as much determined by the stomachs of their horses as by the needs of the soldiers. Field armies in the 1640s, in Germany at least, were primarily cavalry forces. On many occasions armies' fighting ability was compromised due to the loss of cavalry mounts.

The big breeding areas were in north Germany, in Holstein and Hanover, with contracting handled mainly by Jewish horse traders.[14] Smaller and lighter horses came from the steppes of Hungary, Poland, Moldavia and the Don basin. By an accident of history, we can see exactly the type of horse produced, because Gustavus Adolphus's stuffed horse *'Streiff'*, which was mortally wounded at Lützen, can still be seen inside a glass case at the Liverkammer museum underneath Stockholm's Royal Palace. (Contrary to the remarks of Jaroslav Hasek's character in *The Good Soldier Schweik*, it was the horse that was stuffed not Gustavus). Strieff was relatively small, which probably means that it was of more thoroughbred Andalucian stock. [There was also some shrinkage in the taxidermy process] Streiff stood 15.5 hands tall, well-muscled, thick set, with strong neck and powerful hindquarters. A fine small head indicates a hefty dose of Arab blood, which is why the height is on the low end of the range for a mixed blood. Given to Gustavus as a present by Colonel Strieff, after whom it was named, it cost 1,000 Reichsthalers, compared to the regular price for a good cavalry horse of 100 Reichsthalers[15]: about a year's pay. So, capital tied up in just the 5,000 cavalry horses in a regular sized army would be about 50,000 Reichsthalers excluding reserve mounts, saddles, arms, armour, and accoutrements.

Typically Hungarian hussars, Polish cossacks, and Croat horsemen rode lighter faster horses from an Arab/ Turkish stock, crossed with steppe ponies of Mongolian origin; types included Anatolian, Persian, Polish, Crimean, etc., generally referred to as trans-don type; 'small thin light hot tempered with a strong back and firm hoof, rarely sick, impervious to cold and wet and eating almost anything.'[16] Extremely hardy even in deep mid-winter, tough and more wiry, they could forage on any rough feed including the roofs of peasant cottages. They stood at medium height of about fifteen to sixteen hands.

Horses presented a major logistical problem for commanders, which increased over time as the importance and numbers of cavalry grew. Horses need rest and lots of food, both on active service and in winter when there is no grass. They are temperamental animals prone to illness and injury especially under difficult conditions: horse care was a vital part of a commander's decision-making. General Cromwell's rapid rise to prominence during the English Civil War was due in no small part to the Cambridgeshire man's expertise in horse breeding and horse care. General Franz von Mercy's Imperialists won two major battles at Tuttlingen and Mergentheim because he exploited his adversaries' need to disperse cavalry formations to find grazing and fodder at the end of the campaigning season. Campaign strategy was also determined by this 'grazing' factor, particularly as to winter quarters. Ramsay commented on Mercy's army in December 1644, 'the Bavarian army were always afraid of passing the Rhine, and of being undone for want of forage, and provisions, which was so great, that from Philipsburg to Mentz on this side of the Rhine there was nothing sowed, and nothing for horses to eat but in towns.'[17]

In the same campaign year the French army of 'Turenne finding that there was no danger of the Bavarian army's passing the Rhine, and that all his cavalry was perishing for lack of forage, kept only three or four regiments of cavalry, without baggage, which he put in the towns, and furnished them with straw, but with very little oats, and sent the rest of the cavalry away to the hills of Lorraine…'[18] An army's requirements for fodder was a major determinant of strategy, not least for when and where to go into winter quarters. In Spanish Roussillon in 1639 the absence of the French cavalry who had been sent back to Provence for forage had nearly led to disaster for the infantry positioned at Salces; when the Spanish attacked in force the French under Marshal Schimberg had to flee in the night to avoid annihilation in the plain. They were only safe when they reached the hills in terrain unsuitable for cavalry actions.. It was risky to put horses out to pasture in forward areas, especially when the exact whereabouts of the enemy were known, a lesson taught to the Franco-German army at the battle of Tuttlingen 1643 where von Mercy pretended to go into winter quarters before doubling back round a screen of forests to ambush Rantzau's helpless French army, which was dispersed in winter quarters. France's army was annihilated. At Mergentheim 1645 Franz von Mercy surprised Turenne while his cavalry his horses were being bloodied; heavily outnumbered in consequence, Turenne was driven back several hundred kilometres into Hesse having lost most of his infantry

As a result of these hard learnt lessons, going into winter quarters would often involve a strategic retreat by the French army to the left bank of the Rhine in the latter years of the war 1643–46 to keep out of reach of the enemy: yet another factor making the war difficult to win. Turenne noted in this regard that a commander should 'gain command of a tract of territory in which you have all winter to refresh and remake your army.'[19] Turenne found his safe haven and base area by clearing Spanish garrisons and territory on the left bank of the Rhine in the winter seasons of 1644 and 1645 up to the Mosel and the border with Luxemburg.

Food supply

The regular availability and provision of food was the most important element in the maintenance of an army. For a soldier, carrying food was just as important as carrying a weapon; Bernard Shaw's observations in his play 'Arms and the man' about a soldier storing chocolate rather than munitions is accurate. In the 'hierarchy of needs' it was no contest. Military historian Creveld writes in

'Supplying war' that, 'armies could and did follow the call of their stomachs by moving about freely to whatever region promised supplies while largely indifferent to their own communications with non-existent bases.'[20] Traditionally armies took what they needed as they went along. They simply took over houses and demanded sustenance and shelter; or they stole it and helped themselves. Spanish armies set up in advance *etapes* along routes of march and their well-organized commissariat carefully planned supplies in advance as well as routes of march for Spanish units. However, it seems that efficiency declined throughout the war; the increasingly bedraggled Wallenstein and Gustavus's armies would draw large lump sum contributions from towns and cities as well as regular contributions and quartering rights. Both armies had well-organized commissary arrangements but they broke down from time to time notably during the prolonged fighting around Nuremburg in the summer of 1632.

Given that household incomes were at subsistence level for a large part of the European peasantry the effects an army's stay in a region could be devastating, especially if the stay was extended. Braudel reckons that for an artisan in early modern Europe, let alone a peasant, that well over half of his income, about forty-five per cent would be spent on food for himself and his family. Of this amount seventy-three per cent of calorific content was cereal, which left people vulnerable to poor harvests and price rises.[21] For poorer families the percentage would be higher; consequently, the vulnerability to price rises and poor harvests would be higher too. In early modern Europe, for society at large as well as for armies, 'No issue was more urgent…more difficult to resolve than the matter of grain provisioning.'[22] According to Braudel, meat consumption had also declined markedly since 1550. However, food shortage was at times also an aid to recruitment.

Military historian Creveld writes in 'Supplying war' that, 'armies could and did follow the call of their stomachs by moving about freely to whatever region promised supplies while largely indifferent to their own communications with non-existent bases.'[23] This is not completely correct because Swedish army movements were based on well-provided magazines and river lines. Mediaeval armies took what they needed as they went along. They simply took over houses and demanded sustenance and shelter; or they stole it and helped themselves. Creveld's comments are correct for some armies during the war, but not for all armies at all times. Spain's commissariat and staff organisation was excellent. But sometimes even good systems broke down under the stresses of war and shortage of cash. Random pillage or foraging of food was commonplace for armies on the march or in retreat when it was difficult for logistical organisation to keep up with the necessary movement of the army. But organised provision of supplies was more prevalent than is often thought, because unfettered looting would drive away regular supply. However, billeting of troops on peasant families was only slightly preferable to civilians than out and out pillage because according to a contemporary 'The soldier consumes in just one week what the farmer expected to feed himself and his children for one month'[24]

In the Dutch army 'Soldier's rations consisted primarily of bread, beer, cheese, butter, bacon and salt herring....to encourage the supply of food stuffs, the field deputies could pronounce exemption from duties, which meant that all goods could be transported to camp without being subject to tolls or other levies.'[25] The most pressing problem for any army was bread, because soldiers at the least needed plenty of this carbohydrate staple to cope with the exertions of hard outdoor life. This required extensive logistical planning for the gathering of grain and the baking process, which if done in the field as the Dutch army liked to do, 'required six horse-driven mills and twenty iron field ovens...to guarantee the supply of the Dutch army's daily needs'[26] about 30,000 lbs. per day for 20,000 men. Alternatively, the food could be supplied from nearby towns or transported by wagon, or in the case of the Dutch, by barge. Colonel Monro of the McKay regiment was well aware of efficiency in logistical matters at Werben 1631, 'having a first commodity of transportation by water on the river Haggle (Havel) running into the Elve (Elbe) at the leaguer whereupon all provisions could be brought for maintaining of its army,' Swedish control of the major north south river heads from the Baltic and the North Sea was a great boon to Swedish logistics. Not least in calculation was the need for tens of thousands of heavy iron cannon balls and thousands of barrels gunpowder and beer for the troops. A single siege might consume as many as 10–20,000 cannon balls. They also controlled the Main for much of the war; this river was exploited by Torstensson for the purpose of moving the army's artillery from Wurzburg to Mainz rather than the undulating muddy tracks of the Taunus mountains.

Alternatively, the food could be supplied from nearby towns or transported by wagon, or in the case of the Dutch, by barge. There was always the problem of shelf life: Six days. This problem could sometimes be alleviated by double baking bread into rusk. Destruction or capture of an army's base of grain or bread supply would terminate an offensive, as happened to the Spanish army in 1628. The lack of bread destroyed armies quickly while the lack of nutrition in the form of vegetable or meat would do it more slowly, by lowering resistance levels to infectious diseases and dysentery. Sickness was a significant daily attrition on armies of the period.

As Jomini noted 'Navigable streams...render the transport of supplies much easier and free the roads from the encumbrances of the numerous vehicles otherwise necessary'. Access to rivers and river transportation greatly eased transport problems and reduced costs. When the Dutch army moved [circa 25,000 men] 1631, they needed 894 wagons and 232 barges. Transport costs as a percentage of a supply contract *without* the availability of barge transport might reach fifty per cent. Not surprisingly supply by barge was much more efficient and reliable, as well as being less vulnerable to ambush, (although large riverine convoys were captured on occasions on the lower Rhine). One barge would suffice for twenty or thirty wagons. Barges could be towed against the current by horses to cover about twelve kilometres per day. This accounts for the positioning of supply hubs or encampments on major navigable rivers. For example, Gustavus positioned his fortified magazine on the confluence of the Main and the Rhine. When marching from Wurzburg to Mainz, the logistical problems were greatly alleviated by General Torstensson's use of barges to carry the artillery train. The camp at Werben was on a river. Armies advanced, when possible, along river lines such as the Neckar and Weser, the Oder, and the Elbe, the Rhine, and the Main. "Key to Wallenstein's entire provisioning system was the port of Aussig on the Elbe, the point of dispatch by water for foodstuffs, goods, and war matériel from Wallenstein duchy of Friedland and across Bohemia and Silesia on to the German battlefields."[27]

Bread was the basic essential for the supply of an army. Without carbohydrate an army cannot function. There was always the problem of shelf life: Six days. This problem could sometimes be alleviated by double baking bread into rusk. When Frederick Henry's Dutch army of 20,000 prepared for its offensive against the French in 1635, 350,000 lbs. of bread were prepared, and 200,000 lbs. of two years old bread rusks was brought out of storage. There was food for about ten days of campaigning. In practice an army could hardly march more than fifty kilometres from a large bakery.

Rusks were ordered by General de Bergh when he invaded the Dutch republic with a combined Spanish and Imperial army in 1629 and threatened Utrecht, the second largest city of the Republic. Supply was the main problem for the invasion which based it supply magazine at the Rhine crossing at Wesel. To solve the capacity problem of supply by barge to Wesel and onward convoy to the army at Amersfoort, bread was baked into rusks. More importantly, for relatively long trip, rusks, unlike bread, would not become mouldy and stale. De Berg also ordered the recommissioning of two broken water mills to grind flour.[28] However, when Wesel was attacked and captured by a surprise Dutch attack in their rear the Spanish-Imperial army was forced to retreat. So ended the most threatening Habsburg attack of the entire war; Olivarez much-vaunted grand strategy for a combined Habsburg attack on the Republic's weak eastern flank had come to nought. The chance would not reoccur. It had been the original *raison d'etre* for the coup against Matthias in favour of Ferdinand II and precipitation of what became the Thirty Years War.

The lack of bread destroyed armies quickly, while the lack of nutrition in the form of vegetable or meat would do it more slowly, by lowering resistance levels to infectious diseases and dysentery. Sickness was a significant daily attrition on armies of the period. In the hierarchy of needs carbohydrates come top.

Duc de Rohan, the brilliant Huguenot general of the period in his military thesis: *Le Parfait Capitaine* In particular the provision of wheat or bread was the most essential need and de Rohan recommended that 'stocks should be kept in a secure magazine, which is no more than fifteen days march from the army. Distribution had to be tightly controlled, and infringement should be rigorously punished for those officials who cheated. Prices for the troops should be well regulated.'[29] Before retreating in from the Baltic coast in 1644, Gallas ordered large amounts of bready from friendly Hamburg (still under control of their ally Denmark), but the bread ran out when they were bottled up south of Magdeburg. The were doomed when a supply convoy was intercepted and captured by the Swedes; it was one of the problems of a 'war without front' when armies advanced deep into enemy territory.

Food was a vital underpinning for morale and military efficiency. Lack of food was a bigger destroyer of armies than plague. It was also the common complaint as to looting and ransacking by armies desperate for food, eyewitnesses recalled that: 'They set upon us like a set of locusts.... they pinched and pilfered from people cattle sheep bread grain, everything from their farms...', 'they plundered and took away all the grain seed corn and other provisions...', 'They drove off all my cattle...', and 'whole herds of poor people's livestock were driven off...'[30] Both people and soldiers suffered for want of food as it was hoovered up by roving armies and garrisons or soldiers in billets. If contributions in kind failed, for want of organisation or due to shortage, then the soldiers would take matters into their own hands. Most war diaries obsess about food; the plenty or the lack of it. Always tending to be short food, it was a far bigger preoccupation for an average soldier than thoughts of battle or strategy. After Breitenfeld Munro remembers the period the best because 'we found a well provider leaguer for our hungry stomackes, of all good victual where about the leaguer thee was feeding, kine, sheepe, calves, geese, hennes; they left also corn in abundance.'[31] For generals too, strategy was determined by availability of food, and quarters both for the men and horses, whose needs were just as important in holding an army in being. Food supply was a problem which was never overcome during the war. Just before the Peace of Westphalia 1648, Turenne's army turned to farming to feed itself; 'The corn being ripe, the infantry fell to threshing it, while the cavalry went foraging...'[32] The enemy were nearby but that was of secondary importance.

Meat supply for armies would be garnered mainly on the hoof; gathered in by theft or in some cases paid for. Essential for the European market was Transylvania, the major cattle exporters in Europe. Braudel estimates that Transylvania may have sold as many as 200,000 head of cattle into central

Europe *annually*, even before the war: half of the total European cross-border trade in cattle of 400,000 p.a. Poland, Hungary, Denmark, and the Balkans were other major suppliers.

One of the most important aspects of a decisive victory in the field was the capture of the enemy's baggage train and provisions. When this happened there was a double victory because not only was the winner reinforced with supplies, of which it may well have been short, but the enemy would contrarywise be deficient and likely unable to make up the loss quickly: in which case the defeated army would likely fall apart even if was not cut down in a close pursuit. How could the soldiery exist without food? Saxe-Weimar's armies during the Breisach campaign 1638 were always desperately short of supplies. Bernhard of Saxe-Weimar's victory at Wittenweier on 9 August 1638 when he surprised the dispersed Imperialist army by emerging from the woods caught the enemy on the march with their baggage train. Following a near run victory against larger army (20,000 to 16,500) the Weimarian-French army triumphed after turning captured guns on the enemy. Supplies and equipment captured 'included all the Imperial artillery, 11 cannons and 2 mortars, about 2,000 (Turenne put it at 3,000) wagons full of baggage and munitions, 5,500 sacks of wheat and forty barrels of powder, 47 cornetts and 36 flags, as well as the entire chancellery of von Goetz and Savelli, including memorandum, instruction and correspondence with the Emperor.'[33] (*French Gazette*) Much of the Imperial army which lost 1,500 killed and another 1,500 prisoners suffered a significant collapse in numbers of deserters following the battle such that Goetz could not muster enough men for another relief effort for some months. The loss of the wheat that had been destined for the besieged meant that the garrison was eventual starved into surrender; by contrast the food security for Weimar's besieging army was assured.

Food as determinant of strategy, the 'elasticity of war', and *Mother Courage*

Food and provisions were the abiding obsession for the soldier of the Thirty Years War and in truth his war had more to do with daily survival and the obtaining of food than with fighting which was a rare occurrence by comparison. George Bernhard Shaw in *'Arms and the Man'(1884)* paints the picture correctly when he has the hero more concerned with filling his pockets with chocolate than with bullets. In war time on foreign soil the supply system was always complemented by local provision. Armies would certainly look to winter in well-provided regions, but in summer too they moved on like locusts from one lush and un-spoilt region to another. The main issue was always food, as Spanish commander the Marquis of La Hinojosa commented in his letter to Don Juan Vivas 18 February 1615 'feeding eight thousand men for two months is no joke.'[34] That was written in peacetime in 1615 for troops moving through friendly territory. Not surprisingly during war and in occupation of enemy territory the problems multiplied, and the logistics might often fail altogether. Whole armies could disintegrate for want of food for men or horses. It should be remembered that in early modern Europe a large town or city would have a population of 30,000. An army of 15,000, with its hangers on at least double in number, would be like a large city in motion; two armies manoeuvring against each other in a restricted geographical area would soon suck the place dry of food and fodder as at Nuremberg in the summer of 1632.

Billeting of troops on peasant families was only slightly preferable to civilians than out and out pillage because according to a contemporary 'The soldier consumes in just one week what the farmer expected to feed himself and his children for one month'[35]

In the Dutch army 'Soldier's rations consisted primarily of bread, beer, cheese, butter, bacon and salt herring....to encourage the supply of food stuffs, the field deputies could pronounce exemption from duties, which meant that all goods could be transported to camp without being subject to tolls or other levies.'[36] Except salt herring which was a particularly Dutch taste and an item which they had easy access to, the diet was very similar to that of most armies in the Thirty Years War. Beef and mutton were also consumed when available. Fish was also popular. There were many fish ponds in Germany especially in monastic estates and bishoprics. Bohemia was especially famous for fish pond cultivation. At the battle of Jankov 1645 much of the fighting took place around a series of fish ponds (which are still there).

Memoires of ordinary soldiers from the wars are alike in that they talk as much about food as about fighting. Soldiers reckoned their happiness by the availability of food. Quality of life at any given moment was mainly correlated to the availability of food, shelter, and sex; in that order. For Scot James Turner access to 'meate' was especially important. Curmudgeonly Monro was happiest when food was plentiful. Raymond, a soldier of the time, remembered fondly that 'we had at this league plenty of provisions.... and so long as the money lasted wee had a merry life.'[37] He was happy even though he only slept on straw in an old tent. At other times though the situation would be grim if the logistic system broke down or a locality had been stripped of food. As soldier Hagendorf recounts, 'Stayed put for 14 days; celebrated Christmas with water from the Danube and didn't have a bite of bread. At this time there was such a famine in the army that no horse in the stables was safe from the soldiers.'[38] At times like this, armies would fall apart from desertion and disease. The hierarchy of needs put food before transport, cavalry, or munitions.

Provision of food by army commissariats essentially consisted of one thing, bread. Supplying bread, the normal ration was two loaves per soldier per day.

It was an extraordinarily cumbersome and difficult operation, requiring large supplies of grain, milling facilities for flour and transport, the dependability of which relied on the geography, state of the roads, and time of year. It also needed cash or a willing supplier of credit. An army of 15,000 would need 30,000 loafs per day and loaves are bulky items so a huge amount of transport was required. Hard tack biscuits or dried bread or what the French would call a 'biscotine' or husk, could be a convenient substitute for an army command, being both less perishable and more weight-cubic efficient. Dipped in water or soup it would bulk up; in practice an army's bread supply base should cover no more than a sixty kilometres radius. River communication would greatly ease the transport problem for reasons of cost *and* reliability. Obviously, all these arrangements were very vulnerable to breakdown not least because of the lack of cash. Ambushes by enemy light cavalry of vulnerable supply convoys, a not infrequent occurrence, were probably the least of the problems although the ambush of a large supply convoy to Gallas's army near Magdeburg in 1644 doomed that army to utter disintegration. Gustavus was also forced to retreat from the Alte Veste by food shortages due to Croat foraging.

Contributions were often demanded in kind, Typical of the demands made by armies was this Swedish requisition order of 1637, 'The villages, which are to convey necessities for the maintenance of my horsemen... must scrupulously provide the following, every day: five casks of beer, two hundred pounds of bread, sixty bushels of oats, two hundred pounds of beef, four wagon loads of good hay, a variety of spices for me and my officers as needed, a quart of butter, a half bushel of salt, thirty candles. Such shall be delivered daily and without diminution, and if a village fails to supply what is required, the horsemen will fetch it themselves, which the villagers will not like at all'[39]. Sometimes these orders were issued as part of a *salvagardia* arrangement in which case there might be a disciplinary attachment made to the demands, 'Under penalty of death, no officer or soldier shall demand anything other than what has been declared here.'[40] Again, many histories of the war (especially the sensational and populist accounts from nineteenth-century Germany) emphasise the depredations rather than the orderly management of war, which necessarily involved discipline, without which commissary arrangements would have broken down. For the regular feeding of an army, an absolute necessity to stop desertion and disintegration commanders needed order both to secure contributions but also to purchase foodstuffs.

Tryntje Helfferich quotes the Hessian Mannschaft register/census ordered by Amelia of Hesse in February 1639: apart from the fifty to eighty per cent decline in population 'More striking was the loss of livestock especially sheep and pigs-throughout Hesse but especially in these areas regularly frequented by soldiers. Some areas claimed not a single remaining farm animal or plough, not a single measure of sown grain... Niederaula saw the number of households drop from 835 to 146.... the number of sheep from 183,000 to 0, pigs 2062 to 3...horses 463 to 14, oxen 352 to 4. Even allowing for exaggeration these losses are simply staggering.' (Emphasis added)[41] This epistle of nihilistic gloom is contradicted by several hard facts. If there was no food in Hesse, why did Melander choose to go and quarter in this supposedly devastated area in the winter of 1647: and how could his cavalry commander Montecuccoli manage to buy 1,000 sheep, 150 cattle and 160 pigs in Hesse to feed his troops?[42] No doubt certain areas were sucked dry by armies, but this may have been as much by sale of product as by theft or contribution. Tax avoidance in the supply of false figures was not something invented by twenty-first-century multinationals, metropolitan billionaires, or north Italian entrepreneurs. Interestingly revenue recovery was very fast after the war, as punitive taxes/contributions were lifted.

Nonetheless there were irregularities, In Swabia in April 1632 the invading Swedes hit upon the Benedictine lands adjacent to their newly acquired outpost at Memmingen. They were forced to deliver grain, but 'it did not stop there,' according to the monks because meat, fish, beer, and wine was also demanded, 'and vast sums of money.'[43]: over 16,000 gulden. Not least of the reasons was the profit motive underlying the raising of their regiments under contract. In practice colonels, especially in Imperial or Bavarian armies could not always be easily controlled. Acting with impunity they often exploited the power of the gun to expropriate far more than was their due. Commanders necessarily had to turn a blind eye to the depredations, in a situation where there was no government cash to pay back-wages.

Around Protestant Ulm in 1632 it was reported that soldiers paid for their food, 'They bought up all the available bread, meat, beer, as well as grain and other things.'[44] Patrick Ruthven who was appointed Governor of Protestant Ulm set about raising two cavalry regiments from the area. This was a friendly area and Gustavus was able to link up with the Duke of Württemberg, the main Protestant power in the south west of Germany who had renewed his rebellion against the emperor. He was given a 'great supply of men, moneys, victuals, and ammunition for his armies'[45] noted Munro. Typical of Gustavus financial/geopolitical strategy he fanned out his forces around the Swabish region, according to Monro 'to helpe his contribution as Memmingen, Pibrach, Brandenburg on the river Elve (Elue), as also Middleham, Kawffbire, and Kempten on the Leacke (Lech).'[46] The task of subduing Swabia and linking up with the renascent Protestant forces in Swabia under the Duke of Württemberg, fell to Field Marshal Horn with a detached command. He would in due course be instructed to move across to the left bank of the Rhine to link up with the Rhinegrave and Birkenfeld to attack Alsace which was a mixture of Habsburg holdings and members of the empire.

Attempts were made by Wallenstein to deal with the problem of feeding mobile units by the distribution of dual-purpose hand mills, for milling grain to flour, or charcoal for gunpowder. Sometimes large mobile mills accompanied armies, especially the Dutch army. However, these facilities depended on local supply that would quickly be sucked dry by an army: in any case it depended on the time of year. Other staples, which was the responsibility of the army command, were beer, or wine for French troops. French troops and musketeers received two loaves a day plus 0.75 litres of wine, the size of today's standard wine bottle.[47] 'Decades of war' published in 1622 by Francis Markham, using his knowledge of Europe, surveyed the alternative food packages available for troops at the start of the Thirty Years War. He noted for example that 'half a pound of biscuit and half a pound of butter hath been a fit day's proportion for one man, or a pound of bread and a half of beef or else bacon a full day's proportion; or otherwise, a pound of biscuit and a pound of cheese... or four herrings...'[48] Food supplied to troops would be 'defrayed by their own payes and entertaynements.'[49] Not surprisingly army commanders were desperate for reasons of cash shortage and logistical burden, to shift responsibility for feeding their troops onto 'contribution', under the delegated auspices of local governments in occupied lands.

Parker notes that 'The traditional method of provisioning European armies was primitive; everything necessary for the soldiers was requisitioned on the spot, with or without compensation. The troops made for a village or group of villages and quartered themselves wherever they chose. In inhabited houses, the hosts had to provide free food and room service...'[50] Given that household incomes were at subsistence level for a large part of the European peasantry the effects could be devastating, especially if the stay was extended. Braudel reckons that for an artisan in early modern Europe, let alone a peasant, that well over half of his income would be spent on food for himself and his family.[51]

The Dutch army was always well provisioned and supplied though it was always close to its base of supply and well financed; Dutch strategic decisions suited a defensive strategy and optimized their logistics efforts, besides which the cost of transport on the multiple waterways of the Republic was fast, efficient, and cheap. Their army never fought beyond its borders. The French system of supply was overextended by multiple strategic objectives, over centralised and dependent on cash advances from bureaucrats in Paris, who responded tardily to logistics crises and pleas for help from distant and desperate army commanders. As a result, the system would often break down especially when armies crossed over borders.[52] This had strategic meaning because forays by French armies into Germany cost more as well as causing significant troop reinforcement problems. French armies often had to return to the left bank of Rhine to winter in order to receive new recruits as well as graze their horses in peace. The reason for establishing strongly fortified forward magazines was to enable armies to advance into enemy territory was because of 'the problem of supporting a numerous army in an enemy's country is a difficult one' and 'it will be prudent (for an army) ...not to advance too far from its depots.'[53] (Jomini). This accounts for the importance for France of Breisach, Phillipsburg and Koblenz on the Rhine, and Pinerolo on the watershed of the Maritime Alps. Not surprisingly securing these magazine fortresses was a major gain achieved by the Treaties of Westphalia after tough negotiations.

If an army advanced into what had previously been enemy territory, they would find the area stripped of food supplies; it was such problems that destroyed Mansfeld's army on several occasions, forced Baner's retreat from Bohemia in 1639, and 1641. It caused the devastation of Gallas's army that had marched in support of the Danes in 1643. It was hardly surprising that food ran out when these large moving cities passed over the land like so many locusts. A contemporary recorded that when General Aldrigen moved on Konstanz in 1633 to relieve it from the Swedes, he did so with 'some 30,000 soldiers but including the baggage train around 100,000.'[54]. In 1567 the Duke of Alba, on the march with 8,652 Spanish veterans and 1,200 cavalry, reckoned for planning purposes to cater for 16,000 mouths and 3,000 horses. The danger for armies, which were cut off from their base was that they might be too isolated from local sources of supply. This resulted in armies being destroyed by lack of food, or by consequent disease and desertion. Armies tended to advance beyond their logistical capability while the opposing army strengthened as it fell back on its bases.

However, the large number of camp followers had a purpose because the role of women was in no small part vital to the smooth functioning of the army. Not only did they cook and scavenge for food for their menfolk, but they also operated as a vital sutler service for extra foodstuffs, alcohol, tobacco, and other necessities, filling the gaps between what was and what should have been provided by the state, or by the regimental colonels. Supplying extra food and the little luxuries of camp; 'There are some who sold tobacco and provided the men with pipes when they needed them; others sold schnapps...'[55] Their function was sometimes institutionalised. Gustavus's Swedish army permitted one *vivandiére* per company of infantry, and one to two per company of cavalry. The French army had a plague of them; they would become a formalized feature in Napoleon's army when renamed *cantinières*. Their activities are recorded by Grimmelshausen's Simplicissimus and made famous in the figure of Mother Courage, immortalised by Berthold Brecht in the twentieth-century play. A soldier husband or 'protector' would give them the necessary safety to do their business, which according to varied woodcut prints, was conducted from tents or under awnings with their shingles of trade hanging outside. Naturally, a little plunder and pillage, as well as the fencing of looted goods would supplement these wifely and camp follower activities; such scenes are vividly illuminated in Jaques Callot etchings. Pimping, prostitution, and theft were other sidelines for extra income. Citizens would complain of 'the soldier's abominable wives' who stole food from market gardens and orchards.[56] When their man was wounded or sick his woman would become nurse; if he died, she would likely find a new 'protector' in short order.

The most pressing problem of war was always food supply, fodder, and grain for the horses. As the war progressed and more areas were devastated and depopulated, the provision of food became more difficult and expensive as demand soared. Figures produced by economic historian Braudel show that cereal price, especially rye, soared in the course of the Thirty Years War. This system explains the ability of armies to recruit and keep their soldiers, in contrast to former times-because even when cash payments were infrequent the troops received still a good remuneration in the form of their living costs. In hard economic times in the seventeenth century this was not to be gainsaid especially when the average artisan family might spend well over fifty per cent of his annual income on cereals alone.[57] When wages rose sharply through the war as the economy boomed form the effects of war demand and Keynesian military spending's effect on aggregate demand, labour started to move to the city and recruitment especially for infantry became difficult.

There are other reasons for difficulties in recruitment: as an army advanced it lost men from disease and desertion (itself often caused by supply shortages); armies moved into areas already devastated or denuded of food and other resources by the enemy. Garrisons had to be provided for newly captured towns, new recruits were hard to come by away from base areas, and equal and in opposite effect the enemy fell back on its core economic base and recruitment areas, enjoying shorter supply lines, so in consequence becoming relatively stronger. Establishment of magazines helped armies to project war further, but they were expensive to establish and maintain and being further forward they were also vulnerable to capture, like Wesel in 1628 or Breisach in 1633 and 1638: Magazines were ineffective for supplying bread beyond a range of about sixty kilometres or three days by wagon unless the advance was along a navigable river. The war in Germany was fought over such large areas with the supply bases of the key contestants so far apart. Sweden was based on the Baltic and Stettin in particular, and the Imperialist alliance mainly on Ingolstadt/ Munich and the Habsburg dynastic lands, including Vienna and Prague. It became virtually impossible for either side to bring enough military power to bear to conquer the other. Armies tended to outrun their logistical capacity. It was the rubber band effect. Advances gradually wilted under the strain of logistics before snapping back into retreat before a reinvigorated enemy: the seesaw elasticity of the Thirty Years War.

Once an army marched away from its natural base, it became increasingly vulnerable, and this 'stomach' strategy was well understood by the rival commanders. Hard enough do when the army was static, for obvious reasons, the logistical arrangements to feed an army on campaign, multiplied exponentially. As Germany and Bohemia became increasingly devastated along the main invasion routes this led to difficulties in supplying large field armies. The reality of the war was that offensives always tended to run out of steam and collapse in the face of lengthy, precarious supply lines, as well as local shortages of food and fodder. The military historian Creveld writes in 'Supplying war' that 'armies were forced to keep on the on the move in order to stay alive… the presence of large bodies of troops and their undisciplined hordes would quickly exhaust an area…it was food and forage which commanded the army'.[58] So logistics determined strategy: armies needed to follow a trail of food, which meant that a logical direction of march in furtherance of strategy would often fail for want of sustenance. Sometimes it was the fodder for horses alone that was the main determinant of the direction of march. Often armies *had* to go back rather than forwards, for reasons that had nothing to do with enemy forces.

The idea that armies including Gustavus's only lived by plunder alone is wrong: Regular needs had to be purchased and the private enterprise of sutlers was often more efficient than direct requisitioning [theft] by soldiers. Also, the high command did not want to destroy the economic viability of their base areas by too much random theft and pillage. If they seized everything then foodstuffs would quickly be hidden such that the policy of requisitioning would be counter-productive. Moreover, the value of raising contributions by selling protection under *Salvagardia* was only viable if the soldiery were not given licence to gather booty and foodstuffs by requisitioning. So, discipline was a necessary part of the collection of contributions. There would be little incentive to plant crops or raise cattle if there was unbridled theft; in highly contested areas such as Brandenburg, this was the main reason for population declines as farmers emigrated to pursue other economic activities in booming cities. Theft and destruction might be encouraged in enemy territory as a punishment or a tactic to force the enemy to terms especially if the territory was not going to be put under permanent occupation. It was a way of weakening the enemy. However, if in friendly territory or in areas where permanent occupation was envisaged a moderated policy of organised 'contribution' [i.e. local taxation] and *salvagardia* was the optimum solution. A front-end payment was common, followed by regular contributions. Gustavus collected large payments from Protestant cities such as Ulm, Augsburg, and Nuremberg, where he collected 300,000 in July 1632, 'Contribution' might, depending on the circumstances, be in cash or in kind or a mixture of the two.

Lack of food was the main reason for the disintegration of armies; it was a common occurrence in the war. In the hierarchy of needs food is paramount. After that came good dry quarters. Disease could also destroy armies, but food shortage was the most pressing problem. If troops did not have food even a great leader or general could do nothing with them; Bethlen Gábor, writing to Ferenc Rhédey in 1616 complained '…they [the soldiers] didn't bring adequate food with them, especially the infantry. They were starving, therefore I could not lead them any further. I thought to myself, a malnourished army is a defeated army indeed'[59] The soldier in the Transylvanian army was required to buy his own food and equipment. He might be supplied with shoes and sandals and a roll of baize cloth (rough wool) from which to fashion a garment. It was much easier for cavalry to plunder food *en route* because they could range far and wide.

The extent to which the countryside was impoverished by armies rampaging and stealing is exaggerated; so is the idea that Germany was a completely devastated waste land. In fact, local suppliers traded happily with army commanders, and many did well out of the war, supplying livestock, bloodstock, victuals, and beer.

Transport and logistics

Numbers in the armies were more than just the front-line troops. There were the camp followers, sutlers, wagoners and families. A contemporary record by Burster indicates that when General Aldrigen moved on Konstanz in 1633 to relieve it from the Swedes, he did so with 'some 30,000 soldiers but including the baggage train around 100,000'[60].

The effectiveness of Wallenstein's armies was based on an unsurpassed logistical operation, although the Swedish, Spanish and the Dutch armies rivalled him in this fundamental aspect of modern warfare. His command of detail is revealed in a letter sent to Taxis his estates manager in Friedland: He commanded, 'see that Herr Michna [Imperial quartermaster] receives 17,000 sacks of corn soon, so that they can be here this month; thirdly deliver to Herr Michna 2000 hundred weight of powder [gunpowder] to be sent by water, as well as match-lints that you have, and make 3000 hundredweight of them. also have 10,000 pairs of shoes made for the infantry, so that later I can divide them up among the regiments. Have them made in my towns and markets and pay a fair price for them in cash. See especially that the shoes are always carefully bound pair by pair, so that one will know which belong together.'[61](Wallenstein's letter to Taxis, 1625)

Transport was a problem with lumbering wagons having to move over poor or muddy roads, often churned up by cavalry and artillery trains. In winter many roads, most of which were not corduroyed, would be impassable by an army for practical reasons, which was another primary reason for armies going to winter quarters. In his book 'Supplying War', Martin Creveld writes 'All in all an army of this period [seventeenth century] might easily have one wagon with two or four horses each for every fifteen soldiers'[62] Thus a medium sized army of 15,000 [a size typical of later periods in the war] might require 1,000 wagons with about 3,000 horses plus the artillery train. An army might typically be double or triple in size with camp follows, wives, sutlers, servants etc. In 1638 Goetz's army of 20,000 with eleven cannons needed 2000 wagons.

The issues of logistics and supply are timeless, and the problems of supply and reinforcement were the downfall of such commanders as Hannibal in southern Italy, Napoleon in Russia, Rommel at El-Alamein, Mutaguchi at Imphal-Kohima, Soult at the Torres Vedres lines, Paulus at Stalingrad, and von Kleist's 1st Panzer army in the Caucasus 1943. Even successful armies are vulnerable at the end of long supply lines. The capture of an enemy magazine or wagon train supply was often the main prize of a successful battle or siege for the relief it brought to the logistics effort. Shortage of munitions was a major headache for commanders, but it was the breakdown in bread supply that was by far the greater problem, resulting in the disintegration of dozens of armies. Only Charles I's army at first Newbury, which ran out of gunpowder, suffered the ignominy of retreat in consequence of a lack of munitions. Plentiful ammunition supply, as much as the weapons of war is an essential for the delivery of firepower. At Trenevento 22 June 1636, Leganez's Spanish army expended 30,000 pounds of gunpowder and fired approximately 675,000 bullets (according to Hanlon). A regular siege might expend 10,000 cannon balls.

The logistical capability of the armies during the war, were poor in comparison to fifty years later but there was still some improvement over the period: Increasing organisational requirements required a professional general staff specialised in the various aspects of war, such as food, or munitions, transport etc. Not the least of the supply needs was prodigious amounts of fodder for the supply columns as well as the cavalry horses. By the end of the war the Imperial army employed forty personnel in logistical and organizational roles, often enjoying the rank of colonel.[63]

Military engineering

Tilly moved up with 20,000 troops to confront the enemy, outnumbering Gustavus's 15,000. Gustavus retreated into prepared defensive positions at Werben. It was a fortified town that lay in a loop of the river Elbe, connecting to either side of the loop by strong earthworks dotted with sconces and bastions manned by 3,000 musketeers and 150 cannon. When Tilly's army advanced before the defensive works were finished, Monro described how, 'we with spades and shovels wrought ourselves day and night in the ground, so that before his coming, we had put ourselves out of danger of his cannon.'[64] Werben was a triumph of Swedish engineering, which was a skill that had been thoroughly integrated into the training of large numbers of army officers, many of whom had been sent on training secondments in Holland. Gustavus was an expert himself as was General Horn. During Gustavus's campaigns in Poland General Radizwill accused the Swedes of being *'moles'* because of the effectiveness of their field fortifications in fending off superior Polish forces. Foreshadowing the First World War shovels and military engineering became an important part of warfare. At White Mountain 1620, the five earthworks were wrongly positioned and only partially completed because of the exhaustion and ill-discipline of the army and the shortage of spades. Amateurish Bohemian military efforts descended into farce because 'the spades I had brought to the camp at my own expense had been damaged so much at Raknovic,' lamented Anhalt later, 'that we only had 400 usable ones left. This meant we had to fetch some from Prague, but this took so long that our entrenchment was hindered and remained far from perfect…'[65] A week before, good digging and field works had persuaded the Imperial army not to attack at Raknovic, but the lesson was not learnt. Made in his own forges, Wallenstein issued spades to his troops in 1628 when expecting a campaign year of sieges.

Swedish engineering capability was an outstanding feature of all army operations throughout the war and like the artillery it would be a technical skill mainly reserved for Swedes but leavened with some foreign experts. General Torstensson was given responsibility for the for the engineering corps along with his role in the artillery. Aside from field fortifications, the engineers not only built new fortifications from scratch, e.g. at Gustavsburg, but became experts in bridging, fortification, roads, and siege works. Rapid bridge-building ability would endow the Swedish army with a tactical flexibility that was responsible for several of the decisive victories of the war. After Torstensson's capture at Alte Veste in 1632 engineer Olaf Ornehufvud acted as an army quartermaster, being promoted to chief of fortifications in 1635. Attached to the artillery corps the engineers were later separately incorporated by Ornehufvud as the world's first dedicated military engineering corps. Employing a dedicated engineering corps was another revolution in military operations. Engineers were increasingly seen as valuable military assets which is why they drew the special attention of snipers at sieges. (See sniper section below)

Gustavus was an expert himself as was General Horn.

Early in his reign Gustavus between 1611–14 during the war of Kalmar, contacted Prince Maurice when he sought to hire Dutch engineers. The meaning of engineers for military purposes was skill in the architecture and mathematics of military structures, fortresses and siege works in which architectural drawing, surveying, quantity surveying organisational and mathematical skills were most important. Amongst those recruited were Andries Sersanders who in 1614 developed plans for a seven-sided fortress at Kalmar. Gustavus hired aristocratic French engineer Jacques Prempart.[66] It is likely that other Dutch engineers were employed in the Swedish army, some of them graduating from the Leiden school of military engineering. At 400 gulden per year, they were not expensive, because the wage was less than that for an infantry sergeant. After the boom on fortress construction 1590–1620 there was surplus of engineers in the Dutch Republic. Dutch fortification building wound down and the job became more of an artisan craft for maintenance and repair of fortifications. The more esteemed engineer gained considerable prestige and could enter the inner circles of princes but the low wages for a highly skilled profession are a conundrum, but we must assume that there was indirect recompense in the form of substantial kickbacks from contractors.

Dutch *'engineers'* were particularly skilled in the construction of earthen ramparts which were much cheaper than brick and stone structures; a mere 300,000 gulden might suffice for a fortress. However, they did sag from time to time due to waterlogging and shifting. They lasted just five to six years, whereas a well-built stone based, or fortress might last indefinitely-indeed many are still standing today. Despite conducting few sieges, Gustavus had a constant need for engineering services; in Poland he remained on the defensive behind fieldworks for much of the three-year campaign in ducal Prussia. In Germany too, there occasional siege work needs such as the defensive fortification of Werben for example. Gustavus also used engineers for construction of fortifications to protect key Protestant cities such as Nuremburg and Ulm.

Rapid bridge-building ability would endow the Swedish army with a tactical flexibility that was responsible for one of the decisive victories of the war, notably the battle of Lech in 1632 when engineers built connecting bridges to link a mid-stream island to the east bank of the river. One of the outstanding engineering achievements of the war, the connecting bridges were constructed in secret during the night; the manoeuvre enabled Gustavus to outflank the Bavarian fortified river line and establish a defensible bridgehead across the river Lech. The link to the enemy bank was built flush to the water to hide its existence from the Imperialists until the elite Finnish 'commandos' rushed across to the right bank. This attack turned out to be the left jab, because decisive blow was the double envelopment with a right hook which came in the form of Bernhard of Saxe-Weimar with 2,000 heavy cavalry. Having crossed at a ford further down river the Swedish cavalry slammed into the flank of the Bavarian army. Napoleon with his engineers copied the island-hopping tactic at the battle of Wagram outside Vienna in 1809. Referring to Wagram, the military theorist Jomini would chisel the lessons of contested river crossings in stone in six 'general rules his classic work 'the art of war' 1838; '1. Deceive the enemy as to the point of passage…4. The proximity of a large island near the enemy's bank gives great facilities for passing the over troops in boats and for constructing the bridge.'[67]

Monro describes the use of boat bridges on the advance to Werben August 1631 where Swedish engineering skills were demonstrated. Engineers to also improved the defence. According to the contemporary Swedish army record 'both the town wall and the league wall were so thick and firm of old earth, faced up with new, that no ball (from a demi-cannon) could enter it. The bulwarks on which the batteries were made for the cannon were also very strong and formally built, and they flanked one another, so that none could find but folly in pressing to enter by storm. And betwixt the flankers were left voids, for letting troops of cavalry in and out.'[68]

'I have heard many disparage the arms and organisation of ancient armies, arguing that today they could do little…against the fury of artillery' Niccolo Machievelli, 'The Art of War.'

Published in 1521, the only work released in Machiavelli's lifetime. His aim was to compare apply Roman tactical ideas into early modern warfare. Written in the Socratic dialogue style, Machiavelli focuses much of the work on the firepower possibilities of artillery for easily knocking down the walls of towns. Difficult to load and aim, cannons were lumbering things that were fired once at the start of a battle and normally missed.[69] He was not impressed by the efficacy of cannon on the battlefield and that indeed was, before Gustavus, the common view of artillery before the military revolution. They were a siege weapon. If deployed on the battlefield. 'I would place in front of the entire army.'[70]

However, he understands their potential and suggests the method of dealing with effectively battlefield deployed artillery; i.e to rush them before they can fire more than once.[71] He strongly advises against a mass attack against cannon at the usual slow walking pace. His other critique of mass is his comparison of unwieldy liner Greek -like tercios; he recommends instead the Roman system of small disciplined and well-drilled cohorts or maniples (the equivalents of regiment, battalions, companies, and platoons), that are capable of tactical defence in depth as well as flexible mobile deployment that can react quickly to the exigencies of battle.[72] Machiavelli praises Swiss pikemen being well drilled, cohesive units, and brave in the face of cannon fire.[73] Machiavelli implies that cannon were mainly a defensive terror weapon. Machiavelli was an important part of developing the growing renaissance trend to military professionalism and intellectual inquiry in the context of Roman learning.

Chapter VII
Women

'Old Mother Courage' and *Women at War*

Brecht's 'Old Mother Courage' is probably a reasonable metaphor for the random lot of camp followers in the war. 'Sometimes I see myself driving through hell with this wagon and selling brimstone. And sometimes I'm driving through heaven handing our provisions to wandering souls!' (Scene 9) The presence of women among the camp followers may have helped reduce the level of desertion. English troops who landed on European shores without women deserted in droves. Women cooked washed clothes and scavenged for food. Always living on the existential brink their behaviour was often rapacious, violent, and brazenly criminal, 'like a flock of ravens' according to sixteenth-century contemporary Wallhausen or magpies indeed. But they provided the essential oil for creaking armies on the move, filling in the gaps in victual, clothing, and nursing provision left by inadequate, inefficient, unprofessional and underfunded commissaries that had not yet reached the level of state provided efficiency that would develop through the seventeenth century. Some were married women and others were so-called 'whores' who in the seventeenth century were defined as attached but unmarried women. Prostitution was common and the roles of wife, whore, carer, sutler, and prostitute were often blurred or interchangeable depending on necessity. 'The foe parades down every street. And then with us they take their ease, and fraternize behind the trees.' (Yvette Pottier the prostitute, *Mother Courage and her Children*, Scene 3). So important were women in the structure of an army that contemporary veteran Turner describes how their rank and position was formalised into those who rode in coaches, on wagons or on horses.

Following the Swedish example 'whores' and prostitutes tended to be banned from encampments for reasons of morality and discipline. Health was also a problem; sexual diseases such as syphilis were rife, but the main killer was fever and plague... Widows rarely lacked for a new husband, while the phenomenon of 'May marriages' at the start of a campaign year were well known. The German armies had a special reputation for the large number of camp followers who accompanied them, something commented on by contemporaries as confirmed by archaeological DNA evidence for Scottish and German soldiers from the burial site at Wittstock (battle of 1636): but 'the German soldier no sooner an expedition arrives, saddle themselves with frivolous loose women with whom they contract 'May marriages'...they are needed to take care of clothes, equipment and valuables; and in cases of illness, injury or any other personal harm, the women are needed to nurse and take care of them.'[1] Spanish tercios also had a high level of wives and children in attendance. So wedded were the troops to their women that a proposal by a captain to leave them behind at a river crossing in 1621 to enable a rapid march was met by near mutiny with the troops yelling 'Ho, what the devil, I must have my whore back; she has my shirts, collars, shoes, and stockings.'[2]

As in all wars the structure and mores of society were undone. Solace was found as chance and circumstances allowed, for both men and women struggling to find comfort, security, and emotional harmony in abnormal and violent times. Scottish officer James Turner was not exceptional in his experience at Oldendorpe where he was billeted for six weeks in 1634, remembering fondly how he was 'lodged in a widow house, whose daughter, a young widow had been married to a rittmeister of the emperor (Imperial cuirassier). She was very handsome, wittie and discreet... I became perfitle enamoured...'[3] Not just a soldierly lothario, Turner gave a detailed, insightful, and sensitive account of the role of women on campaign, 'As women was created to be helper to man so women are great helpers in armies to their husbands, especially those of the lower condition... they provide, buy, and dress their husband's meat when their husbands are on duty, or... they bring in fewel for fire, and wash their linens;... especially they are useful in camps and leaguers, being submitted, which should be not refused, them to go some miles from the camp to buy victuals and other necessaries.'[4] Senior officers were not generally attended by their wives on campaign, with the more earthy exceptions of Swedish Generals Baner, Torstensson, and French General Gubriant, whose wives ministered to their needs or on occasions, and even mediated the demands of the troops. Baner's wife, highborn Countess of Erbach even gave birth in her carriage before dying near Erfurt. Torstensson's wife, Beata, suffered the indignity of capture by Croat cavalry in the battle of Jankov 1645.

English armies had a terrible reputation for disintegrating very rapidly when transported to Europe and it is often presumed that this was because they were dredged from the Falstaffian dregs and riff raff of society; sick and worthless vagabonds pressed into the ranks to make up numbers. However, PhD work by Graham Long (Cambridge) in 2019 shows that the army was in fact mainly composed of worthy yeomen. Its social composition was by no means inferior to that of continental armies; why then the poor record regarding desertion and disintegration? Apart from the seriously inadequate logistical, poor in organisation and in finance, we could speculate on the lack of language and social integration upon arrival which meant that they had no women to scrabble and help them to eat and survive. Turner's evidence on this is clear; it took him a year or so to learn how to live well as a soldier. It was the finding of a good woman that made the difference. Once tutored, having found a good woman, he fared well in the wars.

As in most wars women are to a greater or lesser degree the subjects of sexual pressure or violence and other forms of exploitation, which tends to grow with proximity to the battlefront. 'Wartime soldiers are by and large youngish men who have been separated from their real or would-be partners and freed from many social restraints,'[5] writes Harald Welzer and Sonke Neitzel in their analysis of German Second World War *'Soldaten'*. Conditioned to violence under terms of moral reference framed by male group bonding, desensitized by hardship and immediate existential threat, that soldiers turn to drink and to sex is not surprising; 'soldiers live out their violent and sexual impulses…nothing more than a shift in the framework that gives the more powerful the opportunity to do things that they already enjoy doing or would like to do.'[6] Additionally soldiers live under the existential promise of imminent death, which sharpens their appetite for the here and now. Walzer and Neitzel report how Wehrmacht soldiers boasted on secretly recorded tapes as to the casual rapes that they made on road trips behind the lines, stopping to take any Russian peasant girls they fancied. Similarly in 1637 a troop of Swedes entered Lingen village, when a *"fat Finn"* and a *"white-haired"* soldier raped a peasant housewife in front of her husband. Both sides in the war were guilty of callous brutality. At Magdeburg in a particularly gruesome case, six Catholic soldiers of the Bavarian army raped a 12-year-old girl to death in a convent.[7] Soldiering, in the absence of very strong officer led discipline, also attracts, and induces criminality. On hearing the report their commander, General Tilly, a deeply religious soldier, turned away in apparent anguish.

On the roads troopers often behaved like common bandits, robbing people on the roads and country lanes. For some soldiers there was even an unwritten licence to rape, an evil commonly complained of in the Thirty Years War. In general though, it was seldom (for the same obvious reasons that it is underreported today.]); an example 'Hannes Trosten's wife was raped by two cavalrymen near the castle wood on the way back from holy arms giving.'[8] Another witness records how his maid was abducted along with other young women, 'with the unfortunate result that one of them was dishonoured by a soldier in Martin Muller's house at Emerkingen,'[9]. Even if the incidence was not as widespread as wild rumour would have had it, soldiers engendered considerable fear in the female population. Hellgemayr's typical hearsay account speaks of soldiers 'violating women and girls, doing great evil in cloister.'[10] Deflowering of nuns was a constant accusation against Protestant troops, and it may well be that there was the allure of *'forbidden fruit'* fantasy as well as desire, or convenient 'moral' justification for Protestant revenge on an obvious totem of Catholicism.

When a town was stormed the soldiery, fired up by adrenalin plus looted alcohol and lust for revenge, would indulge in unspeakable crimes against women; even had they wanted to, officers could not normally control them as the customs of war gave three days freedom to pillage and rape. The streets of a stormed place soon resembled a charnel house. Making his way out with his family, led by a soldier paid for the service, Friedrich Friese at Magdeburg in 1631 saw 'a maid also in the street who had been carrying meat in a basket; she had been shot and a dog stood nearby eating the meat…we saw many bodies in the streets, including women lying quite uncovered. They lay with their heads in a great barrel of beer, which stood full of water in the alley, into which they had been pushed and drowned, but half their bodies and their legs were hanging out…'[11]. Atrocities against women were common place; the London press on the 24 October 1624 recorded the behaviour of Spanish troops at Bergen in 1624, where 'the Spanish make great outrage and shamefully abused women and maids of then towne… stripping them naked.[12] It seems likely that many junior or even senior officers at colonel level must have been involved in these crimes: *benefits* of war in lieu of or in addition to pay. Women were war loot, just another chattel.

Officers were well aware of the mass rape atrocities. Though regarded as a serious crime not covered by amnesties, senior officers had little control. There were some hangings for the offence but not many in comparison to the number of victims. However, there would be little restraint of soldiers in the immediate aftermath of a sack. Like Tilly at Magdeburg, some senior officers did what they could, but other officers were themselves closely involved in the plundering and atrocities and could do so more elegantly by using their power and greater wealth to take pretty girls and 'gentlewomen' under 'protection'. Nor were the horrors of mass rape visited only on the enemy or the poor. Marshall d'Harcourt described events that were reported to him of his own troop's activities on the way to the Italian front, 'there was a gentleman of birth and position who watched…his wife, daughter and sister violated without daring to say a word; in the lands of Besolles alone seventy women were raped…The men of Condom, who had been taxed only 30,000 livres, paid 64,000 to exempt their women from violation, after which they were pillaged and lost fifteen hundred horses.'[13]It is hardly surprising that troops acted more outrageously in foreign lands, (we know this from the behaviour of travelling football supporters so how do we explain the behaviour of French troops in France). In this case quite simply the French soldiers were passing through French lands that they did regards as foreign not least because the populace spoke a different language in seventeenth-century 'France' there were a dozen and more different language; the idea of 'France' and a French state was only just beginning to take shape; this

Gallic concept was new and under the direction of Richelieu and Mazarin was just reaching the cusp of acceptance among many but not all of the aristocracy. The parochialism was so strong, and the language spoken so foreign that for all intents and purposes French soldiers felt that they were passing through foreign lands. Soldierly excesses sparked a revolution in Catalonia when an Italian regiment of the Spanish army ran amok in the in the small town of Santa Coloma de Farnes as a reprisal following the murder of an unpopular government official and his retinue.

We tend only to hear about the worst of the excesses and violence in respect of women: the saddest of hard luck stories; they were mainly the underbelly and dregs of society. Tens of thousands traipsed around Germany in the wake of their soldier husband or sweethearts. Moving cities in most cases, many children were born, many died. Father Drexel accompanying the Imperialists army's campaign in 1620, noted that on the 2 September he 'baptised two children of the soldier, all sorts of misery and hardships are more and more obvious…' adding further the description of one camp follower who 'was carrying a young child on her head, but her hands were not empty of burdens… one such female soldier would carry on her back, head, both hands loaded, and her legs strung with bundles. I saw another carry a musket just like a man as she made her way.'[14] People flee from invading armies and they still do…the more terrible the army and its reputation the more they flee, as we have seen from the Burmese army's invasion of Rohingya areas in 2017. Villagers, townspeople, and ecclesiastics fled before Saxe-Weimar's advance 'because of the daily and nightly attacks and persecutions of the Weimar riders and soldiers…How often was I discouraged by the terror of the Swedes? and no one can see the daily and nightly long treks of refugees before the eyes without the deepest pity.'[15]

In a battle lost camp followers were at the mercy of the victors who were usually high on adrenalin, alcohol, blood lust. They risked slaughter and rape as well as dispossession of all their belongings and savings. After the battle of Naseby 1645 in the English midlands, Welsh women in the royalist encampment probably mistaken for Irish, were slaughtered. Tartar or Hungarian cavalry were notoriously brutal in their dealing with civilians and were recorded as slaughtering women and children after battles. Apart from cruel actions after battles, some troops spread terror, pillaged, raped, and burnt dwellings as a standard operating procedure. This was particularly true of Croats, Polish cossacks, and Hungarian light cavalry and accompanying Tartars. Gábor and Thurn whose armies invaded Austria up to the environs of Vienna, withdrew on 27 November 1619. Gábor had only the patience and resolve of a plains raider; his troops likewise. They were not supplied enough for a long siege through a harsh central European winter. It was the high-water mark of Bohemian military hopes. Ferdinand made an account of the destruction in a letter to John George of Saxony on 5th November; 'A few days ago the enemy began their retreat, but not before Hungarians had devastated, plundered and burnt everything where they had been quartered...stripped people to their last threads, ruined, cut them down...and so ill treated pregnant women and other women, that many were found dead...'[16] On one occasions the firing of a town had a military value, sometimes accidental sometimes deliberate, such as Wallenstein's firing of the town of Lützen to disrupt the Swedish army attack. At Wiesloch Mansfeld's troops fired the town as a matter of course in their hasty retreat but the smoke obscured their positions and enabled them to make a successful counter-attack against Tilly's advance guard as it emerged from the smoke.

There were dreadful times for women but there was also resilience; the camaraderie and amusements of the camp, an occasional good meal, alcohol fuelled singing and dancing round the campfire. Hastily snatched romance provided occasional relief from the grind of marching and living in the open. Hagendorf lost one wife and eight children on campaign. In winter quarters or on garrison duty a semblance of family life might be had for a few months. Hagendorf records it in matter-of-fact way; he met with triumph and disaster and treated 'those two imposters just the same'[17]; how else except by stoicism could he and his wives deal with such terrible tragedy? But as a victim of war himself, Hagendorf also victimised others; the never-ending cycle of received and projected abuse. Fairly typical of men of the time, (and indeed in our own era), Hagendorf found it difficult to function without a woman to care for him, regretting that he had let go a young woman who, after abducting her, he had taken back to her home, 'which I often regret, because I had no woman at this point...'[18] He married Anna Maria Buchlerin soon after in January 1635.

Hagendorf and Turner both recounted experiences of temporary campaign wives. After the sack of a place, attachment to one soldier might be the best option for a young woman seeking protection. Otto von Guericke at Magdeburg reported how women were raped and 'some were kept as concubines.'[19] Following the sack of Landshut 1634, Hagendorf boasted, 'Here I got a pretty lass as my plunder... when we moved on, I sent her back to Landshut again.' And again, at Pforzheim in 1635 with a different army, the Bavarians, he 'took a young girl out with me here too, but I let her go back in again...'[20]. Imperialist soldiers in 1633 'took more than 140 serving girls as wives, but when they had gone a few leagues...stripped the 'whores' and chased them away.'[21]. All described in such a matter-of-fact way to suggest that this was a common practice; a norm not frowned upon.

Other liaisons amidst the mayhem of war were struck up by officers with the numerous widowed or suddenly impoverished 'gentlewomen' or 'women of quality' as young French officers referred to them. Relationships would be struck up on the route of march, or in garrison and with tavern wenches also. Sex was an abiding interest and preoccupation for all ranks. In the Champagne, senior aristocrat de Bussy-Rabutin found himself at rest for three months and fell for 'a young woman of quality, wife of the governor of Quince'. The young woman threw herself at the very young regimental colonel and began an affair; he was nearly caught *in flagrante* on one occasion, escaping 'totally nude' from the window of the lady over the roofs of the town, amidst a flurry of commotion in the place.[22] De Bussy-Rabutin's memoires of the war period dedicate vastly more space to his romantic escapades than to military matters. Long periods in dull garrison duties meant plenty of opportunities; de Bussy-Rabutin after his timid initiation at Quince enjoyed multiple adventures with towns' women across the Champagne region. Inevitably there were quarrels between officers or officers and civilians and duels followed. de Bussy-Rabutin witnessed a fatal duel fought against the baron de Soude. Apart from a brief military excursion for the relief of St Quentin in 1639, this lothario life was his main activity in that campaign year; then it was back to the court for more adventures at the end of the campaign season. In 1637 Henri de Campion fell for the charms of a gentlewoman, Mme de la Fontaine in the off-season between campaigns in faraway places such as Franche-Comté, Spain, and Italy. There was regular correspondence, and the idea of marriage was in the air but his absence, his losses at gambling in camp and poor prospects after failing to gain a captaincy soured the match. The lady found better prospects elsewhere. There was nothing special about the behaviour of troops in the Thirty Years War, nor the needs of women for food and security, under violent threat, and in extremis.

Sydnam Poyntz was twice fixed up with genteel female brides by his friend, Colonel Butler, one of Wallenstein's murderers. It is *possible* that some women were forced into marriage as at Olomouc, where some Swedish officers married daughters of wealthy burghers who were pressured into church. Poyntz's first wife died in childbirth; the second was genteel and well off. He was to suffer 'the true tryall of fortunes mutability,' He recorded sadly, that 'my wife was killed & my child, my house burned and all my goods pillaged.'[23] Poyntz had married above his normal station because during the war the status of soldiers had risen considerably; when he returned to England, he was quite wealthy. As an experienced office from the German wars he was soon appointed to command the Parliament's Northern Association. Enjoying, power, money and cutting a dash in soldierly society was a potent allure for women and their parents or guardians, especially as the war seemed interminable. Poyntz started the war a lowly runaway apprentice; his lack of education is revealed in his prose. He ended up as commander of the Parliament's Northern Association. Croat cavalry commander Colonel Isolani used his officer charms on tavern girls; indeed, it was his amorous interlude at the inn *Zum Rippach,* which delayed his departure so allowing his troops to accidentally discover the surprise advance of Gustavus's army. Others also exploited their rank for money and status. An example of the shake up in normal marriage strata was the betrothal in September 1640 of '*ambitious*' Swedish General Baner to the granddaughter of the Margrave of Baden-Durlach, whose territories were under occupation. Not only was there a huge contrast in age, but there was a social distinction too, because Baner was from a minor *Swedish* noble family, hardly better than rich peasants in the eyes of central European dynasties. Lower Swedish nobility would not have counted for much before the war, but as the commanding Swedish General Baner was able to restore the Baden-Durlach patrimony; so, the match was permitted.

Tragedy in literature, reportage and biography selects itself; gory and sensational news might sometimes excessively colour the époque to make it look more brutal than it was. Exaggeration of the atrocities in Germany in nineteenth-century German historiography and in popular histories such as those produced by Freytag, has given a false and overwrought gothic tinge. Generalisations are dangerous; it would be wrong to conclude that rape was endemic, but war must surely have led to a big increase in this crime and at certain times and places the practice may have become normalised. In general, officers were outraged by it; Tilly's reaction to the rape of young girls is probably typical of most, who abhorred it but could often do little to control it especially after the blood lust of a sack. Rarer is a good report such as the one given by the good nuns of the Bishopric city of Bamberg in Franconia, who suffered two Swedish attacks and occupation within a few months. '…not a single sister of our convent lost the slightest of her virginity. Though the Swedes visited us daily they always behaved correctly and honourably. Though they had appeared terrible towards us, as soon as they saw us and talked to us, they became patient and tender little lambs.'[24] However they were lucky; the Swedish army was still well discipline with a reasonably high Swedish component at this stage, but later armies took on the homogenised brutality and callousness of German troops inured to cruelty and greed. Nonetheless, Bernhard von Saxe-Weimar a fervent Protestant warlord whose armies under the stress of shortage of pay and logistical support did much damage, was most solicitous to convent nuns; Sister Marian Anna Junius recorded how 'as soon as the gate was opened duke Bernhard came to us with a laugh and gave one sister after another his hand and asked how we lived…the prince sat on the pew before the crucifix and spoke in a friendly manner with the sisters…'[25] When offered a pastry 'the prince laughed and reached into the bowl and took a lemon tart…' Life was not all thin gruel.

The effects of the war on outcomes for women, as for the populace in general, were varied and random. In general, though, war caused destabilisation and brutalisation in society, which had terrible consequences for large numbers of women in war zones, whose lot became more even more precarious. For other women living in the undisturbed regions and cities of Germany, the rise in wage levels and decline in grain prices in the second half of the war would have meant an increased standard of living especially if they were married especially.

Chapter VIII
A Soldier's Life

A soldier's lot: Hagendorf, Turner, Raymond, and Munro

At Straubing, near Munich, Saxe-Weimar's army broke two of the cardinal rules of war. The town was surrendered by the Imperialists who under the articles of surrender were allowed to march out with their arms. Trekking away from the place with the Imperial column was Hagendorf, our itinerant mercenary. 'I thought they would let us withdraw, as it said in the accord,' complained Hagendorf ruefully, 'but after five miles they ordered: "dismount hand over what you've got…"' Contrary to the accord and to the customary rule about *not* re-engaging enemy garrisons, Hagendorf was enlisted into the Swedish army where he was immediately made a sergeant in the red regiment.

War was often drudgery, discomfort, and death in little engagements or sieges, with little of the glamour attached to the great victories. This was the war experience of James Turner during seven years in Germany. After the battle of Oldendorf, he reminisced 'the rest of the summer, next harvest and next winter, I was at the sieges of several towns and castles and at many brushes and encounters and ….: all the time suffered exceedingly great want of both meate and clothes, being necessitated to by being constantly in the field with little or no shelter, to march always on foote and drink water…'[1] There was no pay either.

However, Turner also recounts many happy times as a soldier, but Raymond who was more malcontent by nature wrote that 'the life of a soldier is the most miserable in the world; and that not soe much that his life is always in danger – that is little or nothing – but for the terrible miseries he endures in hunger and nakedness, in hard marches and bad quarter…'[2] He wrote this perhaps in a bad moment, forgetting perhaps the better times with wine, women, and song: comradeship, banquets, laughter, practical jokes, sing-alongs with comrades and camp followers, as they feasted and danced around the campfire or flirted with the serving wenches in township taverns. Even the garrulous old professional Monro confessed that 'we soldiers have not always so hard a life as the common opinion is.'[3] On occasions Monro was effusive about his quarters, for example in Pomerania and in the lush Main Valley. In 1633 he spent a good amount of time around the lush pastures running down to Lake Konstanz, (Bodensee) where the army was 'well entertained and refreshed in good quarters…'[4] Optimists and free spirits such as Hagendorf and Poyntz would surely have agreed. Along with sad memories, often relegated to the back of the memory, they would have spent many hours in future years reminiscing, as old soldiers do, not so much on the bad times but on the 'good old times'.

Life was very hard especially for green troops who had not yet learnt the tricks of soldiering. Despite James Turner's 'two companies'… 'being badly used, tossed to and fro, in constant danger of the enemie and without pay…' the Scots officer reminisced that he developed 'cunning and became so vigilant to lay hold on opportunities, that I wanted for nothing, houses, horses, clothes, meate, nor money; and made good use of what I had learned, that the whole time I served in Germane, I suffered no such miserie as I had done the first yeare and a halfe…[5] A veteran was a good thief, scavenger, and chancer; he needed to be steadfast under fire and lucky. Hardiness was also an essential quality: and the acquisition of a companionable good *'whore'* or wife was a singular advantage in circumstances of health, sickness, and injury. Turner was lucky to survive his first winter when he became sick with fever.

Apart from drinking, gambling, looting, and womanising some soldiers found time for intellectual pursuits. After the battle of Poligny 1628, the Normandie regiment was sent back to Soane in Burgundy for a rest; the army also need to resupply. Henri de Campion took the time to revive his book club with three fellow officers who were both 'spiritual and well educated'. Books formed a major part of his wagon allocation. He recounts from his memoires how 'one of us would read passages from several good books, which we would then discuss and examine, with the object to understand how to live and die well with moral purpose….' No doubt Cicero, Plato and other classics were on the list.

Death and desertion

Armies were 'melting like butter in the sun'; desertion, and attrition

In 1626 Wallenstein pleaded for 100,000 reichsthalers from the Imperial treasury: a palliative token payment to the troops for wages owed, 'otherwise' he wrote to Ferdinand's councillor von Trauttmansdorff, 'the army will melt like butter in the sun'[6] Mansfeld would have agreed; shortage of cash to pay troops and an associated lack of food were the primary issues behind rates of ill-discipline and desertion. Another factor was whether the army was winning; if they advanced, they took towns and villages so there was cash and booty in lieu of pay, but in retreat the dynamic was on the other foot. with little opportunity for loot and no pay there was no incentive to hang around waiting for defeat or death. This is why defeated armies could quickly whither to as little as ten per cent of their former troop numbers could be expected to decline by well over half in a campaign size. French armies often achieved this feat within weeks. Not only were new recruits often unfit for service but they joined up for non-military reasons, including the benefit of signing up bonuses. Desertion was induced by the hard drudge of outdoor living, of sleeping and marching in the cold and the rain, with precarious supplies of food, often without pay. Is not surprising even without sickness and fatigue, or 'temptations' along the march that desertion was so rife. 'These 3 days was a very hard march,' complained Raymond, 'for we end of the day very wet, and came so late to our quarters, laying the night sub dis, having only the panoplies of heaven to cover us.... I had nothing to keepe me from the cold wett ground but a bundle of wett dryed flax, which by chance I litt on. And soe my bootes full of water and wrapt up in my wett cloake, I lay as round as a hedgehog, and at peep of day looked like a drowned ratt.'[7] Nor was there any relief in summer when the plagues would break out, most likely caused by the lack of food and insanitary conditions in camps, especially static ones at sieges such as Alte Feste or Bergen-op-Zoom, where Gustavus's and Spinola's armies reduced by seventy per cent and fifty per cent respectively. At Bergen-op-Zoom Spinola had an absolute loss of 12,000 due to plague and desertion. Soldiers', noted General Hartzfeld, would fall 'away like flies, whether becoming sick or incapacitated or deserting.'[8] Baner, whose logistical arrangements tended to be poor complained sarcastically of his Hessian regiments on one occasion that they were 'empty but for the standards and pennants'[9]

Armies melted away very quickly, some more quickly than others. The English and French armies were notoriously prone to rapid depletion by desertion or disease. A study by Parker titled 'The Universal Soldier' in his edited book on the *Thirty Years War*, shows four English regiments declining from 4,913 to 1,630 between June 1627 and May 1638 with monthly losses running from six to thirteen per cent per month. Four Scottish Regiments had losses running from two to thirteen per cent per month and three Swedish regiments declined from 2,577 to 828, March 1632 to December 1632, with losses running at four to nine per cent per month. A German Guards regiment declined from 1,400 in September 1631 to 600 in August 1636, with monthly loss rates running from four to eleven per cent. When a field army was not quickly employed on active service it might never see action at all, for example Mansfeld and Hamilton's English armies in 1624 and 1632 or Feria's Spanish army in 1633. When the attrition of armies was so rapid, commanders had an incentive to use reinforcements quickly, as the contemporary Dutch military commentator van der Capellan noted, 'Spinola, knowing that field armies are subject to these inconveniences [attrition by sickness and desertion], in particular his Walloons and Englishmen...uses them swiftly as he gets them, as if he were laying them on the butcher's slab.'[10]

Calculations for ten French regiments for the period June to July 1635 show losses of twenty per cent per month. This loss rate was by no means exceptional for the French army.[11] Spanish desertion rates were quite high amongst Walloons serving in the low countries running in 1630 at seven per cent per month in one unit although the rate of desertion amongst officers and NCOs was negligible, which shows that regiments relied on their core of veterans. All armies punished desertion by death, although in practice sentence was often commuted in favour of corporal punishment and readmission to the ranks. The positive motivation for desertion would be very varied including 'better wars and greater rewards in other countries' opined the Spain's Cardinal Infante; or the fighting, which was 'fierce, of long duration and great hardship. The lack of wages causes great miseries…'[12] Other reasons for desertion would include harvest time at home, a relationship with a local woman, hunger, boredom, and fear of plague. If he was lucky enough to capture some valuable booty a soldier might retire and open a tavern. The exceptional French rates of attrition probably relate to the French army's poorer logistical and financial system as well as the dislike of fighting out of country: the factors possibly being related. Upon crossing the Rhine in 1638, a French reinforcement unit for Saxe-Weimar was fifty per cent reduced by desertion in one month. Swedes, Scottish, Spanish, and English also fought overseas but unlike the French they could not walk home.

Soldiers also died in battle: lots of them. Over thirty years 450,000 died according to an aggregation of statistics in well documented battles, the majority caused by sickness; sickness was a constant companion to armies on the march or even for those in quarters. Monro's account of *His Expeditions* is punctuated by the death of his comrades and cousins through 'ague', 'pest', 'feaver' and 'plague'; this passage is typical 'Robert Monro died of the pest…here also did die of the plague Sergeant Andrew Monro, Cull Crags sonne…' Each death was personal to Colonel Monro in his clan-based regiment; he writes with sadness and emotion about each loss, in battle or by sickness; with much spiritual reflection besides.

Sickness and battle death is estimated to have killed 400,000 in Swedish service alone, including Scots, Germans, and English etc.[13] Many others must have died in small war skirmishes. Soldiers that survived prolonged active service were rare; we have looked at the stories of Poyntz, Hagendorf, Fritsche, Turner, and Monro because they were lucky enough to survive. Turner barely escaped death through illness in his first winter. They were wounded, two, two, three, zero, and three times respectively. Turner served a relatively short period, as did Monro, around five years; the others served over ten years each. Hagendorf's survival at Magdeburg from a stomach wound is surprising as was Fritsche's recovery from head wounds at Hildesheim when he was hit three times: 'balls lodge in my head, in my leg and above the eye, from which I suffered …great pain.' For every healthy veteran survivor there were many dead or those pitiable soldiers with limb shorn wrecks.

The allure of booty in holding together an army was noted by a Dutch official during the Franco-Dutch campaign of 1635 'Our army is in good order, good soldiers and very willing for they have been given hope that they shall make good spoils which is the reason none have deserted.'[14] Another thing holding the Swedish army together was the hope of recovering back pay; the total sum would eventually reach some six million reichsthalers (As agreed at Westphalia 1648 following several years of hard bargaining). There were several mutinies which were bought off with interim handouts of cash, but it was made plain to the troops that their only hope of recovering all their backpay was to win the war.

The 'Gunpowder Convention', and the French alliance August 1635-Feb 1636

In August 1635 Oxenstierna having travelled to Magdeburg to deal with complaints by the army, was held prisoner by his mutineering soldiers as ransom for back pay due but unpaid. It was a revolt that was ultimately controlled and supported by the German officers. Oxenstierna escaped with the help of Baner the new commander, and the mutiny was quelled, if only because there was no other potential paymaster. The matter was settled at the 'Powder barrel' convention in August 1635, where Oxenstierna addressed the officers in person and explained the 'dire situation following the Peace of Prague that has divided the evangelical states'. Under the terms of the agreement Oxenstierna would consult with the officers before peace was made. The soldiers in their turn 'agree immediately to remain united until death and not to separate unless both the soldiery and the Swedish Crown obtained satisfaction. He [Oxenstierna] promised them he would not negotiate or agree to anything without the knowledge and consent of the senior officers.' [Preliminary declaration of the officers 30 July 1635]

Oxenstierna told them that they could collect their backpay in Sweden if unsatisfied. How they were to be shipped from the Baltic to Stockholm was unclear! They had to keep fighting because not only was it the only profession they knew but it was the only way to collect their back pay; and there was always the hope of loot. Nor was the threat of joining the emperor a realistic one, not only because they were politically against him but also because the emperor would not pay them their back salaries either. Their only option was to carry on fighting for Sweden and *win*!

In early 1641 Torstensson returned to Sweden on compassionate grounds to nurse his health. However, in May, the death of Baner precipitated a double crisis because the army used the excuse of their general's death to mutiny again in demand of back pay. Duty called. Torstensson was sent by Oxenstierna to take up command in Germany. Arriving with 180,000 Reichsthaler, he soon quelled the revolt with a bit of money and a lot of harsh discipline including four months of drill. Torstensson was a Martinet but with a rancorous, mercenary, and polyglot army he needed to be.

Discipline

Gustavus issued the Swedish army with strict and very detailed regulations in 1632, updating an already exacting code. It consists of fifteen general articles and 150 detailed ones to be sworn under oath. Discipline focused on absolute obedience, punishing cowardice or laziness in the face of the enemy, punishing desertion, strict non-tolerance of pillage or fire, except under orders. Moral discipline was strictly enforced. Gustavus was an enthusiastic Lutheran dedicated to God's service: His army should do likewise. For example

> Article 7 'Whatsoever soldier shall neglect the time of prayers...he shall lye in prison 24 houres...'
>
> Article 53 'He that is taken asleepe upon the watch...shall be shot to death'
>
> Article 89 'No whore will be found in the leaguer...
>
> Article 91 'No soldier shall set fire to any towne or village in the enemies land; without he be commanded by his captaine... he shall suffer death for it.'
>
> Article 99 'No man shall presume to pillage...'[15] (Contemporary translation into English. Helfferich)

The articles were read out in full to each regiment at parade once a month. Punishments ranged from hanging, including decimation by hanging for serious offences such as regimental disgrace in the face of an enemy, to camp cleaning, bread and water, fines, demotion, the wooden horse, running the gauntlet and beating with the flat of a sword. Surprisingly, use of the lash was forbidden. There was the central field Consistory of the regimental Lutheran chaplains who held twice daily prayer meetings and a full service on Sundays. Courtesans were forbidden in the camp and so were unmarried women who were commonly referred to as '*whores*'; 'If any unmarried woman be found, he that keeps her may have leave lawfully to marry her; or else be forced to put her away.'[16] (Gustavus Adolphus 1621) Such provisions were copied by other Protestant armies including those of Brunswick-Luneburg in 1636 and by Brandenburg.

The common gothic picture of the war is that there was no discipline and that soldiers ran amok constantly; this cannot be correct because if this were so *salvaguardia* would have been worthless and the armies would not have been able to either fund or feed themselves because the market for produce on which an army relied would dry up. Wealthy burghers and landowners would not pay unless the protection offered was valuable. We should be cautious in accepting the ultra-gothic and 'doomster' take on the Thirty Years War; that there were many outrages over an extended period is undoubted however, but we must be careful not to apply a 'Red top' bias to the entire picture of the war. When the war was in flux and armies on the march then terrible behaviour was much more likely or in the border regions of territorial control where raiding was prevalent; but for the most part and in most areas, the war was a settled and boring stalemate major battles were rare events. Civilians and soldiers needed to co-exist and trade.

Discipline was accepted even if harsh. It was supervised by the provost-marshal whose duty it was to regulate the camp. Under English military articles from 1531, the duties included the organization and rules pertaining to the placing of tents, the eviction of women, the impressment of horses and oxen, and the suppression of gambling. His tent would be placed in the centre of the camp. In practice enforcement of rules would depend on the circumstances; if food was short then soldiers had to be let off the leash and similarly if they had not been paid. Loot would be a substitute for pay something that he allowed and regulated in Poland on occasions. Sometimes it was a reward and burning and destruction a matter of policy, for example when Gustavus wanted to set an example to Bavaria or at the start of his invasion of Germany when he wished to project an image as friendly liberator rather than a rapacious invader. Monro recounts that during the occupation of Pomerania a few months after the landings Andrew Morton (his clansman) was executed at Statin (Stettin) 'for having contrary to his majesty's articles and discipline of warre, beaten a burgher in the night in his owne house'[17]; despite a good record of valour and pleas for life including local dignitaries and the victim of the assault. Sometimes there were outbreaks of indiscipline; Monro records that at Frankfurt after months of hard fighting and long marches, 'all men that were too careless of their duties, were too careful in making of booty' noted Monro, '…that I never did see officers less obeyed and respected than here for a time…'[18] He may have been frustrated that he was not getting his proper share for we know that he played the same game.

The discipline of Wallenstein's army was also exceptional by the standards of the time. He did not want his armies to spoil a sustainable economic base.

Imperial secretary Khenveller reported in writing that 'he of Friedland maintained exemplary order, so that the land was not wasted and burned, nor people driven from the hut and house; but all was cultivated and harvested… though he pressed heavily upon the empire, yet soldier and the peasant lived side by side, and all commanders have learned this manner of waging war from the duke of Friedland…'[19]

However, the discipline was not uniform. With so many troops under command not even the micro-managing Wallenstein could control the behaviour of all his units all the time, least of all the Croat light cavalry. An example of the damage done by Wallenstein's marauding troops on the march in the Halle region is given in a report by an official to the Saxon elector in October 1625 'the cavalry, including many Frenchmen and Croats, disported themselves like bloodthirsty madmen ...the soldiers descended into the village, tyrannised it, seized its cattle, drew horses out of their shafts, robbed villagers, scoured cupboards and chests, broke everything in two, beat and thrashed the peasants, ravished the women folk, all as though this were the Hungarian borderland....'[20] (Emphasis added) Elector John George would have good reason to exaggerate for political reasons however in a widespread war some thirty years long such grotesque events were bound to be quite frequent even if they were not an everyday commonplace.

Nor was the example of officers very exemplary. Wallenstein dismissed Collaltro from the army for thievery, despite his incongruous position as a colonel and member of the Imperial war council. Of Colonel Desfours, Wallenstein wrote, 'That De Fur is a pest. He promotes every sort of disorder and has done more damage than the whole army...he is fur [a pun on the words for thief or rascal] in name and fact.'[21] However it is significant to note that the implication is that the disorder was down too certain badly led and ill-disciplined units rather than the army as a whole; but there were many other Desfours. However, much Wallenstein might complain and rectify excesses, he needed his entrepreneur colonels who were financiers and partners in his military enterprise. Officer corruption and greed meant that discipline was difficult to maintain because the soldiery, ever alert to the example set from above, followed in that same path even if they did not already have the inclination to do so.

'There are a considerable number of cases of officers illegally driving people from their homes, confiscating items without permission, enriching themselves by failing to report or stealing goods...committing sexual offenses against married women. The image that results is that of a pack of marauding mercenaries...'[22] It might have been written about the conduct of many officers in the Thirty Years War, but in fact this description was given by General Walter von Brauchitsch C-in-C German Army in October 1939 about his troops in Poland in the Second World War. The consequences of manifest criminality for general discipline and the level of brutality were appalling. Social psychologists have written about '*soldaten*' in the Second World War 'once the floodgates of violence are opened, anything can provide the justification for the soldiers to start shooting.'[23] Pecuniary and sexual criminality are the camp followers of war.

The impact of an army of say 20,000 with two or three times the number of hangers on and camp followers passing through a locality is easy to imagine. The camp followers could cause as much mayhem as the soldiers themselves; something that Grimmelshausen depicts in *Simplicissimuss* through the character of 'mother courage' and others. Contemporary woodcuts by war artist Jacques Callot also depict the mayhem and unrestrained pillage enacted on occasions by marauding camp followers. Not surprisingly it was the light cavalry outriders and foragers like the Croats, with their extra mobility and opportunity away from the eyes of senior officers, who gained the most fearsome reputation for looting and rapine. More used to the raiding and looting culture of warfare on the Balkan and Slavic borderlands, discipline declined as the number of Croat regiments increased.

Punishment for ordinary troops was harsh even though it was applied sporadically. The provost's post in the centre of his camp always had a hangman's gallows raised in preparation and as a warning. Miscreants would sometimes be punished for crimes to set an example but even for serious crimes little would be done during the anarchy of war. Enforcement of discipline could be harsh, but it was applied randomly and arbitrarily. Soldiers might be hung or shot. However, the most severe punishment was connected to cowardice or negligence in the field rather than indiscipline with regards to civilians. Rape should have been punished by hanging or firing squad, but the punishment was only intermittently enforced, moreover many of the women would attach themselves to a particular soldier to avoid rape as a means of survival. However, famous wood cut artist Jacques Callot depicted an execution for rape which indicates that such punishment was not unusual. (Lothringian artist Jacques Callot (1592–1635), titled in full Les Misères et les Malheurs de la Guerre from scenes in French occupied Lorraine. Callot witnesses the war from French occupied Nancy during the prolonged proxy war against the Habsburgs whose ally was the Charles Duke of Lorraine. Not an official part of the Thirty Years War until 1635. The duchy lost its independence at this time.)

Even the genial soldierly 'everyman' Hagendorf who acquired sexual plunder at Landshut and Pforzheim regarded the practice of 'temporary wives' acquired by conquest as the norm.[24] Draconian punishment such as execution would be meted out to officers who ran away with their troops or who surrendered a city too easily or who treated with the enemy with a view to defection. This was famously the case in the notorious execution ceremony at Prague in 1632 after the battle of Lützen. Failure for military negligence or alleged incompetence might earn an officer a court martial as it did twice for General Gotz, although he was rehabilitated on both occasions: In contrast he was not punished for his notorious massacres of civilians at Pasewalk in Pomerania and in Hesse.

Alcohol abuse was the most common cause of ill-discipline, individually and *en masse*: it was the natural accompaniment to rape, robbery, and desertion. Drunkenness for an ordinary soldier could also have drastic personal consequences. Our hero Hagendorf was on the march to the west of Limburg in June 1642 when he drank too heavily one night and was left to straggle on behind with a hangover, 'I had a bit to drink in the evening,' he writes insouciantly, 'and then fell behind my regiment in the morning because of a hangover. Three peasants hiding in a hedge beat me thoroughly and took my coat, satchel, everything… thus beaten up without coat or bag, I rejoined my regiment and was laughed at.'[25] He was lucky to survive. When some months later he returned to the town, he had his revenge on the miscreants and recovered damages in cash.

Discipline in line of battle when under fire was the corollary of harsh discipline on the march; Monro in a poetic mood describes how 'our canon begun to roare, great and small paying the enemy the like coyne, which thundering continued alike on both sides for two hours and a halfe, during which time, our Battaliles of horse and foote stood firm like a wall.'[26] But even disciplined soldiers needed sustenance so there was some leeway given at times when funds, supplies and pay was short. The congenital ill-discipline of Mansfeld's troops was perhaps reflected in poor battlefield performance but the morale factor was also missing because Mansfeld was transparently a mercenary rather than representing anything like a cause. Bernhard of Saxe-Weimar's army which rampaged and looted its way through southern Germany in 1634 sometimes fought very well at Nördlingen 1634 despite looting and would fight well when reconstituted in the years following his death. His leadership of 'the Bernadine's' had engendered a cohesive élan and comradeship which transcended the normal cynicism of the soldiery.

After the battle of second Breitenfeld 1642, there occurred an event that was exceptional even in brutal Thirty Yeas War, with echoes of Wallenstein's behaviour after Lützen. Archduke Leopold, who barely escaped the battlefield, was incandescent with rage and sated his desire for revenge for his offended Habsburg pride on the Madlo cavalry regiment. Singled out for special punishment after a shameful flight, they were used as scapegoats for the defeat. Habsburg honour was assuaged when an entire regiment of 'cowards' received Roman style punishment in front of the assembled army, 'The entire regiment was to be decimated i.e. every tenth man to be executed, with the victims selected by all men throwing a die. Captains and lieutenants who were selected would be beheaded but ensigns would be hung like the NCOs and men, because their flight from with the regimental standard was considered especially dishonourable…'[27] Some officers had their sentence commuted to be shot instead of beheaded while a few others were pardoned on account of their previous excellent service and bravery. As for the rest, the troopers, 'all were bound to trees with rope and hanged until dead.'[28] Following the execution of several Silesian and Moravian garrison commanders who had surrendered too easily in the proceeding campaign, Leopold's behaviour signified increased Habsburg viciousness as the war came home to roost in their precious hereditary lands. It was a policy born of rising desperation in Vienna reflecting a realisation that the tide of war was changing.

In such a manner was the overbearing arrogance of Leopold satisfied, in proportion to the hubris and incompetence of the Imperial Habsburg blood flowing through the veins of the real progenitor of defeat. In his vicious pride, he was every inch an early modern Habsburg.

Soldiers in death: Discovery of 'the mass grave' at Wittstock 2007, and Lützen.

The epicentre of the battle at the foot of the Scharfenburg near Wittstock (sixty miles north west of Berlin), is now marked because of a rare discovery at a European battle site in 2007 of a mass grave of 130 bodies packed in the sandy earth. Stripped of everything except undergarments, the skeletons and skulls reveal hideous wounds. Skeletal heads were found, jaws are gaping open, still with the pitiful death screams of agony and despair, bones showing signs of extreme trauma; skulls were smashed by musket balls and bones marked by sword cuts and shrapnel damage[29]; (possibly from fused exploding-cannon balls but more likely from canon-fired grapeshot or hand thrown grenades). Even without scientific analysis it is obvious that the dead were from the victor's side. Who would bother to bury thousands of enemy dead? They would be stripped and left for wolves, wild boar, and packs of dogs, that emerged from the forests at night. But before the wolves arrived, human scavengers from nearby villages would be stripping the bodies of clothes and any remaining valuables. Most bodies would be left naked on the battlefield giving an eerie white sheen in the dead of night; all quiet except for the sound of snapping, crunching, and tearing flesh.

Based on the levels of strontium in the tooth enamel, research has identified the geographic and racial origins of the remains. The grave holds the bones of Scots, Swedes, and Germans from the Danube Basin. Franz Schopper, director of the Brandenburg Monument Preservation Office, has noted that: 'The strontium content of the teeth provides a unique geographic marker, indicating where each of these soldiers originates. It is linked to known levels in the drinking water in areas across Europe in the seventeenth century. We believe there are Scots among them…' which ties in with what we know of the Swedish army units deployed. At least three soldiers from the 140 sample at Wittstock (a hundred kilometres northeast of Berlin) also showed signs of advanced syphilis; a soldier's curse, there was no cure for venereal disease in the 1600s and it was widespread among soldiers.[30] Wittstock hosts one of the better battlefield museums in Germany, with excellent exhibits, and a lecture and research centre.

Similar excavations as Lützen and Wittstock have led to other revelations which emphasise that all battles were not the same. Blocks of earth containing forty skeletons were lifted from Lützen. The Lützen find is unusual because it shows an inordinate number of the skeletons with pistol shot wounds to the head from a sample of forty, which suggests that this is the Swedish blue regiment which was overrun in the mist by Imperialist several regiments include Piccolomini's cuirassiers; it 'could' support Professor Wilson's[31] thesis as to the effectiveness of caracole. However, shots to the head accounted for twenty-seven out of forty cadavers, with a eleven pistol balls found inside the skulls of skeletons. Such statistics do not occur in other battles. Therefore, I would suggest to the contrary; these shots must be fired at point-blank range; one might expect the odd lucky shot to the head but with over half of the wounds accounted for in this manner we must presume that the musketeers were overrun and shot from extremely close range, not 'caracole' range, i.e. beyond the reach of pikes; overrunning was possibly due to the very low pike ratio and being outnumbered, and because of lack support from other regiments, which we know to be correct. However, this still requires some degree of accuracy even at close quarters; accuracy which these weapons did not have, let alone from horseback in the midst of battle.

Another perhaps stronger possibility is that they had surrendered and were then executed on the battlefield; this would account for the large number so balls found in the skulls of the sample of forty. Massacre of garrisons was common after sieges and storms, as was the indiscriminate cutting down of a fleeing enemy at the end of a battle. However, execution of prisoners in battle seems to be uncommon. Given the mist and the confusion the temptation to execute prisoners who would be difficult to guard in the dire and pressing circumstances the battlefield, to prevent them rejoining the battle, must have been tempting.

The general conclusion from the various Thirty Years War excavations of Lützen and Wittstock in particular, reveal that most wounds (death wounds) were caused by deep cuts or penetration by edge or sharp pointed weapons and musket ball gunshots. However, it should be noted that grapeshot from a cannon might be like musket ball wounds. At Alerheim there was heavy fighting in the town with huge casualties resulting from both musketry and grapeshot from cannon. Wittstock would similarly have seen a mixture of weapons causing death; canon, particularly those Swedish guns under Torstensson did play an important part.

Medical facilities for the wounded were poor. Recovery was hindered by lack of medical facilities and the likelihood of infections eve from wounds not immediately life threatening. Monro records the common event of post injury infection in the case of his cousin, Fowles, who was shot in the foot; not in itself a serious injury but 'through the smart of his wound fell into a languishing Feaver'. In great pain, he died six weeks later. Officers and soldiers were sometimes sent to towns where there were better facilities and skilled medical experts, so their recovery rate was higher. Monro for example was dispatched to Copenhagen after being wounded in the knee in the service of Denmark at the siege of Stralsund. There are few descriptions of surgical procedures in surviving testimony, possibly due to squeamishness or fear of the all too real proximity to death and it is the potentially grisly circumstances around being wounded. Monro describes a surgical intervention for a young Hector Monro Catwalls in the battle of Alte Veste, outside Nuremburg 1632 who was 'shot alonst the braines'. 'He lived a fortnight after, which shot was wonderful (freakish); for the side of the head that the bullet lightes on. The skull was whole; nevertheless, through the great torment, the chirurgian (surgeon) having made incision on the other side of his head, to see if the skull was whole, but being found splent on that side, so that his braines could be seen, his wound was incurable.' Surgical instruments of the day were as terrifying as could be expected.

Other points of interest from the excavations were the unsurprising confirmations that most casualties were caused by gunfire, either musket or canister. Nonetheless, there were many horrific wounds caused by edged weapons, revealed by deep scars on bones. Many of these were old wounds, with one cadaver revealing four separate head wounds picked up prior to the battle. To speed reloading in battle, which was a matter of life and death, musketeer had the habit of retain a lead ball in the mouth which could be spat directly down the barrel after the powder had been rammed down. It saved a few seconds in scabbling around his pouch. At Wittstock several balls were found in the mouth cavity of the skeletons; killed during the act of reloading their weapon.

The soldiers and why men fought

Recruitment: Who fought and what did they fight for?

The war was a political and religious struggle. It would be wrong to characterise all German soldiers as fair-weather mercenaries. However, captured prisoners would often defect *en masse* to their captors, something quite natural given the choices. Defection would after a battle secure food and safety. Desertion rates of the new recruits in the weeks following would be high especially if the captured soldiers were culturally very different from the army which had captured them. For example, nine companies (about 1,000 soldiers) of Italians of the Spanish army's garrison captured at Oppenheim 1632 joined the Swedish army but deserted rapidly. After Breitenfeld 1631 a large number of the 9,000 captured Imperialist Bavarian troops, many of whom were Protestants, enrolled with Gustavus. At Rheinfelden 1638, 3,000 captured Imperialist infantry were co-opted into Saxe-Weimar's army and similar defections occurred after second Breitenefeld amongst the 5,000 captured by Torstensson's army. Most mass defections by prisoners were of infantry for the simple reason that they could not flee so easily as a cavalryman. Foot soldiers had little practical choice because they would face being destitute tramps, far from home, if they were released. In practice the only prisoners who were kept were senior officers with a ransom or exchange value such as General Torstensson after Alte Veste Prince Rupert after Vlotho 1638 and Imperial commander Hartzfeld after Jankov 1635.

In an exception to the rule, though some changed sides after Nördlingen, the Spanish and Imperialist army also massacred many of the surrendering and helpless Protestant army who were trapped on the low ground at a bottleneck by the bridge. Poyntz recorded that 'the dukes' infantry which were in the bottome were all cut downe and themselves out of order lost their courage and fled, and john de wert followed the duke in slaughter six English miles…'[32] Sweden's army was almost eliminated, 8,000 men were dead and a further 4,500 captured. High casualty levels were not just the result of battle; but confirms that surrendering men were deliberately cut down. Hagendorf was captured again. He noted bitterly that 'The Spanish butchered everyone,'[33] wrote Hagendorf bitterly. Wanton massacre of the losing side was common after storming of places, but it seems to have happened on the battlefield as well; at Lens Grammont admitted that after defeating the Spanish left wing, 'We had little mercy and many were killed.' Again, cultural difference may have been an issue; the captured enemy would also be harder to assimilate as recruits; empathy and sympathy would be less. Alien to Spanish or Catholic soldiery, Scots soldiers of the Monro's Mckay regiment were wiped out at Nördlingen. There may have been an element of revenge because Scots soldiers were themselves notably savage. Many of the captured men changed sides, including Hagendorf, who rejoined his old comrades in his fourth defection of the war. He was happily reassigned as an officer to the Imperialist regiment where he had previously served. Hagendorf who had escaped being massacred, happily recalled that 'After the battle all those who had previously been in the Bavarian and Imperial armies, but had at some point been captured, now returned to their old regiments… The captain, who had been captured with me at Straubing (nr Munich), gave me back my position of captain.'[34] Again the loyalty and comradeship of his former comrades seems to have transcended every other consideration. Cultural and racial affinity was a factor in the post battle choices.

But the emotions of loyalty to the emperor or to the Protestant cause were marked in many officers and units of the respective armies; determined fighting and acceptance of heavy casualties demonstrates more than just bovine obedience to military discipline. Partisan attachment was also driven by traditional religious and dynastic loyalties. At the storm following the siege of Rheinfelden by the Imperialists in 1633, Captain Zinckh cried out to the commandant of the town Colonel Von Anlau 'Cousin, you are a villain, serving against your emperor and your fatherland.'[35] He skewered the poor commandant on his partisan a type of halberd carried by infantry officers). Motives for war were not mutually exclusive, and were often mutually reinforcing. Taking booty from the heretic was doing God's work.

The religious bias of foreign soldiers was very marked amongst foreign recruits to the wars with Irish, Poles and Walloons tending to fight for Catholic nations while Protestant soldiers from Scotland or England fought mainly for the Protestant powers. Nevertheless, the Spanish were permitted to recruit from Britain during the 1630s at the time of the friendly neutrality between Charles I and Spain; around 4,000 Irish fought in the Spanish army of Flanders. Some of them were to be redeployed to the Spanish fronts which opened up after French entry into the war. Ironically this religious divide was not so well observed in Germany itself especially in the Imperialist Armies of Wallenstein which relied on very large numbers of Protestants both at senior officer level and in the ranks, even forming the majority. It was however one of the complaints made by his enemies at court; hypocritical complaints because the Imperialists would later employ a Calvinist turncoat, Melander, as his army commander and many other Protestants including Hatzfeld. Battles were preceded in the Swedish camp by regular prayers, psalm singing, mass, and sermons denouncing the enemy. Religious motifs fluttered on battle flags in many Protestant, Imperialist and Bavarian regiments. Religious feeling was well represented in the banners, flags, and call signs adopted by the various armies. Flags often depicted religious motifs on the Catholic side, including the Jesuit HIS moniker, or biblical sayings or exerts from Psalms for Protestants. Soldiers were especially harsh on towns and villages of the opposite religion even if they despoiled their own from time to time. Maximilian's Bavarian and Catholic League army maintained its religious character throughout the war. Officers had to be Catholic, and the majority of non-Bavarian/German troops were from Catholic countries such as Italy, Hungary, or Croatia.

The Protestant Scots fought in Germany in large numbers; economic factors were primary but the cultural tradition of mercenary service as well as dynastic support for the Stuart Queen of Bohemia and religious sentiment were not unimportant in the mix. Captain James Turner's cynical dictum from the war 'I had swallowed without chewing in Germanie a very dangerous maxime which milaterie men then too much followed, which was that so we serve our master honestlie it is no matter what master we serve.'[36] was a comment the mercenary tradition in Germany not on the Scots who served Protestant or anti-Habsburg powers almost exclusively. even if their masters were very varied including Denmark, the Dutch, Sweden, and France. They also served in Russia, initially under contract via Sweden. Catholics mercenaries such as the Irish, Croats, Poles or Italians were only found on the Catholic aligned Spanish or Imperialist side, except where the French entered the war after 1635.

German soldiers were the mainstay of all armies and recruitment in the German area of the war and in Alsace and at times in Italy during the Imperialist intervention at Mantua. Most German recruiting was put out to the 1,500 private contractors and subcontractors spread around Germany. With depletion rate of two per cent per month on average, recruitment was a continuous business except in the winter months when armies usually dispersed into garrison and winter quarters. French armies depleted even more rapidly; even per cent a month or higher was not unusual. Given the cold, the rain and the deprivations including food shortage as well as the lack of regular pay it was hardly surprising that soldiers deserted and became sick from depleted immune systems or lack of hygiene.

Partly because of parochialism and the divided religious and political loyalty in Protestant polities, Protestantism was not always a rallying flag of loyalty. Many German states and their Protestant subjects disliked foreigners and felt a sort of traditional 'feudal' loyalty to the empire, which was a natural, historic, and legitimate political entity. Despite Ferdinand II's autocratic actions, the empire still maintained a great store of legitimacy which is why the Peace of Prague 1635 was initially so successful in drawing back Lutheran loyalist states. Even William of Saxe-Weimar, Bernhard's brother was drawn back to the fold. However, Ferdinand's peace policy did not go far enough in reaching out to Calvinists or Saxe-Weimar and unlike Wallenstein, he did not understand that he would need to treat with the interveners as well. The genie was out of the bottle and could not easily be put back. Trampled over by foreign armies of French, Swedes, English, Hungarians, Italians, Scots, Croats, and Poles and many others, the first strong stirrings of German nationalism became evident during the war, and it would seem obvious that the empire would be the recipient of that feeling. Indeed, it was the fear of unification under a single polity which drove intervention by France and Sweden who wanted to maintain the empire's fractured polity. As it turned out unity in the long term would come from the most unlikely source, the weakest of the major Protestant entities, Brandenburg.

Imperial armies had no problem in recruiting Protestants; they needed to because they were far more numerous. After the siege of Wolfenbüttel Dec 1627, Hagendorf noted that, 'the soldiers defending the city pulled out; but for the most part enlisted with us.[37] With Danish prospects dwindling rapidly, it was hardly surprising that the defenders defected to the Imperialists. However, committed, if *your* side is obviously losing, you desert it for basic existential reasons. Perhaps typical of many of the German Protestant troops, Hagendorf, the itinerant everyman of the soldier profession fought Pappenheim in the Valtelline under Venetian-French colours but then joined Pappenheim later in his career; captured at Munich by the Swedes he enlisted for them in the 'Red' regiment. Hagendorf not once in his memoirs gives out a clue as to any ideological or religious loyalties, though he confesses sadness at the destruction of his home city of Magdeburg in which event he took part. There must have been many like him, which is hardly surprising: Given the Byzantine political structure of Germany and the constantly shifting political-religious alliances, steady loyalties of many ordinary men and women were hard to come by. It was too soon to talk about national loyalty except for a few polities in Europe, such as the Dutch, the Swedes and perhaps the English, Scots, and the Spanish-but mainly a Castilian phenomenon.

As the war wore on, the main reason to join up was a combination of economic desperation combined with economic hope, at a time when plunder was regarded as a bonus of war. Sometimes they were just hungry. Hagendorf must have been typical of many. In 1627, on 3 April,' he recorded, 'I enlisted with the regiment of Pappenheim at Ulm as a private, for I had become completely down and out.'[38] In desperation many would have joined for the signing on bonus before doing a moonlight flit. Count Mansfeld could always impress his employers by his ability to muster troops quickly, which he did by offering particularly generous signing on bonuses of twenty-eight florins for cavalry as well as the promise of fifteen florins a month: A similar strategy was employed by Wallenstein with *handgeld* (bonuses) reaching thirty-six florins by the late 1620s as he sought to raise mass armies. With his superior logistical system, the chances of the recruits staying was higher. Riding skills would enable the cavalryman to earn between two or three times more than infantry, as well as a superior lifestyle. Recruitment became more difficult as the war progressed, especially for infantry, as high demand in war related labour markets offered rewarding and less risky employment in the booming German economy. The idea that the economy was booming flies in the face of the received view of 'Germany's tragedy' but an upcoming book by the author will challenge this view.

There is evidence that soldiers carried considerable amounts of booty with them in their wagons, a point, which was noted by aggrieved Swedish soldiers whose booty was stolen from the baggage train by allied Saxon soldiers who fled the battlefield at Breitenfeld 1631. As with prize money for sailors there was the lure of the lucky jackpot: 'The fury past,' recounts Munro of the storm of Frankfort 'the whole street being full of coaches and rusty wagons richly furnished with all sorts of riches, as plate, jewels, gold, money, clothes, mules and horses for saddle, coach and wagons, whereof all men that were careless of their duties were too careful in making of booty,'[39] In a zero sum game of chance, the Swedish army had captured the plunder removed by the retreating Imperialists whose baggage train was trapped in the city. At a time when the average artisan might be paying over two-thirds of his annual income for food (according to Braudel's figures) there must also have been many instances when soldiers joined just to get an occasional ready meal. However, the draw of loot must have been high; even ordinary soldiers such as Hagendorf, Munro and Poyntz accumulated savings of thousands of reichsthalers. Mostly hard won after storming attacks, the loot might easily be lost or stolen. Poyntz won and lost great fortunes in the war; Monro had his bag of plunder stolen by fleeing allies in the Saxon army at Breitenfeld. The most mercenary plunderers were the Hungarians but in truth all armies except the Dutch, because they never fought beyond their borders, were highly incentivized by the prospect of loot; when an army was retreating and the prospects of loot fading desertions ran high. Rape and pillage kept morale high; Bethlen Gábor remarked in 1616 that 'nothing upsets them [the soldiery] more than not letting them pillage and plunder like they used to.' Even Gustavus was forced to licence pillaging on occasions to keep his underpaid troops happy, for example in Poland and in Bavaria.

Gábor's light cavalry hussars enjoyed the thrill of riding into the rich and fertile lands of Austria, including the suburbs of Vienna. There were rich pickings. When they had had their fill, they tended to want to go home; fighting was incidental to their main purpose and was mainly directed at small columns of enemy and especially isolated wagon trains. A Hungarian officer György Krauss described the rampaging Hungarian, 'The soldiers left nothing untouched, opened and robbed even the graves, turned everything over and searched where something could be hidden. They even searched the cesspits and took all the grain and wine and other provisions of the people, and left nothing for them, completely ignoring their please and entreaties...'[40]

The border between hunger/survival and death by starvation or related illness was very narrow for most people in early modern Europe. In an army there was always a reasonable chance of being fed however inadequate the commissary or 'contribution' system was. That pay was always late or sometimes never paid must have been well known to most recruits so the lure of regular food, a signing on payment, and booty, as well as the possibility of pay sometime in the future must have seemed attractive for many.

One of the common assumptions about the war, that the army was composed of thieves, vagabonds, starving peasants, and the general dregs of society is not borne out by the facts. From studies of recruits, it seems that the type of person recruited was very much representative of society in general and that temporary economic hardship was often a motive for joining up. In a study of the Bavarian army of 1635, less than three per cent was without employment or a skilled occupation.[41] Surprisingly, in a survey of recruiting in one sample of the Thirty Years War it was found that fifty-two per cent of recruits came from towns and this was in a society where only fifteen per cent of the population was urban. Many of the best troops had previously enjoyed artisan and craftsman status. Hagendorf had become a lute maker in Italy between stages of military employment and after the war he became a respected town mayor. It is certainly true that some criminals and social misfits were often drawn to or forced to join the army, however in France the main outlet for penal military service was in the Mediterranean galleys. The same applied to criminals in Spain and Naples. The Swedish army was largely composed of ordinary peasant stock. English troops were largely of yeoman stock and a leavening of apprentices such as Sydnam Poyntz who would eventually become the commander of the Northern association in the English Civil War after picaresque experiences in the German wars.

Senior officers drawn from the nobility had a complex series of motives for fighting, ranging from career to dynastic loyalty, religious belief, or entrepreneurial drive. Not an unimportant point was social ambition and peer pressure; what Parrott[42] refers to as '*cultural validation*'. Reputation and honour, which are unfashionable values today were of the highest importance to nobility bred in the knightly traditions evolved from the mediaeval époque. Some of the nobility like Lichtenstein, Wallenstein, or Collaltro financed regiments to advance their status at court as part of their schemes for advancement to high office. Other officers from distinguished military families raised regiments to further their military careers; soldiering is what they did. Frederick Schomberg a scion of a famous Palatinate military family was typical; apart from wanting to fight for his elector and the restoration of the disposed Palatine he needed an occupation to further his career; there were no other career options in his occupied patrimony. Exiled in Holland with the Palatine court he volunteered for the Dutch army in 1633 at the age of eighteen after attending military academy in Leiden. In 1634 he was an officer in Phul's German infantry regiment at the disaster of Nördlingen, before purchasing an infantry captaincy in Von Rantzau's French command in 1635. Schomberg, scraped together money enough to bring a regiment of two hundred troopers into the service in Westphalia, at the behest of countess Lowenstein who advanced 20,000 guilders for the purpose.'[43] in Westphalia. He entered the Dutch army and participated in several sieges such as the capture of Hulst in 1645. It was designed for service in the French army. He ended up as a Marshall of France surviving battle, disease, and politics. Like so many fingerlings born into a river, only few aristocratic scions became 'big fish', though many tried. Like many sons of middling aristocrats, passed over and poor second son Lieutenant Henri de Campion was frustrated over his lack of advancement. He would eventually follow his ambitious elder brother in intrigue and rebellion against Mazarin.

The town clerk of Olomouc, Friedrich Flade, described the manner of the 'contribution' negotiations following the surrender of the town: it provides an interesting sidelight on the corruption of war and the power of soldiers. 'Once Colonel Miniati marched out at the appointed time with the Neu Krakow regiment (Polish raised Imperial troops)...(Torstensson) demanded that the city pay 150,000 Imperial talers ransom at once. This was an impossibility so we bargained for a day and a night, at last reducing it to 30,000 by secretly promising 4,000 Imperial talers to the commissioners, to be let off the rest. … soldiers especially their officers stole noteworthy precious items and whatever they could find from the leading burghers' houses.'[44] Colonel Miniati was executed for cowardice.[45] Money was not necessarily a prime motivation for going to war except for professional mercenaries such as Mansfeld but once war was in progress the motivation of money became ever more important; officers and soldiers became inured to the pecuniary advantages; Poyntz and Turner are typical in this. Moreover, unpaid soldiers, notably in the Swedish army after 1639 needed to continue fighting to recoup their wages; in the meantime, they sought whatever recompense passed their way.

The sack of Donauworth by Gustavus's army in 1632 is instructive of the some of the more basic motivations which were revealed after a storm, Monro confirms the atmosphere of blood lust in the first moments when at the sack of Donauworth in 1632, the 'enemy,' according to Monro 'were pitifully cut downe the most part of them in the fury. The towne also was spoyled and quite plundered.'[46] The Scots were prominent in the pillage of the town. 'Sir John Hepburn being thus gotten in,' reported the *Swedish Intelligencer* journal 1632, 'and having first cut to pieces all resistance, his souldiers fall immediately to plundering, when many a gold chain, with much other plate and treasure, were made prize of.'[47] Monro describes the aftermath where Gustavus clearly enjoys the camaraderie of drinking after a victorious battle, not unlike the celebration after a football match 'he [Sir John Hepburn] made his way to a handsome house which had escaped the cannon-shot, and where he found Gustavus with Frederick of Bohemia, the bearded Augustus of Psalzbach, and other men of rank, resting after the fatigue of the past night, with armour unbuckled and flagons of Rhénish before them'.[48]

Then there was the problem of large families and the problem of primogeniture. 'Numerous second and third sons served in armies of the emperor, Sweden, or Spain, men who would receive a pittance from family lands which had been settled on their older brother – enough perhaps to set themselves up as colonel proprietors.'[49] Officers also enjoyed good pay. A colonel received about 1,000 gulden per month, and a captain 150. While a lieutenant only made eighteen gulden per month it was three times better than the pay of a pikeman.[50] [Gulden: Reichsthalers approx. 1: 0.75] It was often noted that officers wore finery while their men were in rags. Generals received up to 4,000 gulden per month: Officers also received the lion's share of loot.

The aristocracy fought in war because war and chivalry were in their DNA; a continuum from the age of knights, the aristocracy justified itself and its privileges including exemption from tax on the basis that they provided military services in lieu. In an age-old primeval process, proving yourself as a man meant becoming a warrior, whose achievement were lauded and idolized in print and pictures. However, it also became a matter of honour, status and self-respect. None more so than young bucks of the French aristocracy where the likes of de Bussy-Rabutin enjoyed the camaraderie of army life; it also helped them to enjoy romantic escapades as they moved from garrison to garrison. Tax free status for services was a central tenet of aristocracy; for example, in Hungary various junior grades of soldier were induced into a lower order aristocracy in return for military service. Gustavus Adolphus was also a typical alpha male; he positively enjoyed war and the life of the camp with its camaraderie and drinking, though he rarely overindulged. He liked to be in this thick of things which is why, even before his death in battle, he was twice seriously injured by gunshots in the shoulder and the hip. Condé [the younger] was similarly engaged with the pursuit of martial glory: filled with a sense of glory and destiny Condé (later 'the Great') revelled in dangerous combat.. Others liked to play the game of war but avoided becoming too near to it, such as Cinq Mars, Gaston d'Orleans and Louis XIII himself.

Melander was a career soldier from humble origins. His motives though were far from mercenary because he was a genuine believer in the concept of empire and his defection from Hesse derived from political and moral differences with Calvinist Princess Amelia. He was also a malcontent. However, Melander's motivations were mixed. His defection to the Imperialist gained him honours and advancement, despite being a Calvinist. Von Arnim is another example of a career soldier and 'political general' who developed a strong belief in a German/third way-neutralist solution to the war; his instincts found a natural home in Saxony; Schwarzenberg, chief counsellor to the Elector of Brandenburg held the same views. Bernhard of Saxe-Weimar may also have harboured similar ideas but that is not so clear: his yearning for honour, status, money, and a principality to call his own, co-existed with a fervent and radical Lutheran belief. A cynical Oxenstierna 1633 was askance at the greed of the German princelings when Gustavus held court in Mainz in the winter of 1631–2: he noted 'There is scarcely anyone of rank, any well-known officer or official who did not aspire to a few abbeys, monasteries, domains and so on; and the more exalted the person, the greater the aspirations.' (Langer 157)

The bastard Mansfeld, was a genuine mercenary also craved social recognition and territorial acquisition. Baner was a Swedish career soldier, who was interested to make his name and fortune from war. He raised his status by marrying into the Protestant house of Baden-Durlach, who wanted liberation and restoration. Köngismarck was a German soldier whose ambitions were certainly very pecuniary as were Wrangel's. They plundered Prague for money in the last days of the war. Coming to maturity in the cynical last phase of the war when the 'entrepreneurial' culture of war was well established, they all amassed great fortunes. The former accumulated a fortune of two million reichsthalers while the latter built a large baroque palace in Stockholm, the Skokloster, and bought vast estates. Many Swedish generals and Oxenstierna accumulated *latifundia* in the Baltic. Saxe-Weimar accumulated a fortune: when he died, he passed on his 'business' to his four loyal colonels including Erlach, a minor Swiss nobleman, who still retained the governorship of Breisach and military control there. This 'Breisach' trump card ensured the continued special 'quasi-independent' status of the 'Bernadiners' in their relationship with the French. Erlach would use his post to set up a military contracting business with his ample finances reflected in a 312,000 livres deposit kept at the Hervart Bank in Lyons. Imperial generals were similarly driven. The rape of treasure and precious artefacts in gloriously wealthy Mantua in 1630 by generals Collaltro and Aldringen, which yielded eighteen million ducats, was probably the richest haul of the war. Italian minor nobility was notoriously acquisitive and corrupt, none more so than Piccolomini. Even the puritanical Tilly under frugal task master Maximilian I accumulated 600,000 Reichsthalers. While many middle ranking officers lost money or even their lives in the high-risk venture of war, the prize for victory and successful insider manipulation of the entrepreneur system, was huge riches, which were unavailable in any other career: Like an investment banker in the recent times?

The desire for adventure and romantic notions of war combined with the humdrum of life certainly took some young men to war. Young James Turner at the age of seventeen was a highly educated young gentleman with a master's degree to his name from Glasgow university, he tired of academic study: So he recounts 'before I attained my eighteenth year of age, a restless desire entered my mind, to be, if not an actor at least a spectator of these wars which at that time made so much noise over all the world…sir James Lumsden was then leavening (raising) a regiment.'[51] This desire of young boys for adventure is a timeless motivation for going to war. It has been estimated by Richard Van Emden that 250,000 under age boys, some as young as twelve, volunteered for the British army in the First World War (the Boys of the Great War 2006). Sydnam Poyntz was another such. He remembered ruefully… 'It is well knowe to most, how mere youth and rashness are of affinite, which may instance myself, for having no sooner attained to 16 years of age, but I began to harbour these conjectures in myself. To bee bound an apprentice that life I deemed little better than a dog's life and base. At last, I resolved with myself thus: to live or die a soldier would bee noble in death as life, which resolution tooke such strong root in me, that not long after I took my way to Dover, thence to Calico…'[52] Englishman Sydnam Poyntz, the war's great chancer, not surprisingly found it quite easy to become a mercenary soldier and changed sides with ease because his main motivation was not religious or ideological. But Scots like Turner tended to be loyal to their clan, kinsmen and the Protestant cause.

According to a bitter contemporary, armies in Germany were 'a medley of nations, French, and Spanish, so that Germany became nothing but a looting ground.'[53] For soldiers like Poyntz and others the allure of booty was a motivation not limited to marauding Croat cavalry. Casual theft, from looting raids, was common. One downtrodden Brandenburg burgher and Lawyer complained 'I had to look on while my whife fastened her bracelets around a cavalry captain's wrists, and I dare not look angry about it.'[54] Pastor Freund noted his losses in one raid in 1631, 'In this plundering I suffered losses in money, linen and household goods…'[55] War attracted and encouraged criminality; apart from financial booty and wanton violence, arson, or destruction of property there was also 'sexual booty' to be had. This could take the brutal form of rape or a more subtle exploitative aspect of war, taking in women 'under protection'. [see chapter VII on women]

France suffered for a lack of cavalry and after formal entry into the war in 1635, desperate and not very successful attempts were made to increase their numbers: riding was for aristocrats not peasants. Overcrowded and poor Switzerland like the wild and remote areas of Celtic Britain had a long reputation for providing mercenary infantry under contract: The tradition continued with contingents raised by both France and Venice. Savoy sent Count Mansfeld with 4,000 Swiss raised soldiers to fight in Bohemia in 1618. However, the Swiss were involved with their own internecine struggles as well as guarding against the Habsburgs, so the proportion of the French army composed of Swiss mercenaries was lower than in former times.

Fatalism and the transitory hand to mouth existence of the soldiery engendered a constant neurosis in the life of a soldier. One of Munro's maudlin diary entries sums it up '… our lives here are but like bubbles of the water, now seene, now vanish.'[56] Motivations for fighting were mixed and changeable. Daily contact with the great existential question led men in many different psychological directions, for solace in drink, in women, in religion, in wanton criminality of all sorts, in hate, or in the acquisition of loot enough to enjoy bacchanalian excess. Or they sometimes escaped the merry-go-round of death: taking their winnings off the table at an opportune time they married and settled down in a quiet business or farm. Poyntz tried that, but when he returned home, he found that his family had been massacred by marauding soldiers and his property destroyed.

The rewards of murder

Assassins in the Wallenstein conspiracy, a judicial murder sanctioned by the emperor went on to high command and fabulous riches. Fortuitously there was a lot of money to be sequestered from the so-called traitors; Wallenstein was not the only fabulously wealthy *'rebel'*. Enormous estates belonging to Counts Trcka and Schaffgotsch would be included in the carve up. Their great estates were parcelled out to his treacherous generals and colonels. Gallas, Piccolomini and Aldringen received estates worth 500,000, 215,000 and 94,000 gulden respectively. [1 Gulden = 0.75 reichsthalers]. The murderous cabal in Eger received estates worth respectively, 225,000 gulden for Butler, for Leslie 132,000 and 178,000 for Gordon. Devereux, Macdaniel and Geraldine received 40,000, 30,000 and 12,000 gulden respectively. A hundred and twelve other soldiers were still waiting for their payment three years later.

Wallenstein elicited much sympathy. Von Arnim, who knew him well, was at the time of the murder negotiating to defect with the Saxon army in support of Wallenstein and the Emperor. Arnim's comment on the murder was typical of the sentiment at the time in much of Europe outside militant Catholics circles and self-interested courtiers in Vienna. Honour and morality were not altogether missing amongst soldiers; Von Arnim wrote bitterly of the murder, 'I know of no instance where such a thing has happened in the realm of a Christian Emperor.'[57] Even the emperor was shocked at what he had done. 'They painted him blacker than he was'[58] murmured the emperor on receiving the news. But like McBeth he had to continue the travesty; a sudden revelation of personal guilt? But in character. He seamlessly ascribed blame to the poisonous influence of courtiers. A general feeling of guilt only grew in proportion with the failure to find any proof of treason. Piccolomini provided a phony document to back up his verbal claims as to Wallenstein's proffered division of spoils, but he was under a cloud when he visited Vienna on 8 April. The emperor and the court knew perfectly well that the pretext for murder proffered by Piccolomini had been bogus and self-serving from the start. In a tradition established through the ages a loaded commission of inquiry exonerated the emperor and found Wallenstein to be a heinous traitor.

Chapter IX
Recruitment

France: Recruitment and officers and the changing role of Europe's nobility

Unlike other European countries France rejected emphatically any idea entrepreneurship in recruitment and the idea of subcontracted proprietorial control. The reason was deeply rooted in the history of the previous eighty years of division and civil strife in the religious wars. After an era of rebel aristocrats acting as warlords, the idea of independent military leaders was anathema to the king and his counsellors. France ran a very centralized military system but on a framework which was antique and mediaeval.

Richelieu opined that 'It is near impossible to successfully enter wars with French alone. Foreigners are absolutely necessary to maintain the army corps, and although the French cavalry fights well, we cannot do without the foreign cavalry …'[1] Having kept out of the wars French troops had less experience than their adversaries. Despite the various military conflicts over the previous decade, Richelieu also had doubts as to the expertise of his troops in siege warfare, 'we are not so accustomed to large sieges as the Dutch. If we fail in our first siege, I fear that we shall lose time and worse still, undermine the ardour of our troops and the reputation of royal arms.'[2] (Richelieu1635 communication to Dutch allies) The French army, even when operating in France, contained many foreigners. Richelieu believed that a fifty per cent foreign component was optimal, and this wish was undoubtedly driven in part by difficulties in recruitment, particularly due to a shortage of highly prized veterans: however only twenty per cent of Louis XIII's army would be foreign. The French army included many Germans as well as Scots and Irish, a tradition that was to last well into the next century; they were known as 'the wild geese'. Richelieu and Louis had a particular regard for Major General Hepburn of the Swedish army and when the Scotsman fell out with Gustavus he sidled over to the French army where he became a field marshal and took charge of a growing number of Scots troops including the *Garde Ecossaises.* Veteran general and military theorist, Duc de Rohan, disagreed with Richelieu's policy, believing that 'the French and German armies abound with good men, and manage easily without auxiliaries.'[3]

The recruitment of officers was quite a different matter. General officer ranks were exclusively the preserve of the nobility, where in Europe there was a surplus of unemployed younger sons of nobility, a prime example being Bernard of Saxe-

Weimar, the 9th son of a minor princeling from the Thuringian mountains, (a poor district). In France the surplus of noble born officers resulted in a surfeit of small sized companies officered by these gentlemen cavaliers, which became victim to regular culls and amalgamations by the high command, with the consequent loss of salary and position for the officers who might only serve one campaign. Prof Parrott the leading expert on the seventeenth-century French army explains how companies became so small from desertion that they needed to be amalgamated to cut the number of very expensive but underemployed officers. Units would decline rapidly in size after the start of a campaign, but officers had no incentive to maintain muster numbers; As a result, many veteran officers left the service unless they had special court contacts, which could help them maintain their position or could offer financing from their own pocket. This meant more instability in the French army. Duty done, and chivalric honour maintained, many them and their personal retainers never came back, which meant a constant drain of valuable veterans.

The problem was exacerbated by the fact that every poor scion of every poor nobleman wanted to become an officer, part of a *noble de l'epee*'s *curriculum vitae* his chivalric badge of honour. But unlike the Spanish army they did not join the ranks of the infantry while waiting their turn for promotion. Many of French officers came from the relatively impoverished nobility that made up at least half of the noble estate. A typical example was the real life Gascon musketeer d'Artagnan, who pulled himself up to become an aid to Mazarin. Due to the need for money to buy commissions or more senior posts, exceptional soldierly talents such as de Campion could not advance his career; de Bussy-Rabutin who had money and the patronage of Condé, had no such problem. The '*intendants*' (military commissioners responsible for finance) were forever consolidating regimental units that often fell in numbers to the size of companies. General Bassompierre in a letter dated April 1638 reported how due to lack of pay, 'companies were so weak when it was time to leave on campaign that there was hardly a third of the intended soldiers; ...he [the king] proceeded to break up Chandenier's company of the regiment of guards, which was supposed to be 200 men and was only 50...the infantry was not as handsome or complete as in previous years.'[4] The popularity of officer positions was also exploited by the regime to raise money; a wealthier nobleman might sometimes use his own money to maintain or make up shortfalls for his company or even an army, as Turenne did on occasion: some aristocrats sponsored personal regiments.

Political unreliability of army commanders was a constant cause of paranoia in Paris; Richelieu had the unenviable choice of either appointing the unreliable elite to military posts to try to win their loyalty to the regime or having them as unemployed malcontents ripe for rebellion. Louis XIII and Richelieu were keen to pair off reliable and unreliable commanders wherever possible. Richelieu's *'creatures'* would be paired with unreliable aristocrats such as Chatillon, Gaston, Montmorency, Maurillac, and Bouillon. Richelieu aimed to keep the aristocracy occupied with war while guarding against the danger that they would turn their armies on his regime. A mediaeval tradition, the role of high command was reserved for the higher nobility, for example, Harcourt, Turenne, or Condé or one of Richelieu's 'creatures' (cronies) such as Gubriante, Breze (Richelieu's nephew), La Force, or Cardinal de La Valette. As prince's of the blood [du sang], Condé and his father were employed, as was Gaston. In many ways the history of Europe in the early modern and modern world up to 1945 is dealing with the need for a *raison d'etre* for the noble warrior elite that emerged in penury from the feudal period. The new merchant class was in the ascendant, and states needed to find roles for Europe's feudal aristocracy, other than the church. With the aristocracy facing increasing financial pressure they also needed money. The answer would be the integration of the aristocracy into newly modernizing states as professional soldiers, diplomats, administrators, and professional soldiers. Similar problems would beset Japan's Samurai class when they were awoken from their mediaeval slumber in mid-nineteenth century. Modern standing armies in continental Europe as well as the constant wars between new 'nationalist' sovereign states were to provide them with occupation, income, and honour for the next 350 years (and even today). The Prince de Condé was an example of this upper echelon who did well out of the war for himself and his more famous son, the 'Great' Condé. Possessing no more than 10,000 livres at the start of the war, Prince de Condé [father of the Great Condé], who was mediocre in military talent, and in the ironic words of Madame de Motteville 'unlucky in war'[5], had amassed property worth a million livres per annum in income.

In Germany, the noble military tradition effectively died only when German chief of staff, Field Marshall Keitel, was hung after conviction at the Nuremberg War Crimes trials. There are many famous names from the Second World War, which can be traced back to senior commanders in Frederick the Great's army; General von Manstein is one of them. Von Arnim, Bismark, and von Moltke are other examples of names dating back to the Thirty Years War. The Second World War was the 'last hurrah' for the Prussian military elite. A tradition died. (But they now go into banking and industry, as can be seen by the roll call of members at the Union Club in Frankfurt)

The route to success was usually built on military entrepreneurship where the aristocracy could raise funds from their stipends to invest in regimental colonelcies. Others started as junior officers, learning the skills of war as well as the skills of business, until they accumulated enough capital, reputation, and patronage to be offered the opportunity to raise a regiment. France did not choose the entrepreneur system but rather awarded its senior officers huge stipends and rewards for victory. If managed properly the rewards of campaign service plus booty could enrich nobleman who survived disease and battle. France's government tried to deal with the surplus of poor nobles by getting them to join the ranks, even hoping to have twenty per cent of regiments staffed from this category. Conscious of the system in the Spanish tercio, it was believed that this would stiffen the moral of the rankers by chivalric example. The Code Michau issued in 1629 set a goal for the 'cavalry and infantry companies to fill with sons of nobility…that in each there would be at least a fourth.'[6] Reduction in costs for paying officers was also a major factor. However, this policy initiative failed; only about four per cent of recruits to the ranks came from this element. Only elite musketeer regiments of the king and cardinal were able to recruit young aristocrats into the ranks.

Rank and file

According to a study carried out by R. Caboche on a sample of 1,429 invalid soldiers in 1648, most soldiers came from the northern half of France.[7] Normandy, Picardy, Burgundy, and Champagne[8] were well represented with ten per cent each and Aquitaine and Burgundy closely followed. Close to the borders of Spain, the Languedoc and Cevennes were well represented, but areas such as Brittany or former Protestant strongholds in the centre and southwest were substantially under represented; this suggests an emphasis on regional recruiting for reasons of convenience and cost; the impressing of men in these areas may also have contributed to the social tensions, which led to peasant revolts in border areas.

Soldiers came from mixed backgrounds. Artisans were well represented so the army was not just a peasant mass: they may have represented as much as seventy-five per cent of recruits according to their 'self-identification', although 'class inflation' may have been at work; only about five per cent classified themselves as labourers; rural and urban recruits were split roughly fifty/fifty.[9] Given that France was overwhelmingly agricultural these figures are surprising and possibly suspect. Alsace and Franche-Comté, which were Habsburg provinces bordering France yielded less than one per cent, despite in many cases a shared racial, cultural, and linguistic background; this is testament to strong traditional and parochial constitutional loyalties, where mediaeval tradition resisted the newer pull of racial nationalism.

Richelieu's efforts to recruit veteran foreign troops meant that twenty per cent of the rank and file were foreign, of whom forty per cent were Germans, twenty per cent Swiss and ten per cent Irish were the main components. There were also significant numbers of Scots following the recruitment of Colonel Hepburn from the Swedish army. There were as many as 4,000 Scots in the French Army of Germany at any one time. National groupings were often consolidated into particular regiments such as the *Gardes Suisses* or the *Garde*

Ecossaises whose steadfast salvoes were noted by Isaac de La Peyrere at the battle of Lens 1648.[10] Other estimates for the number of foreigners are ten to thirty per cent and twenty-five to thirty per cent from academics Parrott and Corvisier respectively. Many French regiments had local roots or were sponsored by the Grandees of the region, such as the Marquis of Persan's regiment at Rocroi. This gave élan and morale to French units, for example the Picardy, the Bretagne, or Piedmont regiments, which all fought at Rocroi; other elite regiments included Champagne, Normandie, Navarre and Rambures, and Lauzières. Richelieu and Mazarin also sponsored regiments of dragoon and fusiliers. Due to heavy losses and the churn created by of consolidation, French units often lacked the high morale of their German equivalents, where for example the Weimarian and Hessian regiments in the Franco-German armies were admired by the French generals for their grit and cohesive professionalism.

According to Lieutenant de Campion who was an active recruiter for the Normandie regiment in the off-season, 'Most of the officers are corrupt, they made accommodations in exchange for money... essentially getting paid for exempting people's sons, then they would go to the local town and buy replacements usually the dregs and children unable to carry a weapon.'[11] Shoddy recruitment incentive by impecunious nobility (of which there were many) would certainly have added to rapid depletion rates but some elite units raised excellent recruits including the Normandy. And sometimes the 'dregs' once trained, can fight well: In recent times, Prigozhin's Wagner Group demonstrated this at Bakhmut and Nelson's press-ganged sailors at multiple battles. However, corruption in recruitment can be a great drag on military efficiency. In the Vietnam war American generals were exasperated by the low IQ of the conscripts, due to the exemptions or escapes of the more intelligent; similar problems of recruitment have been apparent in the Russian army in the Russo-Ukraine War. (2022–)

All for one and one for all

Regimental competition was as fierce as in other armies, but especially so amongst the musketeers of the cardinal and the king. Musketeers were guards but they were also used in combat as dragoons, mounted or dismounted. Family connections and introductions gained admission to these elite units, where entry was highly competitive and the standards of swordsmanship, shooting and riding were exceptionally high. Musketeers acted as elite storm troopers for special missions.[12] For example they made a daring mission to reinforce the besieged Fort St Martin under attack from the English. Musketeers in the regiments of the king and cardinal enjoyed considerable prestige to match their white cross-embossed blue or red tabards.

As these regiments were prestigious enough to attract sons of minor nobility hoping for a lucky chance to become 'something' at court, they soon became a volatile cocktail overflowing with pride; teetering on the edge of 'noble' poverty they were a particularly prickly bunch, who hardly needed an excuse to demonstrate to the world their innate superiority of feeling. Honour demanded that honour be defended. So, the ranks of testosterone-pumped dandies were forever finding reasons to be offended and excuses to whip out their rapiers. Contemporary military analyst Father Daniel Gabriel recounted how 'very often there were quarrels and combats between the King's musketeers and the Cardinals guards.'[13] Officially, duelling was frowned upon, illegal on pain of death, but the rival sponsors of their troops swelled with pride to hear of their exploits, for 'it was a pleasure for the king to learn that the musketeers had mistreated the guards and the cardinal applauded when the musketeers were dominant.'[14] So the squares and side streets of Paris regularly reverberated with the clash and clatter of swords. When in the nineteenth century, Dumas mixed these facts with de Rochefoucauld's possibly fanciful tales of plots involving studded diamonds, the Duke of Buckingham and beautiful English spies, the legend was born. Errol Flynn and Hollywood fame were just four hundred years away.

For all the swordplay, they were 'musketeers'; it was the prestige of firepower and their abilities with a musket which defined them by name and function. As a unit they did not deploy pikemen. The cult of duelling was a sentimental hankering for the chivalry and honour of the imputed glory of a bygone mediaeval époque with its jousting knights. Even then knights could be laid low by crossbowmen, which was the fate of King Richard the Lionheart at some trivial French siege. Displaced by the age firepower, the wafting of swords was not the function of musketeers in battle; but rather it was their job to coldly shoot down the enemy with an impersonal bullet, but prickly and exaggerated sense of honour was the outpouring of chivalric decadence which was still in evidence over three hundred years later at Dien Bien Phu.

Imperialist recruitment; Wallenstein and war finance

Even In 1619 Count Gondomar remarked in correspondence to the king that 'warfare today is not a question of brute strength, as if men were bulls, nor even of battles, but rather of winning and losing friends and trade, and this is a question to which all good governments would address themselves to.'[15] With the cost of regiment at 400,000–450,000[16] Gulden per annum [about 350,000 Reichsthalers] Wallenstein was clearly not offering to fund it all himself; even his fabulous wealth would not be enough for that but he could make outlays for the *startup* costs including the commissioning of many colonels who raised regiments with their own capital and at their own risk for the provision of equipment, food, horses, clothing and signing on bonuses. Food and clothing would be deducted from soldier's pay. Thereafter the army would depend on *'contributions'* made by territories under conquest or control and cash proved by the state through regular income, taxes, and customs duties. The problem was that the cost of armies was so high, in a war that was long lasting, that it was quite impossible for early modern states to fund from ordinary income. Both Denmark and Bavaria were lucky in having large war chests of circa ten million reichsthaler at the start. However Christian IV in four years of war had spent 8.2 million reichsthalers by 1629.[17]

A standard 20,000-man field army cost about three million reichsthalers p.a. Wallenstein would eventually raise an army of about 150,000, the Swedes similarly. Costs for the Swedish army 1630–34 were thirty-eight million reichsthalers. At Heilbronn estimates put forward by Sweden suggested a cost per annum for the Swedish field army of 8.5–9.5 million florins per year.[18] But for small or financially stretched states like Austria, or Sweden with a normal income of about two million p.a.; 'how to finance it' was the major issue. In reality, Wallenstein was offering his organisational skills and his business genius. Nevertheless, the illusion seemed to have persisted in some malign quarters that Wallenstein was offering to pay all by himself from his fabulous wealth. One of his supporters at court, Lord Harrach, his father-in-law, defended him in this, 'He [Wallenstein] complains of the court's belief that he should and can conduct the whole war out of his pocket, says he never promised more than to set up the army and bring it into position, has hitherto sustained it, but that war cannot be conducted by other than a great potentate [the empire] and not a private individual.'[19]

Wallenstein used a combination of borrowing in Amsterdam through de Witte and the levying of 'contributions' to finance the war. Against payment, he supplied much of the army's food and equipment from his own estates and factory or workshop enterprises in the duchy of Friedland, which were geographically well placed, adjacent to the Elbe River. Supplies could be shipped by barge from the riverine port of Aussig, as he advanced his army along the line of the river Elbe towards the borders of the Lower Saxon Circle. Uniquely Wallenstein was not just a contracting entrepreneur general but a major contractor to his own enterprise. His whole convoluted enterprise required accurate accounts of sums owed; in due course his credits to the emperor would be offset in by rent earning conquests and grants of territory. It was a speculative and highly geared military-industrial enterprise. Geared financially and politically. Wallenstein's credit with suppliers and bankers like de Witte and the syndicates in Amsterdam depended on the assumption that his credit was sovereign backed; i.e. by the emperor. It was not, with investors and bankers making the same mistake as banks who lent to EU countries in the euro system. Wallenstein's understanding of the fundamental importance of logistics in war was thoroughly modern and while it lasted, the equal of the Swedish system. Upon invading Germany, Gustavus would largely takeover Wallenstein's system of contributions; and war finance.

Wallenstein was stepping into the shoes of the state because Austria simply did not have the administrative, productive, or financial means to fund all its military requirements. Like most proto-states at this time there was not properly staffed, permanent defence administration. There was the Aulic War council composed of courtiers. Military men such as Colleredo and Collaltro would be drafted into its ranks, but they were notable more for their unctuous and slippery courtier skills rather than for their military knowledge or experience. However, by the end of the war Wallenstein's administration had been replaced by forty-six senior military officials dealing with logistical matters. It was a policy making body focused on strategy but the distance in knowledge and sentiment from Wallenstein led to deep mistrust, tensions and misunderstanding both in Wallenstein's first term as commander and even more so in the second. The council would produce memoranda for the emperor. On top of this structure was the emperor himself who also had direct links to various members of the council because they were his close confidants and companions, who would of course whisper their personal views to the emperor. Another important influence was Lamormaini his Jesuit confessor and the Pope. Other influencing included his son Ferdinand and his brother Duke Leopold. At times the pressure from duke Maximilian whose Bavarian Imperial army commanded by Bavaria's Tilly was the original alliance partner and basis for the success of Imperial arms 1620–1626.

Wallenstein is understood by some to be the originator of the 'contributions' system or military entrepreneurship[20], which became notorious during the war. However, Wallenstein did not invent the method, but he did refine it. His methods aimed at economically sustainable military occupation rather than temporary extortion, inefficient looting, or oppressive methods, which would only have the effect of driving off the population thereby destroying a region's sustainable economic base. Wallenstein subcontracted to other military entrepreneur who invested at the regimental level. It was a method by which war could pay for itself by the quartering of troops on enemy land and the insertion of military power into localities for the collection regular contributions, sometimes with an initial lump sum levy, 'the aim of imposing these extremely heavy burdens was not simply to provide a one-off levy which could meet some outstanding debt of his numerous subcontractors and investors; despite the near confiscatory exactions, it was still conceived as a regular substantial income flow.'[21] These 'contributions' sometimes in kind or in cash would defray a large part if not all of the army's expenses. This practice was contrary to the law of the empire passed in 1570 by the Reichstag, which required payment with receipts at predetermined prices. Nevertheless, it was the only way for the penniless Emperor to fund his army.

There was however one problem with the *salvaguardia* system. A higher rate of contribution could be obtained by promising not to quarter the army in a town or city: After all there was not much point in paying for protection if that meant letting the fox into the hen coup. But that would impact the conditions for the common soldiery who must sleep in the open. Munro complained of the greed for money contributions whereby 'souldiers were usually commanded to lie in the fields, and not suffered to quarter in the townes, which they had taken for feare to hinder the payment of moneys imposed on them…avarice has been the losse of many armies.'[22] There was therefore a difficult trade-off between contented soldiery with lower rates of attrition by desertion or sickness, and the requirement to raise funding for supplying the army.

Local protection warrants called *salvaguardia* were issued in confirmation of payment. The methods of collection would also vary with some regions providing contributions in kind or simply raising taxes on behalf of the occupier rather than the local ruler; as in Brandenburg in 1627. Given the tendency of armies or communities of armies including hangers on of some 30,000–100,000 to move like locusts around the country, there was always political pressure to keep an army off home territory. The principal aim of war was to impose oneself on the enemy, thus securing the double benefit of free maintenance while denying economic benefit to the enemy. This activity in the hands of an itinerant freebooter, such as like Mansfeld, was simply the quick and inefficient rapine and looting of a transient army. It was Wallenstein's genius to turn it into a sustainable 'system' and it was the 'miracle' by which he raised 131,000 troops for Imperial Service with very little direct input from the emperor. How sustainable this system was is a matter of debate. Parrott argues convincingly that the *mass* of the Imperial army, as well as loss of control at the local level, led to overtaxing of occupied lands. A combination of impunity and military power led to exorbitant demands from self-interested colonel entrepreneurs. Italian colonels Piccolomini and Collaltro, for example, acquired a pernicious reputation in this regard. Wallenstein probably understood that his system could not be sustained forever on a hostile Protestant population, which explains his constant pleas for a peace settlement. People would emigrate under the oppressive tax regime of the 'contributions system'. And they did. Mass mobilisation was the necessary strategic method of snuffing out the rebellion entirely, prior to a long-lasting territorial, constitutional, and religious settlement. The aim was to settle the matter quickly because it was not sustainable; when Wallenstein realised in 1633 that the war was in stalemate, he realised that peace was the only option.

The kernel of Wallenstein's system, typical of a modern business and administrative method, was that more could be extracted from the localities over a longer time period if there was regularity, justice, and certainty in the operation of the system. Not too much should be extracted and not too quickly. Nonetheless the burden of this 'contribution taxation' was extremely onerous with an annual tax rate in Pomerania for example at over five times the pre-existing rate.[23] In practice the patience and strains of the contribution system were reaching breaking point after just two years of operation, so much so that even loyalist princedoms were threatening rebellion and non-payment. Resistance was expressed openly at the diet of Regensburg 1629 and again at the Protestant convention in Leipzig in 1630. The *'mulch cow'* did not need to be happy but it did need to be alive and content with the level of protection afforded by the occupiers. Revealingly, in 1621 Wallenstein wrote, 'I have desired and still desire nothing but to serve his majesty and maintain good discipline…either there must be orderly quartering and payment, or a disorderly soldiery… Let your princely grace be sure that a general rising will be caused much sooner if one robs the people of everything than if they make regulated contributions.'[24] [Emphasis added]

To create taxable cash, the economy needed to continue to function, which would not happen if the local populace were terrorised, stripped of their productive assets, and forced to become refugees. Wallenstein was intent on setting up a fair balance between vigorous economic activity and regular taxes [contributions]. His belief in order and good economy accounts for his insistence on high standards of discipline as demonstrated by the Collaltro incident and many others. For example, he ordered the execution of Colonel Gorzenich before the eyes of the army, for plundering.[25]

Fortunes of war were often in flux, so standards of behaviour were never uniform. Wallenstein's system was the optimum one, but it operated best in stable conditions. Retreating armies not expecting to return soon would be tempted to ravage regions on their retreat, to loot as much as possible in a sort of scorched earth policy and advancing ones had little time for niceties in billeting arrangements etc. Moreover, a defeated army's supply and logistic system may well have crumbled if it lost its credit rating with suppliers/financiers or lost its baggage train. Generals often had little option but allow starving troops to sequester provisions, i.e. steal, along the lines of retreat. Discipline soon broke down in such cases. Sometimes both sides demanded contributions, for example in Hesse 1638–40. As the war went on some badly picked over local areas were only barely capable of supporting local garrisons. There was often not enough free cash to support a field army.[26]

However inadequate, the army was also funded by increased taxation from the Habsburg hereditary lands with the emperor providing four million florins from 1625–30, and Spanish subsidies of three million florins were paid directly to Wallenstein's army. 'Wallenstein was never strictly speaking a 'general contractor' independent of the financial support of his master, the emperor even if his army may have approached fiscal and administrative independence at a few points during his first generalship.'[27] Wallenstein provided loans of nearly seven million florins by 1628, some from his personal revenues and fortune and still more provided by the loans raised on his credit by de Witte the Flemish Calvinist banker.[28] Separately from Wallenstein, the Emperor also had to pay 1.2m florins per annum for the maintenance of army garrisons on the Turkish military frontier to guard against raiding and surprise attacks by the Transylvanians.

The importance of financing in directing strategy and even the winning of campaigns at a tactical level cannot be underestimated. In September 1632 the field deputy attached to the Dutch army as a sort of political commissar noted that the taking of the town of Limburg was 'not because of the place's strength [the lack of it] but because of the contributions and other considerations. All the time I have abbots, monks, also nobles and private individuals (i.e. farmers and villagers) coming to visit me in order to come under contribution'[29] The desire to get a *salvaguardia* rather than risk outright rapine and destruction, incentivized the local populations to *co-operate*. Similarly at the end of the Second World War in Italy, wealthy industrialists showered senior British officers with presents, such as boxes at La Scala, and the residency of their best properties in Milan or their palazzos at Lake Como to protect their assets and get preferred treatment.

Swedish army recruitment 1632

The Swedish system was based on conscription lottery according to lists drawn up by regional officials. Gustavus's 'regulations of 1620 made all males over 15 years old liable for conscription. …divided into files of ten men, and each file was lined up before army commissioners in the local meeting hall. One man was selected from the ten, usually a robust peasant of 18–40 years of age, but preferably young. He was then taken to a locally based regiment and trained rigorously before setting off on campaign.'[30] Less than one in ten of the Swedish conscripted men ever returned home so a draft into the army was virtually a sentence of exile and death. After 1634 most Swedish conscripts were used in garrison duty in Northern Germany where the high death rate was in over ninety per cent of cases the result of disease. The great advantage in using Swedish conscripts was that they were forty-five per cent cheaper than hiring in mercenary troops. Only 18,000 Swedish troops returned from the wars from well over 100,000 who went to them.

In the Swedish army the nobility was more 'earthy', and the social system less well developed; while many officer, positions were taken by nobles, Gustavus was meritocratic in his appointments, putting lower nobility into high command, like Torstensson, and Baner. Baner had won his spurs at the siege of Riga 1621

Rival as had Horn, who also went on to high command. Gustavus scoured Sweden for talent and Torstensson, hand-picked for his ability at a young age was plucked from the provinces to work as a page boy. In fact, he was a hostage because his Catholic parents had fled abroad to join the other émigré rebels.

Like other armies the Swedish army needed contributions to survive; they had to live on the German lands, feeding on it like a swarm of locusts. Upon landing in Pomerania in July 1630, this was the priority, as testified by Colonel Monro, 'I sent out parties in the country on military exaction to bring the possessors under contribution too his majesty…the enemy having had a magazine of corne…, (it) was made good for his majesty's use.'

English recruitment and militias in Europe

One underappreciated aspect of the war is the role of local militias, which was sometimes compulsory and sometimes a voluntary civic duty. The picture of the *Night Watch* by Rembrandt gives a flavour of the 'club' camaraderie that was implicit in such duties; particularly important in Holland, the citizens army held off the Spanish for over fifty years before the Thirty Years War started. An addled image of Falstaff's poltroons and misfits, lends itself to lampooning by witty poets such as Dryden, who wrote 'the country rings around with loud alarms, and raw in the field the rude militia swarms; mouths without hands: maintained at vast expense'[31]. Nonetheless, the militia performed a vital function. Towns and cities throughout Europe depended on them. When leavened with veterans they often performed heroic feats in defence of their homes, as at Macau 1621 [China], Breda 1625, Stralsund in 1628, Magdeburg in 1631, Malacca 1640, Salvador [Brazil] 1642, Brno 1645 or Prague in 1648, and many other places large and small. If a town was occupied by an enemy force or if the town/city council did not want to risk a sack, their hold on the militia would often be a decisive factor in negotiating decisions about surrender with the professional army commandant, especially when adequate numbers of regular army troops were not available.

Sometimes militia would also be converted hastily into field units, as when the Swedes invaded Bavaria in 1646–7. In England the much-derided militia were formed into semi-regular units of which London's *'Trained bands'* were the most famous. They formed the core of the Parliamentary infantry at Edgehill, Turnham Green 1642, Gloucester–Newbury campaign of 1643, and Newbury 1644; in the Cropredy Bridge fight, at Basing House, and Waller's Cheriton campaign in the Hampshire in 1644. Later in the same year they also marched all the way to Cornwall only to be surrounded, then abandoned by the Parliamentary cavalry at the battle of Lostwithiel. They were taken into captivity up by the staunchly royalist Cornish militia who fought with great élan in many battles, including the battles of Stratton and Lansdowne, as well as the storming of Bristol. The most famous mass mobilisation of militia was the doubling of the Dutch army from 60,000–120,000 within a few days in 1629 when the Spanish-Imperialist army broke into the Republic's weak eastern flank at Wesel's Rhine crossing. On other occasions militia proved to be inadequate, as in Denmark 1644, when they confronted hardened Swedish veterans. Town and city militia's provided undersung service throughout the wars in Europe especially as garrison auxiliaries during sieges. if their place was stormed they stood to be massacred.

Contrary to the usual legend about riff raff and dregs reminiscent of Fallstaff's ragged platoon of misfits, English recruitment was reasonably efficient. But the picture of recruitment was mixed which is not surprising as it depended on how the Lords lieutenants or deputies in each county, under the instruction of the Privy council, went about their business. There were widespread variances in efficiency and corruption in recruitment policy and implementation. In Somerset those enlisted in the ranks were largely of yeoman stock or apprentices, even gentleman's sons; raising of troops was efficient and easy due to an economic crisis in 1620s. In other places impressment was used indiscriminately against men who had no special connections to the area, misfits, and such like. Graham Long produces solid evidence for his doctoral thesis to show that the process worked quite well, quotas were filled with little social disturbance 'Sergeant Major Edward Leigh inspected 3,000 soldiers in July 1625, he found that less than 1 per cent were considered too old for service and only just over 1 per cent were too ill. Robert Gore investigated 4,700 men at Plymouth in the same month and found only 4.4 per cent had run away, were unfit for service, or were dead.' Although the central authorities sometimes encouraged officials to recruit 'loose and idle people, which may be well spared and yet fit for this service' or to find 'many unnecessary p(er)sons that nowe want unemployment(e)t and live lewdlie & unprofitably in the country'[32], there is no clear evidence that English recruits were of poor quality overall and indeed there were many complaints to the Privy council of labour shortage due to well employed skilled labourers being pressed into service. Recruiting compares well with the continental experience where the major powers had great problems with resistance to conscription being a primary cause of revolutions against Spain Catalonia and Portugal. Resistance in France joined anger about taxes in sparking dozens of 'nu-pieds' or 'croquant' revolts across the country but especially in areas near the borders.

In England, discipline fell apart at coast ports when upwards of 10,000 descended on and swamped the small muster ports of similar population such as Portsmouth. When the logistics failed through lack of funds and organization this led to disorders due to shortages of food, quarters, or pay, especially if there were long delays waiting for shipping or for completion of the muster from other counties. Causes of the failures included Parliament withholding money, and Buckingham's lack of administrative talent. Not surprisingly the logistics trail once in Germany was even worse. Not speaking languages, the English were not experienced at scrounging, scavenging, and looting and had not yet acquired campaign women. Sir James Turner confessed that it took a year to learn the tricks of survival including finding a woman. Women were the essential backbone of armies, but it did not mean they were respected. According to witness John Turner, 'The married soldiers fared better, look'd more vigorously and were able to do more duty than the batchellors; and all the spite was to be done the poor woman, was to be called by their husbands mules, (and) by those who would have been glad to have had such mules themselves.'

Lieutenant Colonel Ralph Hopton was assigned 250 foot from Somerset for the Mansfeld expedition, and his recruits were ideal. Seventeen of Hopton's company were members of the gentry and 212 were husbandmen and tradesmen. Delays had consequences not only for England's towns and villages, but also for the logistical effort. That was the fear of Captain William Courtney in the spring of 1625, who was responsible for transporting 2,000 men from Hull to the Netherlands in exchange for 2,000 veterans of the Dutch service for the assault on Cadiz. He complained of soldiers from Richmondshire (district of Yorkshire) and Lancaster being late, and asked permission to depart without them, for 'There is also seventeen shipps ready victualled for the transporting of those men, which victuals will be lost if the time be delayed'. The wasting effects of delays on victuals were devastating for the Cadiz expedition as well as for European expeditions. In the end a maritime structured supply base in England was of little use for regiments in the middle of Germany. The expedition to Île de Ré in the La Rochelle campaign was also deficient in logistics but much better than Cadiz. Only twenty per cent of the troops returned and the majority cause was sickness, not combat. English command bungling was typified by the scaling ladders proving to be too short to scale St Martin's fortress walls. walls. It was typically amateurish, something not surprising given that the king's favourite, Duke of Buckingham, had no talent except those of 'pretty boy' sycophant and catamite to James I. An unstructured and ad hoc military establishment based on favouritism and patronage was very likely to fail as it had on the Protestant side early in the 1620s. Ernst Count von Mansfeld raised 12,900 English troops for the continent in October 1624 – January 1625, only to be reduced to 500–600 men by May. 'The marquess of Hamilton come then from britine with an army of six thousand foote, …in complete arms being well araide and furnished of artillery, and all things fitting, for the furnishing of an army'; Monro adds that following a 'summer' of both 'famine and plague', they 'died of plague above two hundredth a week.'[33]

If they got to the front they fought well, for example at the siege Maastricht where English troops stormed the city walls, the Dutch could provide logistic support. English troops performed creditably in defence of Heidelberg and in the retreat from Fort St Martin on the Île de Ré 1625; also, in defence. Sir Charles Morgan's forces managed to hold Bremen and Stade against Tilly's victorious Imperial army. Individual English and Scots soldiers found their way into many German units and made names for themselves including Hepburn, Monro, Leslie, King, Ruthven, Poyntz, Fleetwood, Hopton, Waller and many others. Scottish officers in particular were highly honoured in the Swedish army, English officers less so; possibly for political reasons. A typical attack against the Spanish lines of contravallation at the siege of Breda was described by Sydnam Poyntz, then at the start of his military career, shows the élan and determination of English troops in an attack. 'And the Earle of Oxford with 2000 musquetiers and 500 firelocks and 50 with hand granadoes of which I was one, marched towards Breda on a narrow bancke along the river side which leadeth to the towne at the end of which stood sconces [fortified earthworks] behind sconces with canons upon them to skoure and cleanse all that should venture to passe that way, yet not withstanding our English bravery ventured upon that dangerous phase and fiercely into the night charged and assailed the enemies sconces, tooke two of them, and having placed our colours upon the third: the enemy charged so fiercely, …[we] were forced to retreat, which although we did in as goode an order as we could; yet this retreat was very sharpe for us, for we lost more therein than in the assault ….where it was my fortune to escape with life, but to be hurt on the right side with a pike.'[34] At the latter end of the Elizabethan regime, English troop formed two-thirds of the army in Maurice of Nassau's 1597 triumph at Turnhout against renowned Spanish troops where de Vere's English cavalry won the key engagement. Bravery was not wanting as famed knight and poet Sir Philip Sydney had proved when he charged did nobly in a caracole attack on the Spanish at Zutphen 1586; poet John Donne wrote laconically of the heroic defense of Heidelberg by English troops in November 1622, 'Sir Geraint Herbert maintained himself nobly to repulsing the enemy three times but having ease in other parts, 800 fresh men were put upon his quarter (by the Spanish), and after he had broken four pikes, and done very well, he was shot dead.'[35] English and Scots troops also bore the brunt of the Spanish attack at Nieuwpoort three years later in another stunning victory. In 1601 English troops conducted a very professional siege to defeat the Spanish at Kinsale. English troops had a good record so if their performance in the Thirty Years War was mediocre it was down to extraneous political facts especially the incapacity of the regime. It may well be that the corruption and decay of the Jacobean/Stuart era, so exemplified by the dark and cynical plays of Webster and Middleton was the key factor behind the organisational chaos in the 1620s.

England was late to the military revolution not because of any inherent defects in the quality of the English soldiers but through the incapacity of the Stuart regime. The military revolution did not properly catch up with England until the institution of the New Model Army in 1645, but soon thereafter English troops organised by the Commonwealth Republic would perform well, earning accolades from Turenne as infantry at the battle of the Dunes against Condé. At sea rejuvenated and professionally administered navy (including Samuel Pepys) under Admiral Hawk led to the eventual defeat of the Dutch at sea and the emergence of England as dominant world power. Political leadership has a major role in the performance and efficiency of armed forces, something demonstrated by the great success of well-led smaller states in the Thirty Years War – the Dutch Republic, Sweden, Bavaria and Hesse. Not until the emergence of Cromwell and the republican Commonwealth did England start to re-establish its potential as a state, something reinforced by increasing economic-trading success. Resources were effectively mobilised by the state to deliver firepower on the battlefield and at sea.

Political leadership is also a question for our own times as the democratic states struggle to develop the requisite military power (ammunition) deal with Russian fascism. If Ukraine loses it will be down to an utter failure of Europe's leadership; perhaps as a result of Western decadence which Putin has identified.

Uniforms

Another innovation at this time was the introduction of uniforms, which had the effect of unifying the fighting spirit of a regiment as well as being an identifier on the battlefield. However, uniforms were generally not 'uniform' across armies but were more likely an identifier of different regiments or sometimes representative of dynastic colours: an alternative was coloured armbands, ribbons, or leafy twigs stuck into hatbands as recognition signs on the battlefield while this sufficed at the start of the war, the increasing professionalism in arms and the new emphasis on 'the state' and national identification led to the rapid development of uniforms. In a report from James Spans, English ambassador to Sweden in October 1627, he described to Charles I the Swedish army; 'for clothing his army he (Gustavus) hath coarse cloth made in his countrie; and dye it in red, yellow, green and blue, which makes a great show in the fields; and this was never donne before the king's time.'[36] In practice however, new issues of uniform were not the highest priority of armies in the Thirty Years War: The Imperialist army thought little of the matter in the early days because it was under the control of penny-pinching Maximilian of Bavaria. Tilly talked of a 'ragged soldier and a bright musket'[37]. However, following the example of Sweden and Spain, there was increased emphasis on uniform after Breitenfeld. However, an army might only intermittently look smart because it depended on deliveries of cloth or garments. More common and notorious perhaps was the bedraggled look of the Swedish army. Upon invading Prussian Poland in 1626 Gustavus informed his brother-in-law, Elector George William, whose dukedom he was invading that, 'my men, if you like, are poor Swedish peasant louts, dirty and ill-clad but they can deal lusty blows and shall soon be given finer clothing.'[38][Emphasis added]

Munro was also self-deprecating about the shabby look of the Swedish army before Breitenfeld, although observers noted that 'they were not nearly as bad as we have been led to believe.'[39]. 'The greater part of the soldiers were clad in blue and yellow cassocks.'[40] Two months later at Wurzburg Gustavus's victorious troops had clearly come into some cloth because ambassador Sir Henry Vane remarked that 'better men …nor better clothed did I ever see.'[41] He may have been thinking of a comparison with his own tatty English soldiers in Frankenthal some ten years previously. A bedraggled look was often the case towards the ends of campaigns. Poyntz wrote of Gallas's Imperial army's retreat in 1636, with his usual sardonic humour, that 'All the bravery they showed at their coming was gonne, wee could see at their parting nether scarlet coats nor feathers…'[42]

Nonetheless, there was a much greater attention to uniform than in previous eras, as a compliment to regimental pride and morale, as well as for ease of control or differentiation in battle. Spanish soldiers always sported a red sash or red cross on their breastplates: they liked to sport striped hose. Most infantry soldiers would wear a long thigh length cloth doublet and knee length breeches with stockings and shoes. A broad-rimmed felt hat was the typical headgear for a musketeer. Pikemen wore Spanish style helmets in battle with a curved brim and high crown. Officers might have an expensive buff coat, [suede cowhide], thick enough to turn a sword thrust or absorb the power of a spent bullet, and knee length leather boots. Sometimes it was worn underneath their breastplates for extra protection. Officer turnout was usually remarkably distinct from the ordinary soldier, denoting rank, wealth, and much higher pay. In Bavaria, near Ulm, 1633, 30 December, Martin Freisenegger described how 'the troops of the foreign and Spanish regiments mustered… there were half filled companies of blacked and jaundiced faces, starved bodies, half clothed or bedecked in rags and stolen clothes of women. It was the face of hunger and famine. Next to them the officers appeared well fed and gallantly dressed.'[43] This was a sign of the significant decay of Spanish logistics and military efficiency at this time, a few years after the disastrous loss of the treasure fleet at Matanzas Bay, Havanna. However, the army that accompanied the Cardinal Infante across the Alps in 1634 performed well and played a key role in defeating the Swedish army at Nördlingen. Spanish infantry successfully counter-attacked Horn's infantry after they had captured the key Albuch heights position.

Regiments might sport different colours to differentiate themselves or flatter the egos of the colonels. Sweden had red, blue, and yellow regiments: we know that their colours were worn in the form of cassocks at the battle of Lützen where there are descriptions of mounds of yellow clad bodies. By the end of the Thirty Years War, Austrian Imperialists units were often dressed in light grey, if material was available, a tradition which would extend down through to the Seven Years War and Napoleonic wars to modern times. Saxons wore buff colours but made up for the dullness with stripey shirts. Hessians wore dark blue with red hose and cuffs.[44] Some specialist French units such the King's musketeers or cardinal's guard dressed in distinctive clothing, wearing red or blue tabards, emblazoned with a white cross. French troops were also renowned for their extravagant use of fine lace at the cuff and the collar. It was a tradition of French battle elegance that passed down through Napoleon even to modern times when French tanks in the first Gulf War were elegantly camouflaged with what looked like fine chiffon. Napoleon understood that unit élan and pride could be encouraged through differentiated uniforms. Gustavus was well ahead of him in understanding this with his deployment of Yellow, Blue, Green etc units.' Imperialist officer *Oberstleutnant* Giulio Diodati, described how 'a great body with Yellow cassocks' was 'in a moment reduced to a mound of corpses.[45], having been engulfed by three Imperialist regiments. That they stood to be slaughtered *en masse* testifies to their unit élan.

At Marston Moor 1644, the royalist White Coat regiments were prominent; their élan and unit morale was attested to by piles of white clad bodies at the end of the battle. The English New Model Army wore red or *'russet'*, the originator of the famous 'red coats' of the eighteenth century and worn today in ceremony. 'I had rather have a plain, russet-coated captain…' [Cromwell]. This was in contrast to Prince Rupert's 'blue coat regiment'. Red was used as a uniform colour in major battles of the eighteenth century, nineteenth century, in the Crimea at Alma, Balaclava, and Inkerman, during the Zulu wars at Isandlwana and Rorke's Drift 1879, and for the last time just three years later at Tel ab Kebir 1882. However, French units still marched against machine guns in 1914 wearing bright red pantaloons and blue jackets, while Jean de Lattre, later a five-star general, (later the commander in Indochina 1953) wore a similar uniform but with a helmet little changed from the battle of Waterloo. He also suffered an old-fashioned near death wound when he was plugged in the chest by an Uhlan's lance.

Regimental colours

The esprit de corps of a unit was an essential element in retention and continuity of trained personnel. Each regiment, operating like an extended family, tended to take on a particular personality. The heart of the regiment was the colours that provided a visible rallying point in battle; the colours embodied the honour and spirit of a regiment. A tercio's second officer 'was responsible for the company's flag. Given the significance of the flag in the Spanish tercios, this responsibility could entail hefty sacrifices…the flag was the most significant symbol of unity'.[46] When reporting victory, a general would emphasize three points, the cannon taken, the number of casualties inflicted, and the battle flags taken. In a throwback to mediaeval feudalism and chivalry, particular attention was also given to the names of fallen senior officers; aristocrats. especially. This tendency decreased over time although battle reports early in the English Civil War focused on losses amongst 'persons of quality.' Many Thirty Years War battle reports led with such news. The loss of a standard would denote the destruction of a unit, or its loss of honour. Unfashionable as a value today, honour along with religious belief was uppermost in the thoughts of early modern military aristocracy. Captured battle flags would be proof of victory to be paraded in the home country to raise morale or rally support amongst the populace. Exploited for political purposes, captured enemy colours would become focal points for victory *Te Deums* in great Catholic cathedrals such as *Notre Dame* or similar Protestant services in the churches of Stockholm. A contemporary print of the *Te Deum* service to celebrate Condé's victory at Lens 1648 shows the captured enemy flags being paraded into Notre Dame.

An instruction to the colour bearer in early seventeenth-century Germany intoned, 'you are to serve as a model for martial courage. Never yield or give cause for the army to lose heart and flee. If the enemy cuts off your right hand, grasp the colour with your left. If you lose both your hands, hold the colour between your teeth. You are to protect it as long as you live. If God forbid, you have to give it up the struggle, wrap yourself in the colour and die.'[47] Some did just that; a note attached to a captured Imperial flag on display in the simple whitewashed Swedish church at Riddarholmen near the Royal Palace in Stockholm reads 'Imperial colour in which the ensign wrapped himself after the loss of a battle, allowing himself to be killed out of zeal for his religion.'[48]

Religion was indeed a motivation during the war, and the flags themselves often carried denominational motifs or inscriptions. One of the Duke Baden-Durlach's battle flags at the battle of Wimpfen 1622 was decorated with these words, 'Friend of God and enemy of all priests'. For the Imperialists Ferdinand ordered that all regimental flags should be decorated with a picture of the Blessed Virgin, often with sunrays emanating from Mary. Polish flags were similarly decorated, [see Polish flags captured by the Swedes in the Armémuseum Stockholm]. Religious inscriptions were made in Latin or German, *Deo duce* ('God is our guide'), Pro *imperator meusque vitam et sanguinem* (*'My Life and blood for the Emperor'*), *In hoc signo vinces.* (In this sign – the Holy Cross – you shall conquer*).* The Jesuit-led Counter-Reformation resulted in flags being inscribed with the moniker IHS for *Iesum Habemas Socium (*we have Jesus for a companion). Imperialist Cavalry guidons always depicted the double-headed

Imperial Eagle on one side, while religious motifs with suitable inscriptions usually occupied the other. By way of variety a captured Croat flag of Draghi's regiment hanging in Stockholm's Armémuseum shows a large F for Ferdinand under a crown, which probably reflects the fact that they served him directly and personally because they were not members of the empire, but rather vassals in the emperor's patrimonial Croatian dynastic territories. On the reverse side of the flag is a ship, which probably denotes their coastal Croatian origin, and the Latin inscription, '*Spes Mea in Deo*' In God I place my hope][49]. Flags of Spanish or Austrian tercio often incorporated barbed crosses representing the crown of thorns against a chequered background.

One captured cavalry flag preserved at the Armémuseum, Stockholm, has a scene of Golgotha, 'the cross surmounted by INRI. Before the crucified Christ kneels a bare headed soldier dressed in three quarter length amour, lace collar…and his left hand is extended towards Christ'.[50] It was a flag of Piccolomini's regiment captured at second Breitenfeld. Protestant flags were similarly decorated with religious mottoes normally taken direct from the Bible but never in Latin. Some academics argue that the war had nothing to do with religion or that religion became less of an issue as the war progressed, but even towards the end of the war new Imperialist and Bavarian battle flags were decorated with religious motifs, Virgin Marys and crosses, and quotations in Latin from the Bible. A Bavarian flag captured late in the war, decorated with the Virgin Mary, intones in Latin, 'in this sign you shall conquer' (See the flags in the Armémuseum Stockholm). Another Bavarian infantry flag celebrates the link between Ireland and Bavaria with representation of St Patrick on one side and the Virgin Mary on the other. Captured by the Swedes at the battle of Oldendorf in 1633, the regiment was populated by many of the Irish volunteers for the Catholic side in the war.

The importance of flags cannot be underestimated. Not only for their functional importance as a rallying point but as a matter of honour to the unit and the army as a whole. At the battle of Edgehill, the King's Standard was captured. Royalist Captain Smith chased it down 'presently he charg'd in with his rapier at the footman that carried the banner saying "Traitor deliver the standard" and wounded him in the breast, whilst he bent forward to follow the thrust, one of those cuirassiers with a pollax wounded him in the necke through the collar of his doublet, and the rest gave fire at him with their pistolls, but without any further hurt than blowing off some pouder into his face.'[51] Having recovered the Standard, Captain Smith was knighted by the king on the battlefield. Luckily for Smith pistols were not very accurate even at close range something that was noticed at Lützen where eight shots were fired at Wallenstein, only one of which caused a minor injury.

Prince Rupert's diary recorded of the Edgehill battle, that '70 of ye enemyes colours were taken and eight pieces of cannon'[52].

Chapter X
Sieges and Fortresses

Siege Warfare; what were fortresses for Napoleon's maxim XL: 'Fortresses are equally useful in offensive and defensive warfare…they are excellent means of retarding, embarrassing, weakening, and annoying a victorious enemy.'

The Thirty Years War was mainly a war of sieges. Despite the impression we may have of great deciding battles like White Mountain, Breitenfeld and Nördlingen; the reality was that these were the exceptional events in an attritional war of siege and skirmish. A German, Captain Fritsch, of the Imperial army wrote a memoir of his twenty years' service in the wars, but as Mortimer points out his accounts of twelve battles are cursory, and of the capture of seventy-five towns and cities he usually says nothing more than that they were taken. Occasionally he adds 'and we killed everyone within' or such variants such as 'everyone who was found in arms was killed.'[1] This passage demonstrates that major battles were a relatively rare event, about one battle every two years in his case; most of a soldier's *active* service was spent in sieges. However, there were many soldiers for whom garrison duty was their only experience of war because only about twenty–thirty per cent of troops fought with the field army. As a cavalry trooper rather than a foot soldier Fritsch would be more likely to have experience of battle and less chance of garrison duty. Only very occasionally was a storm and sack involved in a siege, where, under the rules of war, the garrison could be put to the sword, something commented on in such a matter-of-fact way that it can be taken as a commonplace and accepted aspect of war. But storms of a city were also rare as most places surrendered on terms as soon as a breach was made in the walls and the summons to surrender issued. Like an annoying pawn in chess, a fortress will likely be taken in the end, 'a fortified place can only protect the garrison and arrest the enemy for a certain time.' XLV (Napoleon maxim XLV)

What were fortresses for? Von Clausewitz describes a fortress 'as plainly composed of two different elements, the passive and the active. By the first it shelters the place, and all it contains; by the other it possesses a certain influence over the adjacent country, even beyond the range of guns. The active elements consist of attacks which the garrison may undertake upon every enemy who approaches within a certain distance.'[2] More than this the fortress can also be a protected forward base for mustering, logistics/magazines, and provision of a springboard for attacks or invasion of enemy territory. Gustavus used Mainz, Gustavsburg, Frankfurt an der Oder and Erfurt in this manner. Frankfurt an der Oder was a base for Swedish advances down the Oder into Silesia and thence to Moravia and Vienna. For the French in occupation of the fortresses of Pinerolo and Susa, these forward bases to support advances on the eastern side of the Maritime Alps, into Piedmont or the Po valley. Breisach would serve the same purpose in respect of advances into Bavaria. German soldier Lazarus von Schwendi writing in the 1550s said of fortresses that their purpose was 'to have to conquer one fortress after the other with great loss of time, soldiers, and money, and to exhaust himself. also, the enemy usually has trouble in provisioning, occupying himself. and relieving the conquered places, and the lord of the land can aways hope for, or rather await, an occasion to bring what was lost back under his control.'[3]

He also noted that it was ' better to lose a city, than to put everything in danger and loss'. However, 'it is a great advantage for the weaker, to know how to make good use of the defensive war'. This was the normal rationale used by risk averse and mediocre commanders. There is a trade-off, as a losing side can trade space for time by defending a fortress, but he also risks losing the garrison and its magazine. You cannot be sure of the amount of time gained. Gustavus failed to relieve Magdeburg which was quickly stormed by Tilly in 1631 even at high cost rather than subjected to a long siege which would have benefited Gustavus more.

A definitive list of a fortress's defensive functions is given by von Clausewitz, for whom they were; 'the great and most important supports for the defensive. 1. as depots of stores of all kinds…2.as protection to great and wealthy towns 3. As real barriers, they close the roads, and in most cases the rivers, on which they are situated…as tactical points d'appui…for the flanks of a position…5. As a station (or stage) …on the line of communication…6. As places of refuge for weak or defeated corps…7. Fortresses which the defender leaves in his front break the stream of the enemy's attack like ice breakers on the piers of a bridge…'[4] In the Thirty Years War fortresses protected 'taxable territory'; they also forced the enemy to capture them so tying up valuable resources in soldiers, supplies and time. For the occasional 'pawn' sacrifice of a garrison or two this was well worthwhile, because the enemy's resources so engaged would be ten times greater and often the losses of men by desertion and sickness in long sieges could be devastating to an army as Spinola discovered at Berg-op-Zoom 1622, Aldrigen at Mantua 1630, and Gustavus at Pskov 1616 when they lost about two-thirds of their respective armies. The great captains of the war such as Gustavus, Wallenstein and Torstensson tended to avoid sieges and their few military setbacks were marked by failed sieges, at Pskov 1616, Stralsund 1632 and Brno 1645 respectively. The Duc de Rohan, the brilliant Huguenot military leader wrote of battles and field engagements in his memoir on the military art; 'to give battle is the most prestigious and important thing about war. Winning one or two battles captures or overturns entire Kingdoms. All wars have been waged with battles since antiquity, because these are the quickest way to victory. Today, one fights more as a fox, than a lion, and sees more sieges than battles.'[5] On the narrow frontages in Flanders and the Dutch lowlands sieges of fortresses were necessarily the central part of warfare, but there were so many of them that war became an attritional slog without end. For Sun Tzu 'a siege is a disaster...the skilled general will subdue the enemy without fighting, overcomes walls without an attack.' What is clear is that sieges, especially sieges of strong fortresses, were very risky. A decision to besiege a place had to be carefully calculated but even de Rohan would admit that some sieges were very beneficial. Of the Capture of Pinerolo by Richelieu's French forces in 1628 de Rohan the great captain and military theorist noted, without this Pinerolo's magazine, sustained campaigns in Italy would have been impossible. A major strategic gain, no less a 'by acquiring this fortress the French have gained such easy entry to Italy that...they will always be in a position to hold in check the Spanish forces in the Duchy of Milan.'[6] Similarly, the longest siege of the war at the Breisach crossing of the Rhine, a veritable 'Gibraltar', paid huge dividends in enabling France to wage an indirect strategy by attacking the empire's key ally, Bavaria. Taking the huge rock that rises from a flat plain on the right bank of the Rhine and its extensive modern works around its bases and bridges, was a remarkable feat which took nine months and many battles in the surrounding area as Saxe-Weimar fended off relieving Catholic, Imperialist and Lothringian armies.

The strategies of siege warfare

The number of sieges to land engagements for the period of 1618–79 has been estimated at twenty-two major sieges to seventy-seven land engagements. However, this begs the question as to what a siege is; is it the investment of a place that holds out for a long time or is simply the capture of a 'place'? Some sieges lasted nine months (e.g. Breisach 1638 and Breda 1625), others a few days. The emphasis on the figure of twenty-two is surely wrong by a large margin, because the point of most of the war's campaigns was to take 'places' (in the words of French military historian Parrott[7]). An army in an attacking campaign would take many towns compared to battles fought. In Gustavus 1631 campaign he took Frankfurt an der Oder, Spandau/Berlin, Erfurt, Fulda, Hanau, Wurzburg, Frankfurt, Oppenheim, Worms, Bacharach, Mainz, and many other places on account of just one battle at Breitenfeld. This is not untypical following a major battle with a decisive result. Torstensson, after the battles of second Breitenfeld and Schweidnitz in 1642 took Schweidnitz, Breslau, Oppeln, Troppau, Glogau, Neisse, and Olomouc and many other places besides. There was rarely a long siege because most places surrendered easily. The figures are misleading because the function of winning major land battles was to give the victor strategic space to capture many places where garrisons were demoralized by the defeat of its field army protector.

A few commanders, notably Tilly, Gustavus, Horn, Baner, Saxe-Weimar, Torstensson, de Melo, Mercy and Turenne clearly saw battle and the complete destruction of the enemy army as a way of forcing decisive strategic shifts in power. They were all aggressive generals; but even battle committed generals would find that most of their time was taken in the capturing of towns and cities, the garrisoning of the same and the extraction of supplies and money from many more. It is probably testament to two factors, firstly that armies were of such a size that they could no longer live off the land as they did during the early stages of Thirty Years War 1618–48 and required well protected magazines as the basis for advances. Secondly the widespread development of modern fortification a made quick storming assault almost impossible or impossibly expensive in men. Other commanders focused on sieges especially the Spanish with their experience of the campaigns in the low countries. Typical was General Spinoza, the Genovese banker turned soldier, famed for his capture of the massive fortress system of Breda which he strangled into surrender in the nine-month siege of 1624.On the Flanders front and in Artois there were so many fortresses and fortified cities in this densely populated region that advancing by one-by-one conquest was the only way to capture territory and the geography of Lombardy was similar in its effect. There was only one major field engagement in Italy during the Thirty Years War despite incessant fighting. On the Dutch–Spanish border there were no field engagements during the Thirty Years War except the small affair at Kallo 1638.

From their experiences in the Italian wars of the sixteenth century, Italians first developed the ideas of complex outworks(sconces) and geometric patterns to exploit fields of fire and herd attackers into killing zones. Development of artillery with ranges of 1000+metres and the increase in the firepower and accuracy of muskets in early modern Europe meant that modern aspects of trench warfare were developed at this time: experiences of which would become familiar to a confederate soldier dodging sniper bullets and listening for mining in the lines outside Petersburg [Virginia] 1865, a French soldier burrowing towards the Malakoff at Sebastopol in 1855, or the cowering front-line infantryman 1914–18. As in later times there was thrust and counter-thrust, sallies launched across no man's land, in attacks and counter-attacks on strong points: for the defenders the 'sally' was an especially important tactic, for by using surprise from behind secure fortification, they could inflict damage and delay on the enemy's approach works and forward batteries. Enemy's morale was also undermined.

An attack against the besiegers outer defence lines was called a sally or a sortie. an essential tactic in defending a city, William Frederick of Orange explained 'I would also risk my men in the outworks with sorties, alarms and mining, because if one is chased into the ditch [and] the counterscarp [i.e. covered way] is lost, it is done and over for those within.' Defences of fortresses or field works were always constructed with 'sally ports'; to enable these counter-attacks, as described by Monro in the defences built at Nuremberg. A smart sally by the Bavarian defenders at Freiburg persuaded Turenne that the French attack should be abandoned.

To protect against sally the front of the approach saps might be fortified at regular intervals and the head of the sap would be protected from musket fire by gabions (mantels). Such straw devices were similarly deployed by the Vietminh during the siege of Dien Bien Phu 1954.[8]

For the besieged, the outworks were a way of delaying an enemy's approach to the main defence and city walls, so much hard fighting would take place around outlying trenches and earthworks. The aim of the desperate besieged was to play for time and to stop the enemy's guns from drawing in too close to the main defence of the town, a breach of which would bring forth a summons to surrender and the appalling choice which would then face the fortress commander-surrender and risk execution for cowardice or resistance so risking a storm and massacre of the garrison. When the guns had made a breach in the main defence then a town was usually doomed. Alternatively, the breach would be made by mines: as in the First World War and wars dating back to antiquity, the horrors of mining and counter mining were commonplace in the war and specialist miners and mine technicians were hired with special payments and bonuses. Fortress defence varied and were most advanced in the Dutch Republic, Flanders, and Artois. Either built of stone or simply of sloping earthen ramparts, the design became standard, with five-sided bastions projecting from the main line of the walls, at a musket shot distance from each other, (approx. 225 metres). Beyond the bastion there may well be ravelins, hornworks, lunes, and *demi-lunes*, usually in geometric shapes which from above look like overlapping star busts.

Monro comments on the defence of the fortress of Spandau 'being of strength one of the fastest in Germanie, fortified well with fosse and counterpartes of ree stone, and an earthen wall above having some one hundred and fifty pieces of cannon upon it'.[9] It was delivered to Gustavus without a fight.

Earthen works were cost effective and quick to develop and earth absorbed cannon shot very effectively, however the maintenance cost was much higher because earthen structures only lasted ten years.[10] Then there was a ditch and in between the bastions, *ravelins* jutted out with 'covered ways' to provide infantry protection behind a parapet. The crown of the ramparts in front of the covered way would be sown by thousands of pointed stakes for the same barbarous purpose as barbed wire entanglements in front of the trenches on the western front 1914–1918. Bastions and *ravelins* would provide each other with enfilading covering fire from muskets and cannon and drive the attackers into killing zones between overlapping fields of fire.

Most Dutch troops were in garrisons, about 30–50,000 out of a total 70,000. There were 33,399 field troops out of 77,000 in the Spanish Flander's Army. Troops were distributed in 208 garrisons around the Spanish low countries. If it came to a siege, professional garrison troops would normally be supplemented by the town's militia on a ratio varying from 1:1 to 1:3. The Dutch could also count on a well-established militia system which was well developed in a country with advanced civic culture where corporation pride is exemplified by Rembrandt's picture; 'The Night Watch'. Most of the sieges and concomitant trench warfare that occurred from 1618–48 covered the same ground in Artois and Flanders as the trench warfare in the First World War.

In contrast to Germany, sieges would be the norm in Flanders because of the multitude of fortresses and the nature of the land which was crisscrossed by canals, watercourses, marshes, and dykes; there were almost never pitched battles. Mauritz of Nassau died in April 1625 at Breda. It was 'the town he had captured thirty-five years earlier when he began his chain of conquests. Since then, he had taken thirty-eight towns and forty-five forts by siege, and five towns and ten forts by surprise. Twelve times he had relieved fortresses under enemy siege.'[11]. The process of siege had become formulaic, as Marshal la Tavannes wrote in the early 1620s, 'nowadays the besieger has the upper hand.... the Spanish and Dutch officers have made the capture of towns an art, and they can perfectly predict the duration of the resistance of a fortress, however strong, in terms of days.' Their only hope of relief was with the 'help of an entire army, not just small detachments.'[12]

The Dutch never willingly fought a battle in open field in the whole course of the Thirty Years War. After their defeat at the only open field battle, at Kallo, was forced on the Dutch once they had been prized out of entrenchments. Unable to reach their evacuation barges in time the retreating Dutch were overrun despite their attempt to dig hasty field entrenchments. Sensibly the Dutch only fought when their advantages and strengths were in play. Why take on the Spanish Tercios in open field if you did not need to? The French army on the other side of Flanders and Artois battered away year after year, siege after siege, only making some more rapid progress towards the end of the conflict after the expenditure of vast resources over a decade. (In the same place this must sound familiar to students of the First World War, with names such as Ypres, Amiens, and Arras.)

The progress of a siege

The approach to any city about to come under siege would begin with skirmishing on the approaches and around buildings on the perimeter. An example is the advance by the royal French army to the siege of the major Huguenot controlled stronghold of Montauban in August 1621, 'marching with the battalions in file because the surrounding countryside is a mixture of vineyards and cornfields bisected by rough and uneven tracks. When they could form up, the king's army halted, and detached from each corps of the regiment, a hundred musketeers and a hundred pikemen to form a storming party which chased the Montaubanese enemy right back to their counterscarp (outer parapet defence) without which they could make no further resistance, except to fire a few pistol shots and firing on them when the enemy left their houses (in the suburbs outside the wall); they would fall back to the next house firing several shots on the chasing soldiers, abandoning their houses without destroying them, enabling the King' men to take quarters there, and there were several score soldiers killed in the action…'[13]

The process of siege warfare was an arduous one and often very costly for the attacker in men, material, and treasure. A typical siege would begin with blocking off roads and rivers, if possible. A gradual strangulation would be set in motion, with the noose tightening as supplies, communication or reinforcement was cut off. Towns lacking in modern fortress defence would often extend out beyond the city walls; in that case the suburbs would be pulled down or burnt to deny cover to any attacking force by opening the field of fire for cannon and musketeers; 'this day the garrison have fired most part of the suburbs and drawne their people into town;' reported royalist observer Baille at the siege of York 1644, 'our men fall into the suburbs and beat them in when they sally out either to fire houses or fetch goods; but whilst the fire consumes the houses, they will not suffer our men to quench it, for if the houses could have been saved, they would have been a great shelter for our men in their approaches…'[14]

The first task on setting up a siege was to do what the Roman army did every night which was to set up a defensive encampment to house the bulk of the besieging army, to be ready against attack by a relieving army. Only after this would the siege lines be constructed, and additional secondary encampments be set up. Along the lines intermittent strong points sconces or redoubts would be established much as blockhouses and pill boxes would inform the modern defence systems of the First and Second World Wars or the First Indochina War. Teams of diggers eight-strong would systematically dig trenches throwing up spoil to one side all under the direction of experienced trenchmasters or engineers. For protection wicker gabion would be 'stuffed quite full of small wood or branches…. (they would roll the baskets) before them as they advance'[15] (along the approach to the city defence/walls) using its shelter to dig unharmed. Trenchmaster Frank

Muller also noted that the gabions were also incorporated into the walls of the encampment; the diggers 'fill it (the gabion)with earth giving it now and again a blow with a spade or mallet to settle the earth'. A typical early seventeenth-century encampment was described by a contemporary as 'nearly ten foot high and fifteen thick at the bottom…there are two-foot terraces for the musketeers to step upon, to fire out the breastwork. This breastwork was five feet high.'[16]. Such works could be very large; at Kinsale in 1601 the English encampment was two-thirds the size of Kinsale the object of the siege. Another impressive fortification and camp built on the lines of contravallation was described at the siege of Érsekújvár in 1621(Neuhäusel near Pressburg in modern Slovakia). It was reported to Bethlen Gábor whose forces were defending the modern fortress against the Imperialist army; 'the first fortification at the German camp is made high like a castle. The rest are on ground level with thirty-two canons in three rows.' Much of the fighting would revolve around key redoubts in the besieger's lines when the besieged forces launched surprise sorties.

Then batteries would be set up and trenches dug in parallels. Further parallels would be constructed and zig-zag communication works (traverses) moving forward and constricting the besieged town to the point of strangulation. As the parallels moved forward so would the screened batteries of siege guns – protected by gabions (earth filled wicker baskets) – until the city and defence came under withering cannon fire from short range. The outworks and lines of circumvallation would sometimes run for tens of kilometres, perhaps 20 km, e.g. at Breisach. The lines were interspersed with earthwork forts/redoubts (sconces) in geometric patterns. The sconces (redoubts) were often for the dual purpose of guarding against sallies from the defenders and repelling attacks from relieving armies; so, the sconces would often face in two directions, like mini fortresses. Finishing these lines of contravallation at the siege of Ghent was an essential first task as Frederick William reassured the estates in a letter dated 30 July 1644, 'The entrenchments of our camp are now complete, and one is starting to finish the camp with outworks thus hoping with God's help to be in [a state of] complete protection (against attack) from the outside within a few days.'[17] This was of particular concern for the Dutch army, which did not like to do battle in the open field.

Whenever confronted by a powerful fortress, Gustavus moved on to easier pickings rather than risk a long siege which would break the momentum of his strategic plan. Gustavus's impatience was noted by Monro, 'against either town or fort I never did see in his majesty's time one breach or shot entered….'[18]. Gustavus excelled in open warfare and a war of sieges would bog down the campaign, which he was clearly determined to finish as quickly as possible. Monro was 'appointed by his majesty to be captaine of the watch being ordained to oversee the making of batteries; also, I was command to set forward our workes, but for entrenching, and for running our lines of approach to the sconces, wherein I was busy the whole night, his majesty having rested the whole night long before day to visit the workes and finding them not so far advanced as he expected, he falls a chiding of me…' Gustavus's hot temper was followed by an apology when informed of the lack of spades He was noted Monro 'ever impatient when the works were not advanced to his minde.'[19]

Nevertheless, Ingolstadt was an exception in that Gustavus had little need for long sieges because he either stormed the places quickly or used his reputation for terror to induce a smart surrender as Munro further explained, '…his fortune being such, and his diligence so great that his enemies did ever parley before they would abide the fury of his cannon, as at Brandenburg, Demmin, Frankfurt, Mainz, Donauworth, Augsburg and divers more; and in my opinion, the terror the cannon breeds is as much feared as the execution that follows.'[20] Swedish use of cannon was certainly a war-winning instrument both on the battlefield and at sieges, and its potency was well recognised by contemporaries. Gustavus lived dangerously as usual but even his nerve may have wobbled a little when one of his entourages at Ingolstadt, a young paladin, the Margrave of Baden, had his head removed by a cannon ball. Then on reconnaissance another cannon ball strike smashed away the leg of Gustavus's grey horse. At Ingolstadt Gustavus's attempt to suborn the place by treachery within failed. Then his storm attack cost a thousand men. He abandoned the siege.

The Swedish army moved on mopping up town after town. As there was no hope of a relieving force arriving in good time, towns and cities quickly surrendered; the brief siege and capture of Straubing and Augsburg was the common currency of military activity in the war. Long hard-fought sieges were a rarity because of the cost in treasure and men, as well as the risk to defenders who might be massacred in a storm attack. All options were dangerous for defending commandants who also risked execution if they surrendered too soon. The Swedish army moved on towards Munich but the Bavarian capital, possibly under orders from Maximilian did not risk a sack. 'After fourteen days the Swedes arrive', wrote Hagendorf, 'besieged the city, and bombarded it. So, we had to surrender because we had no hope of any relief.'[21] Hagendorf duly joined the Swedish army.

Assault

Taking the 'covered way' at the counterscarp was the primary objective of any assault launched from saps, which were zig-zag approaching trench works from which assaults were launched. They were constructed in zig-zags to avoid enfilading fire from the defenders along the trench. Outworks such as *ravelins* and *demi-lunes* might have to be taken before the main walls could be approached. In practice, attacks had to take one obstacle at a time. A covered way was the outer parapet entrenchment, often laced with cannon embrasures, with sloping sides facing slightly downwards; this was called the *glacis*. The glacis would also be covered by cannon and musket fire from the main walls so it was a death-zone onto which the full firepower of the fortress would be focused. Once the covered way was captured, cannon could then be trained on the base of the main walls to create a breach. Firing from close range the work would be quickly done. So as the trenches and saps came nearer to the *ravelins* and outworks, the intensity of the trench fighting would increase because the ownership of the 'covered way' determined the outcome of the siege; hence the importance of extensive outworks and strong points beyond the main defence. As William Frederick of Orange explained 'I would also risk my men in the outworks with sorties, alarms and mining, because if one is chased into the ditch [and] the counterscarp (i.e. covered way) is lost, it is done and over for those within.'[22] The essential principle behind modern fortresses was 'defence in depth'. Breda siege works had thirty-two major redoubts and mini fortresses surrounding its main defence; Breda's capture by Spinola, regarded at the time as a phenomenal achievement involving 80,000 troops. It was captured despite a fierce defence and attempts to storm the siege works from outside, including the sort of attack described by Poyntz above. Breda's surrender was recorded by Velasquez. However, its effect was ephemeral because it did not break the Dutch defence lines because there were so many other fortresses. Such a strategy was futile; Spinola knew it, which is why he returned to Madrid.

Once the breach was made the defenders would be called on to surrender; an offer often accepted to avoid the risk of the garrison's massacre under the normal rules of war. It was also the moment at which a commander could surrender with honour to avoid being executed for cowardice or treason by his own side. Sometimes in the war, more was expected of a commander, so he might hope to defeat a storm before surrendering. To his superiors he could excuse himself by claiming that he had run out of shot, food, powder, or matches; or he could point to the number of cannon balls fired by the enemy.

Such moments of negotiation about surrender after being formally summoned were fraught with tension and danger for the defenders. At Magdeburg, the city council took too long to argue over the whether to surrender. Miscalculating, they were caught off guard when Tilly's army attacked. Similarly at Tienen 1635 in the Spanish Flanders, there was confusion between the when the Franco-Dutch allies about whether there had been a surrender. It led to the brutal sack of the city.

A contemporary print of the battle of Breitenfeld. Note the billowing smoke of battle and the prominence of the cannon and musketry.

A matchlock musket was a heavy weapon and needed a rest. With a large bore that could take down a horse, this weapon was simple to operate and cheap to manufacture. Pouches of course powder for a single shot hang from the bandolier.

A Benin brass figurine of a Portuguese soldier firing an arquebus; the choice of subject denotes the great impression made by firepower on the tribes of Africa.

Located in northern Morocco, the Battle of the Three Kings 1578 The cannons lined up in a line in front of the armies normally fired once and were then forgotten. Clumping of cannons in batteries would come later with Gustavus Adolphus when artillery could fire three rounds per minute.

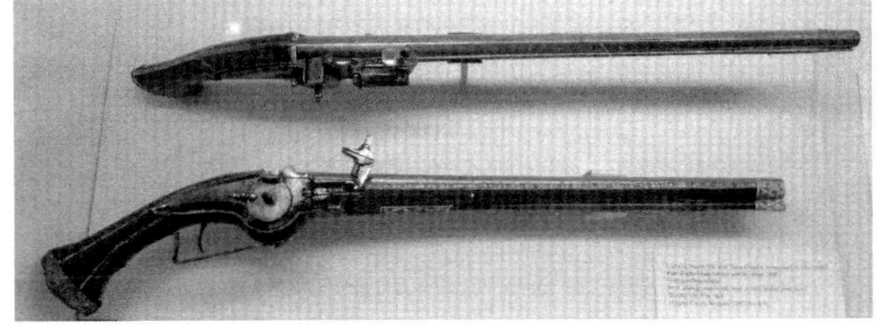

A pair of wheellock pistols which became standard cavalry equipment. In 1643 Montecuccoli, a renowned Imperialist cavalry general, noted: *'Cuirassier should be equipped with breast and back harness, a helmet, together with two pistols'.*

Late 16th Century Japanese ashigaru armed with matchlocks take cover behind protective shields.

Late 16th century demi-culverin-9 pounder. They were painted in bright paint representing the colours of their armies. Sweden sported blue and yellow. Gustavus's standard gun was the 9-pounder; his use of bronze reduced the weight of the transom, and shortened the barrel length to enable greater mobility.

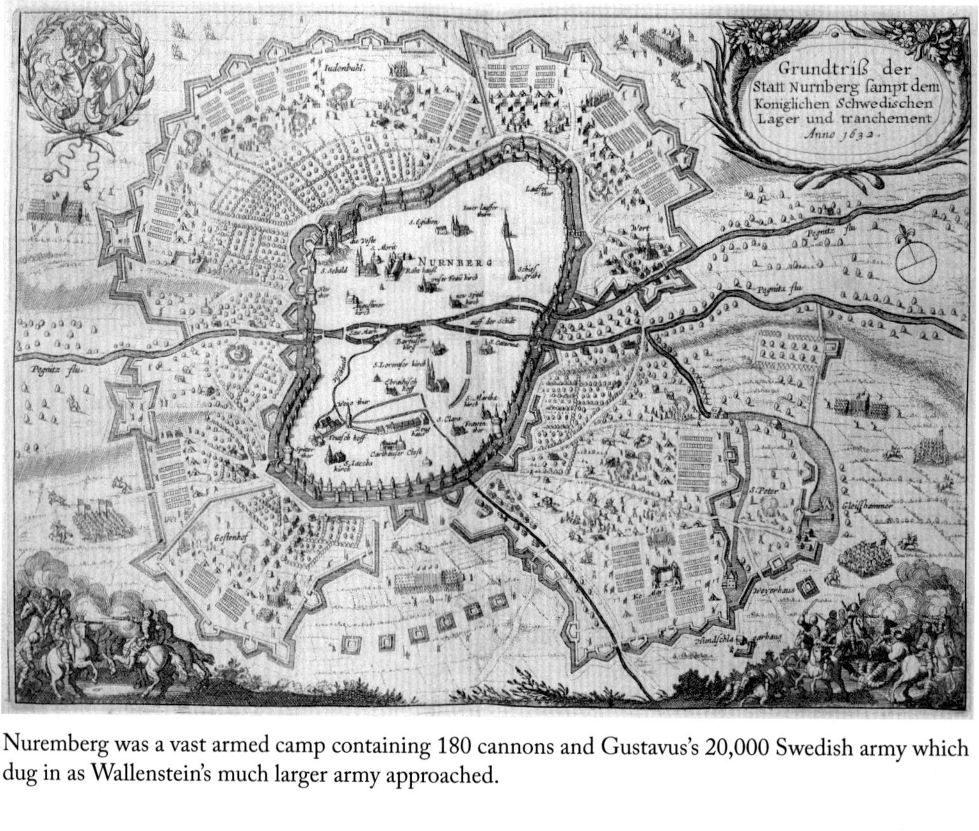

Nuremberg was a vast armed camp containing 180 cannons and Gustavus's 20,000 Swedish army which dug in as Wallenstein's much larger army approached.

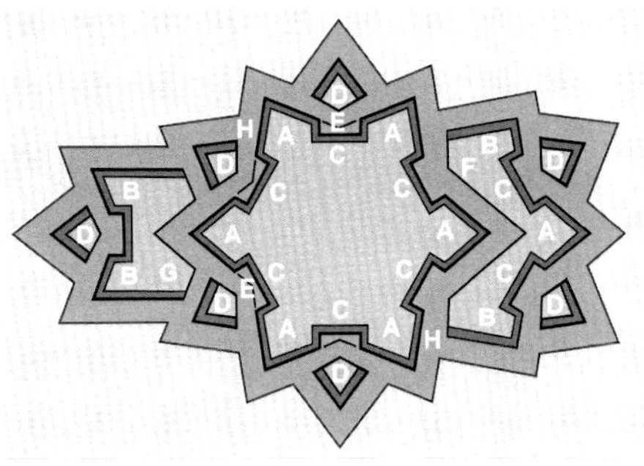

Fort Boutange (Groningen) in the Netherlands is an example of an early modern fortress town with ravelins, bastions, and crownworks. (Modern photograph)

Made in Nuremberg circa 1580 this is a rare example of a matchlock revolver. Unwieldy and expensive to make, the concept did not catch on until advances in percussion cap technology and manufacturing in the 19th century;

Ming troops firing volleys by rank in a print of 1649. They may have learned these techniques from the Portuguese or while intervening against the Japanese invasion support of the Koreans in 1592-98.

The arquebusier is wearing a breastplate and the classic Spanish Marion helmet. Spanish arquebusiers carried an arquebus, breastplate, and two matchlock pistols.

Niccolo Machiavelli 1469-1527 is famous for 'the Prince' but the only book published in his lifetime was '*The Art of War*'; his treatise reflected on Roman practices.

The duc de Rohan. Protestant leader and general who wrote *le Capitaine Parfait* in which he recommends principles of warfare based on Roman practices; published in Geneva 1631. His Valtelline campaign in 1635-6 which optimized the use of interior lines resembled General Jackson's valley campaign in the Shenandoah.

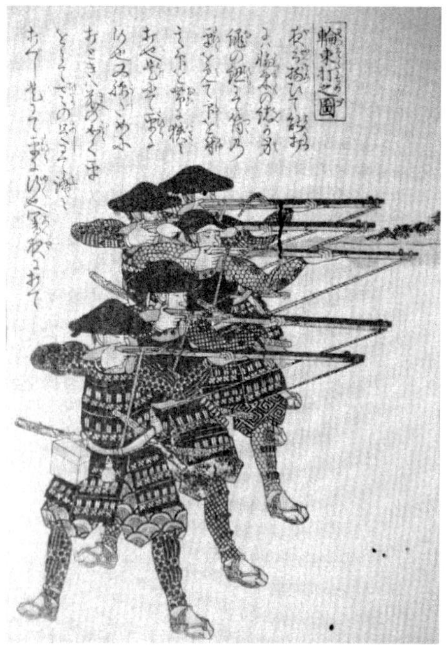

Japanese matchlock musket armed *ashigaru* firing a volley.

Himeji castle, the largest and mostly original castle in Japan. Note the sloping wall. If you have no time to top on your Shinkansen trip to Kyoto, glance right as your speed past.

Gorgio Basta 1550-1607 Imperial commander for Habsburg troops during the Turkish Long War 1593-1606; he wrote three books on military matters; *Il maestro di campo generale...(Venice 1606), and his posthumous work Il governo della cavalleria leggiera* (Venice 1612) Many senior officers of the Thirty Years War served under him, notably Wallenstein, Tilly, and Isolani.

Prince Maurice of Nassau who developed theories of warfare based on Roman military practice. Future great commanders who served under Maurice and took part in the counter-sieges of Breda included Turenne and Gustav Horn. His ideas formed the basis of the military revolution and informed the military ideas of Henri IV, Gustavus Adolphus and other Protestant princes.

Slow-to-load 16th-century cannons were mainly used as siege artillery. Very heavy with long barrels and huge wooden transoms. Lined up in front of an arm they would tend to fire one round and then be left idle for the rest of the battle as the infantry locked horns. The concept of rapid-firing field artillery in battery using brass cannons was introduced by Gustavus.

An ornate gilded closed burgonet with visor as would have been worn by a wealthy nobleman such as the rebel Comte de Soisson. After his victory La Marfee, near Sedan, 9th July 1641 'as was his habit he used the muzzle of his wheel-lock pistol to raise his visor but the pistol accidentally detonated: the bungling Bourbon blew off his own head.'

Johan von Wallhausen was a prolific military writer of training and tactical books and the first director of a military school in the Dutch Republic. He produced 11 texts between 1614-17. He recommended a higher ratio of muskets.

At Werben Monro described how, '*we with spades and shovels wrought ourselves day and night in the ground so that before his) coming (Tilly), we had put ourselves out of danger of his cannon.*'

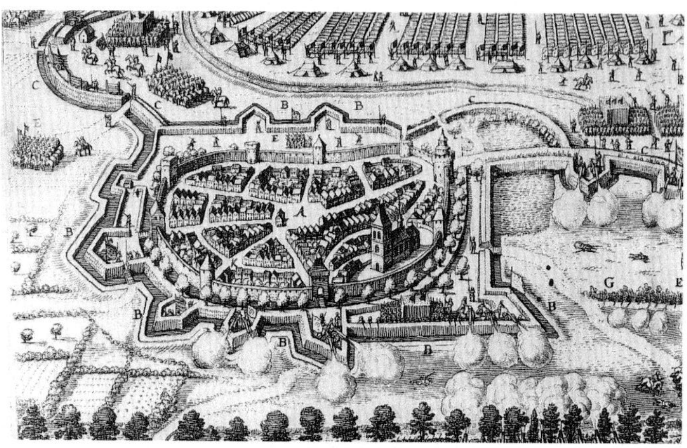

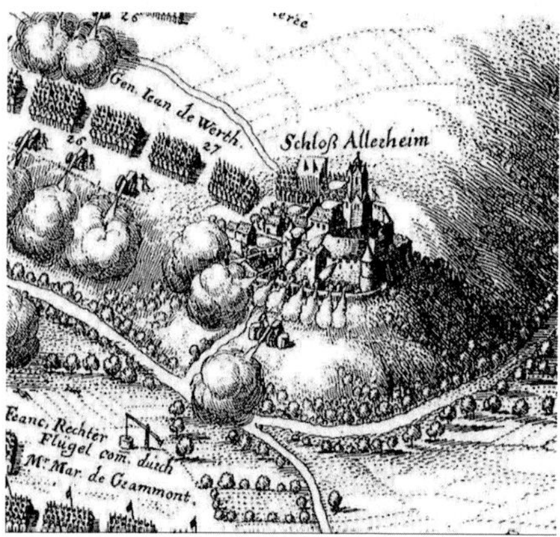

At Allerheim 1645, Conde made a frontal attack against masked cannon and lost 80% of his infantry in a pyrrhic victory. Cardinal Mazarin told Queen Anne, '*Madame there are so many casualties that we can scarce rejoice*'.

Photo taken from the fosse of the great Spanish fortress of Salces on the Mediterranean coast of Roussillon. After a mine was exploded. de Campion, armed with a pike, entered'*with difficulty through the breach, followed by the most resolute of our soldiers. An enemy captain who guarded the breach with many soldiers, rushed at us violently but he was soon killed along with his most determined men*'.

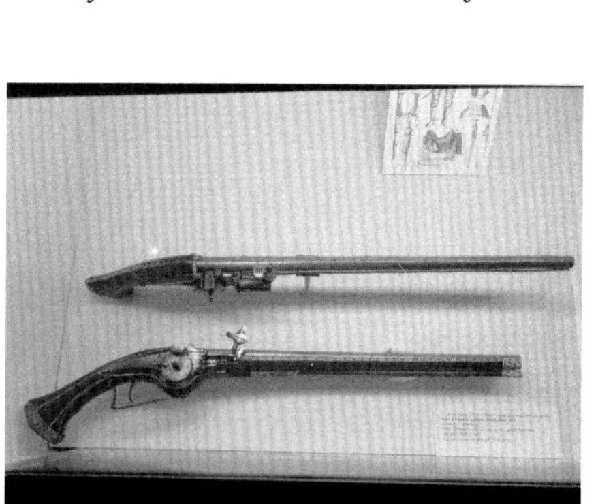

Developments in wheellock pistols from the mid-17th century led to a revolution in tactics. The lance was jettisoned and caracole tactics took over.. It was for the lack of such a thigh guard that poet Sir Philipp Sidney lost his life in a caracole charge at Zutphen in 1586.

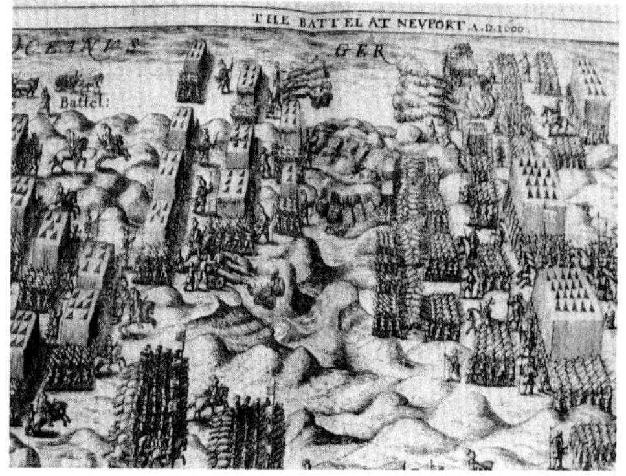

At the Battle of Nieuwpoort 1600 the Prince Mauric's Protestant forces including a large contingent of English were formed up in the small Roman style formations won a spectacular victory over veteran Spanish Tercio,

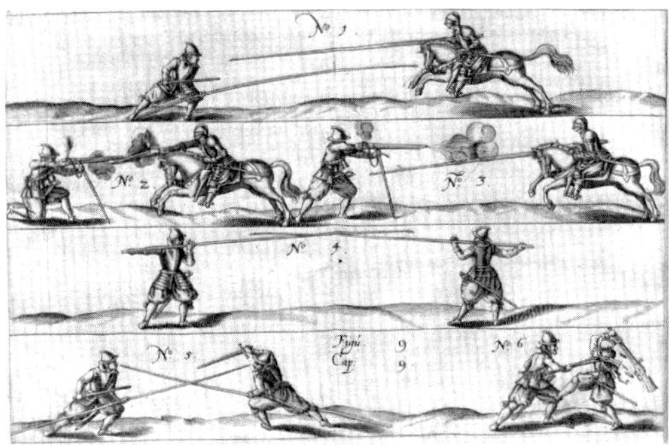

Combat techniques for infantry and cavalry from John von Wallhausen's 'Ritter Kunst'; the art of cavalry warfare. Note how the butt of an arquebus is used to brain the enemy in frenzied infantry combat.

The fortress of Himeji in central Japan was much fought over. It still stands in its original condition; note the sloping wall to help deflect cannon shot.

The Battle of Nagashino 1575 where Nobunaga's *ashigaru* (peasants) musketeers placed behind bamboo defences obliterated the famed Samurai cavalry of the Takeda.

17th century lobster pot type helmet: the face and neck were protected against sword slashes but a pointed sword thrust or pistol shot to the face would likely be fatal or cause serious injury.

Lobster pot type helmet for Harquebusier: the face and neck were protected against sword slashes but a pointed thrust or pistol shot to the face would likely be fatal or cause serious injury.

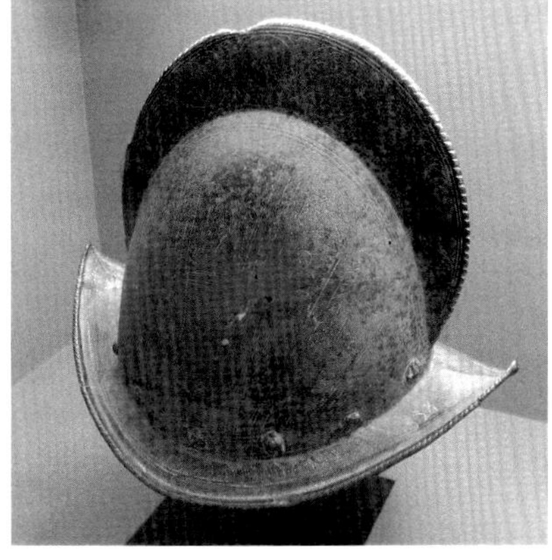

Classic Spanish style Marion helmet which was worn by Spanish soldiers and conquistadors.

Leather guns developed as a cheap a close infantry support weapon for use in Poland 1626-9; after proving to be unreliable they were abandoned in favour of small bronze 3 pounders.

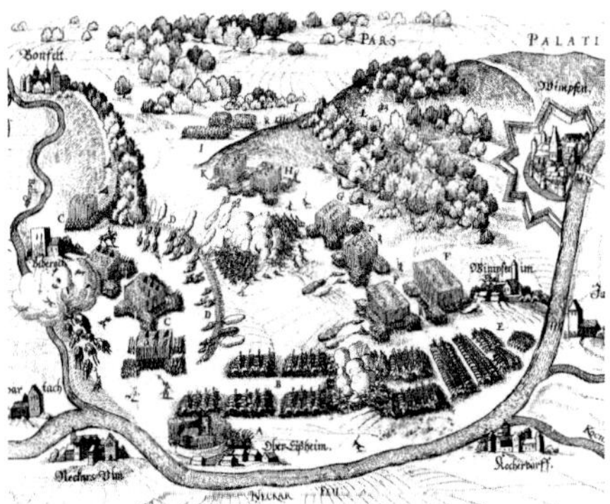

At Wimpfen 1622 the Protestant Margrave of Baden aimed to use firepower from specially designed battle wagons to but Tilly's veteran tercios carried all before them.

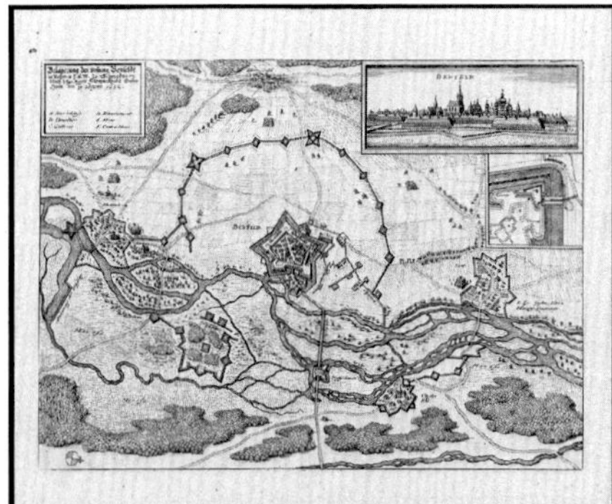

Siege of Benfeld 1632 by Swedish General Gustav Horn. The strong Imperialist fortress was captured after a hard three-month siege. Note the ravelin and bastions, as well as the fortified lines of contravallation around the city.

Sebastian Vranz's canvas of the much-celebrated battle-duel of Lekkerbeetken 5 February 1600. A throwback to the medieval age of chivalry when 22 cavaliers from each side to fought each other to the death.

Polish cavalry; typically flamboyant, with a winged hussar's helmet to go with the twin feathered wings, leopard skin cloaks, and scarlet apparel.

At Sekigahara 1600, the Tokugawa eastern army decisively defeated the Western army; '*Musketfire and the shouts echoed from the heavens and shook the earth, the black smoke rose, making the day as night.*'

Sallies

As they inched forward towards the enemies' outworks and main position, the trenches would become ever more vulnerable to the garrison's 'sallies' or 'sorties', so redoubts called *'corps de garde'* were constructed at regular intervals to provide protection for men and gun batteries. The point about sallies is that defenders enjoyed chances to outnumber and overwhelm the enemy at key points, because the whole besieging army could not be held in exposed forward positions, quite apart from the supply problems that would pose. the purpose of raids or sallies by defenders was to spike the enemy guns and pull down their defences to cause damage and delay to the siege works. Munro describes how at the siege of Donauworth in March 1632, the besieged enemy, 'sallied out bravely, and did beate the Swedes, that guarded the cannon, from their cannon, which they nailed.'[23] Once a spike was 'nailed' into the touch-hole to crack the barrel, the gun was a write off; and it would take time and more casualties to drag up replacements. William Farrier describes the death of a Spaniard after a failed sortie from Kinsale in 1601, 'there was a very lusty Spaniard…who drove a spike into a culverin…he was slain sitting astride the piece.'[24] Besiegers tended to dig forward at least two saps and probably more from different directions to spread the enemy resources and keep them guessing as to where the main storm attack would come from. Where at Lerida 1644–5 there was only one sap thrown forward, because of the exceptional rocky ground, the defenders were put on notice, the defenders could focus their efforts and resources so making the sap hard to defend. Lerida was held despite attacks from two of France's best generals, Harcourt, and Condé.

A rare first-hand account of trench fighting in the early seventeenth-century is the Comte de Bussy-Rabutin's account of a major sally attack at the siege of Mardyke 1646 (a fortress outwork of the Dunkirk defence system);

'On the night of the 12/13 Castelnaut made a lodgment in the enemy defence but with the loss of many Swiss (mercenary soldiers) the following day at eleven o'clock in the morning the enemy made a large sally again the Duc of Enghien's trenches…. I was breakfasting with four comrades when I heard that the enemy had sortied from their entrenchments. I mounted my horse and put on my breastplate, intending to go to fight at the head of the trench…. which the enemy had already occupied and were destroying because it was made of sand, with little resistance from the Swiss…the enemy already occupied the trench. I led my men into the trench and we killed without stopping, coming face to face with the Duc Enghien who was mounting (the works) hardly meeting resistance from the other side…

'…The prince seemed to me to be an incarnation of one of those paintings, when the artist in a triumph of imagination depicts mars in the heat of combat.

His shirt was covered in blood which ran down his arm to his epee hand. I asked him whether he was wounded and he replied., "Not me" he exclaimed "it's the blood of those bastards." He told me that he had re-established the Swiss (mercenaries)at their posts...

'...I went back to my men at the head of the trench and found my cornet who was wounded with two musket shots, he was carried back to the camp. Six troopers were wounded and ten dismounted'[25] When the prince reappeared and calmly said 'come gentlemen follow me' the attack on the enemy was resumed on the contested counterscarp of the fort. 'The sortie had lasted an hour; all the while Condé had ridden exposed alone the trenches amid a hail of musket shot and canon fire.'[26]

De Rochefoucauld who was also in the fight remarks laconically, 'I received three musket shots'[27]

Fights and raids around the trenches were vicious affairs where the raiders would often arm themselves in a manner more suitable for hand-to-hand combat, with wheellock pistols, carbines, halberds, half-pike, axes, swords, clubs, and knives: All less unwieldy than full length pikes or arquebuses requiring a rest, which were weapons suitable for formal battle rather than hand-to-hand combat in confined spaces. Where muskets were employed, after discharge, they would soon be used as club to brain the enemy. Grenades were widely used.

Sorties made by the enemy, often a night or in the early hours were often frenzied affairs, trench warfare in confined spaces. Sometimes a sortie could be just a small raid on a trench, but the sorties referred to at Turin, Mardyck, and Kinsale involved hundreds or thousands in what became in effect small battles.

Life in the siege lines

The experience of siege for the attackers in their trenches and open-air encampments could be even more moral sapping than for the defender, with boredom, filth, disease, and death by sniper fire to cope with. It was often miserable and boring work involving much digging, although the professional soldier Monro noted that 'my souldiers once getting into the ground, we fortified ourselves against their cannon...the spade and shovel are ever good companions in safety'[28]

As usual the poor provision of food was high on the list of a soldier's grievances. Scottish mercenary James Turner complained, 'the whole time of the siege, my best entertainment was bread and water, abundance of the last but not of the first; but this proceeded from want of money 'we for the laager was plentiful enough.'[29] Towards the end of the failed siege of Bergen-op-zoom in 1622 an Italian deserter came over from his trenches to the town and when asked where he came from: He replied *"D'infierno" (Hell!).*[30] In a scene reminiscent of the First World War, foot soldier Fritsch describes how after a failed assault at Paderborn he was wounded and saved by an officer who, 'took hold of me by one foot and dragged me as fast as he could under continuous heavy fire from the enemy. He ran with me to the approach trench and threw me in.'[31] On another occasion at Gottingen 1641 he had to take charge of repulsing an attack on his redoubt.

Snipers

Sniping as a constant feature of siege and trench warfare just as it was in the First World War across 600 miles of the western front. Famously depicted in stories and films about the siege of Stalingrad, sniping has always come into its own in any static phase of war. Crossbows were used in mediaeval times and then muskets. Snipers will aim at any target but if possible, they normally shoot by hierarchy of value which meant that generals, senior officers, or engineers are especially prized; the higher the rank the greater the prize. In the next century Charles XII of Sweden would be cut down in the trenches

Richard the Lion heart was fatally wounded by a crossbow bolt during a minor siege in 1199; in 1573 Takeda Shingen was reputedly killed by a sniper during a siege; at least that is the chosen story portrayed in the film *Kagemusha* by Akira Kurosawa.

The siege of Magdeburg lasted a long time. Starting at the end of 1630, the city was sealed off. Then the net tightened as the spring campaign season got underway in 1631. The Imperialists started to draw in the net by attacking the outer works. It was a costly process foreshadowing the modern period trench warfare at Ypres and the Somme, as Imperialist soldier Hagendorf witnesses recalled, 'We set ourselves up in the local villages and blockaded the city of Magdeburg for the entire winter, staying encamped in the villages until the spring of 1631. There we captured several entrenchments in the forest in the front of Magdeburg. There our captain, along with many others was shot dead in front of an entrenchment. One day we captured seven of their entrenchments. Then we moved in close and built up the whole area with our own entrenchments and saps, but it cost us a lot of men. The 22nd of March Johann Gaslgart was brought in as our captain: the 28th of April he too was shot dead in the saps'[32]

One of the typical soldier's tasks was also the digging of trenches and redoubts, mostly at night; Germany soldier Fritsch recounts: 'so I completed my redoubt before daybreak'[33] In daylight, the hail of sniper shots would have made the job suicidal. Fear of snipers was just another part of the misery of trench life, along with a lack of good hot food. Specialist sniping with long, rifled matchlock weapons, forerunner of the American long rifle, increased throughout the war.

Munro describes how he was wounded by a sniper and saved by his armour on the siege lines at the Altenburg outside Nuremburg, 'being taken notice of, as a chiefe officer, the enemy commanded out a single man with a long peece, who from a tree aiming at me, shot me right above the haunch-bone, on the left side, which lighted fortunately for me on the iron clicket of my hanger [metal fastener for armour between back and front armour]...taking the force of the Bullet, which being battered flat with the iron entered not above two inches in my side.'[34] The Thirty Years War accelerated sniping and the deliberate policy of targeting officers, something that would become contentious in future times' (for example in the American War of Independence) As we have noted engineers were also high value targets. Monro's old comrade Sir John Hepburn was killed by a sniper shot before the walls of Saverne (Lorraine) in 1636. Ordinary soldiers could also be targets. Monro recounted how; 'One valorous young gentleman' during a pause in the fighting at Alte Veste 'out of resolution to shew more courage than was needful in open view of the enemy flourishing his sword and crying aloud Vive Gustavus, he was shot through the head...'[35]

De Bussy-Rabutin describes the regularity of the toll taken by snipers; from excess of pride. Senior officers self-selected as targets by their gorgeous military attire similarly British officers in the Great War self-selected by being taller as a result of their superior diets and for walking into battle sporting a cane. To take cover or show too much fear or to take precautions would involve a loss of honour. A particularly French obsession, honour, had a cost. At the siege of Lerida in 1647 De Bussy-Rabutin hosted a dinner party in a forward area for chevalier de La Valliere who had been away from France for two and a half years and was due to return on leave. The mood was festive. Also at the table was the Marquis de la Trousse his replacement, who persuaded La Valliere to go 'for a moment' to inspect the forward trenches so as to acquaint him with his duties. The inexperienced Marquis de La Trousse, 'with affectation as to his courage exposed himself unnecessarily by walking for inspection on the reverse side of the trench so exposing himself to unnecessary danger. The chevalier [Valière] not wanting to do anything less than the Marquis suffered a shot to the head from a musket and died instantly'[36] It was a sad story of excess pride. Hardened to the serendipity of war the dinner party continued as if nothing had happened. Another of the party immediately left to approach the Prince Condé to secure La Valliere's governorship post. He got it.

De Bussy-Rabutin recounts other 'sniper' stories of sieges at Mardyck, '1 October, the camp marshal, Laval, was wounded in the head by a musket shot and died shortly afterwards...

7 October in the morning, the chevalier de Chabot, marshal of the camp was also shot in the head at the entry to the bridge; he died of his wound a few days later. These deaths shocked everyone...'[37]

For obvious reasons engineers with their drawings, notebooks and maps fluttering in the wind would become a target of preference; their profession advertised itself. They need to be in the front trenches and saps to make their observations, inspections, directions, and plans. At the siege of Ostend 1601–1603, Spanish snipers killed twelve engineers.

Special large calibre 'long guns' were developed especially for use in sieges. In Hungary and Transylvania, a hereditary caste of retainers called 'Gunmen' developed; they would deploy 'long guns' in defence of fortresses against the besiegers who did their best to hide behind entrenchments. This was not always easy to do especially as defenders normally had height advantage. In the siege of Malacca in 1606 Admiral Cornelis Matelief de Jonge describes how the Portuguese defenders firing from the heights on which the monastery of Sao Paulo was located… 'wounded many men every day with their harquebuses and long guns.'[38]

Life for the besieged

Life for the besieged was not pleasant either: Threatened with starvation, and with the constant anxiety of enemy attack, stress levels were high. If the place were to be stormed no quarter would be given to the garrison and under the rules of war the populace would have to face three days of uninterrupted looting and rapine. Male civilians would most likely be taken for soldiers and so cut down, while women could expect to be raped unless they quickly chose the lesser evil of finding a *'protector'* in short order. Fear of all of this would surely have driven besieged citizens to church prayer, but even this might be a mixed blessing. During the siege of York 1644, Thomas Mace, a clerk of Trinity College Cambridge, observed wryly, 'by shooting against and battering the church, in so much that sometimes a cannon bullet has come in at the windows, and bounc'd about pillar to pillar, (and even like some furious fiend or evil spirit) backwards and forwards, and all manner of side-ways, as it has happened to meet with square or round opposition amongst the pillars, in its returns and rebounds until all its force has been quite spent…;[39] the church as a life threatening pinball machine. You would have to be unlucky to receive a direct cannon ball hit, but it did happen; news of such a dreadful, dismembering event would spread around the town and increase the general terror still further.

At Kinsale the besieged Spanish soldiers and the Irish citizens, under a hail of English plunging cannonballs from a nearby hill, were 'enforced to stand in their cellars, for they can't go well in the streets.'[40] More likely was death from collapsing masonry. But the big killer was disease and plague induced death on a population expanded by an influx of refugees, consequent hygiene problems and weakness caused by a dearth of nutrition. Long sieges wreaked terrible havoc on civilians as at La Rochelle, Mantua, and Malacca, where civilian population deaths from disease and hunger of over seventy per cent were recorded. At the first siege of Malacca by Dutch Admiral Cornelis Matelief de Jonge in 1606, the besieged suffered terribly, losing 5,000 out of 12,000 civilians. Commentator Aquino Torre de Tombo noted that the Portuguese commander, Andre Furtado, 'braved this siege with a hundred and eight men: more than five thousand died of plague and starvation because they even reached the stage of eating dogs and rats. Andre Fortado made some sorties…'[41] Borschberg, Admiral Matelief de Jonge…all long sieges had a similar impact; shortage of nutrition made the people weak. In overcrowded and insanitary conditions, often made worse by an influx of refugees, the grim reaper's bacilli made merry on the fragile and skeletal bodies of the populace.

'We were so terribly fired on with bombs that we hardly noticed the shooting of heavy cannon; so many died…'[42] recounted a Catholic citizen of 's-Hertogenbosch in 1629 after Prince Frederick Henry's surprise siege on the fortress which was widely believed to be impregnable. In the first ten days of June 1,000 cannon balls and 'bombs' from mortars were fired at the city. Sallies did some damage, but morale crumbled as the trenches of the enemy zig zagged nearer the citizens started to beg the commander to surrender of the garrison. Nor was there hope of relief. The fear was that the storm would see them massacred, raped, and looted of every chattel; it was a common story, although the garrison commander had to be wary of surrendering to soon lest he was executed for cowardice.

Sometimes the besiegers were crafty in the aim of their canon, looking to target for assassination the commander of the place; at the siege of Marburg 1684 the Hessian gunners nearly succeeded in killing turncoat general Melander as he dined; training their cannon on his rooms, the gunners fired in sync; the table was smashed and many severely wounded as a rain of balls crashed into his lodging's dining room. At Kinsale in 1601 Patrick Strange recounted how 'in the night Don Juan expected no such matter the cannon lighted up the house where…his council were in consultation…'[43] On another occasion in the low country a fellow diner of the Duke of Palma was decapitated at the luncheon table, with a piece of his skull taking out the eye of another; after a quick wipe down of the blood and gore spattered table, the meal resumed.

During a siege the citizenry would often be engaged in civic duties and all things necessary to defend the town or city and survive. At La Rochelle women were used to dig defences. Men were inducted into the militia and trained. An account of siege preparations is given by a Nun before the siege of Villingen in Swabia in 1633 as they awaited the attack of the Duke of Württemberg's Protestant forces… 'Colonel Escher organised everything, appointing watches and instituting good military order. …he had big gabions woven (gabion is a wicker basket filled with sand or earth), assembled, and arranged… in various places. …had fortifications and batteries set up at intervals in the city, with canon and guns emplaced on them. He had a powder mill built in the city and gathered large supplies of powder, lead, iron, stones, and lead bullets… he had the gates bastioned, leaving only the upper and lower gates open, and had the bridges raised elsewhere, as well as letting water into the moat…He turned citizens young and old into dragoons, organising them into troops… Everyone knew what was required of him day and night.'[44] The siege started at the end of November 1633 and was reactivated on the 11 January 1634. After two days of bombardment a breach was made on the 13 January; the Nun's journal stops abruptly after she is called away to make confession in preparation for what was to come. Religious enemies were obvious targets for enraged Protestant soldiers after a storm. Rape and pillage would be their entitlement.

For civilians there was the constant fear of the assault and what would happen to them. Women were particularly fearful because the attacking soldiery would not only be uncontrollable but had rights under customary law to sack the city and rape the women.

Storm

Instead of a siege of attrition, a general assault or probing assaults might be attempted early on to snatch a quick victory, so saving the costs and dangers of a long siege to morale and health of the besiegers. Gustavus did this successfully at Riga 1621 and Frankfurt an der Oder 1631. Both were old-fashioned fortresses with curtain walls but in 1632 at Ingolstadt, which had the benefit of purpose made modern defence, he failed at a cost of 1,000 men. On other occasions the general assault was a last resort, or it followed from the establishment of a breach when the enemy had declined the opportunity to surrender. For the common soldier an assault against a fortified city was the most dreadful ordeal because they must run unprotected into the mouth of the enemy's masked guns and muskets, which could only be reached by clambering over spiked abatis and through ditches.

At 7 a.m. on 19 May 1631 Imperialist General Tilly ordered the storm of Magdeburg 1631, large rich city, and ally of Gustavus. It was an old-fashioned fortification with curtain walls. Equipped with scaling ladders the storm was made by the whole Imperial army; other attackers made waterborne assaults. It was a risky plan, but the soldiery was provided with 'Dutch courage'. 'Before the attack the general [Tilly] had all soldiers and officers provided with fine Renish wine to give them courage' [Ackerman] 'There was such a thunder and crack of muskets,' recorded Ackerman 'incendiary mortars and great cannon that no one could either see or hear and many supporting troops followed us, so that the whole rampart was filled, covered and black with soldiers and storm ladders. Eventually after several hundred men had fallen, we broke in over the defence, putting the remainder to flight to the precinct gate and into Lackermacher Street. In assaults of this kind our soldiers brought some four hundred storm ladders over the earthworks and up to the walls.'[45]

At modern fortresses they would have to enter killing zones of crossfire from bastion mounted cannon loaded with grapeshot. Charmier described what happened at Montauban in 1621 when the French army tried to storm the capital of the Huguenots, 'the ditches and the counterscarp were soon filled with multitudes of dead bodies…when their captains pressed on their companies to the assault and encouraged them by example, crying "come follow us!" the poor fellows were overheard to answer, "where the devil will you lead us?" What else can we meet with in these entrenchments but present death.'[46] The attack failed, and the siege was abandoned a few weeks later.

At the formidable fortress of Salces in Spanish Roussillon 1637, two squads of twenty-five men led by lieutenants were to be the assault troops to rush the breach after the explosion. Elite troops were chosen from the Normandie regiment; Henri de Campion would lead one of them. Following the enormous explosion, the assault group led by Major Troisville wearing a breastplate and with an epee in his right hand, led the way. Following on behind was de Campion armed with a pike, 'following with difficulty through the breach, followed by the most resolute of our soldiers. An enemy captain who guarded the breach with may soldiers, rushed at us violently but he was soon killed along with his most determined men, the rest ran back across the courtyard. We pushed on vigorously but as we crossed the courtyard, a volley of musket fire rang out from the central keep, one shot of which passed under de Troisville's right arm behind the breastplate and killed him'[47]. In the sheltered lee of the citadel the advance party was cut off from the main body of French. Someone needed to report back; Campion volunteered. He was wounded slightly in the leg as he ran the gauntlet back to his commanding officer who he discovered in a burnt and blacked state after an explosion of gunpowder; hardly had he reported than a white flag broke out over the citadel.

Batteries would be moved forward to a point where a breach could easily be established or tunnels dug to place mines under the walls; the 'place' would be summoned to surrender under the normal terms of war, i.e. to march out with drums beating and to march away free. The alternative was to face a storm and risk the sack of the town and the butchering of the garrison. Storming of a town or city was a hit or miss affair, success depended on both luck and the élan of the troops. The main attack would aim for the breaches but scaling ladders were also used for attacks on old-fashioned city walls and this was the method chosen at Bristol and at Magdeburg. German Imperialist soldier Fritsch describes his part in the storming of Neckargemünd in the Palatine in 1621 'where Captain Kogler fell down on top of me from a ladder during the assault and lay dead.' And at Rheinfelden in 1633 'where I was first up the ladder with fifty men'[48] It helped if the ladders were long enough which was a problem for the English when Buckingham sought to storm Fort St Martin on the Île de Ré.

The raison d'être for the massacre of a garrison following a storm was the fact that heavy casualties had to be taken in any storming action, therefore giving the storm troops the moral right to seek revenge and recompense, in lives and booty. Right of sack under *customary* war law obviously reduced casualties by encouraging most towns and cities to surrender. These concepts of *Jus in bello* did not change during the war and were even supported by humanistic Catholic theologian Francisco Victoria who noted that sacking of cities and the killing of the garrison was 'necessary for the conduct of war...as a spur to the courage (morale) of the troops.'[49] At Magdeburg there were 2,000 casualties in the storm attack, so the subsequent anger of the troops was understandable. The fact that civilians would be caught up in the mayhem simply reflects the reality that the decision to resist would often reflect the democratic intent of the inhabitants. Magdeburg's rebel population was known to be both recalcitrant and fiercely Protestant. Once the blood lust adrenalin and fury of the troop was up, and sustained by captured wine cellars, the storm would turn into a carnival of death, rape; and pillage for three days. There was little any surviving officer could do to order restraint even if they wanted, which they did not because they wanted their share. Following behind the attacker's camp followers would pick over the upturned city.

It was a matter of fine judgement when to surrender: 'It was a tricky decision for a commander. If he was later held to have surrendered too early he could be court-martialled and even executed for cowardice or treason. If he left it too late and the town was successfully stormed the opportunity to negotiate terms would be lost, the garrison forfeited its right to quarter and could be put to the sword and the town would usually be plundered and possibly sacked.'[50] garrison commanders were regularly executed for cowardice, incompetence, or surrendering too soon. For example, Colonel Miniati was executed on Duke Leopold's orders in 1642 after surrendering the powerful Moravian fortress of Olomouc too soon, and John George executed the commander of Leipzig's garrison in 1632.

Although a storm of a city would be a way of offering a monetary bounty in the form of loot to soldiers grown weary of pay arrears, the example of Magdeburg shows that it was sometimes a costly military option and not just for the losses incurred in the initial attack. Re-establishing discipline and order was a major problem and there was the danger of plague or cholera outbreaks from unburied carcasses. Soldiers with plenty of booty might retire by desertion; many became drunk. Munro describes how an army was gathered up in preparation for the next march after Gustavus's storm of Frankfurt an der Oder in 1631,'The next day his majesty appointed General Major Leslie as governor over the town, giving him orders to repair the ruinous works and walls, as also orders were given for burying of the dead, which were not buried fully in six days; in the end they were cast by heaps in great ditches, above a hundred in every grave. The next day we were ordained to assemble our regiments, and to bring them together in arms, that they might be provided of what they wanted of arms, having lost many in their disorder.'[51]

The main reason for a determined defence was hope of relief while sitting tight behind strong fortifications. The length of the defence was normally a matrix between these factors, defence strength and likelihood of relief, as well as the importance of the place: After all few garrison commanders really want to be heroic in the defence of an irrelevant place. Most sieges then were short affairs, unless the fortress was particularly well fortified or in a strong geographic position. Unlike the borderlands of the Dutch Republic there were few modern fortresses in Germany. Sieges in the empire were a different experience to those on the Franco–Flanders or Franco–Spanish borders, where specially constructed, well garrisoned fortresses of modern design required the full panoply of siege warfare and might take a field army the whole fighting season to capture just one place. Ingolstadt was the only modern fortress in German; it was never seriously besieged. But even modern fortresses needed determined defenders; Denmark's new fortress of Christianspries (Kiel) surrendered to the Swedes without a fight. At Kinsale in 1601, the Spanish expected to be relieved by a general Irish uprising led by O'Neal, but the rising failed so that town surrendered soon after having held out for a hundred days. A besieging army would often choose heavy casualties in a quick storm following a concentrated artillery bombardment on a particular weak point, rather than risk greater losses through plague in an attritional siege. For example, 2,000 men lost in the storm of Magdeburg in 1631 was a relatively small price to pay for taking such a city compared to the 7,000 plus that were lost to disease by Spinola at Bergen-op-Zoom 1622. Rupert's army, ordered to go to the King's aid before London, needed to storm Bristol quickly in 1643. Storms seemed to be the preferred option in Germany, but on the Flanders or Artois fronts the fortresses were designed too well, making an assault infeasible, so a siege was often long and might take up most of the French or Dutch army's campaign season, either in besieging a fortress or trying to relieve it. If there was no chance of relief the defenders could still hope that logistical attrition, winter, or plague would induce the besieger to retreat.

Prince Rupert chose to storm Bristol in 1643 but lost 500 elite Cornish infantry and their three esteemed commanders. Likewise, in attacking the city in 1645 the Parliamentarians chose to storm the defence where the royalists held them at bay 'two hours at push of pike, standing upon the palisades,'[52] before being overwhelmed. Gustavus preferred to pay the premium of heavy casualties rather than waste time; at the strategically located Frankfurt an der Oder, on the main invasion route to Silesia and Moravia, he lost 800 men. However, he lost over 1000 men in a limited storm attack on one outwork at Ingolstadt. It compares well to the failed three-month Swedish siege of Brno in 1645, which cost 10,000 men. However, some fortresses such as Brno were so well protected that a storm had no chance of success, so a long siege was the only option. Key fortress cities experienced the fiercest sieges.

However, the norm was less exciting. Monotony *was* the norm in regular siege warfare with its formulaic procedure for investment, siege works, digging parallels, and breech by canon or by mines, followed by summons to surrender, then agreed terms with honours of war. Often, towns or cities did not even bother with these formalities. If a campaign had started off with the sack of a city or if there was no hope of relief then towns and cities quickly came to terms: thus, Tilly and Wallenstein made a triumphal and fast progress through the empire after the Battle of the White Mountain because their enemies had been cowed into submission. The Protestant armies under Mansfeld, the Margrave of Baden, and Christian Halberstadt were simply too weak to offer any possibility of relief, similarly Saxe-Weimar's army before Regensburg in 1634. Demoralisation was the key factor. An exception was Heidelburg where patriotic and religious zeal bolstered by enthusiastic English troops led to a robust defence.

Similarly. after first Breitenfeld Gustavus had been able to move across Germany picking up important cities with little effort except for the Marienburg fortress perched on a steep cliff above the city of Wurzburg. The important cities of Erfurt (key to Thuringia) and Wurzburg (key to Franconia) had both surrendered without a serious fight, as did the city of Mainz. This willingness to surrender had been encouraged by the storm and sack of the fortress of Marienburg followed by the storming of the Spanish fortress of Oppenheim upriver from Mainz, where garrisons were massacred. Tilly's beaten field army was too distant to help. Also, in the north some remaining Imperialist holdouts like Kolberg in Pomerania surrendered when it became obvious that relief by Tilly was out of the question. Likewise, after the Imperialist victory at Nördlingen 1634, the town of Nördlingen immediately surrendered. Victory allowed the emperor's forces to quickly retake many cities, rolling back the Swedish conquest of Germany. After second Breitenefeld Torstensson invaded Silesia. At the start of this invasion there was a bitterly fought siege of Torgau, a key city *en route* to the frontier. The place was sacked, and the garrison butchered, following which the Swedish army was quickly able to round up other towns and cities in Silesia, whose citizens were in any case Protestant sympathisers. Gustavus stormed the fortress of Marienburg at Wurzburg and massacred the garrison '*pour encourager les autres*; this too had a salutary effect on other town and cities called upon to surrender. Other famous scenes of early modern butchery after a storm included Haarlem 1572, and Drodhega. There were many others.

At Tienen a Franco-Dutch army besieged the city in 1635, but due to a misunderstanding the French troops had not had news of the surrender before they stormed it. Rampant French troops brushed aside the Dutch guards posted at the doors, much like latter day ineffectual Dutch UN blue-helmets at Srebrenica in 1995; they entered the church, '.... forced past the sentries shot dead the soldiers among them, took out of church and carried off those who were found therein.'[53] (Frederick Henry to SG Heylissen 10 June 1635) The description of what happened is abbreviated and leaves open the question of what happened to the unfortunate females. No doubt some of the women and young girls were carried off to be brutally gang raped and murdered. One shocked officer wrote afterwards 'I cannot tell you how horrified I was to see one of the poor nuns running about in panic with a knife buried in her head. She cried out between the tears 'messieurs save my life, I beg you!'[54]

After the storm – sacking, raping, looting

The sacking of city was a grotesque carnival of horror. Magdeburg's sack is often taken as the worst example; after the storm, the streets soon resembled a charnel house. Making his way out with his family, led by a soldier paid for the service, Friedrich Friese saw 'a maid also in the street who had been carrying meat in a basket; she had been shot and a dog stood nearby eating the meat… we saw many bodies in the streets, including women lying quite uncovered. They lay with their heads in a great barrel of beer, which stood full of water in the alley, into which they had been pushed and drowned, but half their bodies and their legs were hanging out…' And '… The fire meanwhile got out of control mirroring the soldierly debauchery, gold lust, and revelry.'[55] Tilly had completely lost control of his soldiers. This Armageddon was as much a catastrophe for him as much as for the Protestants. Only the cathedral and the Catholic monastery, crowded with terrified citizens, were spared. '…General Tilly was concerned for the beautiful cathedral and detached 500 infantry to fight the fire and was there himself; he saved not only the cathedral but also the beautiful monastery and all the houses on Cathedral Square.'[56] (Ackerman)

In truth, the sack of towns and cities was not an unusual occurrence during the Thirty Years War. Henri Campion witnesses the horrific aftermath of stormed towns. The French army captured the Chateaux de Curlaon, then attacked an attractive little town called Lous-le-Saunier where a breach was established after only eight hours. The town was stormed, and the soldiers set fire to it; 'the soldiers behaved as badly as can be imagined…' Remembered Campion, 'on all side there were scenes of licentiousness. Most of the women were raped violently and belongings thrown into the flames, or pillaged. All this filled me with a pity that I am not able to express but it was impossible to prevent'[57]. The same horrors were meted out to the small town of Orgolet. 'I have never seen such terrible things as were suffered by their [Franche-Comté] poor country which was entirely ruined.'[58] Soldiers had to be ruthless, but they were not without pity. Bernhard of Saxe-Weimar much to his bitter chagrin failed to keep a strong hand on his troops who ran amok, sacking and firing Pontarlier: he lamented 'I can no longe abide such Godlessness with a clear conscience.' Tilly likewise wept after the storming of Magdeburg having heard of the rape and murder of a child by six soldiers.

Monro describes the pitiful detritus of war, human and material, after the storm and sack of Donauworth 1632 'rifled wagons, dismounted cannon, broken drums and arms, and terrified citizens wandering wildly among dead and dying soldiers'

For the unlucky attackers at Magdeburg like the wounded Hagendorf, denied his share of the booty by injury, he at least had the solace of his loyal camp following wife; 'my wife went into the city, even though it was completely on fire, since she wished to fetch a cushion and cloth for me to lie on and for the dressings. I also had our sick child lying with me. But then there came a great outcry in the camp that the houses of the city were all collapsing on top of each other so that many soldiers and their wives who had wanted to loot were trapped…Yet God protected her…My wife also brought me a large tankard and four measures of wine and had in addition, also found two silver belts and clothes, which in later redeemed for twelve thalers at Halberstadt (Amid the carnage there was kindness). That evening my companions came by each honouring me by giving me something a thaler or half a thaler.'[59] He was taken to lodgings in Halberstadt and surrounding villages with three hundred wounded from his regiment alone, all of whom recovered. Hagendorf's evidence is testament to relatively efficient care for the wounded as well as very high casualties in the storm, because three hundred men might represent some ten to twenty per cent of men in the tercio depending on its size and battle strength. It is also evidence of a soldier's mutual insurance system in the case of wounding.

After the storm of Magdeburg, gradually the fighting and the initial blood lust gave way to darkness and sleep, but the city burnt. Friedrich Freise remembered the tragic firestorm 'This night at eleven o'clock, the entire city of Magdeburg was ablaze…In the camp which was some distance from the city, it was so bright that you could have read a letter by the great glow of the fire.'[60] Even in the seventeenth-century age of firepower, sometimes storms of fortresses involved mediaeval methods. Gustavus's 1615 siege of Pskov revolved around attacks on the Varlaamskaya Bastion situated on the apex of the wall system along the riverside, which was captured and lost on the 17 September after a furious bombardment. Gustavus led an attack in person on 9 October. An all-day struggle, the defenders, apart from using muskets, resorted to mediaeval methods using stones, logs as well as boiling tar and oil; the bastion was captured again but retaken. After a prolonged siege from 9 August–27 October and three costly assaults, the last of which saw hundreds of his troops occupy a key bastion only to be blown high sky by a mine sprung by the defenders inside their own Varlaamskaya Bastion, the Swedes withdrew.

At Aschaffenburg 1631, General Torstensson was concussed by a stone dropped on him as he scaled a ladder.

Sieges and *salvaguardia*

Cities that surrendered on terms were usually tapped for money in return for *salvaguardia* (a sort of guarantee of safety, i.e. a military protection racket) It was a variant of the 'contribution' system. This system also had one other effect and explains why military discipline was often harshly enforced. If the soldiery was allowed to rob and rape with impunity then the value of the *salvaguardia or* 'contribution' would be reduced by the notoriety of the army. It was one good reason why discipline was enforced. Cities would more readily surrender and pay up and keep on paying if they were getting value for money. The cities were tapped for sums ranging from 30,000 to 300,000 Reichsthaler. Again we must question the idea of a total and permanent gothic holocaust in the Thirty Years War because commanders had a strong incentive to impose discipline.

The matrix of factors which determined the outcome of an early modern siege

There was a complex matrix of factors, which determined the outcome of a siege.

1. Was the fortress modern or did it have curtain walls – if curtain wall were there extensive earthwork and sconces, ravelin, covered way etc.?
2. Was there the possibility of a relief for raising the siege?
3. How quickly would any relief force arrive? Major field victories had a major impact on sieges, often leading to a *'falling domino'* effect as cities gave up hope amidst collapsing morale, as after Breitenfeld and Nördlingen.
4. How big was the garrison? Was it proportionate and large enough to the defended area? And large enough to make sorties too disrupt the siege?
5. Was there natural topographical strength in the fortresses?
6. Was the fortress capable of repulsing a storming action and how modern and in what condition were the defensive works? Were there *'trace Italienne'* or modern geometric hornworks and sconces? Storming actions rarely took place on the modern, newly designed fortresses of Flanders: These places required carefully crafted formal sieges.

7. Did the besieged place lie on the coast? Who controlled the sea? Could the place be supplied and reinforced by sea, or conversely could naval resupply be cut off by a blockade? Though blockaded by deep draft Dutch warships, Malacca would be supplied for a while by fast shallow draft vessels, until the siege drew tighter.
8. How much food was there for the troops and population in the besieged place? Sometimes, cities would be made more vulnerable to siege because refugees would pour in from the surrounding area overwhelming the city's ability to provide food and water: such tactics had been used by the besiegers since antiquity, 'Alexander the Great, anxious to conquer Leucadia…turned all the inhabitants [from the area] into Leucadia; at last, the town was so full of people that he immediately reduced it by famine.'[61] Defending garrisons might expel hostile citizenry in anticipation of siege as a matter of policy, as did the Swedes at Olomouc. At La Rochelle and Malacca citizens were not allowed out by the besiegers: standard policy under customary war law. The statistics for the death of civilians due to disease and malnourishment could be appalling.
9. What was the ratio of besieging troops to the length of the lines of circumvallation? At Breisach Saxe-Weimar's lines had to cover 20 kilometres of besieging hornworks.
10. Did the besiegers or besieged have enough trained engineers, miners, and gunners? Expert Jesuit gunners were crucial to the successful defence of Macau 1621 and Dôle 1636. Shortage of expertise and siege experience was a problem for the French in the early stages and the English in their siege efforts, for example at La Rochelle.
11. What was the morale of the garrison and the population-how prepared were the population to hold out and join in the fighting and digging? Having heard of the recent slaughter of the garrison at Glogau by Torstensson's Swedish army, at Oppeln and Trrachtenberg in Silesia 1642 the garrison troops mutinied to force the hand of the commander.[62]
12. What extent of privation would the population accept? If the population were in favour of negotiating surrender, how far could the defence continue in the face of civilian hostility? But morale was also a factor in defence. Condé in a letter to Mazarin noted the effect that a mobilised local population would have on the effectiveness of defence, 'the enemy fortresses are defended by the townspeople as well as the garrisons, whereas in our fortresses the citizens are our mortal enemies.'[63]
13. What was the reputation and power of the besieging force? Had they been brutal in previous sieges?
14. How important was the place under siege? Did it warrant a fight to the death? an energetic determined commander such as Colonel Escher could

in 1633 galvanise the defence and determination of the citizens as at the small town of Villingen, which was far from the main areas of fighting and lacked any strategic importance. Torras, the commander at St Matin would late take over the defence of Brno. A great talent as a soldier in defence he inspired the citizens.

How capable and determined was the town's commander?

15. The commander had to weigh up the risk of surrendering too easily against the risk of a sack. This was not just about having care for the lives of the citizens and their property but also for his own life. It was a matter of fine judgement. Surrender too soon or too easily and he may well be executed for cowardice: surrender too late and he would be cut down in the sack. Execution was the fate of the Saxon commander who surrendered Leipzig too softly in 1633. At Olomouc the commander, Mianati, entered surrender negotiation very quickly; his troops marched out on terms, but he was arrested and executed. Likewise at Havanna when Admiral Juan de Benavides surrendered the Spanish treasure fleet to Piet Hein 1628 without a fight, he suffered a tradition death; three fast cuts of the throat.
16. What was the strategy of the besieging commander? During the siege of Breisach, Saxe-Weimar conducted a brilliant aggressive campaign against relieving armies.
17. Did the besiegers have enough troops to seal off the place? At Pskov Gustavus was unable to seal the city so he had no other option but costly attacks.

The defenders needed to calculate this complex and dynamic matrix of factors, always against the background of fear and paranoia in the absence of good and regular information about the outside world. The cost of miscalculation was high, because the soldiers in the garrison would be slaughtered if the place was successfully stormed, and the attacking soldiery would have three days of free plunder and rapine. 'When rape occurred during the sack of a city it was regarded as legitimate if regrettable.'[64] Violent despoilation was standard practice. Even Grotius in *De Jure Belli ad Pacis* was resigned to it.

The attackers, though they would have better intelligence on the outside world, could only guess at what was going on inside, although deserters would probably make good this deficit. It was often difficult in the absence of intelligence, or a message slipped through the siege lines, to know how close to relief they were or how close to exhaustion the attackers were

18. From the attackers' perspective the above considerations were reversed. More importantly sometimes; how much food was there for the besiegers? Besieged cities were sometimes magazines stocked with food. In a strange twist the Spanish besiegers were forced into a truce at Casale 1630 in return

for which the French defenders gave them food. A most bizarre agreement, the Commander Toiras promised to surrender the citadel if Richelieu's relief army had not arrived by a given date. Umberto Eco in his novel, *The Island of the Day Before* lampoons the truce agreement, 'This was not waging war, it was playing dice, interrupting the game when the opponent had to go and urinate. Or perhaps it was like betting on a winning horse. And the horse was the approaching army, whose dimensions increased gradually on the wings of hope, though no one had seen it.'[65]

19. How thick were the walls? Smolensk was the focal point for military effort in Russo-Polish wars because the great fortress and city dominated the White Russian plains. Between 19 September 1609 and 3 June 1611 the city had withstood a prolonged and ferocious attack from a Polish army well equipped with siege guns and mining engineers. Smolensk's fortress had been modernised in the gunpowder era after it was captured by the Lithuanians in the fifteenth century. Not a modern fortress but formidable nonetheless, its walls were 6,575 metres long, 8.5 to 12.8 metres high and 3–7.5 metres thick, (similar to Pskov). There were thirty-eight towers including nine gate towers, so the average distance between the towers was 158 metres, which meant that covering fire could be given from two towers against assaults on the wall. In 1633 Russia's siege failed when Polish Cossaks cut the besiegers' supply line.

The decision whether to storm or not was difficult to judge; a failed storm would be costly, depressing morale then leading to more desertion. It would correspondingly raise the morale of the enemy. If the storm succeeded the town might be destroyed and the economy of the place ruined thus depriving the besiegers of its usefulness. In 1631 the Dutch commander Frederick Henry did not enforce the sack of Maastricht even following a breach established by English soldiers, after terms had been offered. The city was needed, and the citizens were Dutch, besides he had to appease the Stadholder of Gelderland who had aided him in the capture of Venlo and Roe.

Technical expertise in siegecraft and fortress building

As a technical discipline sieges and fortress building became a highly specialised profession, which combined the skills of architecture, construct, geology, and mathematics. Some of the same skills attracted people into the related science of artillery fire and trajectories. Fortress technicians and designers were highly prized, the 'golf course' builders of their day, attracting the attention of many academics and scholars including many highly educated clergymen. Italian engineers dominated the profession in Europe in the sixteenth century, hence *'trace Italienne'* and then Lorraine became a hub for skilled designers including Jean Appier, 'Hanzelet', who published an influential book on artillery and fortresses, *La Pyrotechnie de Hanzelet*. He made his name building the mole at La Rochelle for Richelieu which blocked Buckingham's relief efforts. Comtois priest Capuchin Pere Eustache, a renowned artillery expert helped defeat the French siege at Dôle in 1636: similarly, Jesuit mathematician Padre Rho at the siege of Macau 1622 under the tutelage of Jesuit Adam Schall, who had written a treatise on gunnery. His well aimed cannon drove off the Dutch attackers with one divinely inspired shot hitting the attacker's gunpowder store thus blowing forty soldiers directly to the afterlife. The day before another plunging shot had crashed through a Dutch ship and sunk it. Another Jesuit nicknamed Cosmander, and a renowned mathematician was appointed by Joao IV of Braganza to restore and improve the dilapidated and old-fashioned fortifications on the Spanish border after the Portuguese revolution in 1640. Constructed in the most modern *trace Italienne* style, Elvas, over the border from Badajoz stands as testament to the effort; a sleek, low-slung fortress, it blends seamlessly into the undulating landscape with the cannon embrasures positioned in perfect fields of fire. The Spanish had their artillery and fortress experts Ufano and Lechuga but at the tail end of the Thirty Years War experts and engineers for the Spanish front had to be sent for from the Flanders because of a shortage of skills. Modern fortification technique was introduced into the Caribbean in the late sixteenth century by Italian architect Bautista Antonelli, who under orders from Philip II supervised the construction of new defence at St Juan, Puerto Rico and two new forts at Havanna. It took forty years to finish. The Dutch and the Flemish became the leading fortress designers as massive expenditure was dedicated to a fortress barrier by Oldenbarnevelt in the early seventeenth-century with correspondingly large sums spent in the Spanish Netherlands, e.g. at Antwerp and along the Spanish Main. Johan Mauritz of Nassau was himself an expert. Sweden also developed excellent military engineering skills. Gustavus directly and Marshal Horn were prolific developers of fortress fortifications as well as battlefield structures: engineering skills in the Swedish army tended to be built into the training curriculum of officers with quite a few including Horn, de La Gardie and Lewenhaupt being trained in Holland. A Swede Olof Ornehufvud became chief of fortifications in 1635, and the Swedes were the first army in the world to establish an independent engineering corps at this time. The skills became universal due to publishing of technical books and the printing of detailed etchings of structures including cut away drawings, as designers sought new commissions.

The great age of building which would inform the golden age of fortification took place in the Dutch Republic between 1570 and 1610. The Dutch Republic had both need of fortification to defend itself against a Spanish army that it could not match on the battlefield as well as the riches to pay for the vast array of work across the country including the chain of works along the Maas and Rhine rivers to guard its southern flank and more intermittently along its eastern flank to Germany. There were thirteen major fortresses along the southern flank including 's-Hertogenbosch captured in 1629 along with many lesser works and six major fortresses on the eastern flank. Apart from the border fortresses, most towns and cities were also heavily fortified, including Amsterdam, with a huge, fortified circumference and Utrecht. Powerful Holland helped fund key fortresses in the neighbouring province of Overijssel to the east which acted as a first line buffer to any army attacking from the empire. Decisions on design were made by the Council of State in which the stadtholder, such as Prince Maurice, with his own military knowledge had an important say after which the construction work went to tender with the chief engineer and the 'controller' (quantity surveyor) also involved in the council's decision. The professional and technical process by which the construction of fortresses was contracted and controlled is again testament to the military revolution taking place in military administration. From 1621, the estates of Holland paid for all four estates controllers and eight out of twelve engineers.

To contain his whole army Gustavus in 1632 set up field works in a large defensive perimeter attached to the fortifications of Nuremburg, which had been dug by 6,000 conscripted peasants. 'this leaguer [laager]' attested Munro, 'being accomplished in ten days, and in full defence, with Skonces, Redoutes, Fossies, batteries, and being fortified round with stakkets (stockades), ...and ... sorting ports gates for making sorties).'[66] The earthworks were lined with 300 cannon taken from the city's arsenal; meanwhile, as Wallenstein's larger, newly raised army approached, the Swedish cavalry was kept outside the perimeter to forage freely, ready to provide support to incoming the relieving units ordered to concentrate on Nuremburg. This feat of construction demonstrated the organisation and engineering capability of the army.

It was a professionalism that was a studied imitation of the Roman army. This harking back to Roman military tactics and traditions was the fad of the era for Protestant military thinkers such as Maurice of Nassau, Jacob von Wallhausen's *La Milice Romane* (1616), and later the Duc de Rohan, with his treatise *Le Parfait Capitaine* – commentaries on the Gallic Wars of Ceasar (1636). The classical trend had begun in the renaissance with Machiavelli's Libro Dell' Arte della Guerra (Art of War, 1521), in which contemporary warfare was compared to classical warfare. A standard text book for military theory was *'Les principes de l'art militaire'*, 1641, by Jean de Billon; he suggested a ratio musket-pike ratio of 3:1, but French army regulations still stipulated 1:1 in the 1640s although in practice the ratio probably increased in favour of muskets. For military thinkers the Roman example of a modern military state has continued to have an influence with Fuller and Liddell Hart writing books respectively, on Julius Ceasar and Scipio Africanus.

Frenchman Vauban is the renowned fortress builder/siege engineer of the later seventeenth-century: But he was only building on a very profound and extant body of knowledge and experience. Vauban is overrated in history; he was a French aristocrat prominent in the reign of Louis XIV. He was marked out by history because he basked in the glow of the Sun King.

Mediaeval forts are surrounded by so-called curtain walls interspersed with towers. The walls are straight, thick, and mainly built of stone except the massive forts of the Polish Baltic where great edifices of red brick are testament to the former power of the Teutonic knights. They could be battered down by battering rams or more likely by catapults called trebuchet firing massive stone slingshots. Most towns and cities in early modern Europe were defended by such mediaeval walls. Monro described approaching the walls of Landsberg in, just to the north of Frankfurt an der Oder recounting that 'a draw bridge which was taken up at our arriving'[67] Most of the sieges of the Thirty Years War in Germany were conducted against such defence which in the age of gunpowder and modern siege guns meant that sieges would be brief because a breach could quickly be made. However. a revolution in fortress design and building had started to develop from the mid-sixteenth century. Italian architects schooled in mathematics started to produce defensive systems which could counteract the supremacy of the siege canon. Artillery fortresses countering like with like and defended by soldiers armed with hand-held firearms, arquebuses, were being enabled to fend off attackers from behind strong defence in depth. The method and technology of modern fortress building developed rapidly in the late sixteenth century under the threat of war as well as the reality of attritional war in the low countries. The long bitter sieges of Haarlem and Alkmaar 1672–3 were pointers to the future of siege war in the region. The two-year long siege of Ostend 1602–4 became a celebrated event for Spanish forces; unfortunately, there was always another fortress to bear evidence for von Lazarus's dictum on sieges and exhaustion. The technology, mathematics and geometry of fortress building disseminated rapidly from Italy to France to the Dutch Republic and spread rapidly across Europe. [see final chapter on state modernisation and the military revolution].

Troops were well aware of the potency of modern artillery fortresses compared to those with old-fashioned curtain walls. At Esztergom [a strategic fortress on the Danubian border with Austria] in July 1605 an Ottoman war council met to discuss whether to start a siege or raid Austria, some favoured a siege but others representing the janissaries disliked trench fighting which a long siege must entail. According to veteran officer Abdülkadir Efendi 'they brought up Esztergom's invulnerability[68]: Esztergom is a strong fortress… with [walls] four or five layers [thick]. Its ordnance is very great…. [Moreover] each of its four bastions is a fortress…; the inner fortress is [also] strong and difficult [to assault].'[69] Sieges were not one way traffic, canons could shoot back and with the modern configurations arising from bastions, infantry approaches to the wall would be caught in a deadly crossfire of grapeshot.

The idea of building large fortresses was especially attractive to the smaller states of Europe who saw it as a way of retaining their independence and deterring attack. In northern Europe the Dutch built huge fortress lines, meanwhile in Bavaria, Demark and the Palatine took up the theory by constructing major fortresses. Christian IV of Denmark constructed Christianapreis and various others to defend the neck of country at Schleswig Holstein. Frederick V Palatine built fortresses Frankenthal and Manheim. Maximilian of Bavaria constructed Ingolstadt. Italian renaissance was not just about painting but about education in general including mathematics, science, and engineering. Italian dukes developed a fascination for artillery both a way of defence and a method for the reduction of their enemy's castles. This led to siege guns and fortresses such as Casale, Pinerolo, Piacenza. However, all this activity was based on a flawed idea of defence, as if there was one magic bullet that could solve a strategic problem. With great perspicacity, Parrott notes that 'historians have missed the essential point that fortresses could succeed in their defensive purpose only in conjunction with field armies able to relieve the garrison placed under siege. This essential lesson was ignored by rulers of second- and third-rank states, who constructed fortifications to project both military effectiveness and dynastic status but without incurring the huge and unsustainable additional costs of maintaining an effective field army.'[70] The Palatine, Bavaria, Hesse, Denmark, Luxembourg, and Parma were all overrun and occupied by the enemy despite strong fortresses. Nevertheless, the Dutch who maintained a strong army never fought in the field but used their army to shadow and threaten an invading army or block it with earthworks or uses of flooding by opening the dykes.

The low countries were a special case. What kept a state in being and its territories or vital interests intact was the strength of its army. Fortresses even if they could hold out, could be screened off and quickly become an irrelevance. This was the fate of the Palatine which became a big loser in the war. Hesse might have disappeared had not the 'army in being' exiled itself to the northern coasts; the army's existence made its isolated fortresses relevant. If the army had not existed then Hesse Darmstadt the rival Lutheran state would likely have taken them over. Bavaria survived appalling depredations and the capture of Munich because of its powerful army. Luxembourg lost its independence. Parma's army was crushed in the first days of its war with Spain; overrun and occupied but Parma was restored thanks to its powerful friends. Besides Spain never bothered to attempt to take the fortresses.

In the face of modern fortresses, the Spanish would often just screen them off which might a most allow a small garrison the liberty of a few miles of countryside. Spanish General Cordoba did this with Frankenthal and Manheim. The former fortress was surrendered by the English in 1622 after several years of siege as a political settlement with Spain. However, the Palatine had been completely occupied and Heidelburg captured. Frederick's army was destroyed at the White Mountain outside Prague in 1621. Denmark lost its modern fortress at Christianapreis after Christian IV lost its army at the battle of Lutter. Bavaria was laid waste many times, despite the fortress of Ingolstadt. Ingolstadt was bypassed by Gustavus, who went on to captured and loot Munich.[71]. The Duchy of Parma was occupied by Spanish troops who simply screened off the fortress city of Piacenza. Pinerolo fell quickly after the defeat of the Savoyard army. The military strategies of Prince Maurice and later Henry of Orange was to avoid open battle at all costs; they only wanted to fight behind trenches and redoubts because they knew that if the army was obliterated in a pitched battle, even the much-vaunted defence line would collapse. For lack of a strong army Montauban, the Huguenot fortress city would be captured in 1628.The battle of Nieuwpoort in 1600 was an accidental battle entailing a rare defeat for the Spanish tercio, but it was not repeated. The Dutch fortress line on their southern border only held because there was a strong army to support or relieve its fortresses. Even though Breda fell in 1625, the length of the siege owed much to the fact that a Dutch army was trying to interrupt the siege. The effort completely exhausted Spain's military capacity and the most tangible result of the siege was a superb painting by Velasquez of Spinola taking the surrender. Soon after Spinola was returned to the court in Spain where he headed the opposition and called for a change in policy.

Fortress defence systems in the First World War were sometimes little different; Fort de Douaumont was a classic bastion, a five-sided polygon. It was an outer defence of the classic bastion of the old seventeenth-century fortress of Verdun which entertained five more bastions at the angles of its escarpment line along with ravelins and *demi-lunes*. France held Verdun because it had an army that could defend the country; when in the Second World War army was defeated the huge cost of the Maginot defence system was utterly wasted. Fortresses without strong field armies are just useless dead weights waiting to be captured which was the fate of Frederick Palatine's superb fortresses at Manheim, Frankenthal and Heidelberg. Where field armies were on hand then fortresses could provide a block on the enemy or a base and magazine for counter-attack such as Bavaria's modern fortress at Ingolstadt. When the corpulent duke of

Parma decided to invade Spanish controlled Po valley, he discovered that the stronghold of Piacenza afforded him only a token foothold in his principality.

Drawing on mathematical, geometric, and engineering principles, the new breed of specialised fortress builders designed fortresses which combined defence in depth with walls that were impenetrable or shot deflective. Wall profiles were now low and with flared gun embrasures to allow cannon to be aimed at arc of ground over the glacis or the outside terrain; the walls were also slightly sloped to deflect and reduce the power of cannon balls. Walls were made of stone or brick back by earth of to give immense absorptive depth. Parapets tended to be of brick to prevent deadly stone splinters. Designs would include outworks sometimes in multiple geometric layers. Such arrow shaped works were called ravelins. The central bastion which would be the design building block for architects such as Bachot, might be a five-sided polygon, onto which various defensive shaped structures would be added or indeed additional bastion bolted on at the angles to the structural frame. Other shapes were called 'hornworks' or *'crown work'*. The geometric design would often be in the pattern of layered stars with ravelin and *demi-lunes* almost the out works.[72] The concept behind such works was to expose and drive attackers into deadly crossfires, as well as reducing so-called 'dead zones' in which the enemy could shelter from fire. Behind the ravelin or outworks there was the scarp and counterscarp in between which ditches often filled with water. In major systems there might be major outlying forts to give defence in depth to the central place, the idea being that an attacker would be worn piece by piece long before he even approached the main fortifications; defence in depth. Dunkirk for example had major outlying fortresses at Mardyke and Furness, both of which had to be taken in 1646 before the central works of Dunkirk could be engaged.

Geometric draftsmanship and surveying were essential professional skills. Fortress engineers all worked with the contours of the land to extract maxim advantage from nature. As if they were golf course designers, they knew how best to mould the fortress into natural contours and geographical strong points or the reinforcement of weak points. Guns located at the central bastion had to be able to enjoy a clear field of fire over the outworks and onto their glacis, the better to sweep the enemy clear as they approached the first defences. Other tricks were the use of water in nearby rivers to divert into moats and ditches; Simon Stevin was an expert in the new specialization of sluices and hydraulics. Other specialist skills included in the title *engineer* was explosives; particularly important for mining and countermining. Mining to explode a breach and starvation became the main method to force surrender because the storming of a modern fortress was odds against.

There were many short cuts to improving the defence of mediaeval city walls which still accounted for the majority of defence. Wall could be reinforced by building up earth bank behind old city walls; bastions could be added and an out defence line of redoubts ravelins and redans made of earth could be constructed. Ghent provided itself with an earthen defence system for the meagre cost of 300,000 guilders. However, these earthen defence had a short life, perhaps only five-seven years and would then need repairs of replacement; maintenance costs were high. The more solid and permanent bastions constructed in Amsterdam's defence system required florins, 2,000,000 each. We can estimate that earthen ramparts were perhaps ten times cheaper than permanent brick and stone structures. Given that every small town was fortified the total Capex defence bill for the Republic was vast, excluding the cost of maintenance. Earthen ramparts were common; some of them still exist; a prime example is Bourtange; they were also effective because of their ability to absorb canon balls' energy. Engineers were constantly required to put in hand maintenance works and improvements to old defence; in water the logged Netherlands foundations often crumbled, and walls fell down. More solid and long-lasting defence would have ramparts faced with stone or brick as well as the counterscarp and a paved parapet.

The labour-intensive process of building defences was either contracted or by forced levy or by volunteer civilians in times of crisis. Sometimes the army was used. Comte de Bussy-Rabutin describes how he was employed at one point in 1647 to use his troops to make earthen repair and improve the defence at newly captured Courtrai, '...on the 18th July [1646] we went over to Courtrai to repair the breaches in the wall and to construct several new defensive outworks.'[73]

The attacking army need fortress engineers as much as the defender, in fact more because there were considerable amounts of construction to be set in hand. These works could be huge. At Breisach Saxe-Weimar's lines were 20 kilometres long while at the siege of 's-Hertogenbosch the Dutch lines of contravallation were about 40 kilometres long. The attacking army need to be secured in a fortified encampment with ramparts and firing step and embrasures for canon. The trench lines had to be interspersed with redoubts of all shapes and sizes, star, lozenge, square, or pentagonal bastions. Lines of circumvallation had to face two ways to prevent surprise attacks by the enemy from its relieving forces. Using draftsman skills, the engineer needed to draw the defences of the enemy then plan the zig-zag traverses and saps to approach the enemy fortifications at their weakest points. Numbers of these avenues needed to be constructed to keep the enemy guessing as to which one was the focal point. At intervals more redoubts needed to be built to ward off sallies; then batteries had to be moved forwards into gabion protected positions as the lines drew in tighter on the enemy defences. It was dangerous work. The new breed of fortress engineers needed courage as they were required to go to the front lines in daylight. At the siege of Ostend 1601–3, seven out of the twelve 'engineers' engaged would be killed. With their white, paper charts, maps and drawings flapping in the breeze the snipers on the parapets of the enemy outworks would easily recognise a valuable target. This was the fate not just of junior engineers but even master designers were closely involved with sieges; renowned master engineer Jacob Kemp was shot while inspecting the lines at Grol in 1595.

A skilled profession, the going rate for *engineers* was about 400 guilders per annum, but this reduced to 200 after the Twelve-Year Truce in 1609. Wealthy Holland paid higher than other estates. Simon Stevin only earnt about 600 per year despite his renown. As the war progressed the status of engineers declined somewhat. Regarded increasing as an artisanal skill as the seventeenth-century progressed, it did not attract people from the regent class, although some engineers would become prominent in civic life and local government. Alternatively, in France, the fortress engineer was regarded as a sort of early modern 'rock star' attracting the elite a culture of technical military excellence in engineering or artillery which has extended through Napoleon into modern times. Vauban was a count. Many of the renowned military engineers were ennobled or came from the ranks of minor nobility; they could expect to meet with and dine with high nobility even with kings. In England too the Dutch engineers who attended Charles I during the civil war were accorded high status and honours. In the Dutch Republic hydraulic engineers who managed and built the dyke systems were also esteemed not least because flooding was also a defence system for the Republic.

Fortresses on the Spanish Main

The programme developed by Philip II in 1588 called 'A defence plan for the Caribbean' in response to successful English attacks, was already in progress but now accelerated due to the renewal of war. Fortresses were *very* expensive, 'these forts were built according to the latest designs in military engineering, featuring lower walls, triangular bastions and other refinements.'[74] ' in more remote areas…. building material, labourers, soldiers, supplies, food, and ordnance had to be brought in.'[75] The monumental defences of Havanna, many still in place, took forty years to build and were garrisoned by 600 regular troops as well as ten companies of militia. The advent of the Thirty Years War necessitated a major upgrading of defensive capability, something that was accelerated after the loss of the treasure fleet to the Dutch at Havanna in 1628. At the narrow mouth of the harbour the modern defence of Fortaleza de San Carlos de La Cabaña is a formidable structure towering over the harbour. Emphasis was placed on modern fortresses and bastions with thicker reinforced sloping walls to deflect shot: Reflecting the increased firepower of enemy ships, many more cannons needed to be mounted. Building of course was not the only cost. Other capital and inventory costs included expensive cannon, stores of gunpowder and shot;

and this is not to mention increased running costs involved in maintenance and larger garrisons. Seventy per cent of garrison troop officers in the colonies had been diverted from the Flanders front and although foot soldiers were also sent from Andalucía this would hardly have helped the shortage of naval and military personnel in Spain.

Cartagena's fortress is one of the most famous and well preserved; it was completely upgraded with major new forts added between 1631 and 1634. After a major attack on St Juan by the Dutch in 1625 in which the town was sacked, though the citadel held out, new defensive walls were built and a rampart added along the harbour side in 1634. Vera Cruz constructed defensive walls in the 1630s with a large battery constructed in 1635: [Still standing]. Other major works during the Thirty Years War were undertaken at Santa Marta, Maracaibo, San Antonio, Santiago de Cuba, Panama, and Santa Catalina. The latter island was held for a while by Anglo-Dutch privateers until expelled by a Spanish expedition from Cartagena in 1640.

Even on the Pacific coast of Mexico a stronger masonry fortress, San Diego, had to be built at the main port of Acapulco after a Dutch raid destroyed the old fort in 1615. Other Pacific cities had already increased spending after *'El drakes'* raids of the previous century. From the 1620s French British and Dutch raiding by officially encouraged privateers as well as the creation of settlements in the Antilles, St Kitts, Tortuga, Nevis, Tobago, Providence Island [off the mosquito coast], Barbados, and Espanola led to attacks on various of the weaker cities in the region like Maracaibo, Puerto Cabello and La Guairá. Santiago de la Vega, known now as Spanish Town-Jamaica, was also raided.[76] In 1641 Santa Catalina Island off the coast of Nicaragua was recovered by the Spanish from Anglo-Dutch corsairs; thereafter the Spanish built nine cannon mounting forts on the island. All this enemy activity produced a climate of fear and demands for better protection by the local authorities, in the form of stronger fortresses, more galleons and soldiers. The shock caused by Pietr Heyn's assault on the treasure fleet at Matanzas Bay near Havanna in 1628 stimulated further construction. Besides the Spanish Main, raids by the Dutch in the Pacific in 1623 and 1643 led to the works at of Valdivia, on the Pacific coast, as well as the fortification of Lima's port of Callao at the cost of 876,000 pesos.[77]

The cost of trying to preserve Spanish power in the Caribbean was an enormous drain on the treasury. Apart from the transfer of the Fleet of Flanders from Dunkirk to the Caribbean, which undercut naval power deployed against Dutch North Sea and Baltic shipping, several special armadas in 1629 and 1631 were sent to the Caribbean to remove nascent French, Dutch and English colonies. A few colonies were destroyed including those on Nieves, St Kitts, Tortuga, St Martin, and Trinidad. Admiral Don Fadrique's much lauded armada in 1632 cost 716,000 ducats of which only twenty per cent was recovered in freight revenue.

What might seem like irrelevant pinpricks on the outer skin of the Spanish power structure was to deprive the Spanish armies and navy in Europe by the diversion of troops, resources, and treasure for Imperial protection. Vast expenditures on defence on the dozens of towns along the thousands of kilometres of Pacific coast, along the Spanish Maine and Caribbean islands, were out of all proportion to the actual threat. The economic war of attrition and the eventual victory of the Dutch, French and Swedish alliance in the Thirty Years War was due in no little part to the long-range wars fought on the *'fringes'* of the world. The Dutch strategy was for *indirect* war, but it was not less effective for that because it optimised Dutch attacking and defensive capabilities, while stretching the resources of the enemy. Nevertheless, the vigorous and effective action taken by Spain belies the image of inevitable decay and decline in Spanish capability.

Portuguese forts of the Estado da India (Asia-including Macau- and East Africa)

The Portuguese were prolific fortress builders around their Asian, African, and south American Empire. They built new fortresses or adapted existing defences of the towns and cities which they captured to make them artillery fortresses. Portugal's main contribution to the captured places was the construction of bastions to mount cannon; old-fashioned walls were kept presumably because it was too expensive to convert them to modern sloping defence although elements of trace Italienne design might be added so that many forts were hybrid. Trace Italienne design or elements of it were introduced in the mid-sixteenth century but the fortresses never reached the level of geometric complexity to be found in early seventeenth-century Europe because the enemy, usually local states/ sultanates simply did not have enough cannon or naval power to pose the same sort of threat.

Most fortresses were islands or peninsulas connected to a hinterland. Portugal's so-called empire was actually a trading network and with only a few excepts such as Mozambique and Ceylon there was no attempt to seize territory, which would have been beyond the resources of the small European state. Portuguese power like the Dutch and British later on, was based on sea power where modern vessels after about 1620 would mount as many as forty cannon. One broadside (i.e. half the cannon complement) of twelve- to twenty-four-pounders deploying more firepower than most large size European armies. Between 1600 and 1610, the Duch established naval control in Asia starting with the straits of Malacca. In naval battles there, modern Dutch ships well provided with cannon would defeat Portuguese ships armed with six guns and taking one hour to reload. Firepower blew away Portuguese control of Asian sea routes. By the time the Portuguese modernised, their fleet with powerful, heavily gunned galleons in the 1620s, it was too late. The Dutch had already established control.

The purpose of the forts was to act as centres for trade and protectors of Portuguese communities and factories (godowns-warehouses) where traded goods could be stored until the next export ship arrived. Where a fortress could not be built for example in the tidal rivers of south east which flowing down from the Himalaya, the Portuguese would tend to rely on undefended Portuguese trading communities. Tidal river were unsatisfactory locations for forts because for half the year they were hostages to fortune because ships could not move against the flood, moreover on these low, mud-bound mangrove coasts there were no safe anchorages to withstand the monsoons and cyclones that sweep through between June and October. Such tidal rivers included the Ganges, (Hoogli), Brahmaputra (Calcutta-Sandwip), Karnaphuli, (Chittagong-Diangia Bangladesh), Irrawaddy, (Thilawa-Burma), Sittang, (Pegu-Burma), Mrauk-U (Kaladan River Burma), and the Mekong (Phnom Pen Cambodia).

On occasions the fortresses might be captured by the regional power sometimes in combination with the Dutch or the English in the case of Hormuz. The strategic hub of Malacca was captured with the aid of the Sultan of Jahor's manpower and logistics in 1642. The key of course was sea power; control of the sea around the target fortress was a necessary precursor to an attempt at capture. This would sometimes be preceded by a sea battles as off Jask in 1621, off Goa, off Malacca, off Manila, off Mrauk-U, off Batavia, and Moçambique, 1616–48.

Fortalezas de Estado da India

Philip III noted in 1607, 'Ever since the discovery of India, experience has demonstrated the importance of fortresses; and now this seems even greater with appearance of the [Dutch] rebels in these parts.'[78] As a trading empire based on coastal forts security in the face of local land-based powers was essential, because the Portuguese could always count on their dominance at sea to bring relief. Although the Portuguese presence was for the most part tolerated and mutually beneficial to the indigenous, local difficulties and flare ups occurred, but the artillery fortresses were strong enough to deter jealous and hostile powers. However, the arrival of the Dutch, posed a particular threat because their powerfully armed ships challenged Portuguese sea power, moreover there were possibilities of coalescing with local powers with jealousies and grudges against the Portuguese.

Fortresses defended by powerful cannon were the basis of Portuguese Imperial power and still the most material evidence of Portugal's imprint on the world.

Cartographer and historian José Manuel Garcia says of them that they were 'a network of interests of political, military and economic which was a grand extension, and strong expression of maritime domination'[79]. Fortresses were always located on the coast in the Estado. The only exception in Portugal's global empire were the upriver fortresses beyond Luanda in southwest Africa (Angola) forts such as Muxima and Cambambe which were slave trading hubs. Portuguese interests around the globe were always based on maritime prowess. In a world without formed states the Portuguese were able to takeover key coastal cities in Asia using their firepower and indomitable aggressive will. Vasco da Gama and Albuquerque were brutal and outstanding warriors driven by a crusading spirit and an insatiable appetite for power, money, and glory. Most of the places taken were ruled by Moslems so the happy coincidence allowed the invasion of Asia to take on the mantel of a crusade. There was also a quest to find a mythical 'Prester John' an Asian Christian and it seemed at first to the early crusaders that the Hindus were indeed Christians before better acquaintance with language and culture revealed the mistake.

The size and range of the Estado da India at its peak is hard to estimate. A good way to look at it is from the collection of contemporary illustrations of Portuguese fortresses published in circa 1612; apart from this there are other diagrams of fortresses published between 1550 and 1634. The number of fortresses, excluding settlements without defence, was seventy-three. Categorisations are difficult but I have grouped the fortresses into three categories, islands close to a littoral (18/24.6 per cent), peninsular, i.e., land with water on three sides (20/27.4 per cent) and coastal forts which face the hinterland directly behind (28/38.3 per cent). Another salient fact is the split between *trace Italienne* defences in the modern geometric style and curtain wall fortification. Calculations on this are necessarily difficult because of definition as well as hybrid development. However, this split is roughly 41.5 per cent *trace Italienne*, 43 per cent, curtain wall, and hybrids 10.7 per cent. The modern style fortification was introduced to the Estado as early as 1558 although the style was rudimentary compared to what was being achieved fifty years later. A few forts had stockades rather than full brick fortifications. They included Gaulle in southern Ceylon and the newly founded Syriam in Burma. Other non-Estado towns without fortification and outside the Estado included Hugli, Chittagong and Darran in the Bay of Bengal. To protect its valuable Camphor trade to China, the Portuguese built forts Lifau and Belibo in Timor. There are several islands in the Celebes, northern and southern Maluku with Portuguese fortifications including Serapua near Ambon, on the Banda 'Spice Islands', Calamata and others on the sultanate islands Ternate and Tidore (North Moluku), and Sanana in the Celebes; (remote and picturesque places visited by the author).

Most fortresses were square with four bastions, but the number could be much higher for example Colombo, St Thomas de Mylapore, and Chaul thirteen, Damao ten, Aden nine and Malacca even some forts were triangular and other had octagonal shapes or hexagon or were irregular rhomboids. Some fortifications were shaped into hillsides and rocky outcrops. Ten of the fortresses had citadels and several had a square citadel-fort within more extensive outer walls. Settlement was normally outside the fort except in big, fortified places such as Goa or Malacca. Malacca also had suburbs.

Bastions were gun platforms so the number of them is an important indicator of the number of guns in the defence. Each platform might carry three to four guns. Tricornered Batticaloa had three bastions and eight guns in total. Colombo had 200 cannons of all calibres.

The extent of fortification normally went with the importance and trading wealth of the town and city. Surprisingly some of the most important places such as Goa and Macau were not especially well protected. Goa was defended by a fortress at the harbour entrance but was such an extensive city that it was not walled. Macau was not permitted by the Chinese to build fortifications under their licence to occupy Macau however as the Dutch threat increased, this policy changed, and the Portuguese built fortifications in spite the Chinese regulations. Philip III (II of Portugal) was increasingly concerned about the defences of the Asian empire as it came under pressure from the Dutch intrusion into the region. He needed modernising proto states needed to make inventory of their assets updated records as to the defence; Philip gave orders for an updated survey of colonial fortifications:

> 'I have information that the sketches done of the Kingdom's defence are very damaged, and does not leave a proper record, being so old and unworthy; therefore, I recommend you order it to continue the sketches to be redone, so that the defence that need it are maintained.'[80]

The information as to the defence were contained within the sketches *Plantaformas das Fortalezas de Índia* and it is these which enable an assessment of the Estado system of fortifications. The two main works of record are the *O Lyvro de Plantaformas das Fortalezas da Índia 1612* and the *Lyvro das plantas das Fortalezas 1650.* The provenance is not clear, and several cartographers were involved. Philip IV (III of Portugal) 1632 ordered a review of all.

> '…the plans of all the fortresses, cities, and proofs of the state of India with those of the barracks and the height at which they are and all that there is in them, artillery, prices, people, masters, and vacancies, food and expenses, and all that is beyond the crown of Spain, by António Bocarro, keeper of the tower of Tombo, and chronicler of the said state'[81].

The Spanish kings took a close interest in their Asian possession but except for one campaign to the Malacca straits early in the seventeenth century there was no other attempt to coordinate Spanish and Portuguese fleets which remained. In the sixteenth century there was also a joint attempt to capture Ternate and Tidore. However, the sheer difficulty of communication and coordination meant that both were failures. By 1630 Spain had no money to spend on defeating the Dutch in Asia. Aid to Portugal was focused on saving Brazil's sugar economy.

At the centre of Spanish power in the Philippines was the capital and main naval base at Manila. Geographically optimal for its centrality to the island chain, Manila, located on the west side of the islands also boasted a huge, sheltered horseshoe bay guarded by the uplands of Battan at its northern neck. This harbour was vital given the violent typhoons, which regularly sweep in on the east coast bringing devastation to Luzon; fortunately, the width of Luzon at this point weakens the storms before they reach the harbour on the west coast. By 1600 there were seventeen main forts and settlements that were large enough to justify defending with regular troops. The recommended garrison at Manila was 600, plus four galleys for plying the islands.

Following Dutch attacks on Manila in the early seventeenth century, large sums were spent on improving the defence in a modern geometric style. Already by 1620 Manila boasted a modern fortress, including eleven artillery-mounting bastions with several outworks also in the Italian style: a typical colonial city with whitewashed fort, angled walls, and bastions topped by sentry cupolas. Inside the fortress you can still see typical whitewash houses window grills and churches of a Spanish grid planned colonial city. The church of St Agustin completed in 1607, which still stands, with its cloisters and dark mysterious atmosphere, is especially worth visiting. The city fortifications are still there, adjacent to the port.

Württemberg's castles and the legend of Konrad Wiederholt

Konrad Wiederholt was born into a gentleman's family in Hesse and like his brothers he became a soldier variously serving for the Hanseatic League and Venice, where he became acquainted with Magnus of Württemberg. This patronage was his pathway into the militia of the Duke of Württemberg firstly as a lieutenant and then as a major. He was given command of the Princedom's most important castle at Hohentwiel. It was one of a clutch of seemingly impregnable-looking castles raised on pinnacles of rock in the south east of the Black Forest; they included Hohenneuffen and Hohenzollern. In the event only Hohentwiel held out. Castle defence depended mainly on the steadfastness of the commander; many would simply surrender from despair at any possibility of relief surrender.

After his army's defeat at Wimpfen 1622, the Duke of Württemberg had to go into exile and his territories which included eleven monasteries and their territories and five bishoprics, controlling some thirty per cent of his territory. Having been secularized these were subject to the counter reformation. The duke went into exile at Strasbourg and was forced cede his princedom to his son. The liberation of the south east by Gustavus's forces who captured Munich, Ulm and Augsburg led to the return of the duke who raised 5,000 troops to recapture Imperialist held towns in his princedom. supported at times by Swedish forces under General Horn this task was largely achieved and the Swedes moved on to capture various towns on Lake Konstanz including Meersburg, Radolfzell, Buchhorn, (Friedrichshafen), and Mainau Island.

The defeat of Saxe-Weimar and Horn at Nördlingen in September 1634 was followed immediately by the advance of the Duke of Lorraine and Werth against Württemberg. They sacked and burnt the towns of Waiblingen and Herrenberg, and powerful fortresses were also taken, but Hohentwiel held out. Duke Charles and Werth moved on and crushed a Württemberg army under the Rhinegrave of 6,000 at Wittstât on 28 September 1634. Swedish conquests in the south west and at Lake Konstanz were eradicated, because isolated Swedish garrisons were withdrawn from the lakeside. After three years of lake warfare 1632–4 with attack and counter-attack, blockade, and counter blockade the lake campaign was over.

It was Major General Ruthven who first arrive on the lake to take Radolfzell's surrender. Violating Swiss neutrality, Konstanz was besieged by Horn and Wrangel, but a storm was repulsed with 1,000 dead. With the help of Imperial flotillas, attacks on Überlingen and Konstanz were repulsed even though the Swedes built a twenty-two-gun warship *Drottning Kristina*. The Swedes evacuated Überlingen, Meersburg and Buchhorn. Überlingen had previously been captured by Wiederholt in a surprise attack.

Wiederholt, a local Protestant warlord, was not content to just defend. It would be wrong to call him a mercenary because he was always an anti-Habsburg fighting for Protestant interests and indirectly for the Duke of Württemberg. He raided far and wide collecting contributions from ninety estates and conducting a sort of guerilla war against the Imperialists between 1634 and 1648. In this time five sieges were repulsed. Additional efforts to suborn the Protestant Wiederholt were made with the active mediation of some of his relatives.

To no avail. Wiederholt remained loyal to his masters, although who the masters were became a moot point because he would join with Saxe-Weimar and after his death he transferred his loyalties to the French. All may have been done with the tacit agreement of theDuke of Württemberg. He would be duly rewarded and ended a very rich man whose inheritance was bitterly contested.

Chapter XI

Military Frontiers and Defensive Barriers

Hungarian/Croatian military frontier against the Ottomans

The other strategic problem for the Habsburgs was the need always to keep a substantial fortification and garrison system on the Ottoman frontiers not far to the south of Vienna. The Turks were the traditional threat to Habsburg hereditary interests and any actions in the empire risked a stab in the back, either from the Turkish army in full force from their territories that ran over the Sava River, to the east of Zagreb and northwards to lake Balaton and Buda over the Bosnian mountains to the Croatian coast at Zengi. Another source of raiding into Royal Hungary was border raiding from the Ottoman satrapy of Transylvania [a Calvinist Hungarian state, part of the former Hungarian kingdom] formed after the battle of Mohacs 1526. Transylvania bordered Royal Hungary on its norther edge above Buda from its borderland region of Tokaj [famous for sweet wines]; the Principality of Transylvania also bordered Poland to the north, Turkish controlled Moldova to the north east and Wallachia to the south of the Transylvanian Alps with its mixed Vlach [Romanian] population.

War on two fronts was the abiding danger and one of the main reasons why Vienna was always short of money in their quest to impose themselves militarily in the empire because the empire was required to garrison 120 castles and fortresses with Imperial troops, 12,000 each from Germany and Hungary, half cavalry, and half infantry. The financial cost of this standing army in garrison was considerable; it would account for fifty per cent of the budget of the Hungarian estates and a further contribution of about 750,000 Rhénish florins per year from the Upper Austrian estates to make up the other fifty per cent balance.[1] Further contributions would be made from the Moravian estates to cover expenses related to the building of the modern fortress of Neuhäusel in the mining area of what is now Slovakia, some fifty kilometres east of Pressburg [Bratislava]; it was a forward defence for a line of attack by Ottoman forces against Moravia and especially its capital Brno. At this time and until the end of the First World War the north bank of the Danube east of Austria/Moravia and north of Hungary was integral to the kingdom and occupied by ethnic Hungarians. (It is now Slovakia)

Dutch fortress defensive chain

As Dutch economic success built up over the last decades of the sixteenth century, the economy started to spin off huge flows of surplus cash and tax receipts. Still in an existential war with Spain Oldenbarnevelt decided to spend the money in building a strong defensive system of fortified towns along the Brabant border with the Spanish Netherlands. These needed huge numbers of cannon which were produced at a newly founded National Artillery Foundry at the Hague in 1589.

By 1599 there were seventeen fortress towns along the main battle front with many subsidiary fortifications in addition. Some of these fortresses boasted dozens of subsidiary fortresses and powerful outworks. They included towns such as Deventer, Berg-op-Zoom, Nijmegen, Breda, and Maastricht. Deventer for example had eight bulwarks and ravelin which were developed over a period of fifty years. Breda was similarly endowed with outer works, including 'ninety-six redoubts, thirty-seven forts, forty-five batteries.'[2] Fortification varied hugely in size and sophistication.

Spinola was unsuccessful in his attempt to breach the fortified line at Berg-op-Zoom in 1622. His army suffered huge casualties, over 20,000, from disease and desertion; he retreated. The town could be resupplied by water. The barrier was never penetrated even after the loss of Breda in 1624 because there were so many other fortresses. Flooding of the countryside made passage of armies impossible, and the Dutch controlled the waterways and the sluices. Moreover, the exhaustion and attrition involved in the nine-month siege so weakened the Spanish army as to prevent the exploitation of the victory.

Battle of the Slaak 11–13 September 1631

The campaign years of 1630 and 1631 were frustrating and fruitless for the Dutch. Ambitious plans to capture Dunkirk, Hulst or Bruges gave way to doubts when the Spanish blocked their advances: Dithering over strategy between the push and pull of the various provincial estates' strategic priorities also confused matters. A powerful fishing lobby, including the dreaded fishwives, whose livelihoods and husbands were being put at risk by attack on herring 'busses'. They demanded Dunkirk as a target following continued heavy losses caused by 'Dunkirkers' (Flemish privateers) who 'lie before the mouth of the Mass and here in view of Scheveningen and are hanging about so that the fisherman do not dare put out to sea.'[3] [Tobia van Eyck to Count Floris] Friesland wanted troops in the north east to counter the Imperialist threat. Zeeland wanted an invasion of Flanders. Holland and Zeeland wanted naval war in defence of trade and to attack the Spanish-Portuguese colonies. Frontier provinces such as

Brabant just wanted land war. Meanwhile Richelieu demanded action, any action that would justify his annual subsidy to the Republic of one million guilders. However, there was pressure to do something before Spanish reinforcements arrived, troops released by the termination of the Mantuan war under the Treaty of Cherasco. Barged to Zeeland and thence to Flanders in the vicinity of Bruges, the Dutch army did eventually ship out in early June 1631. However, Frederick Henry was forced to withdraw because of 'great hunger in our army by reason of the inaccessibility and great distance from which the *vivres* (provisions) must come, which one believes to be the greatest reason for the withdrawal.'[4] (Deputy Bernhard Sloet letter to the States of Overijssel)

Spain and Olivarez were also frustrated. Years of attrition to break the Dutch defences yielded them nothing. Their attempted invasion with a combined Habsburg army under de Berg and Montecuccoli which was launched from Kleve in 1629 against their weak eastern flank, failed when logistics broke down after the Dutch captured their base at Wesel. Captured in Wesel was two and half weeks' supply of rye and buckwheat enough for 110, 000 six-pound loaves of bread for the Spanish army. Without bread and the possibility for resupply the campaign which had shown much promise after the capture of Amersfoort which threatened the Republic's second city of Utrecht ended the most serious threat to the Republic.

Unable to penetrate the Dutch defence lines, in a last desperate effort, the Spanish under Baron de Moncada, a Sicilian aristocrat, decided to outflank the Dutch fortress system from the sea, this time by establishing a fortress in their rear. Commanded by Spanish General de Moncada, Marques de Aytona, the Spanish sought to take control of the Scheldt and isolate Zeeland.[5] His aim was to take the star-shaped fortress of Willemstad, opposite Holland, at the entrance to the Volkerak. This fortress commanded the complex network of connecting channels and islands leading to Middelburg [Zeeland's main island]. If Zeeland could be conquered, Antwerp would be free at last to trade, moreover, the Spanish would be able to establish a base in the strategic rear of the Republic's main lines of defence and fortification. It was a strategy akin to the Anzio landings in Italy in the Second World War when the allies, blocked on a narrow front by strong defence made an amphibious lunge to go around the German flank; but that campaign nearly ended in disaster because it was underpowered. Would the Spanish attack be powerful enough?

As a strategic concept the Spanish had a fine plan, but it required command of the waterways and overwhelming sea power [which the allies enjoyed at Anzio]. Would a force of thirty-five ships and fifty barges carrying about 6,000 Spanish soldiers and sailors be equal to the task? They were operating against a savvy riverine foe in their home waterways around the Scheldt. These were waters controlled by the pugnacious Zealanders. In a preliminary move, a first attempt to land at Zeeland on the 11 September, to establish a base on Tholen Island was foiled in the muddy shallows by an Anglo-Scottish regiment from nearby Steenberg in Brabant. They waded the eastern shallows at low tide to cross over to Tholen Island, then formed up on the threatened western shore line. Around the porous borderlands of the Netherlands, accurate intelligence on Spanish plans had leaked out. de Moncada's campaign had been thoroughly compromised before the outset. The Dutch were ready. Unlike the Anzio landings strategic surprise had been lost at the outset.

Nothing daunted, de Moncada tried again the following day, the 12 September. On a misty night, the Spanish succeeded in slipping into the Mastgat from the Oosterschelde without problem but only because the alerted Dutch had already decided to let them through before closing the net. As the Dutch fleet of fifty shallow draft emerged through the early morning mist, they were ambushed, The Spanish found themselves bottled up by the Dutch fleet including Dutch warships or heavily armed barges as they aimed to pass through the Slaak by the shore of Anna Jacobapolder. Fleeing in panic, many of the barges beached themselves on the northern shore of Anna Jacobapolder where the fleeing soldiers were shot down or rounded up by English Scottish, and Dutch soldiers.

A crushing victory little remarked on by historians now but should be because it was the moment that sealed the Republic's strategic victory in the war in the Eighty Years war, something that took a further seventeen years to seal at the Treaty of Munster January 1648. The scenes from 1631 were depicted in contemporary prints, specially minted silver coins and Dutch broadsheet flyers broadcasting the '*Triomphe*'. It was the most notable Dutch triumph in the war to date, and a victory which crushed Spain's dangerous strategic sally.

Dutch naval forces annihilated the Spanish barge fleet, capturing eighty-three sailing barges and transport ships, 4,000 soldiers and sailors. 1,500 Flemish and Spaniards were killed, mostly drowned. Just two ships of the force escaped, including the hapless commanders Moncada.[6]

The battle of the Slaak was a one of the most decisive victories in the Dutch phase of the Thirty Years War: the last major attack on the Dutch provinces, Spanish hopes for freeing Antwerp from decades long blockade were in tatters. Like the assault at the Dardanelles or at Anzio, the concept was brilliant, but strategy was not matched by sufficient force, operational skill, or determination. Even if Moncada had been able to establish an island fortress in the Scheldt channel it would have been difficult to sustain it in Zeeland's back yard without additional commitment of substantial land and naval forces. A miserable effort, it was the last Spanish fling at the Dutch. Such an expedition could not be done on the cheap. Moncada's force was badly underpowered for such an ambitious venture, which in the circumstances was '*grandiose* strategy' rather than grand strategy.

How effective were the chain defence systems? The Dutch example and others

The empire's military frontier was no doubt an effective deterrent to localized military raiding but not completely so because raiding was a continuing feature of life on the frontier even after the ending of the Long War [1693–1606] with the Ottomans. Raiding parties could and did easily slip through the gaps in the defensive chain to loot, murder and burn the defenceless villages behind the frontier. Low-level warfare was permanent. Raids and counter raids by various sizes of raiding parties crisscrossed the military frontier's; objectives were loot and ransom money. Border areas became wastelands; raids had to go deeper but depth meant higher risk.

Despite the frontier Bethlen Gábor's large armies had no difficulty in passing through the frontier, not least because many of the fortress commanders and borderland magnates were Calvinist and had thrown in their lot with the rebellion of the Hungarian Estates. Even later there was no difficulty for Gábor's successor György Rákóczi. He would similarly pass through easily in 1645 with his large army even without the collaboration of district captaincies on the frontier. They did not stop to capture these fortress chains. Despite the ease of passing through or round the military frontier, the fact was that invasions by Gábor and Rákóczi were just very large raids. Their cavalry armies of up to 30,000 cavalry, travelled light without big supply trails and gun trains which would extend for miles behind the vanguard elements of regular armies. Each horseman would take one or two remounts with him. Transylvanian and hussar armies lived 'on the hoof', looting and gathering food supplies as they went. If Gábor's army had been a regular army, then ignoring the military frontier would not have been possible because supplies lines could easily have been cut by local garrison forces half of whom were cavalry. In truth the Transylvanian army could not operate in any other way. The idea of taking a formal west European style army over rugged terrain and poor roads for 1000 kilometres, the distance between Alba Iulia and Prague was unthinkable not least because Transylvania was a poor state with a population of one million and a society and military culture entirely linked to the horse.

The Dutch line held successfully throughout the eighty-years' war with Spain although it came under pressure in 1609 just before the signing of the twelve-year truce. However, like the Maginot line the entire Dutch defensive system could be outflanked. Although the Spanish tried to nibble at the fortresses on the left flank of the Dutch line they only once succeeded in flanking the defensive system in this way.

When Frederick Henry took Maastricht in 1632 this victory after an extended and bitterly contested siege he effectively sealed the eastern end of the line.

He had already made sure of sealing the other end of the fortified line by the capture of 's-Hertogenbosch in 1629 and the important victory at the battle of the Slaak in 1631. Luckily for the Dutch the Imperialist never established a strong enough hold in north west Germany next to the Dutch eastern frontier despite Spinola's capture of Kleve in 1614; a strategic place that he was unable to exploit after the war with the Dutch re-commenced in 1621. When the position in Kleve and the crossing point at Wesel was exploited in 1629, it was too late. Had the Spanish and Imperialist forces of the respect Habsburg regimes focus their strategic ambitions on the Dutch eastern flank it might have changed the direction of the war. The Dutch fortress line to the east was too dispersed to offer any real resistance to an invading army. Dutch defences would be outflanked in 1672 the year of the Rampjaar, when France occupied much of the Republic only to be blocked by Amsterdam's water defence.

When an Imperialist army outflanked the Dutch fortified line then burst through into the eastern provinces in 1629 and threatened Amersfoort and Utrecht it seemed that the Republic was doomed. The main army was entrenched far to the south at the siege of 's-Hertogenbosch. Unfamiliar to open warfare the Dutch army, if it came away from the siege, might have to attack a veteran army in the open field; if destroyed the border defences would avail them little, and surrender might be the only option. The story of the German panzer armies outflanking the Maginot line are very similar; in Vietnam the Ho Chin Minh trail outflanked the DMZ and the Vietnam People Army skirted round and attacked the American base at Khe San. Post war French forces1945–54 set up the de Lattre lines around the Red delta with hundreds of fortified block houses, but Vietminh forces still infiltrated in such large numbers that they could take control of fifty per cent+ of the delta. Moreover, the Vietminh held down in static positions some 500,000 troops leaving only about 30,000 for aggressive mobile operations, but even these would be pinned down at Hoa Binh, Na San and lastly at Dien Bien Phu. It is the fundamental problem of the static linear fortified defence. If breached or outflanked only a superior mobile army will prevent total defeat and given the fact that basic strategy and tactics have been attuned to static warfare, defeat is likely. But not always.

Following the failure of the siege of Stralsund in 1628, Wallenstein and the Emperor were considering what to do with the huge Imperial army. Apart from the decision to intervene in the Mantuan war with two corps, and to send a corps under von Arnim to Poland, the Spanish were also pressing for cooperation in attacking the Dutch whose army was preoccupied in the siege of 's-Hertogenbosch. It was hoped that this an attack on the open flank of the Dutch would cause the siege to be relieved. After considerable diplomatic pressure and correspondence with Wallenstein and the Emperor, a further corps of 16,000 troops under Montecuccoli was sent into Westphalia to join the

Spanish army under Bergh, which had moved over to the flank of the Dutch fortress system. The Habsburg's combined Imperial-Spanish army, 16,000 Spaniards and 8,000 Imperialists, using the town of Wesel in Kleve (with its bridge over the Rhine) as a base, invaded the eastern part of the Dutch Republic, and captured Amersfoort.

The panic that this caused provoked the Dutch to raise a nation in arms. Henry was not to be bluffed out of his siege. The national army, which was bolstered by militia units, grew within weeks to the astonishing size of 128,000, including temporarily drafted sailors. Perhaps Rembrandt's *The Night Watch* were in the host, which included 13,000 Danish, German, Scottish, English, and French mercenaries recruited from the recently disbanded Danish army, following the Treaty of Lubeck. It was a force that the Spanish could not match, nor was the invasion from the east sustainable for logistical reasons not least because of the vast quantities of bread that needed to be milled for the large, combined army of 24,000.

Facilities in Wesel were too limited to cope with supply of bread on this scale, even though some captured watermills were put into commission. The long flank route for supplies was simply too long to keep the Spanish army in motion given the lack of local supplies. Especially problematic was the supply of fresh bread before it spoilt. Because of the slowness of wagon transport, a range of 60–70km- from a bread supply base was the maximum optimal range. Spanish troops had to depend on a long supply line from the south Netherlands running over 80 kilometres through Roermond, Venlo and Gelder to Wesel. Recognising the Spaniard's logistical difficulty, the Dutch estates evacuated the regions around the Imperial army to prevent trading with the enemy, although in this they were not entirely successful. Peasant farmers continued to sell grain to the Spaniards.

After Amersfoort the Spanish Imperialist army threat switched to the key city of Utrecht, which caused panic in the estates of Utrecht and Holland. In the Dutch camp at 's-Hertogenbosch the mood was gloomy: every soldier knew that their strivings in the trenches was about to come to nought, baring a miracle, because the siege would have to be raised to save the nation. On hearing the news, the Dutch soldiers 'hung down their heads like bulrushes'[7] in the morass in which they toiled. But holding his nerve, the indomitable Frederick Henry resisted political pressure for the abandonment of the siege to go to Utrecht's relief, believing the garrison to be strong enough to withstand until he captured 's-Hertogenbosch. Making up for his lack of flare with true grit, it was his finest moment as commander; 'denuding this army of more men, because for the advancement of our approaches, which have now been reached as afar as the town moats, (we) ourselves require more men, all the more because the enemy is gathering near Herentals. (another relief column).'[8](Frederick 14 August),

The Spanish army advanced too slowly to retain the initiative. Besides the supply situation deteriorated, Bergh's position became untenable when Ernest Casimir's commando raid by 2,500 Dutch troops, operating behind enemy lines, surprised and captured the Spanish army's weakly defended and ill prepared supply base at Wesel. 1,600 troops surrendered. There were not many successful surprise attacks on fortresses in the Thirty Years War, but this was one of them. No doubt glad to take part in some war of movement after the stultifying slog in the trenches, and lucky to be chosen to be taken out of the line to perform the service, Hexham described the attack with gusto, 'downe goes the bridge the horse (cavalry) stood before the port enters, the trumpets sound tantara, they scowre the streets, and drawes up in bataile into the market place de coup en pied, with their pistols in their hands. The Spaniards fled the Towne to the Sconces, our foote (infantry) follows the horse, besets the wall, and possesses all the guards, breakes downe the bridge, which lay over the Rhyne, and draue downe the streame towards Rees & sets fire on some sloopes and punts, which were on the other side of the water.'[9] From the evidence it seems that the Spanish guards on the gates were gulled into believing that the cavalry so boldly presenting themselves at the gate were Imperialists, so they lowered the draw bridge to let them in. Failure of vigilance or intelligence as to enemy movements, and lack of password security cost them dear. A pious and quite puritanical Hexham in the manner of a future Cromwell, thanked the Lord for his 'glorious work' and sang 'forth thy praises with the rest of the people.'[10] Wesel's governor would pay the price of the debacle with his head.

The Spanish invading army was not powerful enough nor its logistical lines secure. When a Dutch commando-style raid captured Wessel, the invasion was soon terminated. Nor would the invasion necessarily have succeeded because Amsterdam was a huge fortress system which would have been impenetrable except to the largest, well supplied and determined army. To the south of Amsterdam, the sluices would have drowned out the land forming a barrier running down to Dortrecht. The heart of the country and most of its population and economic capacity lay behind the barrier. Moreover, the attacking army was underpowered and when a huge militia army of over 100,000 was assembled the refusal of the Republic's military leader Frederick Henry to panic, meant that the threat was stared down. Never powerful enough nor supported by reserves, de Bergh's army was probably never expected to do more than an extended raid with the hope that 's-Hertogenbosch would be relieved. But the 'raid' did show up the strategic weakness of the Republic and reveal what might have been achieved if the Imperialists in Germany and the Spanish had more effectively cooperated and coordinated their strategies.

The fundamental vulnerability of the Dutch defensive line would be amply demonstrated in when Louis XIV army led by two great generals Turenne and Condé stormed through the eastern borders to capture Utrecht, thirty-six fortresses, and the eastern provinces of the Dutch Republic in 1672 (the year of the Rampjaar). Brought to heel, the Republic was forced to submit to an ignominious peace treaty at Nijmegen in 1678; it could have been worse. The comparisons to the history of the Maginot line and the French surrender are palpable; that there was not a complete surrender rested on the fortunes of geography which enabled the flooding of the Holland line to protect the heartlands of the Republic. The problem with chain defence systems is that they can be outflanked; moreover, they absorb huge resources and can lead to a false sense of security. Not all physical barriers were a waste. Except for the occasional raid, the Great Wall of China served as an effective barrier for some centuries. Eventually penetrated in 1644, it would be the weakness of Ming field armies which lost the empire to the Manchus.

Zasechnaya Cherta (the Great Abattis line) origins

The Great Abattis line was constructed from 1533 and finished in 1566; it runs in an arc running from in a line from the south of Kursk east toward Voronezh and Saratov on the Volga. It guarded against the Tartars whose raids into central Russia secured a flow of slaves and loot to Constantinople. Built from the plentiful forests of Russia, the line consisted off abatis driven into the ground, sometimes in multiple lines, and interspersed with wooden towers and stockaded strongpoints. The length of the line was about 600km long. Constructed to protect the heavily populated Muscovy region against Crimean Tartar raids which had developed in number and size since the mid-fifteenth century. Manned by 35,000–65,000, the garrison forces were backed up my mobile forces based at Tula numbering between 6,000 to 17,000. Tula was some 150km behind the open left flank of the line to guard against flanking sweeps by Tartar raiders. Tula would become the centre of the arms foundry business in Russia. New fortified cities developed included Serpukhov, Kolomna, Zaraysk, Ryazan and Belyov. Tambov and Ryazan were other major fortified cities behind the middle of the line, blocking the trail that led to Moscow. The vulnerability of the system was exposed when the Crimean Khan's army rolled over the defence and ravaged Moscow and the Muscovy region in 1571; an estimated 150,000 were hauled off into slavery, sold mainly into the Constantinople slave market.[11] Usually forced to convert to Islam, slaves mainly bought by the ruling classes were used as domestic servants, agricultural workers, concubines, or sex workers, and as soldiers.

The Abattis line was south of the Oka River line defences with extended for 250km but incomplete defences had provided an easy way through for raiders. From 1633 a new and additional line starting some 600 km south of Tula near

Voronezh and running up the Don River in an inverted L shape which left a gap of 450 kilometres to the Volga fortress line. As a result of the new defence lines, very large raids decreased but small raiding parties ensured that there was devastation and slaving enough to compensate. Perenkop the start point for the raids in the north of Crimea was 1100 kilometres from Moscow.

From 1500 to 1633 there were thirty-eight raids excluding minor ones. Size of raiding parties varied but could be as many as 20–30,000 even in the first half of the seventeenth-century. The main aim of the raids was to capture slaves for Constantinople's thriving slave market where needs included manpower for the Mediterranean galley fleets, as well as for domestic service and concubines. In 1644/45 the number of captives taken was 10,000 and 6,000. It has been estimated that 20,000 of the population was lost to slavery every year. Galloping through the Russian defence, each rider brought two spare horses. On the return journey the horses if still alive would be loaded with booty but most importantly the Tartars brought back slaves in a 1:3 ratio/captive to Tartar horseman.[12]

A major raid made at the same time as the siege of Smolensk 1632–3 by the Russians during the Thirty Yeas War, was another factor weakening the Russian army; many troops deserted from the main army to go to the south west and protect their homes against Tartar raiding. The raiding was probably encouraged by the Poles, but the Tartars would hardly have needed encouragement when forearmed with the knowledge that the abattis line had been denuded of troops.[13]

Zasechnaya Cherta [the Great Abattis line] in Russia does not seem to have been very successful in stopping raids but there were occasional successes when the Tartars overreached themselves. A major invasion in 1571 saw 150,000 slaves being captured and the Moscow suburbs and city burnt and pillaged.[14] When in 1572 the Crimean Khan supported by the Ottomans repeated his invasion across the fortified lines, they were crushed at the battle of Molodi just 40 kilometres south of Moscow near Podolsk; the Khan escaped with only 20,000 of his original 60,000 troops, losing his son and grandson in the battle[15]. It was a salutary lesson and there were no major raids for ten years thereafter. Fortress cities established at the end of the sixteenth century (see above) proved the Russian state's increasing determination to end the 'Steppe harvesting' of slaves. Only in 1598 was there a major success in turning back and defeating a large raid at the Oka line [Bank line] barrier just south of Moscow,[16] but the raiders had already passed through the abattis line and the Belgorod line; again, the main defence for a nation was a strong and victorious army not a static defensive barrier. But after the 1572 defeat, there was an interval before the raids continued though on a smaller scale in 1591, 1592, 1614, 1618 and 1632, when a Russian force was defeated outside Livny. It was a force weakened by the war with Poland at Smolensk. However, there were dozens of smaller raids even in the first half of the seventeenth-century with as many as an estimated

20,000 persons a year lost to slavery.[17] Raids did not stop until the Crimea was captured in 1783.

Defensive lines serve a political purpose and have an obvious simplistic appeal to rulers and the fearful populace of a state, whether it is Imperial China, the Habsburg empire, the Dutch Republic, or Imperial Russia; [or even Trump's wall with Mexico] Impressive in scale and cost they were less than impressive in actual effectiveness. Except for the narrow fronted Dutch lines, they did not stop or deter large armies or even determined raiders. As the battle of Molodi 1572 showed the key to defence was a strong army to which a defensive line can only have a supporting role; lines may delay and obstruct but generally they cannot stop; moreover, they were usually outflanked.

Even a strong army could not stop swift raiding by well mounted light cavalry. However, there were benefits to the establishment of chain defence because they made raids riskier; raiding may have been worse without them. Some sense of protection helped to give confidence to local populations as well as providing temporary refuge for when the scourge was over. However, this protection was sometimes not enough in the border areas of Hungary to prevent Ottoman raiders from imposing 'taxation' behind the military frontier; i.e., 'protection money.'[18] It is possible that the existence of the military frontier deterred Transylvania from developing a regular army with infantry and artillery because such attachments would have required a long wagon supply chain easily cut off by the garrison troops. Light cavalry alternatively could come and go as they pleased; but as a mere raiding force effectiveness was thereby limited. The Dutch defence system supported by a strong army was successful in shutting out the mighty Spanish army, but they were lucky that the Habsburgs did not coordinate their forces for a big push from the east. They lost their chance; after the entry of Sweden and the victory of Breitenfeld 1631, the opportunity never arose again. Lucky too were the Habsburgs. They faced their existential threat during the Thirty Years War with an unusually quiescent and troubled Ottoman state on their southern border. Had the Ottomans exploited the problems of the Habsburgs and rolled northwards with 100,000 troops, the military frontier would have availed the Habsburgs very little....and world history would be very different. After 1633 raids into the Muscovy area ceased for a while as the army modernized and improved its capability but numerous raids official and unofficial continued. Nogai Tartars rode for fifty-five days up the Muskarsky trail, taking high ground between river basins. Advancing through Livny, Tula and Serpukhov to the environs of Moscow, about 1,000km from their starting point at Perekop on the Crimean isthmus. As the Russian state modernised its armed forces, the line was moved down to 300km below the Great Abattis line in 1650. By 1680 it had been lowered again to the Izium line with Russian fortresses just 150km from the Black Sea. In the seventeenth-century, Peter the Great and Catherine the Great would be taking the fight into the Crimea.

Along the Volga fortress cities guarded the flanks of Russia at Saratov, Tsaritsyn [Stalingrad] and Samara, all established at the end of the sixteenth century; inland fortresses were constructed on the abattis line at Livny 1586, Voronezh 1586, and Kursk 1587. The point was that lines effectiveness and the ability to advance them depended on a powerful standing army. However, raiding would continue into the late eighteenth century. As at Kursk 1943, Putin's barrier of defences in Zaporizhzhia oblast in occupied Ukraine, laded with huge deep minefields and anti-tank traps/bunkers in multiple lines has been highly effective. similarly formidable were Rommel's defensive wall at el Alemain. effectiveness of barriers depend on a complex matrix of topographical and military factors, the most important question being, 'can it be flanked'? El-Alamein could not be flanked because of the Qattara depression; so it was only broken by great superiority in men and material, something not available to the Ukrainian army. Defensive barriers are optimal when they are short, flanked by impassable geographic barriers, offer defence in depth, and are back by a strong army.

Name of fixed defence systems in military history:- effectiveness evaluation based on length of time in operation and effectiveness in stopping incursions/attacks. 1–3, 4–7, 8–10	Poor 1–3	Good 4–7	Very good 8–10	Method of penetration and comments
Roman defences against the Barbarians-*Limes Pannonicus/Limes* *Samatiae*-30 BC to circa AD 400 420 km long		5		So long that it was hard to maintain and finance-easy to penetrate and or outflank. Eventually overwhelmed by numbers and economic and political collapse. Weakness-great length, remoteness, topographical difficulty, shortage of manpower relative to length
Hadrian's Wall AD 122–410 117 km. Stone wall and intermittent strong points and forts.			9	Eventually collapsed as the Roman empire declined due to economic problems and internal strife; but like Roman defences in Germany and the Pannonian Limes, it was effective for a long time, 300 years, but was abandoned when the Roman empire was collapsing.
Great Wall China Variously from 7th century BC. Ming 1368 to 1644/21,000 km/2200 fortifications			7	Eventually penetrated at weak points after centuries 1644-Ming militarily weaker (and internal strife/decadence) than Manchus; weakness-great length, remoteness, shortage of manpower relative to length.
Military frontier-Habsburg Balkans 15th to 17th century 1000km + Major 120 forts and strongpoints defended by 22,000 permanent troops, 50/50 infantry and cavalry.	3			Easy to penetrate or outflank by light cavalry. Eventually Habsburg modernisation and declining Turkish power-economy led to victory for the Empire. Weakness-great length, remoteness, topographical difficulty, shortage of manpower relative to length.
Russian Zachesnaya Cherta (Great Abattis line) 14th 18th centuries Circa 700 km and guarded by 35–60,000 troops.	4			Easy to penetrate or outflank, by Tartar horsemen. Eventual Russian victory was due to improved military and greater resources. weakness-great length, remoteness, shortage of manpower relative to length. Felled trees barricade on raised ramparts, ditches, palisaded strongpoints, watch towers and interspersed with natural features of lakes and marshes. The width of the abattis approx. 200 m. Interspersed with kremlins in major garrison towns and cities such as Tula, Orel, Kursk, Voronezh, Belgorod, Simbirsk

Dutch defence lines 16th-17th . 80 years war. Circa 200 km southern border defence. Intermittent but densely populated fortified towns and subsidiary works, and the Dutch Waterline, flood/dyke defences) protecting Holland's eastern flank; Amsterdam to Dortrecht. started 1629; length70 km.			8	Very effective network of fortress defences in Brabant bordering Spanish Flanders, with 13 main bastions, eg Bergen op Zoom, and Breda, and multiple subsidiary fortifications. But danger of flanking weakly defended eastern flank province of Utrecht remained. Spain could not must enough resources to break through in a war of attrition. The Dutch deployed circa 70,000, including a mobile army of 20,000 excluding militias. Spanish troops in the army of Flanders approx. 75–90,000 excluding militias. On several occasions some 30,000 extra troops deployed on the Dutch eastern flank but never strong enough to overwhelm fortress and flood defences.
Gustavus's defensive lines in Poland's ducal Prussia 1625–29/circa 170 km. redoubts, Teutonic forts, and masked cannon.			8	Effective use of interior lines with fast stressars (flat bottom sailing barge) to counter threats on exterior lines; Swedish artillery, musket firepower, and entrenchments kept larger armies at bay; Forward fortresses at Mewe, Stuhm, Strasburg, and Wormditz acted as breakwaters to Polish attacks in front of 7 other garrison towns along the fortress line.
General Lee's confederate defence lines, June-March 1864–5 trench systems, redoubts, cheval de frise, and masked cannon around Richmond and Petersburg, circa 90km; American Civil War.		7		Effective in holding off a Union army more than double the size, but eventually outflanked by superior manpower and attrition. Circa 60,000 and 120,000 troops confederate/Union. Overwhelmed by Union economic and logistic power just as the confederate supply and logistics spiralled downwards resulting in 25,000 desertions. Weaknesses also increased as defences lengthened to prevent outflanking-so manpower to length became an increasing problem.
WWI defence lines on Western fronts 1914–18 760 km of trenches and barbed wire usually dug in three lines and interspersed with strongpoints with cover from machine guns and artillery.		7		Very effective as shown by the casualty figures in stalemate for most of the war but eventually vulnerable to firepower, high explosives, and tanks in well organised attacks. Victory of resources and firepower superiority. Undermined by German economic weakness and internal collapse-revolution.

Hindenburg Line; as above. Arras to Reims approx. 170 km		6		Defence in depth, three trench lines, deep bunkers to protect troops against artillery, barbed wire. However, tanks and concentrated firepower in rolling barrages would defeat it.
Maginot line 1925–40, France. Concrete fortifications, gun, machine gun turrets. Never tested in battle, mines, and barbed wire. 432 km.	2			Outflanking was easy by attacks through the Ardennes and Belgium. The most notoriously useless defensive line in history
Rommel's defence line El Alamein 1942. 80 km. Very deep minefields and barbed wire covered by the famously deadly 88mm anti-tank cannon		6		Fairly short and protected on the flanks by Qattara depression and the Sea to the north. Eventually penetrated by overwhelming firepower, manpower, airpower, and attrition tactics. Victory of resources and logistics capacity and determined attack in attritional warfare.
Defence line at Kursk 1943; defence in depth with antitank traps, pill boxes, barbed wire, mines, and entrenchment. 576 km long defended by			10	Hard to outflank. Very effective in degrading German power and opening the way for a counter-attack. Attrition: the victor won by military superiority and resources incl manpower with huge reserves of tanks, aircraft, and cannon. Germans 0.9m/Soviets 1.7 m and respectively 2900/5100 tanks.
West Wall/WWII-Siegfreid Line 1940–45. Length 630 km with 18,000 bunkers. Hedgehog tank traps and ditches copied by Russians 2022–2025		4		Penetrated by huge firepower and overwhelming resources ad outflanked.
De Lattre lines in Indochina 1952–54. Concrete fortresses place intermittently; protected by rings of barbed wire, typically four machine gun posts and a 75mm cannon in a turret with covering fire from a battery of 105mm howitzers. 378 km long.	3			Easy to penetrate for infiltrating Vietminh units entering the key Red Delta area, but made rice trade to Vietminh difficult. Not enough resources for effective defence amid an often-hostile population. Weakness-great length, remoteness, topographical difficulty, shortage of manpower relative to length. 1200 individual fortified blockhouse and 250 clusters of blockhouses (3–6) protecting fire bases of mutually supporting 105mm cannon.

DMZ Vietnam. 10 km wide strip some 100 km long between north and south Vietnam.	2			Easy to outflank along the Ho Chi Minh trail in Lao and Cambodia. Not enough resources for effective defence amid a hostile population Weakness-great length, remoteness, topographical difficulty in mountainous jungle terrain, shortage of manpower relative to length.
Zaporizhzhia-Donetsk, 2022–23 Russian lines of defence on the Mariupol front. Approx. 230 km			9	Impossible to outflank due to the Dnipro River, defence in depth/10 km deep belts of mines and three main lines as at Kursk with anti-tank traps, pill boxes and protected by massed artillery. Outflanking possible in Kherson-but logistically constrained by Dnipro River and similar defences. Similar to Kursk in WW2 or El Alamein but with Ukraine lacking in manpower, ammunition, air power, Ukraine's attack was bound to fail despite superior precision weapons. With fewer manpower resources and limited ammunition, attrition is not a good strategic option for Ukraine.

Chapter XII

Fortress Campaigns 1632: Ingolstadt and Benfeld

The siege of Benfeld is little covered in histories of the Thirty Years War. It is a seventeenth-century classics of the genre, little known because a few days after its conclusion the battle of Lützen would take place some 1000 kilometres away. At that battle the hero of Sweden and Protestant Europe, Gustavus Adolphus, was shot down in the fog and smoke cloaked battle that was a most brutal and defining point in a most prolonged and bloody war. So, the history and significance of what happened at Benfeld has been entirely lost. In this section we look at a campaign leading up to a siege; it includes the short siege of Ingolstadt earlier in 1632 which is also little noted by historians. These sieges are instructive because a siege was normally much more than a simple attack on a walled town or city. Major sieges were normally part of a wider campaign and strategy; the groundwork and manoeuvres leading up to a siege had to be carefully choreographed.

After wintering at Mainz in 1631–2 impatient Gustavus broke out early from winter quarters to launch a fast and full-blooded strike at Bavaria to destroy Tilly's Bavarian Imperialist army and knock Maximilian's Bavaria out of the war. He was also determined to recover from a sharp blow to Swedish military prestige when Tilly launched a surprise strike at an exposed Swedish column at Bamberg where a corps under General Horn, with incomplete field defences, had been driven off from the town with some considerable loss.

United with Horn's battered corps, Gustavus drove south. Confronted by Tilly's army on the strong river line at Lech on the border with Bavaria, Gustavus's full genius was deployed in outflanking and smashing the Bavarian army on the Lech. Famed General Tilly was mortally wounded in the fight while Maximilian scuttled from the battlefield leaving Munich defenceless against a rampant Swedish army. He holed up in his powerful new fortress and magazine at Ingolstadt. Gustavus followed.

Maximilian was safely established in fortress, hoping no doubt that he would not be bottled up in a long siege; he spent his time frantically begging for help, even penning a pleading and unctuous letter to his erstwhile political enemy Wallenstein, '…I would entreat your honour not only to have the goodness to grant the bearer, von Toring, a friendly audience … Written this day in my fortress of Ingolstadt April 1632. P.S. the enemy grows daily stronger and is far superior to us in numbers. If your honour does not make speed and force a change, he will break through. He now lusts after the Danube and Austria. Your honour's most well disposed uncle.'

As for Ingolstadt, its investment would have taken some months because Ingolstadt was one of the few modern fortresses in Germany with 'trace Italienne', low profile, star shaped defences, and hornworks. The place, which served as a major Bavarian logistical base, was never seriously besieged during the entire war. Ingolstadt also deployed a huge garrison of 10,500 troops. A siege would have broken the momentum of the Swedish advance on Munich. The old-fashioned method of capturing fortresses by treachery was tried but the plot was discovered, 'Then we went back through Ingolstadt to the other side of the river, for the Danube River runs near Ingolstadt.' Hagendorf informs us, 'The residents of Ingolstadt then fired heavily on the Swedes with cannons, so that the king's horse was shot out from underneath him. An attempt was made to take the fortress by treachery. Count Farensbach, was caught in a failed plot to deliver who would some days later be judged by the sword at Regensburg…'[1] Then a Swedish night time probing attack by 1,500 men on the key sconce giving access to the bridge before the town was decisively beaten off 'with musket and with fire-workes (grenades)…leaving three hundred men killed about the Skonce…'[2].

Not surprisingly Gustavus moved on to easier pickings. He realized that a long siege would take many months so costing him the momentum that he craved. Bypassing Ingolstadt which was a powerful modern fortress, magazine, and rallying point for the Bavarian army, Gustavus moved on to the capital Munich where he feasted on that city's wealth, its brimful magazine, hundreds of cannons, and cultural treasures.

Failing to take Ingolstadt however had a cost and consequence because the possession of this one powerful fortress enabled Maximilian to maintain a strategic and logistics base in Bavaria even in the darkest times which would become the mooring point for his defeated or retreating armies to recover from their losses. In the longer-term Maximilian's retention of Ingolstadt paid rich dividends for his pre-war investment enabling him to stave off defeat for much longer than might otherwise have been the case as well as keeping an important magazine as a base for the future recovery of his principality. Conversely for Gustavus, Ingolstadt would have been a major gain because it could act as a very defensible magazine in south central Germany and springboard for an offensive against Vienna in either in the Autumn of 1633 or the spring of 1634. Gustavus needed a finely balanced calculation on the pros and cons of tying his army into a static and risky siege. Alternatively he could execute the sort of mobile warfare that better suited his army and would yield other rich pickings, as well as opportunities to smash the enemy's main field army. There was no right answer.

Gustavus's impatience was noted by Monro, 'against either town or fort I never did see in his majesty's time one breach or shot entered....'[3]. Gustavus excelled in open warfare and a war of sieges would bog down the campaign, which he was clearly determined to finish as quickly as possible. Nevertheless, Ingolstadt was an exception in that Gustavus had little need for long sieges because he either stormed the places or used his reputation for terror to induce a smart surrender as Scottish Colonel Munro further explained, '....his fortune being such, and his diligence so great that his enemies did ever parley before they would abide the fury of his cannon, as at Brandenburg, Demmin, Frankfurt, Mainz, Donauworth, Augsburg and divers more; and in my opinion, the terror the cannon breeds is as much feared as the execution that follows.'[4] Swedish use of cannon was certainly a war-winning instrument both on the battlefield and at sieges, and its potency was well recognised by contemporaries. Nevertheless even the largest siege train would not enable Gustavus to quickly deliver Ingolstadt. Gustavus lived dangerously as usual but even his nerve may have wobbled a little when one of his entourage at Ingolstadt, a young paladin, the Margrave of Baden, had his head removed by a cannon ball. Then on reconnaissance another cannon ball strike ripped a leg off Gustavus's grey horse. Even with cannon, troops, and munitions aplenty there was no chance to breach Ingolstadt's superb defences save by a very long siege of attrition, which would take months, and even then, might not be successful. He chose to snap off Duke Maximilian's Bavarian capital at Munich instead.

At Munich, Gustavus was accompanied by a jubilant and gloating Frederick V Palatine, who enjoyed the *schadenfreude* of the moment by prancing through the corridors of Maximilian's palace: no doubt Frederick bathed in the warm glow of revenge for the looting of the fine library at Heidelberg which had been sent to the Vatican. In the event it was Gustavus who orchestrated the reciprocal looting for the benefit of Sweden. (Frederick had formerly been exiled from his principality by the military actions of Bavarian General Tilly and Spanish General Cordoba) In general, Gustavus allowed his troops to operate a brutal regime in Bavaria, probably because of the principality's Catholicism as well as in revenge for the rapacious behaviour of Bavarian troops and elector in Protestant Germany. 'At this time, much robbing and plundering took place, particularly in the countryside,'[5] The brutality of the conflict led to a sort of guerrilla war with peasants ambushing isolated parties of soldiers, killing them then mutilating their bodies. On one occasion fifty Scots soldiers died in this manner, having their eyes gouged out and suffering other revolting mutilations. According to an officer in the Swedish army von Chemnitz, some soldiers were 'set upon... and most cruelly executed...(they) cut off their hands and feet, poked eyes out, cut off noses, and (pardon the liberty) private parts'.[6] (von Chemnitz would become an important constitutional expert and an adviser to Swedish crown)

Gustavus was hard on Bavaria as an act of deliberate policy because he hoped to knock Maximilian out of the war and destroy the wealthy principality's will to wage war. As always for Gustavus and any army on campaign, the key emphasis was on the collection of food, and fodder. '... at that time a strong force of Swedes came, 4,000 on horses and on foot, with large numbers of wagons, and they threshed all the grain in the field around our village... and took all to their camp. They also took the hay from our village, as well as cabbages in the gardens, the apples and pears, the whole lot. They left us not the least thing.'[7] Bavaria as an enemy land was fair game, although friendly territories could also suffer random theft by their own soldiery. Where there were excesses however, including serious crimes against Bavarian citizens, there was punishment by hanging which included five Swedish soldiers and others in 1632[8]. Harshness against Bavaria was necessary because Maximilian had ordered uncompromising resistance against the invader. So, to induce towns and cities to offer contribution required special measures. When '*salvaguardia* terms' were agreed Maximilian was furious, 'he accused his people of disloyalty, ingratitude and malice.'[9] Some of Maximilian's peasants revolted also against Bavarian troops in 1632 and 1634[10], seeing little or no difference between them and the sometimes rapacious Swedes. Many Bavarian farmers ignored Maximilian's injunctions and complaints, happily sold grain, and produce to the Swedes.

Around Protestant Ulm at this time, it was reported that soldiers paid for their food, 'They bought up all the available bread, meat, beer, as well as grain and other things.'[11] Ulm was a friendly Protestant city in a sea of Catholicism area, but further to the west, Gustavus was able to link up with the Duke of Württemberg, the main Protestant power in the south west of Germany who emerging from the ban of empire had renewed his rebellion against Ferdinand. He was given a 'great supply of men, moneys, victuals, and ammunition for his armies'[12] noted Munro. Württemberg raised 8,000 men for the Protestant cause. Typical of Gustavus financial/geopolitical strategy he fanned out his forces around the Swabian region, according to Monro 'to helpe his contribution as Memmingen, Pibrach, Brandenburg on the river Elve (Elue), as also Middleham, Kawffbire, and Kempten on the Leacke (Lech)...'[13] Risings in the south and linking up to friendly Protestant Imperial cities was exactly what Gustavus had hoped and planned for when he invaded north Germany in June 1630.

Gustavus's troops conquered much of Swabia but failed to suppress all the banditry and low-level guerilla warfare against his troops and their supply lines as they foraged and requisitioned foodstuffs. Rumours of an Imperialist advance on Ulm impelled him in May 1632 to take the defences of this important allied city in hand; General Ruthven as appointed its commander of the city;

he quickly raised two additional cavalry units. At his point, Gustavus decided that he must hurry back in the direction of Bavaria in the face of rumours that his key ally Saxony was negotiating with the emperor through the restored offices of Generalissimo Wallenstein. Fearing for his communications back to the coast and indeed for the stability of his alliance structure on Germany with the moderate Lutheran states, he needed to be nearer to Saxony and ready to take on a resurgent Wallenstein led Imperialist army. Moreover, the wealthy Protestant stronghold at Nuremberg had yet to be taken into safekeeping and by taking it in hand Gustavus could secure 300,000 Reichsthaler in funding at a place more strategically convenient for both watching Saxony and as a jumping off point to invading Austria by the direct route through Regensburg and Passau. Just 230 kilometres from his magazine at Erfurt, it was an excellent alternative to Ingolstadt although that fortress would lie uncomfortably on his lines of communication.

Not wishing to abandon his extensive gains in south west Germany as well as the possibilities of invading Alsace and on the left bank of the Rhine, Gustavus restarted his 'starburst' strategy, tasking Field Marshal Horn with a detached command to subdue Swabia (Württemberg) and link up with the renascent Protestant forces in the south. He would in due course be instructed to move across to the left bank of the Rhine to link up with Gustavus's to main paladin allies in Alsace, the Rhinegrave Otto Ludwig and Count Birkenfeld. They were to secure the left bank of the Rhine up to Trier and Koblenz then attack Alsace which was a mixed kaleidoscope of Habsburg holdings and members of the empire. As a territory holder in Alsace General Birkenfeld would be a useful ally in conquering for Sweden this rich province. Meanwhile the Duke of Württemberg moved back to take further places in Swabia and threaten the Konstanz area providing a distraction and diversion from Horn's efforts.

After securing the left bank beyond Sweden's main base at Mainz, at Koblenz and Trier, in a battle at Wiesloch to the south of Heidelberg on 16 August 1632, General Horn defeated the capable Count Montecuccoli. The victory created the all-important strategic space for the next phase of Horn's campaign; he then crossed to the left bank of the Rhine, having captured the small Rhine harbour at Kenzingen on the 5 September.

He joined his allies on the other side. Birkenfeld, like many Protestant paladins in southern Germany, had rallied to Gustavus after the spectacular victory at Breitenfeld. He had spent the early months of 1632 capturing small townships around his patrimony based at Bischwiller in Alsace. In another victory which secured Horn's flank, General Patrick Ruthven defeated a force under the duke of Baden near Kempten on the eastern side of Württemberg.

Horn captured Kitzingen on the Breisgau side of the upper Rhine on the 5 September. With his rear covered, and the west bank in the hands of allies

Horn crossed over to the west bank with about 10,000 troops he was soon establishing close contact with his Sweden's allies in Strasburg which lies twenty kilometres to the west of the city and on the same river that feeds into the Rhine near Breisach. Strasburg was a good choice of base; an enthusiastic Protestant ally the city was full of goodwill for the venture against Benfeld. This powerful fortress city was a Catholic Bishopric loyal to the emperor; not only a rich territory but a great danger to nearby Strasburg; Benfeld was a thorn that had to be removed to secure Alsace's rich territory. Willingly the citizens of Strasburg would provide cash, munitions, and victuals, and even four cannons at a critical moment in the siege. Strasbourg was a most conveniently located logistics base and magazine for Horn's assault on the fortress of Benfeld.

And Horn needed all the help he could get because the fortress a mighty edifice consisted of a modern, low profile 'five point' star-shaped fortification in the *trace italienne* mode with sloping sides to deflect shot; it had been twenty years in construction. Horn placed his main camp on the eastern side of the fortress with direct road link to Strasbourg and near access to the Rhine for ease of supply. A contemporary map of the siege shows the usual fortified line of circumvallation around the fortress. The map shows parallels constructed on the south east side and a subsidiary camp guarding the supply road to Rhinau on the Rhine. The south side of the fortress was protected by seemingly impassable and extensive marshland though which ran three main streams and a myriad of rivulets punctuated by an occasional small island. The contemporary publication, *Swedish Intelligencer*, described it thus, 'five cornered, the walls strongly beset, with towers and roundels the bulwarks thick lofty with the wett ditches about the wall was strongly pallisaded with some outworks to it.' From contemporary prints we can see how accurate the description was. The place whose circumference was not long was adequately defended by 800 musketeers and 140 cavalry besides the local militia. Additionally, the fortress was 'excellent well provided… of victuals and ammunition.'

Luckily Horn was a highly skilled soldier with training and experience in the engineering of siege warfare. He had partaken for example in the siege of long siege Riga in 1621 at which he was wounded as well as many subsequent smaller sieges. Earlier in life he had studied siegecraft under the master tutelage of Maurice of Nassau, the foremost expert in Europe. In the late twenties, while Gustavus was battling the Poles round Danzig, he had commanded the defence of Swedish Livonia (Latvia) against the Poles. Married to Swedish Chancellor Oxenstierna's daughter in 1628 he was a most trusted regime loyalist and Gustavus's military deputy. At Breitenfeld 1631, Horn's fast reaction in refusing the Swedish left flank upon the disintegration of their Saxon allies, both contributed significantly to saving and winning the glorious Swedish victory.

Horn moved to surround Benfeld; by the 8 September the place was sealed shut.

One weakness of the fortress was the extra mural suburb attaching to the southeastern wall which had not been completely cleared by the time the siege began. However, as this suburb backed on to the miasma and rivulets it seemed that no great danger from this 'dead zone' and blockage to a clear field of fire. However, Horn's experience came into play; he understood the opportunity of a covered approach provided by Benfeld's suburbs which could be exploited by driving a covered gallery over the rivulets from the least expected direction of attack. Further, to ease the problem posed by the rivulets, and moat water Horn ordered his 'spade men' (as described by the *Swedish Intelligencer*, a London news-sheet), to dig out alterntive channels to divert the water impediments.

The Imperialists were not slothful in trying to raise the siege. Apart from numbers of sallies from the town, Count Solms, sibling of an August Imperialist family, swore to raise the siege. With six thousand men and a thousand cavalry Count Solms approached the Swedish lines, however Horn gathering in his troop, forced back the Imperialist horde to a town some twelve miles distant. Maintaining his efforts, but with other demands on his troops, Solms had difficulty billeting and holding together his scratch force. He made constant summons for reinforcement from outlying Imperialist garrisons round Alsace but raids in force made by Swedish forces kept the Imperialists on the run, unable to muster safely within range of Benfeld.

Meanwhile the digging and construction of the covered gallery continued. Intermittent sallies from the fort at night saw trenches being filled in. But the works were only delayed. By mid-September the gallery had been built from the south south east over the rivulets and was approaching the outer moat covered by the suburb buildings, now mostly ruined. All the while during construction cannon and sharpshooters put the diggers under fire, however Horn provided covering fire to sweep the ramparts. His cannon protected behind gabions in their gun-pits played upon the enemy's artillery, dismounting many; Swedish fire was said to be so intense that 'there was no man ...able to appear upon the bulwarks... though the town had kept some pieces of canon yet un-dismounted upon their walls yet hardly durst a cannoneer try by them'. Such was the effectiveness of the covering fire that thirty Swedes had already tested the defences on the 13 September by moving into a dead zone under the walls of the town.

On the eastern end of the siege Horn drove forward trenches, traverses, and saps towards the enemy outworks on that side of the city; an alternative line of approach to the fortress it kept the enemy guessing as to which line of attack was the '*schwerpunkt*'.

On the 26 the gallery went over the outer moat and into the suburbs where Swedish musketeers digging out loopholes with their knives and swords gave covering fire to the spade men. Horn's pioneer used rubble to fill in the moats and as a base for the planking of the galleries. To maintain the works and protect the labourers, Horn constructed a large redoubt half way across the rivulets and moats.

By the 8 October, Horn's works were near enough to mount a furious assault on the town, but it failed. On the 13 October Benfeld's commander sought to play for time by offering a truce while an expected relief force was assembled. The truce was refused.

With about 7,000 troops in his Imperialist army Count Solms mounted an attack on the Swedish lines on the 15 October, coordinated by a sally from the town. Once again, the attacks were fended off.

Following this attempted relief the Rhinegrave Otto Ludwig beat up the mustering places of the enemy, disturbing Solm's plan for further relief efforts. Riding out with 500 horse 500 dragoons and one thousand command muskets he ambushed elements of the retreating enemy. He cut down 300 of the enemy and took 150 prisoners. With a remarkable persistence Solms refused to give up; stripping garrisons as far away as Frankenthal, Heidelburg, Colmar, and many smaller places he hoped to bring about 10,000 troops together, but this never proved possible. Reinforcement was demanded by the Imperialist forces at Konstanz by threats from 10,000 Württembergers who feinted in that direct under the rejuvenated and restored duke.

At Benfeld an attack from a hundred horse from a sally port was beaten back. The gallery came ever nearer such that labourers could start to dig a tunnel beneath the thick walls. Defenders responded by counter-mine digging. A troglodyte tussle ensued.

France sent a welcome reinforcement of 600; not yet officially at war, Richelieu nonetheless was completely aware of the strategic importance of this fortress magazine. Strasbourg sent four more cannon.

More assaults were launched on the fortress ramparts with an ensign heroically snatching an Imperial standard amidst a hail of shot.

On the 25 October Horn went into the gallery directing the mining himself.

On the 26 October instructions were given to prime the mine with gunpower.

By the end of the 27 October the mine was set and the tunnel tamped so as to send the force upwards; just the fuse trail led back to the gallery. Perceiving that the mine was ready to be blown, fortress commander Bulach sent out a letter heralded by trumpets, asking for leave to request delivery of the said letter to the Bishop of Strasburg. Bulach explained the dire situation in the fortress with a suggestion that he receive leave to surrender. A three-day truce was requested to give time for delivery, consideration, and reply; a last desperate effort to buy time the offer was refused. In the mould of Gustavus, Horn held up the message, refused the truce, and demanded immediate capitulation. It was a canny move by the commandant Colonel Bulach who was trying to finesse that fine and deadly line between surrendering properly and honourably, so obviating the risk of execution for cowardice by his own side and seeing his breach overwhelmed. In such an event the garrison would be massacred, the place subject to rapine and looting for several days; he himself would likely be cut down or skewered in the melee.

On 27 October evening the mine was sprung. A breach appeared through a cloud of dust and falling masonry; the Swedish army sprang to the attack and was met at the breach where ferocious fighting ensued all night, all day and into the night again.

Horn fed men into the gaping tumbled wound of the fort to relieve the fallen, the injured, or exhausted. Even dismounted troopers were deployed into the firestorm. The soldiery, bursting with adrenalin, anger, and greed for booty, pleaded with their Horn not to accept an armistice so as to secure the rights of pillage and rapine.

However, on the 29 October, with no hope of relief and the Imperialist commandant's own troops started hanging white flags from the walls. Terms were negotiated and agreed in thirteen points, covering the manner of the garrison's withdrawal. Freedom of religion was granted including the Catholic one, and the usual rights to liberty and free enjoyment of property and chattels were granted to citizens, officials, and soldiers alike. Prisoners were exchanged without ransom. Wounded soldiers could freely be transported out or could tarry until recovered. However, except for private chattels all munitions, victuals, stored weapons, and defenders' artillery became the property of the Swedes, except two pieces; (in time honoured tradition). The administration of the town would be given up to the city of Strasbourg, a fact not pleasing to a citizenry jealous of their status and independence as the bishop's seat.

At the appointed time on the 30 October, 400 of the garrison marched out with 120 horse; another company of foot soldiers (about 100 men) defected to the Swedish army. They marched 'out with colours flying, drummes beating, matches lighted, bullet in the mouth…. with two field pieces; pledges being given'. The facts imply a casualty rate of about three hundred killed and wounded.

Benfeld would remain in the possession of Sweden until the end of the war, being eventually handed back in 1650. Its possession guaranteed that Alsace's political colour would in the main remain attached to Franco-Swedish cause despite the furore caused the controversial defection of Bernhard of Saxe-Weimar from Swedish to French service. Keeping hold of the fortress meant that great stores and a strong garrison could always be maintained and dominate the area. Alsace was swiftly brough under Swedish control as all the small towns roundabout, with their small garrisons were captured by the Rhinegrave's cavalry. About a week after the fall Field Marshal Horn would learn of the death of Gustavus Adolphus at Breitenfeld. Together with Bernhard of Saxe-Weimar he was elevated to be the joint commander of the Swedish armies.

In due course the securing of Alsace was an inestimable benefit to the anti-Habsburg coalition. Saxe-Weimar would use it as a logistics base for his astonishing and brilliant campaign in 1637–38 which was one of the crucial turning points in the course of the war. Alsace would be ceded to French control under the Treaties of Westphalia.

The siege campaign and sack of Leicester 1645

Charles I left Oxford in the new campaigning year on 7 May with his sights set on taking back control of the Midlands. However, it was a slovenly beginning. Prince Rupert had been champing at the bit to get started. Meanwhile, Cromwell with the New Model Army had been active in attacking royalist assets around Oxford. Firstly, he beat up several elite royalist regiments, taking several hundred prisoners, then he moved on Bletchford house which surrendered when summoned despite a strong garrison of 150 musketeers. Its governor, Colonel Windebank had a young wife in tow, so he surrendered without a fight which relieved Cromwell who 'did much doubt the storming of the house, it being strong and well manned'[14]; Saving himself from being killed by the storming party under the rules of war, Windebank was duly shot by the royalists for cowardice. Cromwell moved on to Brampton-in-the Bush 18 miles from Oxford where he captured another 250 prisoners. However, he failed to storm Farringdon Castle near Oxford, where the officer leading the assault was pushed off a ladder with a pike and landed in a ditch.

The king marched to Stow-on-the-Wold and towards Worcester into Staffordshire, capturing a number of places *en route*, all the while drawing in garrisons from around the midlands and the north, such as Cheshire, Derbyshire, and Lancashire etc. By 13 May the King's army was in Droitwich, by 25 May at Burton-on Trent, and by 27 May in Ashby de la Zouche.[15] Loughborough was next; The direction of travel pointed to the county city of Leicester in the central midlands. Picking up the trail Cromwell and Fairfax started to rally a Parliamentary army of about 14,000.

Leicester's defenders under Colonel Grey, the younger brother of the Earl of Kent, tried desperately to pull in reinforcement meanwhile, having picking up rumours of an imminent attack. There was a garrison of 950 infantry and 100 dragoons plus 1000 militia men who had been called into service. Other nearby Parliamentary garrison, for example at Cole Orton with 350 soldiers and plentiful cannon, declined to participate in the dice game of war.[16] The garrison totalled about 1750–2220. They faced about 11,000 men equipped with twelve cannon and two mortars, a battery of which was soon erected by Prince Rupert on top of old Roman earthworks. The city's defence were not strong with one section, the Newark quarter on the south east, being particularly weak because one of the Aldermen hold property there and did not want it bisected by a wall or diverse constructions. Outworks on the western side of the city included three major hornworks. Preparatory to a siege it was normal to knockdown houses abutting the walls or interfering with the field of fire or likely to be used to give shelter to enemy marksmen. After the war, tailor William Summer, petitioned the mayor and aldermen concerning his terrible losses. He claimed compensation because his townhouse had been demolished and his orchard cut down before the assault took place because they had compromised the defences. During the fighting his son was killed, his possessions were ransacked by royalist soldiers, while 'with the fright whereof your petitioner's wife hath beene distracted ever synce'. Other petitioners Frances Stevens and Constance Brewin petitioned money in compensation for their loss of their husbands had both served and died during the assault. The two widows who had 'falne into great want and povertie', were claiming as of right 'as by Ordinance of Parliament is mentioned to be allowed'.

On 30 May, Rupert called on the city to surrender by formal summons. There were divisions in the siege committee, but the response was defiant. With time up mortar bombs rained down on the city and the cannonade to open a breach began at 3pm. Attacks would be made from the east of the city because the river Soare and its rivulets in flood during the spring made attack from the west impracticable

Impatient to succeed Rupert ordered a night attack against a breach in the curtain wall which had been quickly blocked up by a breastwork of woolsacks which were plentiful in a country famous for its sheep. Royalist troops, including Prince Rupert's Blue Coats advanced in four columns against the three bastions guarding the west side. There was heavy fighting around the woolsack barrier where the royalist were twice repulsed. With the focus on the woolsacks other attacks stretched the Leicester defences which enabled Astley's regiments to break into the town where fighting continued in the streets. Another hornwork was captured using grenades and likewise at Gallowtree Gate, grenades were the essential weapon. With the gates open cavalry rushed in to add to the mayhem in the streets. Major Bunnington of Rupert's regiment was 'shot in the eye just as he was on top of the ladder.... 'Cavaliers swarmed through the city, capturing the Roundhead's main battery. 'In the meantimes,' it was recorded that, 'the foot gott in and fell to plunder, so that ere day fully open there scares a cottage unplundered. There were many Scots in the towne, and no quarter was given to any in the heat.' It is likely that the Scots tag was just an excuse for anyone to be cut down, men and women. The darkness of night hid the horrors of the sack. After plunder soldiers turned to the drink in the cellars, both beer and wine. We have no information on rape but there must have been many. Shaping his usual dig at Rupert Clarendon the king's counsellor wrote that 'the conquerors pursued their advantage with the utmost licence and miserably sacked the whole town without distinction of people or places to the exceeding regret of the king'; mere crocodile tears because this was the normal usage of war. A London newspaper *Mercurius Civicus* referred to the action as 'The bloudy massacre' of Leicester, but as with the gothic tales of the siege of Magdeburg and the German wars (the Thirty Years War 1618–1648) the horror and casualties were probably exaggerated by deliberate propaganda.

The story of the sack was used as evidence in the 'first war crimes trial in history when Charles I was brought before Parliament charged with waging war on his people after his raising his standard against Parliament in Nottingham August 1642 following his failed attempt to arrest the five members. At the trial a husbandman from Rutland (adjacent to Leicestershire) accused the king of failing to stop barbarities during the sack, claiming that he overruled the tender mercies of a royalist officer saying, 'I do not care if they cut them three times more, for they are mine enemies.' Other testimony from former royalist soldiers supported the evidence.[17]Solicitor General, Oxford educated John Cooke had his home in Leicestershire and it seems likely that he was able to collect evidence from around county and the city. Still current today as an important plank in war crimes law, Cooke invoked the doctrine of 'command responsibility', the same law that skewered Milosevic in the Hague; in the arraignment it was written 'he the said Charles Stuart, has been and is the occasioner, author, continuer of the said unnatural, cruel and bloody wars and therefore guilty of all of the treasons, murders, rapines, burnings, spoils, desolations, damages and mischiefs to the action acted and committed in the said wars…'[18]

Symmonds recorded that 200 soldiers were killed on each side and there were an estimate 400 townspeople slaughtered in the sack. There must have been at least as many wounded, probably more.

Nine cannons, dozens of barrels of gunpowder 400 horses and 1000 muskets were captured. Charles levied 2000 pounds on the city.[19] Typical of the tide of war five great estates, including Burley house were abandoned to the victors. Belvoir castle remained unbowed. It looked like the royalists were achieving a major strategic victory in securing taxable territory in the Midlands. Meaning to stay and to stamp royalism on the county, Charles installed a garrison of 1500, a number he could ill afford with the Parliamentary army fast approach from the south. Recruiting locally began in earnest.

Little did the royalist army and Charles I realise that within few weeks their army would be destroyed and with it any hopes for a royalist victory in the civil war. His army advanced to meet a Parliamentary army thirty per cent larger, having failed to order General Goring to join them from the west country with 4000 seasoned troopers. The battle of Naseby would settle the Civil War.

French strategy, tactics, and manners in the war

Flanders and Artois were where most of the French military effort was made in interminable sieges. Siege warfare accounted for about 90 per cent of military operations in Flanders or Artois. A siege would require about 15,000 soldiers, the size of a large army corps. To complete a long siege, it would often be necessary to amalgamate two armies because of rampant desertion. Given the quality of fortresses in this region and the expertise of defenders, one siege might take up most of the campaigning year especially as the French started the campaign season late and finished early.

There was little progress made in the first years because there were many dozens of fortresses along the Franco–Flanders border in Artois. In addition, the focus on the attack and occupation of fortresses or 'places', as Parrott[20] refers to them, was no more than a formulaic approach to warfare, which would end in a sort of swap process at the future peace negotiation. If the enemy made the occasional counter-attacks and got a place back in return, it meant that for every two steps forward there would be one back. For most of the war with Spain, the French were attacking but the Spanish needed relatively few men in defence, moreover the Spanish offensive in 1636 captured a string of French towns and fortresses that took some years to recover.

The strategic issue for France seemed quite easy, i.e., to cut the Spanish lines of communication, and launch cross-border attacks on Spanish possessions and interests along the thousand-mile line of communication to Flanders. However, the Spanish possessions were quite difficult to get at. Geographical factors also made long distance supply to France's border areas difficult, so Le Tellier set up a magazine system, as Gustavus had done in Sweden. Local supplies and magazine storage became one of the key functions of army and regional intendants. Magazines to service the main 'fronts' were the responsibility of Le Tellier who 'created some permanent stores in key fortresses, such as Dunkirk, Arras, Breisach and Pinerolo.'[21]

The strategic use of interior lines, i.e. switching fronts as Richelieu had done between La Rochelle and Italy in 1629, was never done again despite the extraordinary success of that campaign. The reality was that the short duration of the campaign season was linked to the shortage of finance and supplies, which meant that the campaign season could not run on for too long. Unlike the super long campaign season of 1629 [when there was only one army to finance] there was no chance to switch armies between fronts even if that was practical on French roads, and with organisational, recruitment, and supply constraints. Campaign seasons had to be short because there was not enough money for long ones, so unlike other armies, only very limited objectives could be achieved in any one campaign. Progress in the war was necessarily slow.

The priority for French strategy was to attack Flanders, which was the hub of Spanish north-European operations, which offered the most immediate threat to Paris. As a result of the alliance with the Dutch it seemed sensible to attack the Spanish Netherlands from north and south simultaneously. In practice this was not as logical, practical, or attractive as it first appeared because the Spanish benefited from interior lines, being able to quickly reinforce threatened points in any direction; they also had strong fortress defence on their southern Artois/Flanders border, multiple river lines and forts in defence of the northern border. A further problem was that the Dutch never fought outside their fortified lines; they were culturally not attuned to offensive operations in the open field; standard strategy developed by Maurice of Nassau was defensive.

France reinforced the Dutch alliance through annual subsidies that varied between 1–1.5 million guilders, although actual payments were often about ten to twenty per cent lower. The benefit to France was that while the Dutch army would threaten and besiege a city on the northern border of Flanders, they would draw off any relieving army from the towns and cities besieged by the French in Artois or Southern Flanders or Luxemburg. However, the prioritisation of Flanders gave some advantages to the French, including the fact that northern France was near to the entrepôt of Amsterdam where any of the military resources could be bought and supplied by sea with relative ease; the battlefields were also not far from Paris which made communication, supply, and control easier.

Lastly, the king needed to be occupied. He loved to play at soldiers as he had done from an early age. It was simply easier and cheaper to manage a royal progress nearer to home on the Artois front, in easy reach of Paris. However, the presence of the king would unbalance overall military provision and strategy itself, because resources had to be concentrated on his bit of the campaign first, to the detriment of all other fronts under the centralised funds budget-cap system. Money had to be lavished on his tented pavilions, his attendants, and the lavish supply of fine foods and wines. In essence, war was still a mediaeval summertime amusement for the French court. Louis XIII enjoyed the pomp, paraphernalia, and parades. He enjoyed the 'toy soldiers' aspect of it all and would frown and criticize any deviation from an immaculately paraded army. De Bussy-Rabutin was severely scolded for leading his men on foot one occasion rather than from horseback. Although the allure of Flanders was obvious, it was a slow attritional strategy because it favoured the defence and would absorb resources disproportionate to possible gains. It was a very slow and painful way to win a war; taxes to pay for it triggered in 1648 the civil war known as 'the Fronde'.

An indirect strategy of knocking out the Viennese Habsburgs first would have better served French interests and increased the likelihood of a short victorious war. A focus on Germany would also have made better use of France's alliance with Sweden, a far more effective land power than the Dutch. Eventually the major French breakthrough in the war was achieved on the German front when Bernhard of Saxe-Weimar, who had been induced by Richelieu to defect with his army from his Swedish allies, launched an astonishing campaign that ended in the capture of the key fortress and Rhine crossing at Breisach in 1638. Mazarin changed the strategy after Louis XIII's death to focus more aggressively on the German front with a surge in numbers and military expenditure.

Conclusion on sieges

Evolution of military tactics and technology, the impact of Sweden

From the perspective of military history, the battle of Breitenfeld has rightly been seen as a very important signpost of the future. Concentrated firepower and tactical flexibility in linear formations had shown their superiority when the morale status of the troops was equal. Veteran tercios had for the first time been met by veterans who were their equal; the difference lay in leadership and tactics. Firepower won over mass in the infantry battle. With tragic irony, the tercios' discipline and martial pride only made them better targets for Swedish firepower. This accounts for the very heavy death toll.

In another textbook victory, battle of Lech Gustavus used mobility and combined arms to forge a victory against a Bavarian army entrenched behind a river line. He pinned down the enemy entrenchments with an artillery barrage: then using an elite Finish 'commando' unit he secretly constructed bridges with his specialist engineering unit, then stormed the far shore using a forested island as cover, The landing spot chosen for a bend on the river was then held against enemy attacks, by using cannon crossfire from each wing of the bend. In a double flanking attack, Saxe-Weimar's cavalry struck the Bavarian flank having crossed a ford further down river. The battle would in time win Gustavus control of Bavaria and the entire south and west of the empire, including Alsace.

The second point about these battles was the superior use of excellent brass cannon, both at the army level, when deployed in batteries and as mobile close support for the infantry. Organised as an elite unit of the Swedish army under the supervision of outstanding young General Torstensson, the artillery arm would become the key to Swedish military success over the following twenty-six years. The value and effectiveness of lighter and powerful Swedish guns was certainly believed in by the Swedish army. General Leslie, sent by Gustavus to advise the Czar in 1631, informed the Russians that Gustavus 'in the current war won victories with these cannons, and with this intervention has been able to travel a great distance, and we expect that he will be able to advance even further.'[22] In reporting on his defeat at the battle of Breitenfeld Tilly emphasised the superiority of the Swedish artillery.[23] Imperialist armies would adapt rapidly.

Munro's analysis which notes, 'the fourth helpe to this victory, was the plottons of musketiers, his majesty had very wisely ordained to attend the horsemen, being a great safety for them, and a great prejudice for the enemy, the musket balls carrying and piercing farther than the Pistolet.'[24] This and Swedish mixed arms capability seems to be the only possible explanation for the poor showing of Pappenheim's brilliantly led veteran cuirassiers. As in Poland, use of mixed arms was a key ingredient of Swedish military success, including the posting of small cavalry units behind infantry. As Montecuccoli would later advise, 'a small squadron of cavalry, acting promptly can wreak havoc amongst large infantry battle lines.'[25] However, when the Swedish cavalry arm improved the supporting musketeer units were dispensed with. Nonetheless all armies would copy Swedish tactics of intermixing musket units if they perceived that their cavalry was weaker or at a disadvantage.

Swedish forces had been deployed in two lines with a reserve behind them. Tilly was much criticised by contemporaries for his lack of reserves and his deployment of his forces in one line. Imperialist General Montecuccoli writing in his treatise *Sulle Battaglie 1642* noted that Tilly, 'placed his whole army along a single front and found himself in a bad way as a result.'[26] However, in using tercios his front was already overlapped by the more thinly deployed and outnumbering Swedish-Saxon army. It can be argued that the main decider in battles was the battle worthiness of troops rather than tactical deployment as such; however, the victory of the Swedes in a *veteran*-on-*veteran* fight suggests that tactical deployment and maximisation of firepower was the key difference. In copying the Swedes thereafter in deployment of infantry and cannon, the Imperialists and Bavarians seem to have drawn that conclusion. Nor is it a coincidence that the storm of firepower unleashed by Sweden at Breitenfeld led to the rapid adoption of battlefield entrenchment by the Imperialist Bavarian army as standard operating procedure. From a political viewpoint and as a marker in the development of modern warfare, the battle of Breitenfeld was one of the seminal events in seventeenth-century history.

Attacking mass versus firepower/battle tactics and deployment

The one major problem in the development of linear formations, often in accompanying fieldworks, deploying optimised use of firepower, is that infantry contests became firepower slugging contests. The weight of tercios operating *en masse* as a sort of phalanx had the potential to win battles by smashing the enemy centre; they were also invulnerable to cavalry attack. When tercios disappeared, there was no longer offensive or breakthrough capability in infantry attack.

The stalemate in the infantry battle became a standoff firefight by troops in linear formation *without* the depth and mass or élan or equipment to penetrate the opposing line. Also, the use of artillery as a defensive weapon and the decline of the Tercio meant that infantry lost its battle-winning role which the Swiss pikemen and German Landsknecht had given it in later mediaeval and early modern times. English archers at the battles of Crecy, Poitiers and Agincourt had already amply foreshadowed the use of firepower behind fieldworks against dense mass. Despite the demise of the tercio, a future great commander, Napoleon, would in effect reintroduce elements of the tercio concept by his use of attack in column formation following on from a massed artillery barrage.

New linear formations were vulnerable on the flanks and in the rear. In the early modern period, from about 1632, the answer for attack minded commanders was the cavalry attack on the flanks of linear formations; in many ways a reversion to the methods of Alexander the Great and Hannibal. The defence against cavalry attack and outflanking or penetration would be the infantry square, a tactical concept which would be handed on down to General Slim in the Burma campaigns for his 'box' tactic whose strategy was passed on to General Salan in French Indochina for his victory at Na San in 1953. The strategy relied on the attacker failing to bring along enough supplies for a protracted stand-up fight. When general Giap brought up enough artillery, food, and ammunition to Dien Bien Phu then the 'box' system failed. War is a game in constant flux between different strategies, tactics and weapons, measures and countermeasures and counter-counter measures and so on.

Such is the constant reinvention and recycling of military tactics. In essence battlefield dispositions had not changed since times of antiquity. The battle-winning importance of cavalry increased as the war progressed as it was realised that outflanking infantry formations was the only way to win a decisive victory because 'In time of battle it is almost impossible for a battalion or body of either horse or foot to stand when it is charg'd in front and flank…'[27][Sir James Turner]. The crushing victories by Torstensson at second Breitenfeld, by Turenne at Alerheim and by Cromwell at the battles of Naseby 1645, and Marston Moor 1644.

Chapter XIII
The Propaganda War 1620–1627

For the first time in European history mass media became a battleground for the opposing sides. The development of cheap printing technology now put books and news pamphlets, sometimes illustrated, within reach of a wide number of people. This went hand in hand with the development of secular education, and the reading of the Bible in colloquial languages. Education and learning were spreading out from the courts of kings, castles of noblemen and knights to the merchant classes; attendance at universities increased. It was the ability of ordinary people to read the Bible, which became the motor force of the Reformation and the subsequent proliferation of Protestant theologues like Zwingli, Melanchthon, and Calvin. Monasteries no longer enjoyed a monopoly of learning or book production; the scraping of quill pens on vellum came to an end. Any doubts on the revolutionary power of printing technology in early modern Europe can be laid aside by a visit to the superb Plantin-Moretus Museum in Antwerp, site of the first mass market printing presses. Equally impressive is the Gutenberg Museum in Mainz, home of the eponymous bibles.

The battle for minds on the Catholic side was instead taken up by the Jesuit movement, which was based on rigorous development of educational and intellectual abilities. The explosion in demand and interest in the new medium led to a corresponding explosion in its exploitation to feed the hungry demand for news and information. Efforts of states to produce and distribute this propaganda were matched by a booming print industry across Europe where the profit motive was equally as powerful as the political one. Vendors and newsletter writers were hungry for information with which to feed their subscribers. Propaganda was not just with words. In 1622, as Tilly's army advanced across Germany in pursuit of Mansfeld and the various Protestant paladins, the Pope was assembling another army, Sacra *Congregatio de propaganda fidei*, (a missionary organisation) to move in behind them to take over the secularised Protestant bishoprics and spread the Counter-Reformation.

From the outset both sides in the Bohemian conflict looked to win over the newly liberated masses to their viewpoint by political polemic and black propaganda. The vicious exchange of polemic was started by Frederick V's propaganda chief with the publication of captured and compromising Habsburg diplomatic letters. After the battle of the White Mountain in 1621 the Imperialists captured wagon loads of compromising diplomatic correspondence from Frederick V and his foreign policy adviser Christian Anhalt. Compromising details of his negotiations with foreign powers, with the princes, were widely broadcast. Especially embarrassing, the Habsburgs seized on Frederick's desperate pleas to the Ottomans for intervention on the Bohemian side in exchange for becoming a satrapy. In an age when the crusades and Turkish depredations were a near and loathsome memory, this propaganda coup helped lower still further the tattered reputation of the 'Winter King'. In 1625 some of Ferdinand's letters were discovered revealing compromising correspondence with Spain; they were published in *Chancellerum Hispania*. In 1627 Comenius's correspondence was captured including Frederick's letters. His critical and insulting comments on his allies, were widely published. It is all reminiscent of the Wikileaks scandal today, and similar in effect to leaks of vile terminology used by senior US state department officials about their 'allies'.

All states started to employ propagandists to write a wide variety of texts, some long, learnt, and well-informed pieces, others short polemical pamphlets: different types of polemic for different audiences. Centres of publishing in Antwerp, Amsterdam, Mainz, Heidelberg, Leipzig, Hamburg, Paris, London, and Cologne turned out publications which were disseminated all over Europe either by clandestine distribution or through the normal channels of private enterprise. These publications *could* be sold; such was the hunger for information. An example of early journalism were the illustrations and articles produced by Matthias Merian and Johann Philipp Abele in *Theaterum Europaeum*, printed in Frankfurt.[1] It was a sensation retelling of the black legends of the war; as if it needed further blackening, the Imperialists also issued the *Acta Mansfeldica* 1622, which detailed his atrocities.

Highly intelligent, educated and politically motivated Jesuits were widely used as polemicists. Maximilian employed the Jesuits Jakob Kekker and Adam Contzen as propagandists. In 1624–5 Contzen published two major anti-French propaganda works *Mysteria politica* and *Adannatio ad Ludovicum XIII regem*. For the more intelligent and well-read readers, European politicians prepared longer more literary polemics, such as the forty-three pages of anti-Imperialist diatribe '*altera secretissima instructo Gallo-Brittanico-Batavia fredericko V data ex belgica Latinam linguam versa, et optimo public evulgata*....' published in Cologne in 1626. Its purpose was to galvanise Catholic opinion and win over political ditherers at the start of the conflict. It was typical of thousands of political spin pieces published in the war. In England, Thomas Hobbes, not yet the famous political philosopher, was commissioned to translate it.

In England society was being torn by sharp religious and political polemic. The country, especially London, inclined strongly towards Frederick V, but was also the target for Imperialist propaganda, which aimed to shift support away from intervention. The political polemic from the puritan movement in England became ever more radical and xenophobic, whipping up religious and political discontent at James I's drift in foreign policy towards the Catholic powers. There was a vast output of news and information, which in turn led to the production in 1620–42 of many works relating to the war including, 'fifty-five plays and entertainments and masques…plus sixty works of prose and poetry.'[2] News sheets called '*currantoes*' sometimes published four times a week when press censorship was partly lifted in 1638. There are 400 surviving London periodicals covering the Thirty Years War.[3] At a distance from the war, news from the continent was amplified even further a relatively isolated island nation. Society was radicalised. Fears and paranoia beset the political classes. Religious sects and the educated mob watched nervously for any signs of subversion by dangerous foreign elements or ideas, 'Popery' and 'absolutism': Spanish and Austrian Habsburg actions stoked their fears. A seventeenth-century version of twenty-first-century 'euro-scepticism', Parliament was infected by this passion; but unfortunately for James I, it was passion without policy.

Pamphlets with biting criticism of his favourites including Buckingham were also widely circulated. Not only was James stung by such criticism, but he also feared the rising political-religious polarisation in English society: a trend that was already apparent had in the late Elizabethan era; from 1618 it festered and fed on the crisis in Europe. James I set up a licensing system and issued several proclamations to control rancorous and 'dangerous' publications: in September 1632 there was a 'Proclamation against disorderly printing, uttering, and dispersing of books and pamphlets'. This was followed in Augst 1624 by a 'Proclamation against seditious popish and puritanical booke and pamphlets;' an even-handed approach which masked the fact that the main political danger came from the Puritans [Calvinists], who were whipping up paranoid anti-Catholic sentiment in opposition to the King's foreign policy and the marriage plans for his heir Prince Charles. In 1623 Cambridge don Joseph Mead complained of censorship in his access to speeches critical of James foreign policy in the House of Lords.

Religious differences as representative of social-political-cultural differences were exaggerated and manufactured for the purposes of propaganda aimed at the respective partisans or near theological allies to rally and motivate the prosecution of the war. Traditional liberties were threatened! Civilians were terrorised, pillaged, raped, and slaughtered! Bolstering domestic opinion, creating a positive ferment for recruitment, stirring battle passions, affirmation of identity, and winning over new allies, were the primary reasons behind the sharpening of religious tension through the use of new publishing media. It was further underpinned by private religious instruction and from the pulpit. Protestant landowning classes across Europe also feared Catholic property restitution. By harping on existential insecurities, a climate of *existential paranoia* was created which posed sharply the *'security dilemma'* to the fragile and suspicious minds of the power elites. Ordinary citizens were similarly polarised by the stimulation of their primordial fears. 'People may respond to this existential dilemma by attempting to inflate their diminished and fragmented sense of self, often by seeking out and identifying a new set of concepts… It is precisely at such moments that people may be drawn to ideological messages that crystallize differences, simplifying what are otherwise more complex and fluid categories… converts are drawn into an essentialist ideology that divides the world into black and white, erasing grey zones – everything and everyone is either "right" or "wrong".'[4] This mentality gripped leaders such as Emperor Ferdinand and Frederick V Palatine who then projected their own psychosis through the media onto their respective theological/ideological camps: military actions and the treatment of civilians would have been harsh enough without such a divide, but the moral constraints which were lifted by propaganda helped give a special brutal edge to the earthly conflict.

One other historical by-product of the media coverage of the war has been to reinforce the 'gothic' image of the Thirty Years War conflict. Uncritical historians have taken the senstionalised output too often at face-value instead of seeing it as it is-sensationalism to sell copy. Historians might in future take the *Sun, Bild, de Speigel,* and the *Daily Mail* or Fox news, CNN, even the BBC in recent times as serious founts of objective information. Let's hope not!

Richelieu's black propaganda; war, foreign policy, and polemic in France

Richelieu employed teams of propagandists and pamphleteers to ward off the scurrilous print attacks of his enemies in the ultra *devot* faction. For the cardinal, the use of the press had nothing to do with some notion of encouraging public debate; it was simply another mechanism for the projection of state power in his absolutist system or in the early days, an extension of the factional infighting in the Royal Council and at court. Another aspect of the increasing use of the printing presses was ability to use this technology to change the nature of the relationship between state and citizen. The state could now send its message directly without the interface of the regional and local nobility, who often had different political agendas. It was yet another method of marginalising the great nobility and the pro-Spanish factions. The Richelieu press pushed a *'Gallic'*, anti-Habsburg foreign policy.

Government propaganda was nothing new in France. The *Mercure Francois* had already been established in 1613, but needing a more regular vehicle for government propaganda Richelieu would found the government subsidised *'hebdomadaire'*, the *Gazette,* through his protégé Théophraste Renaudot. Starting off as secretary to Marie de Medici the Capuchin monk Father Joseph amongst others was employed by Richelieu as his leading penman; the polemical monk would become a lifelong adviser, and in due course a trusted diplomatic envoy. As Professor Nassier notes, 'The aim of the authors of pamphlets was to influence the advice of the king, who in the year 1620 was also unsure.'[5] There was also the wider purpose of social mobilisation for war, including the raising of state awareness amongst the populace with the state channelling information directly rather than in mediaeval reliance on the regional nobility and the church.

To compensate for his previously negative 'Calvinist' image, Sully and Philip de Mornay had been particularly adept at exploiting the press to build up Henri IV's reputation, as a strongman of action, a war leader, and champion of poor people. His image was imprinted on countless leaflets: Legends were created, victories exaggerated. Revolutionary in the scope of its reporting, the *Mercure* used a network of correspondents across Europe. From 1624 Father Joseph became editor of the *Mercure*: the polemical monk would become a lifelong adviser, and in due course a trusted diplomatic envoy; 'The goal of the authors' pamphlets was to influence the King's council, which in the 1620s was itself divided.'[6] Other writers included: 'Paul Hay de Chastelet, Jean de Simond, Jean Sihon, François de Chauvigny de Colomby, Jean Desmarets de Solin'[7] who all became members of Richelieu's Académie Français established in 1635 with the purpose of regularising the French language. A part of Richelieu's state modernisation programme. There was also the wider purpose of social mobilisation for war, including the raising of state awareness amongst the wider educated populace with the state channelling information directly rather than in mediaeval reliance on the regional nobility and the church, which were apparati mainly in the hands of the opposition. Like the internet today, exploitation of new cheap media printing technology was a way of bypassing rivals for power by direct political engagement. In his book published in 1631, *De l'Autorité des Rois* one of Richelieu's penmen, distinguished scholar François de Chauvigny de Colomby wrote that 'It was not enough for the princes to be anointed by the heavens. Their subjects had to believe it too.'[8]

The number of publications in circulation was vast. For 1615 alone there are 386 titles preserved in the French National Library. The pamphlet war reached a crescendo in the 1620s years as the vicious policy debate and political battles developed between the *'devot'* parti and Richelieu's *'Gallic'* faction. The centre for the very active book and pamphlet market was around the Palais de Justice and the Pont Neuf where the tradition is still continued from semi-permanent stalls along the bridge and adjacent riverfront. Numbers of pamphlets dropped off after the *'day of the dupes'* as the *'devot'* party lost power and finance. When he came to power, Richelieu cracked down on unlicenced publications especially derogatory ones about the king and his government. In 1639 caricatures and satires about the king were banned.

The market for the *Gazette* pamphlets was aimed at the educated classes who could afford the 120 livre per annum subscription price: A large sum representing a year's wages for an artisan in Paris. Figures taken from records in Grenoble give some indication of the readership. Given that it was a remote military frontier town the number of merchants and artisans are possibly under-represented. Readership is obviously skewed to the 'establishment-government cadres' at various levels; a *Times of London* readership in a former era.?

Classes of reader	% Purchasers of *Gazette*	% Readers of all the books
Nobles	24	13
Officials	40	30
Administrators	11	19
Lawyers	17	25
Merchants/artisans	8	13

Figures from the Nicolas Library in Grenoble.

Other publications, like polemical short pamphlets, placards, and fly sheets, the *'red tops'* of their day, would have had a much wider audience, reaching further down in society. In printed word or by pictures, etchings, engravings, or woodblock were produced cheaply for as little as one to four sous, well within affordability for the lower orders.[9] The onset of war and the determination of the regime to establish its legitimacy in the face of hostile oppositionist press led to a deluge of printed information supported by pictures. For example, scurrility as to the legitimacy of Louis XIII son, and rumours as to the King's sexuality and the mother's behaviour were countered by mass-circulation etchings showing the king and queen together offering up their child, to the Virgin Mary; printer Bosse's 'the vow of the King and Queen to the virgin'. Even more sharp were oppositionist pamphlets such as *'le Ballet Politique'*, which painted the distressed state of the kingdom with high taxes. In response to attacks on Louis' alleged weakness and to boost Louis's status another print depicts him as a Gallic Hercules slaying an allegorical lion, probably Spain. Underpinning this was Callot's new technology in engraving which improved printing quality by imitating etching without raising cost, there was also rising demand from a seminal increase of interest in religious matters, but coming second in volume[10] was the printing of news sheets about military matters, maps and diagrams of sieges, battles, pictures of commanders and technical drawings of all the new weapons, firearms, and cannon.

With rising national consciousness, there was a hunger for war news, which the press could deliver cheaply and pictorially. The military revolution was as much about cultural and social development as much as one about state apparatus, weapon technology, military organisation, and industrial modernisation. The revolution is bundled in holistic and seamless package.

Chapter XIV

State Modernisation, Military Revolution, and 'Firepower'

Models for the military revolution

A 'military revolution' if we are going to use the term should be a revolution not an evolution Geoffrey Parker's thesis as to the military revolution which he describes as happening between 1500–1800 stretches what might be a description of an exciting and rapid period of development into an 'evolutionary' three-hundred-year odyssey without meaning or clarity. When such a stretch is contrived, we may as well say that the history of the world since Genghis Khan, Julius Caesar or Belisarius has been revolutionary. Parker's narrow causal focus on artillery fortresses skews the whole debate off course into meaningless and muddy waters. Clearly fortresses were a very important precursor to the 'revolution' as polities reacted to the potential of gunpowder and the potential of firepower, but warfare is about more than fortresses however important they are. There was indeed a revolution in fortress design in the sixteenth century as a consequence of the gunpowder and cannon revolution, but that is not a military revolution per se, although it was one of the catalysts to the revolution. The acceleration came in the late sixteenth and early seventeenth centuries under the impact of war and broad and iterative coinciding factors of progress in economy and education. Fortresses dominated the nature of war in Flanders and the Dutch border 1568–1618 but were hardly relevant on other fronts notably Germany and Poland during the Thirty Years War. Moreover, the use of fortresses, i.e., their meaning and iterative effect only became apparent in war. The acceleration in the use of firepower, not just for fortress reduction but particularly in the increased use and deployment of field canon and the introduction of regimental close support canon. Also notable was the tripling [or more] of firearm ratios in infantry units (musketeers: pikemen) in the early seventeenth-century; battle by firepower is the key concept which defines the 'military revolution'. this fact alone is explanatory of the spurt in change that was the military revolution. It was firepower which made modern artillery fortresses necessary and made their reduction so long and complex. Even if we just concentrate on fortresses, we are forced to conclude that the rapid revolutionary phase of their intellectual and physical development after 1570 was already over by 1650 as well as their role in accelerating state formation. Also over, was the fantasy that fortresses were a standalone defence policy; As we shall see only a strong army could keep a nation and its fortresses safe. Fortresses give the illusion of security but not the reality as the empire was to discover in its wars with Transylvania. Denmark and the Palatinate also built strong fortresses, but both were overrun as was Bavaria despite the fortress of Ingolstadt. Hesse did not have strong fortresses; it was overrun but it remained a state in being because it had a strong army. Sweden did not invest heavily in fortresses but in its army.

No one can doubt that all the ingredients for a military revolution were present in 1600, but it took an intense 'era of wars' as Andrew Roberts describes the first half of the seventeenth-century and the Thirty Years War. The military revolution was about firepower, its development, application, and associated requirements for state modernization. The need for firepower and its efficient application required reformed and new state institutions, which had severely lagged the advanced development in technology and capitalist economic systems over the previous 200 years.

Jeremy Black relates military revolution to size, but this is a rather a simplistic a distillation with a focus on one factor. Nor is it a factor of much worth because size. Size is merely a function, available economic resources and population say nothing as to the nature of military operations as such or the radical change in the role of firepower in military calculations. In fact, size in early modern Europe was already a prescient factor in the huge armies deployed by Wallenstein-Tilly in the Habsburg-Bavarian alliance, and later by Gustavus Adolphus, where the deployment of corps size units or indeed whole armies foreshadowed the Napoleonic era.

Much more apposite is Michael Roberts' thesis both for its analysis of the radical changes and rapid changes brought on by military technologies. His time period though drawn from Swedish experience is nonetheless apposite for the changes wrought across the spectrum in Europe; much of it is drawn from the Swedish experience and experiments in military development. A self-defining feedback loop in history but supported by many other factors including the Dutch experience of war after the revolt 1568. Michael Roberts properly understands the time scale and speed of the rapid changes that occurred 1560–1650. Perhaps he needs to ascribe different weights inside his time period because the period 1560–1620 is relatively slow, more of a 'build up period'. The huge catalyst to fire the spurt in innovation in warfare was the Thirty Years War 1618–48; a war that encompassed several other wars, the Dutch War of Independence 1568–1648, The Thirty Years War 1618–48, the Swedish Polish War 1621–29, the Transylvania Habsburg wars 1618–48, the Franco-Habsburg War 1634–48, and the Franco-Spanish War 1634–1660 to name a few. The sheer breadth and scale of the fighting in Europe in the early seventeenth-century accelerated the methods, and the nature of war. That the war was by turns existential, religious, and ideological in nature added to the combustibility of the elements. At stake was both struggle for dominion in Europe as the Habsburg alliance came under threat as well as the entire concept of united Christendom.

So, Roberts from the first was on the right track and he also appreciates the institutional changes wrought by the war. His thesis is supported by Brian M. Downing in his book *The Military Revolution and Political Change* Princeton 1992 where the linkages of political development are properly picked up and analysed, recognising that the Thirty Years War led to economic and political stresses which brought in absolutist fiscal states. With Roberts and Downing in synthesis we have a near complete description and explanation of the 'military revolution' including the rapid advance in state modernisation to which the model proposed in this book readily adapts. 'The military revolution of the sixteenth and seventeenth centuries led to the strengthening of monarchic power in countries relying on domestic resources to finance modern armies.'[1] Others such as Jan Gete make important contributions; 'The fiscal military state with large permanent armed forces, practically unknown in 1500, had two centuries later become the normal European state.'[2]. Gete also understands the 'identity' politics generated the modern idea of nation states a phenomenon to be encapsulated at the Westphalian peace in 1648. Except for Spain, Europe did not have standing armies at the beginning of the seventeenth-century but by 1650, permanence had become a habit and necessity as a result of the Thirty Years War; peacetime numbers reduced as the occupation of Germany was wound down from 1648–1654 but permanent structures as well as the productive arsenals of war remained. Government institutional and decision-making structures also changed in tandem with changes in the function and importance of the aristocratic and feudal elites. William Beik, in his book *Absolutism and Society in Seventeenth-century France: State Power and Provincial Aristocracy in Languedoc*, Cambridge 1985, noted the increasing intrusion of the state in decision-making and most importantly in administrative execution 'one fascinating thing about seventeenth-century government was the any institutional processes and personal networks intermingled and influenced each other... while institutions channels were established firmly enough ...Government was articulated first through royal institutions but while institutional channels were established firmly enough that they deflected and modified the nature of personal influence, personal forms of power...still played a central role in the decision-making process.'

France was a society in transition, where leading aristocrats as well as the 'de robe' or de l'epee increasingly became servants and employees of the state with advancement based on technocratic expertise and education. The state advanced its power over all levels of society, a trend which was already marked in Sweden and to some extent in the empire, a system which would be rigorously enforced by the future powers of Prussia and Russia. The transformation of citizens at all levels to detailed and intimate control by the state (i.e. absolutism) was necessary function of most state inspired modernisation in continental Europe. It was of course, also a progenitor of social stress and revolt which was widespread across seventeenth-century Europe.

This book describes the preceding factors which go into a military revolution in the 1568–1650 period; I am happy to use Michael Robert's time frame and not be fussy about the odd decade. After all the minutiae of definition cover this discrepancy. It is doubtful if Roberts would disagree as to the dates of revolutionary lift off, the point of sharp inflection and revolutionary change coincides with the Thirty Years War, the Eighty Years War between, the Long War and the battle for Hungary, and the various Baltic wars, Kalmar, Ingris and the Swedish-Poland wars. All these wars came together in a great global conflagration, The rate of change settles down to the mere evolutionary after 1648. This book points out the symbiosis with societal, political and institution change, proposing that changes here were just as radical and revolutionary and that such a symbiosis is in any case quite natural. This is not to say that such revolutionary change will always be driven by a continental wide and long-lasting war. Except for quantum, the Napoleonic wars did not engage dramatic changes in warfare, essentially because there had been no preceding economic and technological revolution. This book explains the coincidence of factors which when sparked by the wars of the early seventeenth-century created a fusible combustion into revolutionary change. These factors included, levels of economic development, the availability of the printing press, the intellectual freedoms developed since the Reformation and the Renaissance, i.e. the development of rationality and logic including the rediscovery of the classics. Not coincidental to the military revolution was the recognition by the new military thinkers that Roman concepts of formation and discipline needed to be re-evaluated and rediscovered for the purposes of the battlefield and for the new medium of firepower. A scientific approach for a scientific age. John von Wallhausen was the doyen of Protestant military instruction; he was appointed by the Dutch to be director the Schola militaris in Siegen 1617. He published eleven major works and manuals on the military training and fighting techniques for infantry, with diagrams between 1614–17. Works included: *Ritterkunst* – the art of cavalry fighting, 1614: *Romanische Kriegskunst* – Roman military art, 1616.

The essential ingredients of the military and societal changes were primed and set before the Thirty Years War. The sixteenth century was indeed a formative period. Just as a dried forest is tinder for a conflagration caused by a spark, so the defenestration of Prague provided the detonating explosion that triggered the military revolution as well as the era of rapid state modernisation, a rippling concertina of change in an era which was the inflection point between the mediaeval world and the modern world.

Although we should never become too fixated by strict models and dogmas, we need to give some explanatory credit to Marxist analysis of seventeenth-century development. Simplistic and plain wrong in application on occasion Christopher Hill on the English revolution makes an important contribution to our understanding of European development not just '*development in one country*'; important contributions to our understanding of the period can also be gleaned from works by Rosa Luxemburg, Trotsky, and Lenin and indeed from Marx himself. Rosa Luxemburg points out, with the unalloyed clarity of a Marxist ideologue, that 'Militarism fulfils a quite definite function in the history of capital, accompanying as it does every historical phase of accumulation.'[3] All these Marxists were of course foreshadowed by the Levellers in the Putney Debates in October 1647, less we forget that Marxist theories are little more than an intellectual expression of what was felt emotionally by the peasants and countryside bourgeoisie in their 'croquant' rebellions, by the Levellers, by the clubmen or 'werewolves' in England or Germany, by Czech revolutionaries in Prague in 1618 [men like Comenius], by the revolutionaries in the streets of Barcelona 1640, Lisbon, 1640, in Napoli 1646, Palermo 1646, and Paris in the Fronde 1648. The early seventeenth-century was a time of wars in Europe and the British isles; it is not surprising that it exploited the capitalist developments of the previous two centuries and detonated latent social tensions in a time of stress and social and political change. The reformation had normalised revolution.

In future centuries and bursting from the same model of military, economic and societal development, we have the revolutions in Peking 1911, in Petrograd 1917 in Budapest 1919, Munich and Berlin 1919–1920. Economic development over the period which was the essential precondition for the military revolution without which the rapid combustion could not have happened; economics and finance provide the oxygen which fed the inferno of change, dragging state finances out of the treasure box in a King's bedchamber or his dinner plate collection, dramatically into the modern world. Proper weight needs to be given to the shipping industry, international-global commerce, the quest for new products and feedstock for the economic and state modernisation processes set in hand by the military revolution (see Nick Collin's work Vol II). The international trade in saltpetre for example became important; new colonial adventures and the rapid advance of proto-colonialism was just another of the breathtaking change in the era under review. Rapid and revolutionary in import it ran in symbiotic tandem with the military revolution and state modernisation. Without the radical changes in ship design and firepower the eastern trade and coastal toeholds in Africa, Asia, and the Persian Gulf could not have been won or held.

The model for military revolutions develops in three broad and overlapping phases

1. Economic, technological, social, capitalism-entrepreneurship-markets, political and intellectual preconditions
2. The spark, i.e. long lasting, attritional, total, existential war or threat of it, with attendant need for money
3. The military revolution collateral to the need for state modernization, development of the absolutist fiscal state. This required citizens to be chained to the interests of the centralised state and to be educated by propaganda to identify with the state rather than their feudal domain or locality. To marshal resources efficiently to prosecute an existential war, parochialism had to be replaced by the state.

Capitalism and military revolution

One point not so often discussed by historians looking at this question is the whole economic and technological background to it. It is easy to see the military revolution as something ordained by the newly-awakening kingly states and ordained by state action. We have a fascination for the actions of kings and states; therefore there is a tendency to overweight their achievements. In fact, the hidden hand of capitalist development and its internationalization was the single most important factor in enabling the military revolution. Several hundred years of extraordinary progress in international markets and banking development, transport links for the carrying of primary products and finished goods productive capacity, metallurgy, mining, chemistry, and printing, had transformed Europe. It had also transformed the globe such that east-west trade in primary products finished goods and semi-finished goods (e.g. saltpetre from India to be transformed into gunpowder in Europe) became a global concern. Another war essential, copper was arbitraged between Japan and the European market. Grain, flax, wood, tar and sisal from the Baltic was exchanged for sophisticated products, textiles and luxury goods from the entrepôt at Amsterdam. Sugar or salt came from the Americas. Bullion flows out of the Americas and Japan financed international trade flows and international correspondent banking relations allowed trade to run smoothly and increasingly enable cashless settlement. Financial structures could finance the wars and smoothly reinvest saving flows whether it be the Jewish conversos of Lisbon, the Fuggers of Augsburg, the Genoese bankers, or the Merchants of Venice and Amsterdam. Vast complex and much of it hidden from easy historical view or trackable from incomplete samples. The catalyst of extended and extensive warfare in early seventeenth-century Europe underpinned by capitalists, scientists and innovators caused the transformation of warfare from the myopic boudoir of feudal history to the great continental and intercontinental world stage.

It is worth noting too that it was the industrial and entrepreneurial revolution of the early nineteenth century that provoked the second military revolution and then the third under the catalyst of the First and Second World Wars. Similarly, capitalist productive progress, the microchip, the computer, and the discoveries of digital age have propelled the fourth military revolution.

Globalisation of the conflict followed the globalization of capitalism and trade following the gold and bullion rush of the in the early fifteenth century Americas and similarly the 'spice rush' in Asia in the same era.

'He taketh eke some Malabars aboard
parforce, the fellows by the Samorin sent
when were the Factor-pri'soners restor'd
Of purchase stores he tajeth hot piment:
Nor is the Banda the dried flow'er ignored,
nutmeg and swarthy clove, which excellent
makes new Malucan Isle, with cinnamon
the wealth, the boast, the beauty of Ceylon'

Luís Vaz de Camões, Os Lusíadas
(trans. Sir Richard Burton 1890)
Camões Lisbon 1571

By the early seventeenth-century three more parties had entered the early global trading market and with that went war, firearms, and naval firepower when the tiny European invaders needed to use the advantages of firepower to overawe the overwhelming numbers of the indigenous populations.

We can list the changes brought on in the military revolution 1600–1650.

- A quantum change in the amount of firepower deployed on battlefields – cannon and compared to the proceeding period both in absolute terms but much more importantly in relative terms, i.e. Firepower per soldier deployed. We can estimate this latter change from five times to ten times given the increase in cannon deployed.
- A quantum change in the rate of fire by the introduction of all-in-one cartridges, and better training and drill, by perhaps a hundred per cent or more.
- A quantum change in the ratio of muskets to pikes moving from 1:1 to 3 (or 4:1 in the case of Sweden).
- Quantum increases in the deployment of exploding munitions whether fired by cannon or thrown as 'grenadoes' or 'fireworks'.

- Great emphasis on drill and development of the regiment as the building block of modern armies together with distinctive uniforms and flags – development of brigades.
- Great increase in mixed arm fighting deploying infantry-pike and musketeers, cavalry, light cavalry, dragoons, regimental artillery.
- Radically increased specialization and rising status in the different arms of the military by the incorporation of separate regiments for artillery and engineering and logistics by the end of the war.
- The placement of field artillery in battery and decrease in weight to throwing ratio of about thirty to fifty per cent by improved carriage design/transom design, shorter barrels, and improved metallurgy.
- For the first time, battlefield mobility of artillery with the greater use of limbers to spread the load and development of improved limber designs as well as the militarization of wagon teams and drivers.
- State-organised conscription of citizens became a widespread method of recruitment across European polities.
- Development of detached cavalry column to raid deep into enemy territory to disrupt enemy communications, ambush convoys, relieve threatened places, or even take smaller towns.
- Development of detached corps size armies (by Gustavus in particular) to achieve certain geopolitical objectives, extend territorial control, capture cities, go to the relief or support of allies. Also, to relieve logistical pressure and chaos by choosing different routes of advance.
- Development of strongly fortified forward magazines to support advances into enemy territory.
- Deploying invasion fleets to take the initiative against strategic targets or switch lines of attack against the enemy.
- Much increased emphasis on economic targets and the economics of warfare.
- Indirect warfare, as would be advocated by Basil Liddell Hart, was the quite original strategy devised by Oldenbarnevelt, to defeat the Spanish crown by attacking Philip III's and Philip IV's colonies and trade flows in Asia, China and the Persian Gulf. Dutch attacks would later fall on Philip IV's colonies in Brazil (Portuguese and Spain). War was no longer about tactical forays but about grand strategy.
- Concepts of society government, interstate relations and war changed markedly with the influence of writers such as Bodin, Machiavelli, and Grotius.

The sum of these developments in both firepower and the art of war was revolutionary in early modern Europe, interactively causing radical changes to government and the concept of the state. The influence of new thinking was enhanced by increasing sales of books and literacy as well the mould breaking

Protestant ideas on the vernacular and views on authority. Existential fear in Europe was exacerbated by the religious conflict and the ambitions of nations seeking to extend their interests in world where old forms were breaking down, most importantly the high cost and complexity of societies needing to adapt to the high-cost firepower based military solutions. Cost and enhanced need for tax collection was then a driver to the social transformation including the relationship of the citizen to the state. Feudal models of loyalty and parochialism were changing in favour of the centralised absolutist or 'Kingly' state. Or alternatively the maritime-merchant states of the Dutch and English.

The later sixteenth century and first half of the seventeenth-century as the pivotal to the military revolution

Military Revolution or the ascendency of 'firepower'

We have seen how the ingredients of the military revolution were sown (cultural, political, social, and economic); how the intense period of European continental and global war involving existential, ideological, and religious issues created an explosive mix of circumstances that propelled both a military revolution with a simultaneous and iterative change in the organization of European states. They all modernized in different ways and at different speeds; those that failed to modernize or were simply too small, failed and disappeared. Others that might have disappeared were saved by sheer luck in becoming buffer state creations of the great powers following the Treaties of Westphalia. Left behind in Germany, for example, as one might leave one's rook on the base line of an opponent's chess board, as a piece to be deployed later, was Brandenburg. The weakest electorate would seize its luck under a pair of dynamic long-lived electors [later kings, including Frederick the Great] and become the powerful state of Prussia using the well-trodden tools of modernization already developed by Sweden, Bavaria, Hesse, France, and Austria during the Thirty Years War.

The Dutch Republic and England again under the impact of wars both foreign and civil [in the latter example] developed their own unique forms of modernization moving together in tandem after William of Orange's Glorious Revolution. Spain had already modernized its military by the end of the sixteenth century; but wrecked by overreach and attrition Spain was to go into decline; a fact symbolised by the reversal or slowdown in adult literacy. Based too much on Castille, Spain failed to consolidate its regional political structures into an effective state.

The military revolution can be defined as the decisive switch from steel blade or 'point' weapons [the pike in particular] to firepower. This switch had been under gestation in the sixteenth century with arquebus pike ratios in the leading army of the day. By the end of the seventeenth century the pike had become redundant; it only needed the ring bayonet to finish it off. The flintlock musket derived from the Swedish *snaphance* became the standard firearm for the next two centuries and more. Moving on from the crude match and cord arquebus, firepower came with a much more rigorous attention to drill and formation in order to maximise the effect of firepower through volleys and rolling volleys, something re discovered by Maurice of Nassau based on Roman tradition but in response to the drilled mass of the Spanish tercio.

Rates of fire also increased dramatically as the all-in-one ball and powder cartridge was introduced. If we want a metaphor for the revolution, it is in the pike: musket ratio [or the firepower ratio] which changed from 1:1 in 1600 to 1:3 or 4 in 1650. That was a revolution in infantry firepower alone, but rates of fire increased due to drill and all-in-one cartridge means that firepower deliver increased by something in the order of 600 per cent in the first half of the seventeenth century. Formation in ranks rather than in tercio blocks became the norm; it was in a sense a return to Roman formation systems. Rigorous parade ground training brought troops quickly into line and ready to deliver volleys in optimal formation. Salvo fire or rolling salvo fire were the standard procedures in the Swedish army. However, it was not always effective. Field Marshal Horn having been captured at the battle of Nördlingen, complained that. when his troops fired in salvo at the Spanish as they ascended Albuch hill against the enemy redoubts, that the Spanish ducked behind their defences.

Prince Maurice developed the counter-march to reload system; a major step in infantry tactics, the purpose was maximum firepower delivery by speed of loading and optimised depth in ranks. Jacob de Gheyn's book *Wapenhandelinghe* 1606 became a standard text, and it inspired many others which led to the rapid dissemination of new tactical thinking across Europe; it aimed at firepower maximization. This type of formation lasted through the American Civil War and beyond, until deployment loosened somewhat under the brutal impact of long-range rifles and then machine guns. We see the firepower effect not just in infantry but in the use of the pistol and carbine for cavalry as well as the tactic introduced by Gustavus firstly in Poland and then in Germany, in the Thirty Years War of deploying 'command companies' of musketeers interspersed with cavalry units. Over time cavalry operations would mostly be of a dragoon type with charges becoming rarer. This was exemplified in the American Civil War.

The infantry tactics being developed need discipline and regular troops. The early battles of the Thirty Years War saw the testing on Maurice's concepts; introduced ahead of their time before social and political modernization could develop regular troops from societies far behind the level of education and sophistication of the Dutch Republic. Lower pike ratio and complexity probably led to constant disintegration of the green Protestant armies in the first years of the Thirty Years War. Maurice's victory at Nieuwpoort in 1600 over the tercio had perhaps led Protestant states to jump the gun. As veteran soldier Sir James Turner noted 'It was also important not to change formation style without proper training, 'any new form wherewith your men are not acquainted, you shall not fail to put them in some confusion…'[4] After initial contact most battles probably descended into a confused melee with and therefore fire discipline lost. However, when a veteran and discipline Swedish regular army used these new infantry tactics against the Spanish-trained Imperialist and Bavarian units at Breitenfeld in 1630, the result was a smashing victory. Veteran Scot, Monro describes how the superior and elite Imperialist heavy cuirassier cavalry were repulsed at Breitenfeld, ' then at a neere distance our musketiers meeting them with a salve; then our horsemen discharged their pistols, then charged through them with swords; and at their return the musketiers were ready again to give the second salve of musket among them; the enemy thus valiantly resisted by our horsemen, and cruelly plagued by our plottons and musketiers; you may imagine how soone he would be discouraged after charging twice in this manner and repulsed.'[5] Thereafter the new model of infantry organization would be taken up universally by the Catholic powers in Germany, with the exception of Spain who used the tercio big regiment system until they learnt for themselves the lessons of firepower at Rocroi in 1642.

Changes were not copied exactly and Imperialist regiments of about 1000 remained larger than the 600-man regiments of the Swedes although in practice regiment sizes varied widely. Influences were no just one way, as the Swedes moved to match Imperialist regiment size by brigading their regiments with two regimens per brigade.

With this increased formalisation and organisation in smaller units, came the regimental system, standards, coloured uniforms etc. Army sizes and the cross-continental range of armies as well as the increased duration the campaign year, often running through winter under Swedish generals led to greater emphasis on logistics; forward magazines in specialised fortresses was a concept especially introduced by Gustavus Adolphus and copied by the French. Vast quantities of powder, bullets, cannonballs, grain, beer, accoutrements, victuals, and consumables of all sorts needed to be stored. All this plus storage of specialized infantry, artillery or cavalry equipment required organization and commissariats hitherto fore not envisaged in European armies except for the Spanish army, whose efficient commissariat and *etapes* system had developed from the mid-sixteenth century as Spanish military power was developed for projection on a continental scale.[6]

Another related aspect of change in the Thirty Years War was the development of more mobile canon with standardised calibres. The process was driven by mass production in counties such as Sweden. Producing to standardized diameters, the

Dutch set up a gun foundry in the Hague in 1589. With dozens of fortresses and ships to equip there was no shortage of demand for internal purposes let alone for export. The use of bronze as opposed to steel was a major development as were the incremental reductions in weight of the gun carriage, the weight of the gun, and the length of the barrel. Another development introduced by gunner expert General Torstensson was improved limber design which enhanced the benefits from already reduced gun weight. Limbers which distributed weight over more wheels and allowed for transport of munitions with the gun rather than in separate wagons allowed for battle field mobility for guns to keep up with a moving battle; they came into their own at the battle of Jankov 1645 where the Imperialists were stunned by the rapid deployment of the Swedish army's guns on a distant part of the battlefield. The impact of the cannon cannot be underestimated; previously seen as a weapon mainly for sieges with peripheral use in field battles, the canon became a battle-winning weapon which in some battles of the Thirty Years War, such as Freiburg and Alerheim inflicted as much as fifty per cent of all casualties. The number of cannons deployed by the main armies increased dramatically with Swedish and armies deploying as many as sixty pieces. Because of variances it is not possible to quantify the extent of firepower increase as a result of the increased role for artillery, the use of all-in-one charges, better training by a dedicated corps under a specialized senior commander but we must reckon that it is in the order of 500–1,000 per cent based on casualties caused and the increased number of cannon per combatant.

Modern 'artillery' fortresses and *trace Italienne* systems had developed since the start of the sixteenth century. An aerial view of the fortification of Rocroi [1555] on the French border with the Spanish low countries shows a perfect modern geometric system; successive triangular escarpments and overlapping fields of fire give the impression of multiple stars; the fortifications are angle for deflection if shot and low in profile; a revolution compared to the chain walls of mediaeval towns and cities. Instead of breaches caused by trebuchet, the canon had taken over this function since the fifteenth century. The reaction to this was the *trace Italienne* (introduced increasingly into fortress with increasingly intricate star shapes and overlapping triangular patters of outworks etc. apart from canon, gunpowder could also be used for mining underneath defence to blow breaches. It was certainly a step towards modernity even if still steeped in mediaeval process. Not until firepower came to be used more generally in the Thirty Years War and its quantum improvement in efficiency can we really see the sort of acceleration that could be termed a revolution.

An immediate impression might lead one to conclude that the fortress of Rocroi was the work of Vauban; not at all, the works predated him by over a hundred years because Rocroi fort was constructed in 1555. Not just a tool for defence, the art of fortification was also needed for the construction of the line of circumvallation on behalf of attackers and its defence sconces and outworks. Further the fortress experts were also excellent draughtsmen who would draw models of the enemy's fortress defences, the better to understand their weak points and strong points. They would be experts at the traverses and parallel need to attack the enemy's spot marked out for breach as well as the placement and even the sighting of batteries. What constructions were needed to defend the saps snaking toward the enemy defence would also be their responsibility. On the printed page their elegant designs are things of elegance and beauty. Much of their work involved on highly skilled draftsmanship as well as mathematical skills.

Learning and shared technology via books which was the internet of the day spread technical knowledge quickly; such printing capability arrived at the exact moment when cannon technology threatened the functionality of castles and forts. In essence, the fortress experts and mathematicians of the day were in their printed works constructing a sort of primitive pre-computer CAD method, to enable fortress designers to model visually their constructs for the benefit of their paymasters and the builders. Bachot, writing in his second book *Le Gouvernail d'Amboise Bachot* describes how 'I begin with geometry, as a foundation and support for our perspective, with which we can represent the concepts developed in the art of fortifications, through elevated forms and with the use of shading, to allow the eyes to comprehend the objectives of the design.' Geometry was the device which would present the best way to establish interlocking fields of fire in depth; and to reduce the number and size of 'dead zones' which contrary to the name was the place of safety where defensive canon crossfire however directed could not hit an attacker The Dutch under attack since 1568 from much large and professional Spanish forces were in great need of defence; the artillery fortress with geometric designs for crossfire and low profile angled walls, to deflect the energy of cannon balls, was the answer to their prayers. It may well have been the difference between survival and extinction.

Oldenbarnevelt constructed a host of such fortresses in a chain along the Dutch frontier with the Spanish Netherlands in the late sixteenth and early seventeenth centuries. Even the earthen structures thrown up to enhance the outer defences of mediaeval curtain walls followed the precepts of modern fort design as did the outworks of besiegers in their lines of contravallation. In the early seventeenth century such modern fortresses were constructed by various of the electors; by Frederick V at Manheim and Frankenthal, by Maximilian of Bavaria at Ingolstadt or by the Emperor at Benfeld. As Monro attested Spandau was a powerful fortress, but the elector of Brandenburg was not powerful enough to resist Gustavus. In Italy Parma's two fortresses at Parma and Piacenza survived Spanish occupation of the Duchy but that was mainly because the Spanish did not have enough troops available for this low order priority. They were screened off.

Denmark's Christian IV built a string of fortress on the southern border of Jutland including Christianspries (Kiel) but it availed him little; if they survived it was because they could be supplied by sea. This was a common denominator for fortresses which survived attack by large victorious armies. Dutch fortress Bergen-op-Zoom defied Spinola because it was in the Scheldt delta, which was controlled by the Dutch. An outstanding example of a fortress holding out with the benefit of its coast position and support from maritime allies is Stralsund which faced the full weight of Wallenstein's Imperial army. Had it not been on the coast with plentiful import of supplies and reinforcements Stralsund must have fallen. By analogy, La Rochelle's immensely strong Huguenot fortress would fall to Richelieu when it was cut off from English support by Richelieu's construction of a fortified mole across the channel to the port. Richelieu is famously painted standing defiantly on the mole wearing armour and a cardinal's cape.

Except for Benfeld and Breda, these modern fortresses were rarely taken under siege. The capture of Benfeld was a rare exception; normally armies would march on by as the Swedes did at Ingolstadt in 1632. Where such a system was besieged, as Breda was by Spinola's Spanish, the siege lasted for nine months and involved the concept of defence in depth with a chain of outer fortresses providing an exhausting and fantastically complex campaigns, like giant chess games were required to win major strategic fortresses with modern designs; the sieges of Breda, 's-Hertogenbosch, Breisach and Benfeld are classic examples of the genre; they were rare events. Only attrition and starvation tactics would win it except at Benfeld which eventually surrendered to General Horn under threat of storming after a breach. Developing from the 1550s the accelerating after 1668, such fortification systems served well into the twentieth century and were barely improved upon. However, there was little development after the early years of the seventeenth-century; Vauban merely continued what had already been developed a hundred years earlier.

Chapter XV
Failures and Laggards in Modernisation

Several states failed in their efforts to modernize their administration and their military and this is demonstrated to some extent in the figures of population growth in capital cities which reflects growth in the administration required for a growing and developing state or proto-state as they emerged from the feudal and agricultural era. As we have indicated the rate of modernisation of the emerging proto-states was variable. intimately connected to economic success although the figures for Madrid and Brussels demonstrate that the Spanish government was borrowing its way political and economic collapse.

City	1600	1650
Amsterdam	60,000	176,000
Brussels	55,000	20,000
Copenhagen	40,000	29,000
Hamburg	40,000	75,000
London	100,000	350,000
Madrid	49,000	130,000
Moscow	80,000	200,000
Paris	220,000	430,000
Stockholm	10,000	50,000 (1670)
Vienna	50,000	60,000

Poland

It is worth considering the consequences of failure in modernization. Early Poland was a considerable country with a population of about eight million and a booming export orientated agricultural economy. After victories variously over the Habsburgs, the Swedes 1610, the Russians and a huge Turkish army in 1621, there was surprise when tiny Sweden inflicted so many military humiliations on them. Seemingly recovering later in the century when King John III Sobieski led a dramatic relief and attack on the Ottoman forces outside Vienna in 1683 Poland's problems as a state were hidden from view. Poland's oligarchic magnates dominated the complex constitution using this power to prevent modernisation and the overthrow of their feudal rights. Effective reform was impossible without a consensus of the Polish magnates. Resistance to the Swedes was half-hearted 1621–1629 because the southern magnates were not prepared to put the same funding and intent on protecting the north as they were to defeating the Ottomans in the south in 1621, when a Polish army of 80,000 had been victorious at Chocim. Against the Swedes in the north the Hetman could only deploy about 20,000 troops and in fear of the Habsburgs the magnates prevented King Sigismund from using all the available military aid from Wallenstein.

Winged hussars and Polish military capacity 1600–1634

Poland has long had a fascination and pride in its bloodstock and cavalry prowess, a tradition that continued up till modern times with Poland's recovery of independence, when the legend was renewed by Marshal Pilsudski's victory over the Red Army in the 'Miracle of the Vistula' 1920. Doomed by technology, the imagery of Polish lancers pitched against panzer divisions at the start of Second World War has been immortalised by history. The horse was king and Polish government concentrated too much on their cavalry prowess and not on mixed arms capability and the infantry. Cavalry was the effective arm of war for protecting the state from Tartar raiders and the Ottoman horde invading from Moldova. However, it was a military weak in well trained and armed infantry, who were generally regarded with disdain by the horse bound the Polish aristocracy, one of whom Starowolski said, 'we use them not so much for fighting but as labourers building ramparts, digging ditches, erecting bridges, clearing road from the guns and heavier wagons. If we desire to capture a town, we hire Germans or Hungarians, who are much better trained than our men.'[1]

The pride of the Polish army was the cavalry, notably the famously exotic 'winged hussars' mounted on Polish horses deemed the best in Europe: export of horses was forbidden. Traditionally hussars were armed with the lance, which was rarely used in early modern warfare except by the Poles and the Scots. According to contemporary reports in 1576, troopers were armed with 'helmet, sleeves [chain mail], lance, sabre...sword..., a firearm carried in the saddle, feathers and other ornaments for splendour and to frighten the enemy.'[2]. Little had changed by the 1620s except that two pistols had become the norm. For decoration, they 'fastened to the left side a huge wing made of Ostrich feathers, which covered the whole side of the horse and the rider's leg to his ankles.'[3] Sometimes there was one wing, sometimes two and they might also be attached to the back of the saddle rather than the armour. The armour involved a breastplate and plate to cover the upper arms, groins, and thigh; cuirassier style. Helmets were typical of western European styles with neck, nose, and ear guards. Unlike other nations, other cavalry units, such as cossacks, continued to wear chain mail armour. Some units or individuals carried a weapon unique to the east, a sort of ice axe with a sharp point, which was meant to be driven through the helmet and brain of the enemy. Clearly the assassination of Trotsky in Mexico City in 1940 had early modern Polish antecedents.

Polish cavalry deployed a dress sense and drama not seen again until Napoleon resurrected his famous Polish lancers. Understanding soldiers' vanity, he decked out his elite cavalry units in eclectic and élan boosting finery. Napoleon understood that a flashy uniform boosted the morale and competitive sense of identity in army units. It also helped a soldier to impress the women of the garrison towns. Early modern Polish cavalry cut a dash. They were the pride of the country, 'both an ornament and a defence' claimed the Hetman Sobieski in '...which no other nation other than the Polish have, nor can have.'[4] Writing soon after the Thirty Years War Italian envoy in Poland, Cosmo Brunette, told of the 'grandeur and beauty of this cavalry; to speak of their costumes, their tall lances with long pennants, their tiger skins and exquisite horses and saddles, stirrups, and reins dripping with gold, embroidery and precious stones; to do so would diminish their beauty. It is a chivalry that has no equal in the world; without seeing it with your own eyes, its vigour, and splendour is impossible to imagine.'[5] The dress of the Polish cavalry was not uniform, and the soldiers wore a sort of eastern cassock under their armour if they were heavy cavalry; armour would either be metal plate-lobster style, or even chain mail, something that had died out in western Europe. Around their shoulders they might wear multi-coloured capes, cloaks and colourful oriental patterns for saddle blankets or thick sheep or bearskins. A particularly popular, exotic, and uniquely Polish adornment, was a cape made of jaguar or leopard skin or furs or sometimes mock jaguar spots painted on cloth for the poorer trooper. Red was the predominant colour worn by cavalry. Equipped with scimitars, exotic headdresses, baggy trousers, capes, plumes, wings and feathers, ankle or knee length flared coats, and lances with colourful pennants, the whole aura was oriental and exotic. With their high cheek bones and long flowing whiskers, they could easily be mistaken for Tartars.[6] A French soldier in the Polish army reckoned that 'The beauty of their arms and horses...the wealth of their equipment, surpass everything that one can see in Europe and Asia.'[7]

The Polish army used shock tactics to win battles even against infantry in position. Armed traditionally with a 'super long lance', half of which was hollowed out to reduce weight, the hussars had wiped out a numerically much larger Swedish army at the battle of Kircholm in Livonia in 1605, and again at Klushino in 1610. Naturally, Polish cavalry were much feared by the Swedes whose army of 11,500 had been annihilated at the battle of Kircholm by a mere

3,500 Lithuanian, lance armed, winged hussars. There is evidence that the Polish cavalry was a terror weapon and that anyone impaled by the long lance was unlucky. Terrified enemy soldiers would cut and run. High enemy casualty ratios came in the pursuit after a victorious first encounter when fleeing infantry would be hunted down individually. It was the threat of Polish shock cavalry attacks, mounted as they were on superb chargers bred on the great estates of Poland that induced Gustavus to intersperse his cavalry units with companies of musketeers. This tactic would help even up the contest in Livonia and Prussia from 1621–30. In comparison the Swedish cavalry rode scrawny nags. Firearms were introduced to the Polish cavalry rather later than in the rest of Europe but were not regarded as primary weapons.

Montecuccoli the Imperialist general described how the hussars built up a steady momentum and then charged just a hundred paces from the enemy and 'at fifty paces they run at full bridle in order to deliver their thrust.'[8] sixty paces is as much as a horse can endure so as not to arrive tired and without vigour; furthermore the shorter the gallop the more united will be the troop.[9] Numbers of hussars were reduced to thirty per cent of cavalry in Polish armies, which is probably explained by both factors of cost and effectiveness.

The reason for the Polish emphasis on cavalry was the nature of warfare on the great steppes of southern Poland and Ukraine as well as the Russian marches to the east. The Poles not only deployed heavy cavalry but also excelled in light cavalry, often recruiting on the steppes of the Ukraine from the Cossack communities. These light 'raiding' units were deployed during the Imperialist attack on the rebellious Czechs early in the war. The Poles also had various forms of light cavalry apart from hussars; they were armed with carbines as were the cossacks who were used for raiding, foraging, and cutting off the supplies or communications of the enemy.

Poles enjoyed a special relationship with the horse; bloodstock was in the blood. Training in riding and fighting, including the use of the lance was extremely exacting and they started young; as late as the 1630s it involved deadly jousts using sharp pointed lances and no barrier to prevent collisions. A pool of talented reservists was built up from the so-called Kwarciani who had standing army duties in the rebellious Cossack borderlands. One major advantage for Poland was the fact that it possessed the best and largest horse breeding facilities in Europe. The royal stables alone at Białystok, boasted 3,000 stabled horses of all breeds. Other nobility far surpassed the king in wealth; they controlled private armies of horsemen. The Don-basin type horse was widely used on the steppes; they were known as 'Turks'. Hussar heavy cavalry used crossbred Frisian/Turk-Arab types depending on taste and desired characteristics. The result was a horse 'strong, solid, and fast,'[10] according to a sixteenth-century Papal Nuncio Ruggieri, 'the crossbred type was quite large…slower running than the Turkish horses albeit stronger and prettier.' – A stable platform from which to level lances at the enemy standing at least fifteen hands two inches: all in a great tradition which passed down to the elite Polish Lancers of Napoleon's army and beyond.

However, the impressive the Polish military and economic power was there was not strong centralized state which could dependably call upon a regular and disciplined army. There was no arms industry or capacity for industrial production of weapons except some artisan efforts on some of the great estates. Poland was weak in the provision of cannon; there were no foundries. The muddle over cannon ammunition at the siege of Mewe in 1626 points to a disorganised artillery arm. Imports of small arm weapons came from Teschen in Silesia or from the Dutch Republic. The state did not have the monopoly of violence; the great landlords controlled their own troops.. They were also very weak in artillery. While the royal stables were large that hardly compensated for the lack of firepower under the control of central government. Weak central government under an elective monarchy where the magnates purposely kept the monarchy weak was hardly likely to produce a system geared to efficient. Aristocratic privilege and conservatism blocked effect reform and the move toward a rational modernising state with an effective tax system. A sclerotic state system was reflected in the failure to develop a modern firepower orientated military, which was a catastrophic failing for a country with open flat borders. Failing to reform, the state was carved up, absorbed, and destroyed in the eighteenth century. After a brief spell of independence Poland was destroyed again by Nazi Germany and the USSR. Still wrapped in the romanticism of the horse after the Miracle of the Vistula in 1920, in 1939, Polish cavalry, facing German tanks, charged once again into the dustbin of history.

Surrounded by three large predatory neighbours Poland by 1750 already had a geopolitical problem; its internal structural weaknesses and unfortunate geographic and topographic position doomed Poland to eradication.

Transylvania

Following on from the long wars, Prince Stephen *Bocskai* stabilized a principality devastated by war 1593–1606. Immigration into vacant lands increased and a political structure was established. Population increased to about one million and Transylvania took over the supervision of the voivode of Wallachia with its Vlach (Romanian) population, the remnants of the long-lost Roman province of Dacia. Transylvania was bordered to the northwest by the Tatras, and in the east by the Carpathians and to the south as well as along the Transylvanian Alps bordering Wallachia. About 600 kilometres across and 300 from north to south, total landmass comprised about 200,000 square kilometres. Population was one to two million.

Under inspired leadership Transylvania became an important power in the first half of the seventeenth century. With the ground work led by Prince Bocskai who allied with the Ottomans in order to preserve the autonomy that Transylvania enjoyed under Ottoman tutelage, Gábor and Rákóczi corresponded with the extensive network of Calvinist princes across Europe as well as Lutherans. Gábor as married into the electoral House of Brandenburg, whose ruling family was Calvinist even if their subjects were Lutheran. Gábor, the mysterious and exotic great hope for Protestantism following the Bohemian rebellion was much discussed in the London press and by in correspondence between diplomats. For example, in a 16 August diplomatic note, Viscount Doncaster writing to Sir Robert Norton in London reported that;

> 'The Prince of Transylvania whose nephew is bredde at Heydelberg and who being of the religion [Calvinist] hathe been heretofore forced to put himself under the protection of the Turke for his security from invasion of the house of Austria hath now an army of 30,000 and it is thought will either lead them directly to the Bohemian's assistance or els against some part of the Austrians' territories, which is all one in effect.'

(From Hanau 7 August 1619) Unfortunately, light cavalry cannot be expected to stand in line of battle against heavily armoured cuirassier and harquebusier. When they met the Imperialist army in formal battle they ran away. However, in specific circumstances on the Hungarian plains they could be very effective.

On one occasion the Imperialist army was surrounded in Hungary, only escaping utter defeat by the deft leadership of the second in command count Wallenstein. Encouraged by Thurn, Gábor reneged on the Peace of Nikolsburg and invaded again in the summer of 1623. Typical of the times the London 'weekly news' sheet published by Nathaniel Butter wrote in tabloid fashion 28 October 1623, 'A most true relation concerning the great invasion made by Bethlen Gábor in the emperor's dominions... [Austria] is now a defendant against the incursions made by the Turke and Bethlen Gábor... once again, the approach of Bethlen Gábor fortifies my hopes'.[11] It would be another false dawn but at least Transylvania had become celebrated internationally. Gábor's army, consisting mainly of 40,000 light cavalry but including 3,000 Turkish janissaries and various units of Turkish and Tartar cavalry, invaded Moravia cutting off an Imperialist army corps of 9,000 troops at Göding (Hodonín) on the Moravian-Hungarian border south east of Brno. The Imperialists entrenched and circled their wagons, a familiar tactic in wars on the Hungarian steppe, as on the South African veldt in the face of Zulu attack, and reminiscent of old cowboy and Indian films set in the great planes of the Dakotas.

Transylvania's army

Rape and pillage kept morale high; Bethlen Gábor remarked in 1616 that 'nothing upsets them [the soldiery] more than not letting them pillage and plunder like they used to.' Gábor's light cavalry hussars who enjoyed the thrill of riding into the rich and fertile lands of Austria, including the suburbs of Vienna. There were rich pickings. When they had had their fill, they tended to want to go home; fighting was incidental to their main purpose and was mainly directed at small columns of enemy and especially isolated wagon trains. A Hungarian officer György Krauss described the rampaging Hungarian, 'The soldiers left nothing untouched, opened and robbed even the graves, turned everything over and searched where something could be hidden…'[12]

The backbone of the army was its light cavalry; imbued with the DNA of their Mongol forebears the plains hussars were natural horsemen. Horse and cattle breeding was the business of Hungarians who lived on the steppes of the principality; they exported huge numbers of cattle to Europe. On their small ranches and *latifundia* the Hungarians wallowed in the cult of the horse; like the south American gaucho or the plains Indian they were only 'real men' when mounted; anyone who has witnessed the riding culture of these countries know that the horse and rider naturally move as one, in contrast to the stiff, disjointed, and unnatural manners of European riders. Dressed in their colourful array their preening machismo and egotism drove them forward to raid their enemies, hitting fast, looting, pillaging, and killing. These men proud and independent were not tuned to the idea of formations or ranks or formal military discipline. Loosely grouped in regiments of 500 they were likely officered by the ranking feudal magnate from their district. Many of the cavalry raised were former cattle drovers who had been emancipated by Prince Bocskai in 1602–4; they were called hajdú, many of whom were ennobled and brought into a special military caste with tax fee benefits in return for military service. However, lacking an agricultural base, there was little of a 'Yeoman' class which might have provided the pikemen infantry as it did through the rest of Europe.

Lacking a powerful centralised state, there was little standardization in costume, weaponry, or armour, if any. Hungarian cavalry were a mixture of more heavily armoured hussar units and lighter units of hajdú cavalry-essentially a local feudal militia settled on land in return for military service. They were expected 'to keep good horses, lances and other well-maintained equipment ready for war'[13] hajdú cavalry wore knee length dolman, mainly red in colour, pewter buttoned with classic hussar cross bars might be topped by a light chain mail topcoat. A round felt cap dressed with feathers would adorn the head. Some wealthier hussars in 'heavier units' might sport a breastplate or a cuirassier's helmet imported from Germany. Lightly armoured a hussar might well deploy a Turkish style arm protector called a 'Vambrace' which could parry and defend slashing strokes against vulnerable forearm. A long red cloak sometimes fur lined was commonly worn. They wore long length Turkish style swede leather boots to just below the knee-the heels were shod with an iron horseshoe. The main weapons of the hussar were a curved slashing sabre and a short lance; alternatively, a Turkish style long broadsword might be deployed. Firearms were possessed by some; usually a short carbine or sometimes pistols in pairs either side of the saddle though these were probably owned by the wealthier horsemen and nobility. A particular vernacular weapon of choice was the battle axe or war hammer with a sharp curved spike which could be driven into the skull of a victim. However, it was the lance that was the prime weapon in battle, although this required stocks of lances for replenishment in battle because the lances snapped off upon impact. Describing the battle of Zólyom 1621 in a letter to Bethlen Gábor, István Eghri noted '...and they could not spare two hundred lances – all of the weapons were broken, and they had to resort to swords.'[14]

The tactics of the Hungarian trooper were those of mobility and surprise ambush. When charging they would gallop in several lines from all directions so as to panic and confuse the enemy who would usually flee in terror and expose themselves to being hacked down as they fled. Imperialist commander Basta recorded that a hussar charge 'It is like a summer shower; when it rains it pours but is soon over'. Hussars were expert at picking off unguarded wagon trains or small enemy detachments.

However, if the enemy infantry were well trained it was the hussars who might come off worse; a contemporary recorded the events of the battle of Goroszlo1601, 'Basta [the Imperial commander] sent more and more units which stood their ground against the lancers charge; finally, the soldiers (Transylvanians) could not withstand the fire, so the bridge was taken...'[15] Firepower triumphed.

Hungarian hussars and hajdúk had great warlike qualities and instincts for battle. As the Bohemian army retreated to Prague in October 1620 Frederick of Bohemia recorded in a letter to his wife on 22 October that 'Yesterday the Hungarians defeated sixty horsemen and gained a good number of fine horses; today they have taken a number of wagons with provisions which were being taken to them. Thus, every day we have prisoners...' This was the warfare at which the Hungarians excelled.

What they could not do or do well was stand in battle as Count Anhalt recorded bitterly of the battle of the White Mountain 'so I confirm that when I withdrew, of all our Hungarians, only a hundred were left of the ten thousand, such was the diligence they showed.'[16] To strike hard and fast with maximum surprise the method of the Hungarian cavalry. Typically, Gábor instructed his troops to 'avoid dealing with the Germans, for with time they burrow in trenches, and it takes great effort to get him out of there.'[17]

A further well noted operational constraint to hussars was their refusal to take static positions as guards to wagon trains or infantry. Such slow moving and fixed positioning was a sheer horror for the freewheeling cavaliers of the steppe: sieges likewise as Torstensson was to discover as his army besieged Brno 1645 when some extra help in the trenches would have been welcome. Hungarian cavalry whether in the Imperial or Transylvanian army would often refuse such duties, 'the cavalry did not want to obey the command; some refused to march with carts…and some even opposed the slow march itself – in other words they wanted to do as they pleased. They said that would not be guardians of foot soldiers forever… saying that being last in line would result in getting a bad quarter.'[18] State weakness was implicit in the indiscipline of its main weapon of war. As ever the main day to day concern of a soldiers was good food and comfortable quarters. Even more impossible was asking hussar troopers to dig trenches and engage in the hard graft of siege warfare.

Gábor himself was loath to engage in the details of modern logistics; nor did he have a modern administration or tax system to deal with such matters although the Gábor said of himself that he 'liked to go into battle, and I heard him say, if only someone took care of the accounts, recruitment, and provisioning-apart from that he was happy to manage battles including all difficulties and would never want to stay at home in peace'[19]. Despite his dislike of bureaucratic drudgery, Gábor was adroit in administration and government; he was rebuilding the country from the devastation of the Long War 1593–1606 which had crippled the principality and the Balkans in general.

For the Hungarian troopers whether hussars or hajdúks, a free-spirited life on the hoof roaming and plundering the enemy lands in fine summer weather was the very essence of freedom, happiness, and cultural affirmation. Sleeping rough under the stars and riding freely was the dream of his ancestors; as one of Bethlen Gábor's aristocratic lieutenants, Miklos Zrinyi, put it in his epitaph 'May a casket or the wide blue yonder be my shroud if honour is with me in my last hour. May I be devoured by the raven or the wolf, always the sky above, and the ground below'; a romantic epitaph which revealed the spirit of Transylvania but was it the last cry of a doomed state.' Gábor's troops scored some notable successes at Shut Island 1621 and at Göding 1623 against regular Imperial armies. They were an ill-disciplined plague that could devastate Austria on several occasions in 1619–1620 but before the walls of Vienna they were useless. They would not dig or demean themselves by going into trenches. Similarly, at the siege of Brno in 1645 they added no value except perhaps some cavalry scouting and screening; and they reputedly brought the plague with them to the Brno encampment which hastened the raising of the siege. However, Gábor's troops captured the modern fortress of Neuhäusel (Érsekúvjár) but that was a rare siege success. In 1626 after Gábor had re-entered the war his combined army with Hungarian troops, Mansfeld's remnants and Ali Pashas janissaries faced down Wallenstein's Imperial army. Exhausted by his march from north Germany Wallenstein did not risk a battle with Hungarian cavalry who had twice cut off and surrounded Imperial armies. Resistance on the Moravian borderlands and in northern Hungary [Slovakia] was fierce. While Tilly and Wallenstein destroyed Protestant resistance over the entire empire, Imperial troops leavened by Spanish veterans were fought to a standstill by the Hungarians on the Transylvanian–Hungarian border

As chancellor and key underpinning supporter of the previous monarch Bathory, Gábor instituted many of the reforms, which he was later able to pursue in greater detail from the time of his elective accession in 1613. Raised in a lowly Calvinist noble family he was educated in Germany, and it was this insight into a more advanced society and social structure, which propelled Gábor's drive for modernisation. Like Gustavus and Oxenstierna in remote Sweden, Gábor was aware of his country's backwardness: A thoroughly renaissance monarch he took a keen interest in promoting education and the arts and raising the level of civilisation. His palace became a showcase for modernity and included ornate gardens; horticulture and gardening were nurtured under Gábor and became an obsessive interest for the successor regime of György Rákóczi.

Gábor understood the link between strong economy and military power. Picking up from previous agriculturalists, his primary focus was on increasing agricultural production by efficient and intelligent farming techniques. An educational renaissance, which had flooded in with the reformation, was turned to account in the management of the great estates, (or 'Princely Manors', as they are referred to by Hungarian scholars). Economic wealth was built on professional and technical development of agriculture from which the state extracted tax from surpluses according to strict purchasing and price controls. Gábor insisted on the appointment of educated overseers 'who' according to Gábor, 'should be suited to his post and a clever scholar; and let him educate, teach, and accustom him to tend others, farm, and discuss the laws. Let him be master the custom of that land together with every by-law.'[20] Point forty-six of Gábor's instruction sets out the wide powers of the judges as instruments of central government in legal and financial control, 'Every quarter of the year our court judge should give a summaris… so that he may, when we enquire as to perceptions and expenditures, inform us at all times.'[21] (As above) Regular courts and a permanent legal establishment were innovations that brought forwards the operation of the state. A codified official law book was published which regulated procedural matters.[22] Gábor even handed down minutely detailed instructions for the construction of stables for good husbandry management. His particular interest in horses had a point because it was the cavalry which formed the basis of his power and the status of his regime: he ordered that stable

'...have its pillars set in a strong foundation...stalls must be made for horses in the Székely fashion, and the stalls must be carved into the beams and nailed above and below once again into the floor beams; which must be sunk into the ground nicely level to the ground....'[23]

With plenty of copper from his mines which he encouraged as a source of revenue, Gábor resurrected the foundry which having been started in 1584 had been abandoned in 1600. Production was not very large. However we know that in 1629 twenty-four newly cast guns required gun carriages to be made. There is only one reference to guns being taken on campaign. In 1645 two guns were said to have accompanied Rákóczi's army that joined with Swedish General Torstensson at the siege of Brno. So we must presume that the canon manufactured in Gyulafehérvár (now Alba Iulia in Romania) the capital went to defend the fortresses that Bethlen Gábor was constructing in this period at the border fortress of Oradea 'a monstrous walled pentacle'; Still to be seen at Oradea is the stone carved legend, 'Gábor of Pannonia, descendent of Hercules, built out of love for his country these walls of gigantic strength, ...heaven echoes his merits his divine name will be inscribed in the stars'[24] Production of cannon did not alter military methods or lead to modernisation of the Transylvanian army.

Transylvania benefited from strong demand during the Thirty Years War for its copper and agricultural products which included cereals and horticultural produce. Bloodstock export was banned though some smuggling probably occurred in border areas. However, Transylvania was also one of the major cattle exporters in Europe. Braudel estimates that Transylvania may have sold as many as 200,000 head of cattle into central Europe *annually* even before the war: half of the total European trade in cattle of 400,000 p.a.[25] Unlike Sweden there was little industrialisation or transformative effect on military tactics: this is not surprising because the slow passage of lumbering guns would have denied the Transylvanians of their primary military advantages of speed and manoeuvre. Gábor exploited these advantages to the full; indeed, his military capability exactly matched the narrow strategic space under which he was allowed to operate by the Ottomans.

Underpinning his drive for power and status was economic success: 'His [agricultural]estate policy becomes more comprehensible if we seek the place of the manor in the prince's efforts to mobilise every material resource for the wars of independence. In fact, the revenues of the Transylvanian princes at the time of Barthory came to 5,000–6,000 florins, while his income [Gábor] in 1629 amounted to 164,010 florins and fifty-four dinari derived from the treasuries of the manors.'[26] Gábor's territory was marked out by quite sophisticated modern fortresses which were built in the mid-sixteenth century in a time of wars. Between 1539–1600 eight modest sized bastion equipped fortresses were built with advice from Italian architects, and four other towns had their defences modernised. Perhaps only Érsekújvár with its regular hexagonal bastion defence came up to the top standards in European fortress design; Gyulafehérvár fortress was rectangular; it only had bastions on three of the corners but was defended by a moat.

Transylvania made considerable effort at state modernisation but the army could not be transformed to a modern standard. However, if it had, it would have been impossible to supply it on battlefields in Bohemia or Moravia that were 1000 kilometres distant. Gábor could only project his power with a light cavalry army which could survive on the hoof.

With powerful, ambitious, and potentially unstable neighbours, Transylvania was in a vulnerable position; despite the excellent governance of its princes the future of the Principality would depend on the whims of others. Despite its efforts Transylvania would disappear within two generations. Not so much as a failed state as a small state made to fail due to its geopolitical and cultural vulnerability and the actions of its neighbours. Even had Transylvania developed a modern army on the lines of Sweden, the chances of survival would have been low.

Russia

Russia under the new Romanov regime of Patriarch Filaret Romanov (father of the Czar) recognized the need for modernization having been spurred into action by defeats and Moscow occupation. The Czar's informal alliance with Gustavus's Sweden, in the face of Oxenstierna's scepticism, involved technology transfer and the sale of cannon as well as the loan of Scottish officers to train a regular infantry to replace the 'streltsy' the traditional, partially self-governing, and semi-hereditary retainers of the Czar. Somewhat akin to the janissaries. like the Boyars and the Orthodox church conservatives the streltsy were blocks on progress. Reforms were not fully implemented when the Russians broke the Truce of Deulino 1619 and attacked Smolensk in 1634; strategic mistakes, superior Polish cavalry who cut off supplies, and various logistical deficiencies led to the Russian army being surrounded and forced to surrender. Reform would have to wait for Peter the Great who bullied and terrorised his nation into a brutal modernity off sorts. However, the bovine tradition of rigorous and unthinking discipline, conservatism, as well as a willingness to sacrifice as many troops as it takes is a military culture that persists even in 2023; Peter's first action as Tsar was to massacre and disband the streltsy. Russia was a country so vast and with a weather system so brutal that its ultimate defence was literally its depth; so unlike Poland and Transylvania, reform and state modernization was not as existentially critical for Russia.

England

The dreadful inefficiencies and problems of the English military under the corrupt and inefficient Stuart regime meant was exemplified by poor performance in the Bishops Wars and the disintegration of the armies in Germany and at Cadiz. Reform came with Cromwell/Fairfax New Model Army, the Commonwealth and Cromwell's republic. Improved administration led to an army which performed well at the battle of the Dunes and a navy under Admiral Blake which returned and improved on the standards under in the Elizabethan regime. Authoritarian administration under Cromwell and suppression of the chaotic and centrifugal rule of Parliament helped to establish aa more modern and efficient bureaucratic system under the organizational genius of Secretary of State Thurloe. Cromwell dissolved Parliament three times. Professionalism of the bureaucracy is represented by administrators such as Samuel Pepys. Men of talent came to the fore rather dandies who caught the eye of the king. Under the Stuarts political and administrative incompetence as well as corruption proliferated. When the competent Stafford became chief minister, political mistakes contrived to have him executed with the King's signature on the warrant. Parliament was alienated from the Stuarts by their inconsistent policies as well as deep suspicion as to absolutist tendencies and pro-Spanish policies. Mutual antipathy and distrust led to a spiral of chaos underpinned by irregular funding of the regime. Under the Parliament which established the New Model army and then Cromwell, funding for the army was regularized. When the humble petition was addressed to Cromwell in 1657, Parliament's part in the deal was to provide a regular one million pounds per annum and a further pounds 600,000 pounds for the army. With regular funding and a more professional cadre of officials separate from the court, the performance of the army and navy improved markedly and within a short period of time. The New Model Army and the Self-denying Ordinance was the start of it. The army had a seriousness of political purpose quite different from continental armies where commanders busied themselves with the profits of war, whereas at the Putney Debates colonels concerned themselves with democracy and the rights of man.

These reforms, backed by strong stable government led to and extraordinary economic and trading success resulting in the largest empire in the history of the world. As much a political-social-economic revolution as a military one, it is no coincidence that the rise of Britain as a great naval and military power came on the back of a revolution in governance.

England had time to recover and reform because of its island geography, and because there was non-intervention in the Civil War because Europe was too preoccupied in its attritional Thirty Years War 1618–1648. This non-intervention allowed a Parliamentary system to emerge as winners in the civil war. This event which preserved some essentials of the Feudal representational system would be, with the exception of the Dutch system, quite unique in continental Europe, where some form of absolutism was the norm. England in civil war under the Stuarts was a failed state; luckily for England, that the nation survived and prospered had nothing to do with any innate genius, but to the serendipity of geography and individuals. Complacent in its island there was no immediate threat to trigger reform from outside but the dynamic for change was war within the commonwealth. A hybrid modernisation was the result.

Ottoman empire

Ottoman decline is a matter of controversy and is exaggerated because the Turks deployed the best army in Europe with fine Saphi cavalry and janissaries well trained in firearms. 'Suleyman [the Great d.1575] had left governing machinery of great effectiveness. There was a truly Imperial civil service…they presided over an administration that efficiently transmitted revenue to keep the army going. Up to 100 treasury secretaries kept track of revenues and outgoings, and in the provinces the governors had an equivalent civil service, on a smaller scale. The taxes rolled in, sustaining an army of 200,000: many more than the European states could muster.' Despite fall in standards and corruption under the eunuch system, the army was administered by the Porte well enough that it could finance and sustain huge armies.

Despite this capability there were concerns. Aliz Effendi's effusive criticism on the excessive size of the central army and the cadres of the Viziate, was backed up by the venerable Koci Bey who wanted reform of the fief system of land tenure for the military; Dervis Hasan complained about 'the inflated number of janissaries and the cost to the treasury' there was also a certain 'lack of confidence and nervousness' due the paucity of good intelligence as to western technological developments. Strassburg on a diplomatic mission from Sweden 1632–3 was feted at the Sublime Porte on account 'the reputation of the Swedish armies thanks to their numerous wonderful successes.'[27,28] No doubt they had heard about Gustavus's cannon; Strassburg noted that the Turks had a concern that as no war had been conducted in the west for twenty-five years that they might have fallen behind.

Weakness in firepower was noted by a Grand Vizier in 1602 during the Long War 1593–1606 with the Habsburgs, 'in a field or during a siege we are in distressed position, because the greater part of the enemy forces are infantry armed with muskets, while the majority of our forces are horsemen, and we have very few specialists skilled in the musket'.[29] Later in the sixteenth century the Aulic War council would also note their forces' superiority in firearms weaponry over the Turks. However, there is contradictory evidence which undermines the idea that Ottoman lacked access to firepower or capability in this field. At the Hungarian fortress of Esztergom in 1605, experienced veteran officer Abdulkar Efendi wrote of the disciplined janissary use of salvo fire by ranks.[30] Alternatively, in terms of fighting effectiveness the European troops made an impressive showing, According to Grand Vizier Yemişçi Hasan Pasha, 'Most of the soldiers of Islam are horsemen, and not only are infantrymen few, but experts in the use of the muskets are rare. For this reason, there is great trouble in battles and sieges… so, the musketeer janissaries, under their agha, must join the [sultan's] army promptly'.[31] Troop quality was mixed and inconsistent; increasingly the Ottoman army would rely on hastily recruited auxiliaries, without the drill discipline or skill in musketry of the janissaries. Ottoman decline would not show up for some time, because their army reached the gates of Vienna again in 1683. The truth was that like many European states, Ottoman efficiency and military capacity waxed and waned, depending on its ruler.

The seventeenth-century witnessed massive turmoil during the reign of Murad IV with revolts as well as a virtual civil war between sipahi cavalry and janissaries. Grand Viziers came and went in bloody succession. After the last great flourish and flexing of Ottoman Empire's power which brought it to the gates of Vienna in 1863, the Ottomans entered a period of long-term decline.

The seeds of Ottoman long-term descent into be the 'sick man of Europe' are varied but some of them were apparent in the early modern period. Firstly, the economy was weak, and tax collection remained poor compared to other states. Secondly the education system and literacy were being rapidly outpaced by proto-European states. Under the domination of the madrassas education system, Islamic conservatism would become a major block to reform. When Kemal Ataturk became President, he attacked the power of Muslim ideology and institutions, and even its symbol such as the fez. Literacy remained a major problem long into the twentieth century with literacy at only 8.9 per cent in 1927 and sixty per cent in 1975. Even if we discount distortion in the figures from the switch to Roman and Ottoman script from Turco Arabic script[32], illiteracy and its related economic decline especially its lag in developing heavy industry a major block on economic and social progress in contrast literacy and education combined with state modernization, and the iterative and existential struggle for dominance and/or survival in the European space, propelled European states forwards.

Sultanate of Makassar

This book focuses on the military revolution in Europe which is where the 'take off' in the military revolution and state modernization occurred. However, many of the factors involved in that process were apparent in the Sultanate of Makassar* in the early part of the seventeenth century; factors include included economic success based on an international capitalist trading model, openness to new ideas, and education. As Japan closed itself off to new idea under Tokugawa shogunate, Islamic Makassar grabbed at the future enthusiastically.

Makassar, located on south west coast of Sulawesi Island in the south China sea, (towards the eastern end of the Indonesian archipelago) was not a Portuguese possession but they maintained nonetheless an informal alliance and a large presence of Portuguese nationals, including up to 500 traders. It was the one state in the whole of the east, which took up western technology and military know-how with enthusiasm. Apart from the Portuguese, the English and Danes also established factories there. Spices were shipped in from around the region to Makassar's lively international market, which was the bane of Dutch attempts to monopolise spice distribution and stop 'contraband' trading from the Java Sea region. The sultan maintained strict neutrality in the Thirty Years War; of warring rivals Chancellor Matoaka ordered that, 'The King requires that both may be alike free in the port of Makassar, but is loath prince to displease either, and his affection is very constant to the English, so as no politic prince in Europe could do no more, but his country cannot be supplied without the Portuguese, so the best we can expect is to stand in equal balance.'[33] Portuguese sailings out of Makassar, especially the Japan trade, had a value of 500m *cruzados* in 1634, twelve per cent of Portuguese non-custom port concessionary trade. Strategically positioned as we have noted already, the place soon came under the covetous eyes of the Dutch. In practice neutrality favoured the Portuguese.

Makassar had risen to prominence in a typical regional coincidence of wet rice growing and strategic trading potential such that the population rose to 100,000 by the early seventeenth century.[34] This highly organised state built strategic rice stores to feed its populace in lean years. Like ancient Athens, this maritime sultanate also had a 'zone of influence' including many neighbouring islands to the south, including Lombok, Borneo, Sumbawa, Flores, Timor and Seram.[35] The city became the alternative supply station for pepper as well as fine spices such as mace, nutmeg and cloves smuggled throughout the Dutch security zone around Banda and Tidore: in the other direction Makassar became an entrepôt for the booming market for Indian textiles, from cotton goods to luxury silks. It was also the main regional market for slavery; slaves were captured along the Sulawesi coast or imported via their strong Portuguese connections to the Portuguese slave trading community at Chittagong and the Dutch in India. So, it became a cosmopolitan trading and financial centre, despite the Moslem ban on interest, for many races Portuguese, Spanish, Malay, Javanese,

* 1900 km south east of Singapore/1500 km north west of Darwin (Australia)

Indians, Chinese, English and Danes. Rice grown in its ample hinterlands was exported around the region to other coastal conurbations especially to Malacca.

Between 1590 and 1640, led by unusually curious and enlightening rulers, the city underwent a cultural renaissance based on learning from the west, with European technology, books and scientific instruments being highly prized: This led to quasi-industrialisation with shipbuilding, brick manufacture for houses and fortification, a cannon foundry, musket, and gunpowder production. Armouries contained 2,422 firearm pieces in 1615, and domestic manufacture started in 1620.[36] Levels of culture and education were high. Makassar's rulers had libraries and interested themselves in mathematics and astronomy.

Brick manufacture was especially important for the construction of fortifications, some of which are still standing in what is now a busting metropolis. Under a series of exceptional local rulers, Makassar reacted with urgency to prepare for Dutch attacks in 1615; 'all the land is making bricks for two castles to be finished this summer.'[37] Sombaupu Fort measured a substantial 250 x 500 metres, and the state boasted two other forts of similar size and many other smaller fortifications. Sombaopu, which had walls 4 metres thick, boasted four bastions mounting twenty large European made cannon, while the various forts at Makassar were connected by a fortified seafront some 11 kilometres long.[38] State armouries 'laid ready 10,000 lances, 10,000 cresses with bucklers (shields) to them 'spaces' (lances) as many, 2,444,800 quoyances of rice for store; all this to entertain the Flemings (the Dutch) …'[39] It was not an easy city to take because of its large and warlike populace. Blockades would make little impact on a city with a very extensive hinterland of lush paddy. A large, elongated conurbation along the straight shore it enjoys a sheltered roadstead protected by a string of coral atolls running parallel to the waterfront. Well placed artillery fortresses at either end of the city restricted possible naval attacks by protecting the narrow entrances to the north and south of the coral-guarded roadstead.

The state became Islamic in 1607. Makassar, which was intermittently at war with the Dutch during the Thirty Years War, held their own so well that the Dutch called them the 'fighting cock of the east'.[40] Makassar's inhabitants, and their allies the warlike Bugis armed with muskets and chainmail of their own manufacture, consolidated their power on Sulawesi and outlying islands. One of the main reasons for Dutch hostility was that Makassar's rulers refused to cut off their relations with Portugal, whose key, trading hub at Malacca depended on Makassan rice imports. But in 1615 Makassar resisted proudly, Sultan Alauddin telling bullying Dutch envoys that Makassar was 'open to all nations'. He was a believer in free trade, 'God made the land and sea; the land he divided among men and the sea he gave in common. It has never been heard of that anyone should be forbidden to sail the seas. If you seek to do that, you will take the bread from the mouths of people.'[41] Fine sentiments but it was Dutch made laws of the sea developed by Grotius to protect Dutch interests which prevailed and were then expanded upon by the next maritime superpower; Britain. Never officially aligned with Portugal the interests of Makassar and Malacca were connected, so much so that 2,000 Portuguese emigrated there after the fall of Malacca in 1640. In turn Makassar became the *bête noir* of the Dutch as the last hold out against VOC trading power and the spice monopoly in south east Asia; they were able to fend off Dutch attacks until finally overwhelmed in a fiercely fought siege in 1669. From a teaming and prosperous south east Asian trading network, the city states of Asia went into went into decline; the Dutch closed off development and modernisation by exploiting the military revolution to close down regional rivals in modernity and trade. Even modernizing states can fail if the predator is more advanced and bigger in due course the British empire would conquer India and close down the global dominance of the Indian textile industry though this trope has been somewhat distorted and exaggerated by BLM historians.

Japan

Not all Dutch conquests of Portuguese assets in Asia were achieved with military means. An example of vicious skulduggery in neutral ports was the Dutch a bloodless triumph in Japan, when the Portuguese were suddenly expelled in 1636 by the Tokugawa shogunate in three 'Acts of Seclusion' 1633–39, which was to last 200 years. This was the final chapter in a steady escalation in persecution which had been increasing throughout the 1620s, Catholicism having been first banned in 1614, the Bakufu authorities were well aware that priests continued to be smuggled into the country.

Persecution and suspicions of Portuguese Jesuits mounted on account of the identification of the Portuguese with Jesuits of St. Xavier who had had considerable success in developing Catholicism. With 300,000 converts, mainly in Kyushu Island, Catholics under their converted Daimyo [regional ruler-warlord] came to represent an independent and dangerous power because of their links with foreigners. Perhaps as important in the calculation made by the Shogun was the threat of individual Daimyo in Japan's various islands acquiring independent wealth and power through trade.

A consummate power player and schemer in the Tokugawa family tradition, Iemitsu, set out to consolidate power by centralising the administration, and reducing the power of regional Daimyo. Like Ferdinand II he also believed that religious diversity was politically dangerous, and undermined Japan's unity and strength. Radical changes in Japan's trade policy, which favoured VOC were in part due to the fortuitous presence of an exiled French Huguenot from Brussels, François Caron. Caron joined the staff of the VOC in Hirado, being promoted through the ranks to become senior merchant in 1633, then chief

Factor in 1639. As a fluent Japanese speaker, he had privileged access to the Shogun to whom he was a confidante. When he informed Iemitsu of the history of the Jesuits and the Spanish empire, Caron was pushing at an open door. A triumph for Caron's diplomacy, he successfully painted the Portuguese and their Jesuit friends as politically dangerous 'fifth columnists'. Jesuits were blamed for fostering rebellion amongst the Catholics of Kyushu. Shogun Iemitsu was also given lessons in geography, so he learnt how small the Dutch Republic was and how vast, populous, and powerful the Spanish/Portuguese empires were. Caron wrote of his past dealings with Iemitsu in 1641 'after the investigating the size of the world, the multitude of countries and the smallness of Japan… he (Iemitsu) was greatly surprised and heartily wished that his land had never been visited by any Christians.'[42]

The Shogun drew the obvious conclusions: That the Spanish/Portuguese Empire was a threat. Catholics had suffered increasing persecution for several decades, but under draconian seclusion laws, the 'Closed Country Edict of 1635' Ships' movements were strictly regulated, trade was licenced, and sales were strictly controlled. The new law included the following: '3. If any Japanese returns from overseas after residing there, he must be put to death. 4. If there is any place where the teachings of the [Catholic] priests are practiced, the two of you must order a thorough investigation. 5. Any informer revealing the whereabouts of the followers of the priests must be rewarded accordingly. If anyone reveals the whereabouts of a high-ranking priest, he must be given one hundred pieces of silver.'[43] This naturally pushed Japan's Christians to revolt and drove many expatriate and Christian Japanese communities into mercenary soldiering, usually in alliance with Portugal. Only the Dutch were allowed to keep a trading post in Nagasaki and Hirado Island, off the coast of Kyushu, where the benefits of trade accrued to the Bakufu [Shogunate] rather than the Daimyo. This effectively excluded the Portuguese following on from the Spanish who had already been banned in 1624. Although the Portuguese hung on to some trade, in practice they were hamstrung. The more specific 'Exclusion of the Portuguese Edict of 1639' was the final nail in the coffin, '3. While those who believe in the preaching of the priests are in hiding, there are incidents in which that country (Portugal) has sent gifts to them for their sustenance. In view of the above, hereafter entry by the Portuguese *galeota* (ships) is forbidden. If they insist on coming [to Japan], the ships must be destroyed and anyone aboard those ships must be beheaded.'[44]

The Japanese government issued the 1639 edict following a revolt by Japan's Catholics in 1637. At Hara, the first flashpoint of revolt, 2,000 soldiers trained in musketry by 200 Samurai defended a coastal fortress. The attacking army of over 100,000 made little progress, so they 'requested' help from the Dutch who set up landward batteries, as well as bombarding the fort from the sea. Unwilling helpers, the Dutch found that their guns had too little elevation for a fortress set on high bluffs. Hara was eventually captured in April 1638. Shimabara castle was next. During the siege the castle was bedecked with Christian flags, a red cross on a white background, (like the crosses which emblazoned the sails of Portuguese ships). The fort was defended by over 30,000 Christian inhabitants. They were all butchered when the defence was overrun. Portugal and the Jesuits were blamed for encouraging the rebellion. Jesuit priests were horribly tortured and martyred, and 300,000 other Christians eradicated or driven underground. Individual Jesuit priests moved underground but were as ruthlessly hunted as those in Elizabethan England. Their martyrdom, a story of brutal torture and death, is brilliantly depicted in Endo Shusaku's novel 'Silence' based on the real life and death of Portuguese Jesuit priest Cristóvão Ferreira (c. 1580–1650). 'He (Iemitsu) was cunning as a serpent so that the Christians who until now had not flinched at threats and tortures succumbed one by one to his cunning wiles.'[45] In due course François Caron would become the director-general in Batavia of the VOC's entire operation. At the age of seventy-six when returning to the Netherlands it was some irony when he was drowned by shipwreck off the coast of Portugal, together with all his accumulated wealth.

Faced with this devastating blow to the most valuable trade route in Asia, Portugal responded by sending a ship with a complement of seventy on a diplomatic mission to recoup their trading privileges. Sailing into Nagasaki Bay in July 1640, the entire crew was arrested, even though the ship carried no cargo and was not attempting to trade. Following the Edict of 1639 to the letter, Iemitsu had fifty-seven of the diplomatic delegation and crew beheaded after they had refused the choice of apostasy.

For political reasons Japan turned in on itself and remained isolated for 250 years. Foreign influences were regarded as dangerous and the recent experience of international conquest in Korea had been a disaster. Having been badly burnt by international contact Japan withdrew from the world. Having been a leading exponent of the use in the musket, the opportunity for develop first class cannon from their ample copper deposits was spurned. With their Samurai culture and disciplined armies, Japan might have become a leading military power. However, isolation led to decadence and a significant decline in military capability. Two hundred and fifty years later, they would suffer repeated humiliation at the hands of the USA and the English whose warships shelled Shimonoseki (without response) in punishment for insults to Englishmen. 'Black ships' from the USA which entered in the bay of Shimoda and imposed a humiliating trade treaty on a military weak Japan which had fallen behind in military capability. A satirical poem below lampooned Japan's pitiful weakness; soon this humiliation would lead to the Meiji restoration (of the emperor) when ardent modernisers took power from the Tokugawa.

Breaking the halcyon slumber
Of the Pacific the Pacific
The steam powered ships
A mere four boats are enough
To make us lose sleep at nights.

Nations can slumber and sleepwalk into decadence and fail in their primary duty as a nation. Soon, the Japanese failed state would be resurrected into a leading world military and naval power within a generation. Has western Europe been sleepwalking since 1990?

Small states in the Thirty Years War

Savoy survived as a satrap of France. Despite changing sides several times between Spain and France, the dynastic link though Louis XIII's sister's marriage to Emmanual of Savoy probably saved them. Pulled asunder by civil war created by outside powers, Savoy was eventually brought by Mazarin into the French fold, a satrapy in all but name and official documentation.

Charles Of Lorraine fought for decades to keep the Lothringian free of French control but his alliance with the Habsburgs simply bought him a losing ticket, although the matter would not be settled until the Treaty of the Pyrenees 1659. As a small state encompassing French vital interests on the Rhine there was little prospect of remaining independent.

Venice was geographically tucked away in an uncontested space, moreover Venice was an immensely wealthy state with the ability to buy mercenaries. In her magazines she deployed huge reserves of military hardware; deploying a large naval force, Venice was an important bulwark against the Ottomans; collapsing the Venetian state was in no one's interest. Venice was also a state protected by water and mountains; not just an island, the Po valley and the Delta was not an easy place to campaign, and mountains covered the territory to the north and east. Clever diplomacy operated by the most capable diplomatic corps in Europe also helped Venice's efforts to remain free, something helped by the continued fracture in Italian polities.

Lessons from failed states

The story of failed proto-states of Europe is that there is no perfectly common thread. A powerful and competent executive resulting in a professional army geared to the delivery of firepower on the battlefield was a necessary factor in the existential struggle in the European geographic space. Clearly a successful transformation depended on economic strength, and size was certainly a major factor as was the geographic make-up of the state including its position visa vi other ambitious states. Cultural, social a and political factors played a great role. Sometimes survival was just a matter of luck, the foibles, megalomanias, and fickleness of human beings. Facing comprehensive defeat and probably dismantlement of the geographically diffuse Prussian state in 1762 Frederick the Great's regime was saved by the death of Russian Empress Elizabeth. Her successor Peter III immediately changed sides in the war, primarily due to his personal admiration for 'the Old Fritz'.

National spirit was important for the Dutch, the English, and the Swedes; propaganda and the creation of difference through fear or otherwise became an abiding strategy for modernizing nations. Sometimes this was based on religion.

A combination of luck and geographic positioning, mainly related to the sea or water enabled the survival of number small states; the Dutch, the Swedes, the Danes, the English and Venice. The Dutch and Sweden also had a national spirit. Savoy was married well into French dynastic alliance. Russia was underdeveloped but too large to conquer.

Nevertheless, the lesson from the era was that failed states would probably disappear or be absorbed, unless they became modernized states deploying professional armies and superior firepower. The tiny Dutch state achieved freedom by capitalism and the military revolution; Sweden likewise. Denmark failed to modernize their army, but Copenhagen's Island geography and a superb navy maintained Danish freedom. Modernised to a degree, Transylvania thrived as a satrapy but when it attempted freedom in 1711, a combination of its relative lack of development its small size and population, as well as a vulnerable geographic position, meant that it disappeared from history. England expanded because of its ability to deploy mobile firepower at sea and due to its island geography. Israeli, despite being surrounded by much larger and more populace states has been able to maintain its freedom thanks to its military superiority, its modernised state, and economic success as well as its alliance with the USA.

Taxation, capitalism, and the military revolution

Comparative tax raising power amongst major powers

	1600–1609	1600–1609 per cap	1650–59	1650–59 per cap
Spain	430.8 tonnes silver	62.6 grams silver	412.7	57.3
France	294.2	18.1	1053.7	56.5
Dutch Republic	116.8	76.2	213.9	114.0
Venice	67.6	37.5	68.0	42.5
England	63.7	15.2	196.1	38.7
Poland	15.2	1.6	39.9	5.0
Prussia	3.5	2.4	6.3	9.0
Ottoman Turkey	122.6	5.8	150.1	7.4

Karaman Pamuk 2010

The figures demonstrate rapid growth in state revenues for some of the actors in the wars of the first half of the century. However, each figure for each country needs to be understood in context. Spain was already severely overextended by the end of the sixteenth century; they had already gone bankrupt once under Philip II. Despite desperate measures during the Thirty Years War revenue did not increase; the economy remained depressed after four bankruptcies, debt rescheduling and forgiveness and over taxation in Philip II's reign. The economy was in decline already as epitomised by the decline in wool exports from 400,000 bales a year to 25,000. In 1607 there was a major default under the Lerma regime which threw the economy into depression; despite this under the Olivarez regime which took over in 1617, borrowing soared as Madrid prepared for war and increased military spending not just on the army fortresses, and colonial defences, but on the creation of a modern navy.

Per capital taxation had gone as far as it could do by the end of the sixteenth century; an attempt to increase revenue had led to five revolutions in Spanish controlled territories after 1640. The Catalonian and Portuguese declarations of independence were fatal to the Olivarez regime and the Habsburg dominion in Europe. Tax unification under the Union of Arms programme in 1624 had only been partially successful with widespread resistance from local elected bodies; Catalonia had refused. Olivarez had attempted an absolutist revolution and it failed. Raw dissatisfaction was exacerbated by the fact that Spain's satellites understood that despite Olivarez's efforts the Castilians still occupied all major appointments. A further bankruptcy in 1627 threw military planning into chaos. The loss of the treasure fleet at Havanna to Piet Heyn acting for the Dutch West India Company was ruinous for Spanish credit. Another default in 1647 occurred in the run up to the peace with the Dutch in 1648 at Munster.

With less than half France's revenues by 1650, Spain was bound to lose an attritional contest with France. The three-fold plus increase in French revenue with no corresponding increase in economic growth and wages over the period is testament to exigencies of attritional war; the tripling of per capital taxation explains the huge number of *croquant/nu-pieds* peasant uprisings and eventually the Fronde from 1634–48. France became the classic absolutist fiscal state geared to war. Taxing agricultural products was difficult and hard to do justly, even if the tax farmers were not venal, because of variable and volatile harvests which might vary even in close regional proximity due to microclimate vagaries. Modernization was difficult in a backward agricultural economy. Finessing was not possible, and application of taxes was necessarily crude and inefficient compared to small urban economies. Similar circumstances in a mainly agricultural society would produce the Russian revolution.

The Dutch republic doubling in revenue also experienced far the highest per capita tax take. However, this is reflective of economic growth and very high levels of income. Dutch wages were about five times higher than other countries, so high per capital tax does not imply any undue strain; quite the contrary. Deficits were easily financed through the efficient debt markets unlike France where structural inefficiencies meant that the costs of debt was four to five times higher than in Holland. France with half the per capita tax take was groaning under the strain of it. The Republic meanwhile shrugged off the effects of attritional war in Europe because it was not attritional for the Dutch, who thrived in war industry and trade. In much the same way the USA benefited from the First and Second World War. Dutch ability to tax was easier because it taxed products in an urban setting; economic activity was smoother.

England shows the most impressive growth in revenue collection; it was based on economic growth and increasing tax efficiency; government modernisation accelerated due to the societal impact of the civil wars 1642–50 and Cromwell's subsequent military dictatorship; the trajectory meant that England with its larger population would soon be challenging the dominance of the Dutch in trade, industry, and sea power. England, by state modernising and taxing effectively, despite a Parliamentary system became a superpower because it combined economic liberalism with structures of governance that enabled the firepower revolution at sea and on land. Despite accusations of corruption the state council established by the Rump Parliament was effective in setting up an administration, that for the first time was outside the immediate ambit of the monarch's court. That solid professional administration was put in place was exemplified by professional naval official Samuel Pepys and administrators Marten and Chaloner.[46] After Stuart mismanagement the English navy suddenly became a proud war-winning machine under Admiral Blake. Complaints of corruption against the Stuart regime were also a cover for a political battle over religious tolerance, human rights, and control of state machinery. Under Cromwell's absolutist 'Parliamentary' dictatorship administrative systems continued to develop; when the restoration took place the administration continued and did not revert to the court. Samuel Pepys for example simply switched his former allegiance to the new regime; his work continued as before. On land the New Model Army's superbly organized and disciplined infantry would fight impressively to defeat Condé's Spanish at the battle of the Dunes 1654. Prestige won by Drake and others was regained by Admiral Blake. Still behind the Dutch the English would struggle to overcome the accumulated experience and power of the Dutch but nonetheless fought them to a standstill in a war which was settled by the Peace of Westminster in 1678.

Weber's thoughts on the modernizing impact of hard-edged, better educated Protestants in northern Europe may be overblown but surely there is some merit to the idea that civic zeal in England, the Dutch Republic, and Sweden owed something to a north-European-Protestant ethic. What the English experience does show is a separation of the machinery of government from a highly personalized monarchical court.

Notably, the failure of Poland and the Ottomans to mobilise their states' revenue base was symptomatic of weak central government. Even after a 500 per cent increase in taxation through 1600–1660, Poland's tax raising power was less than one twentieth of the Dutch republic per capital and less than one tenth the level in France. For Poland it would mean extinction in the eighteenth century; small and geographically vulnerable Transylvania would also disappear despite many successful reforms; revenue collection from the cattlemen and livestock breeders on their grasslands cannot have been easy. If we consider the size of Poland's population, we can see that their reliance on population alone, twelve million in 1618, would not be enough to maintain their status. Venice's economic stagnation due to the loss of their spice monopoly through the Levant shows in their figures, taxes per capita increased. Prussia's figures show the first signs of the autocratic grip of the great elector; their progress hereon would be rapid. Ottomans were in a slow decline despite the still impressive absolute size of their revenue base in 1600, the small percentage of tax take revealed governmental weakness.

The spurt in state modernization in the first half of the seventeenth-century, the corollary to the military revolution, is also seen in the populations of European capital cities; concentration of power, money and bureaucracy on central government and the court led to phenomenal growth in the capitols of Europe 1600–1650.[47] Similar growth rates were seen in the populations of leading cities which were modernizing their government and building a centralized autocracy, of Paris, Vienna and Amsterdam for example, and for similar reasons. Paris population doubled to 450,000 1600–1650. Madrid which was already large before the 'era of wars' increased from 50,000–130,000 and Lisbon from 110,000–165,000. Similarly, London increased from 200,000–400,000, a rise attributable to trade but also to the growth of modern government; likewise, Amsterdam increased both as a commercial and administrative centre from 30,000–165,000, although much military and naval activity was decentralized to the different states. Stockholm with a quasi or modified constitutional absolutist model grew from 10,000 in 1600 to 60,000 in 1670. Prussia was to follow the absolutist model developed in the early part of the century; luckily boosted by the Westphalian treaty, and led by a dynamic modernizing elector, the Prussian state's capital Berlin grew from 12,000 in 1648 to 172,000[48]. By 1700 Russia had similarly followed an absolutist model; after the creation of St Petersburg the population increased from zero to 100,000 by 1700; the city was entirely given over to the court and a modernised bureaucracy replete with German advisers, including military and naval bureaucracy. Populations in the capitals of defeated nations or nations that failed to modernize enough, remained flat or even declined, for example Warsaw and Copenhagen respectively.

Taxation is the capital accumulation that feeds a military revolution and its associated state. It can be grown as a by-product of economic growth, or it can be ripped out of the welfare and living standards of the people as it was by the Richelieu-Mazarin regime or by a combination of the two. This absolutist method can indeed lead to rapid economic development for example by the development of heavy industries and weapons facilities, etc. In the case of seventeenth-century France there was only a limited effect whereas for example the military revolution enacted by Stalin's regime 1933–40 was based on a heavy industrial growth through taxation-confiscation under the 'primitive capital accumulation' concepts developed by Yevgeni Preobrazhensky in his seminal1926 publication *Nova Econômica.* Sweden's military revolution was similarly based on industry but with primitive capital accumulation being achieved by a combination internal exploitation of resources sold into the international market, i.e. copper and iron ore. Herring and forestry products were also important exports but later overshadowed by the mineral bonanza. In the soviet case by grain and minerals. Like The USSR, early modern Sweden imported foreign equipment, technology, expertise, and some capital too. Although Sweden also had some internal capacities in metallurgical expertise, they needed foreign capital and expertise for secondary production of refined product, e.g. bars ingots, wire, and tertiary production of weapons and other manufactures,

The remarkable fact of the war was that nations so recently emerging from feudalism, with woefully underdeveloped structures of government, could in the Thirty Years War rouse themselves to such prodigious military efforts, for such a long time. But this epic of attrition and existential struggle came at a price. Revolutions during the Thirty Years War were the manifestation of rapid change, onerous taxation, and social stress. Not for the first or last time in history, state development in tandem with rapid social, technological, and economic change, was catapulted forwards on the wings of war.

Conclusion

The military revolution of the period from about 1550–1650 was integral to modern state formation whether that was in absolutist states, in the consensus states of Scandinavia or in a proto-post feudal representative state such as England. England may not have been absolutist, but economic survival and progress required modern state formation; this process was boosted by regimental and infantry traditions developed by Cromwell and the New Model army through his reign but most importantly by the development of a modern navy, which required modern state structures for a weapon system that was by far the most complex industrial process in the early modern world. Samuel Pepys navy which emerged from the Republican Protectorate was able to develop with sound state structures and well enough to stand up to the maritime power of the Dutch, and eventually defeat them. Competition with the Dutch economic superpower of the seventeenth-century was part of the push and pull of modernization in seventeenth-century England. Capitalist capital accumulation through trade, land enclosures and liberal political-economic traditions propelled the world's first industrial revolution. Being an island was a great help because in consequence England was not overrun by foreign armies.

The pace of modernisation in Europe was not uniform and its manifestation varied considerably from country to country; those countries that did not modernise, or were too small, or who did not fully embrace the military revolution to update their military, would disappear as states. For example Transylvania would be absorbed after the failed war of independence in 1711. Centrifugal forces made Poland progressively and relatively weaker by comparison to its neighbours. That did not matter too much in the seventeenth and eighteenth century but when Prussia, Austria and Russia emerged as militarily powerful modern absolutist states, able to channel their entire nations into total war, then a Poland without natural frontiers, with a weak central government lacking tax raising power, would be absorbed.

Under the pressure of the very extensive wars of the époque, in the late sixteenth or early seventeenth centuries, most of the states of Europe modernised or tried to modernize their political structures and military systems to adapt to the extensive and existential requirements of interstate competition. The coming together of iteratively connected social, economic, intellectual, technological, and political factors accelerated this process. It was the 'military revolution'. During an 'era of wars' to quote Andrew Roberts, they did this by harnessing the potential of existing economic development and private enterprise. The rapid modernization of military capacity in the early seventeenth-century was enabled and even provoked by the hidden hand of private enterprise, building on existing capitalist achievements, in repetitive production techniques, in mining processes–metallurgy, in structures of international trade finance, transportation, correspondent banking, and technological developments. Military revolution has always followed periods of rapid economic innovation stimulated not so much by governments but by the hidden hand of capitalism, including recycling surplus capital through efficient financial systems, bond markets, assientos, and banks in Europe. Correspondent banking, deposit accounts and set off arrangements smoothed trade flows for arms and war materials enabled states to finance larger, ever more modern armies and for longer than would be achievable through current budgetary incomes. Modernizing governments exploited the capacity that was at hand, something that gave stronger economies an advantage so allowing states such as the Dutch Republic and Sweden to develop more power out of proportion to their population. The power was translated into firepower, for the Dutch in their fleets and fortresses, for the Swedes in the cannon which were smelted and cast in their own factories from ores mined in their own country. Modern capitalism underpinned the Thirty Years War and fuelled the long attritional struggle.

Rosa Luxemburg points out, with the unalloyed clarity of a Marxist ideologue, that 'Militarism fulfils a quite definite function in the history of capital, accompanying as it does every historical phase of accumulation. It plays a decisive part in the first stages of European capitalism, in the period of the so-called 'primitive accumulation' as a means of conquering the New World and the spice-producing countries of India.'[49] There is some truth in this assessment, for example Dutch and English merchants did use their surplus to move outwards and conquer other trading opportunities, (initially territorial aggrandisement was not the objective but the suppression of competition would over time become a hallmark of militarized colonial capitalism). However, the new militarism early seventeenth-century Europe was not the result of capitalism but rather the inevitable result of accumulated existential political competition. Human agency simply exploited naturally developed capitalist markets to transform, by taxation and technical appropriation, structures of state aimed at optimising the delivery of firepower on the battlefield and at sea. We know well that non-capitalist-communist or societies which disdain 'interest rate returns' (Moslem societies), have the same propensity to militarism, perhaps even greater. Advances in capitalism enabled the military revolution; it did not cause it.

Another Marxist writer Benno Teschke claimed in his book 'the myth of 1648' discussed the early modern inflection point in statehood and sovereignty suggesting that the dynastic regimes of Europe continued much as before saying that the nature of 'the State' has not really changed. It was still dynastic construct, where the means of violence were not monopolized by the state but personalized by the king, who sold army posts to patrimonial officers.'[50] However even he admitted that 'personalized, decentralized feudal political authority was replaced by more centralized absolutist rule, which was in turn replaced by depersonalized, centralized capitalist political order: modern sovereignty. Absolutist sovereignty. In striking contrast to modern sovereignty, was proprietorial in character, personalized by the ruling dynasty, and rooted in absolutist pre-capitalist property relations.'[51] This analysis has much merit even if it is generalized and does not account for variances the fact that capitalist structures were in place long before the early seventeenth-century. Marxists tend to believe that there has only truly been a revolution if a King's head is chopped off which is why Leon Trotsky believed that the English revolution was worthy of study as the inflection point ushering in a bourgeois capitalist stage of history. Even in Marxist analysis it is clear that a military revolution had run in tandem with a 'capitalist political order'. There were modernised states, or 'sovereignty'as he calls it, at the time of Westphalia 1648 but Teschke argues that it was controlled exclusively by dynasties,

Clearly superior state organization enabled the transformation of taxation and state institutions and indeed the concept of the sovereign state during the 'era of wars' led to permanent military establishments capable of year-round military activity on land and sea. Political decision resulting in extended war in the late sixteenth and early seventeenth centuries provided the existential driver that detonated the archaic and semi-feudal proto-states of Europe into an explosive period of iterative dynamism. Economic strength and an efficient tax system underpinned state power. It is no coincidence that leading nations in the military revolution were the small wealth producing states of the Dutch Republic and Sweden; small, nimble, well governed, these states faced an existential threat, real, presumed, or potential. Rapid state formation and military organization was a matter of survival.

The Dutch needed to build and maintain dozens of fortresses and a sizeable fleet, as well as providing for a standing army that could be rapidly expanded by organizing well trained militia's; the sort of citizen fellowship exemplified by Rembrandt's *Night Watch*. This all required an advanced and well-organized society, and excellent standards of administration. Given the geography of Holland such organisation structures were present from the start due to the needs of water management in the low-lying 'low countries'. It is not surprising therefore that the great organizer and leader of the Dutch estates was the Grand Pensionary of Holland, Oldenbarnevelt, also the administrator for hydraulics and water engineering for Holland's levels, dykes, and canals. The threat of water and how to deal with it was both an existential need and a defence mechanism.

For Sweden the needs for developing a state were different and so also the methods. Existential threats came from the Danes against whom Sweden had rebelled and from whom they had subsequently separated in 1523. Christian IV was not yet reconciled to the fact. However, the most potent threat was from Sigismund Vasa King of Poland, Gustavus's uncle who had been usurped by his brother, Gustavus's father and was determined to try again to win back his kingdom after failing in his attempt 1598–9. Sweden's expertise mining and access to rich copper and iron ore deposits led to rapid economic growth in processing and secondary production, fuelled by foreign expertise and capital, combined with local know-how. Operating with a thinly educated population and administrative capability, Sweden rapidly built up its cadre of technical experts by expanding and improving Uppsala university and opening a university in Dorpat Livonia. Modernisation in state and economic structure, which involved the import of skilled labour from continental Europe, would enable Sweden to build a fleet to rival that of Denmark and to create a highly trained and organised army and officer corps capable of securing a Baltic empire, invading the Poland, and bringing the Habsburgs to their knees.

Permanent military forces, meant training in firing practice, discipline, formation marching, regular pay and quarters. It also meant the ability to reload and fire and listening to orders while under fire. General Wolf's Martinet training of his soldiers had one purpose; to fire the perfect volley and repeat it as soon as possible. His thin red line's single perfectly timed volley against a ragged French attack on the Plain of Abraham (Quebec) in 1759, won the north American continent for the British empire. Something similar vis-á-vis India, plus a little bit of British skulduggery did the same thing at the battle of Plassey 1757. As the age of firepower dawned at the end of the sixteenth century, the issue was already well understood.

The ultimate objective of modernization and the purpose of a state in arms and institutions in pursuit of sovereign objectives and nation state consolidation was to deliver efficiently and with discipline and formation on the battlefields of Europe or on the high seas, at the critical moment, the maximum possible firepower. This requires political organization that turns a peasant into a citizen, ore into a gun, and a citizen into a trained and motivated soldier, and for this the states needs information, effective administration, taxes, education, propaganda, and social organization. A revolution does not take two hundred years. The essence of the military revolution took about from 1600. Thereafter changes were incremental with little in the way of innovation even in the extended period of the Napoleonic wars. Why no existential push to a military the revolution under the threat of Napoleon apart from an ineffectual experiment with rockets? There were no major technical or miliary innovations before or during the Napoleonic wars. Size of armies and the number of cannons deployed was the most significant aspect of the wars; hardly revolutionary, but just an extension of the firepower revolution of the early seventeenth-century. The next acceleration in technological and societal development, the second military revolution, took place from the mid-nineteenth century, and was most notably marked in the 1860s in the American Civil War, then the Austro–Prussian War of 1870 and the Franco–Prussian Wars. It was marked using railways, the telegraph, ironclad ships, repeating rifles, and breach loading cannon. It was preceded by the efforts of industrialists and inventors with development of the steel industry, the chemical industry, explosives, and steam power. The exploitation of technical innovations developed in booming capitalist economies led to the second military revolution.

The third great military revolution, the product of the nineteenth century Industrial revolution, developed out of the First World War through to the

Second World War. It was notable for the use of submarines, aircraft-including jets, rockets, telephones, hand-held radios, machine guns, aircraft carriers, the telephone, high explosive shells, tanks, radar sonar and the atom bomb/H-bomb. Inventors and entrepreneurs by way of example included Nobel, Morse, Watt, Krupp, Ford, Tesla, Marconi, Wright bros, Lenoir/Otto (internal combustion), Rudolf Diesel, Einstein, Turing, computers, Edison, Sikorski (helicopters), Leo Baekeland (plastics), Fritz Heder (artificial nitrates), Frank Whittle, Alexander Fleming, Werner von Braun, and Goddard (rockets)

The fourth military revolution is now in hand and revealed itself firstly in the laser guided technology used in the Second Gulf War and using drones by Azerbaijan against Armenia who were forced to terms after one week, having been the victor in all previous wars. The remarkable fourth revolution (digital) has recently seen the use of drones, lasers, space communication and spying, HIMAR, guided artillery shells, advanced AA interceptor rocketry, NLAW, and Javelins to defeat the Russian invasion of Ukraine. AI is on the way as is autonomous intelligent weaponry. There hardly seems to be one inventor any more but a continuous iterative process involving vast teams of researchers around the world. However, individual inventors such as Turing, McCarthy (AI), Tim Berners, Lee (internet), Werner von Braun, Albert Einstein, and Jack Kilby (microchips) have had a huge impact.

Like the first great modern revolution which we call 'the age of firepower' these revolutions derived from the hidden hand of technological change, entrepreneurial talent in a capitalist system which enables states under extreme existential pressure, such as war, to grab and exploit these factors of science and change. Constant evolution can be accelerated under existential pressure.

Under the pressure of the very extensive wars of the époque, in the late sixteenth or early seventeenth centuries, most of the states of Europe modernise or tried to modernize their political structures and military systems to adapt to the extensive and existential requirements of the interstate competition. The coming together of iteratively connected social, economic, intellectual, technological, and political factors accelerated this process. It was the 'military revolution' during an 'era of wars' 1600–1650. Proto-states did this by harnessing the potential of existing economic development, including an international financial system, and private enterprise; only this could explain the ability of the polities of Europe to conduct an intense war of thirty years duration. Transformation of taxation and state institutions and indeed the concept of the sovereign state during the 'era of wars' led to permanent military establishments capable of year-round military activity on land and sea.

Permanent military forces, meant training in firing practice, discipline, formation marching, regular pay and quarters. It also meant the ability to reload and fire and listening to orders while under fire. No longer a part time auxiliary from a feudal landholding but an appendage of the state, the new soldier would by degrees and martinet discipline be transformed by military drillmasters such as General Lenart Torstensson and Turenne into the disciplined automatons that would characterise the Prussian armies of Frederick the great. As the age of firepower dawned at the end of the sixteenth century, the issue was already well understood. In being able to fire and reload three times for every one of the French Admiral Nelson understood the exact same principle-backed by tactics which optimised firepower capability; well drilled firepower superiority wins. The objective of state modernisation and consolidation was the disciplined and reliable delivery of firepower, at the critical moment, on the battlefields of Europe; or on the high seas.

As part of this process citizens also had to change. This involved both incentives and penalties. Conscription might be imposed by the state, but the state had to become more adept at winning the loyalty of the citizen in this new kind of state. The absolutist state demanded much from its citizens in military services and taxes, unquestioning loyalty, and in some cases overt oppression and quasi-slavery notably in Russia but also in parts of Austro–Hungary and Poland; it did this through oppression, propaganda, and the church. It was not much of a two-way bargain or contract between the people and what became the ancient regimes of Europe. The sins of existential absolutism, of secret police and the focused idea of building societies geared to the maximization of firepower would come at a cost. The French revolution was 130 years away and all of Europe's citizens were demanding a new social contract in 1848 (even Britain had the chartist movement); those that did not adapt would face a bonfire of empires in 1919.

Given that power competition is an enduring and never-ending element in human nature (a point forgotten in the complacency induced by decades of peace in Europe) and the nature of states, there is always a need for security which is the primary responsibility of states. This can be done in two ways; by building military capability and/or by making alliances. In essence military capability means firepower inclusive of these characteristics – accuracy, range, mobility, and speed of delivery. It is clear from the evidence that firepower increased at an astonishing rate between 1600–1650; we can measure it both by the increasing ratios of musketeers in armies and by the rate of fire, there were far more cannon per soldier than previously. Use of cartridges enable three shots per minute. Gustavus's role in this process is well recognized by military historians such as JFC Fuller and Basil Liddell Hart. Fuller in his book '*Armament and History* 1946, talks of the age of gunpowder in the round but recognized the revolutionary role played by Gustavus.

Tellingly it was the Chinese who developed gunpowder but despite this technological lead they failed to develop it and the Mings ended up having to copy the 'military revolution' from Jesuits, Portuguese, Dutch traders; and they still failed in their existential struggle against the Manchus. In China the military revolution was ephemeral in its effect because thoroughgoing state modernisation continued to elude China until the twentieth century. Likewise in Japan where an early lead in the production of excellent firearms and associated infantry tactics became stultified due to cultural and political factors. State modernization had to wait for the Meiji Revolution and the band of modernisers, oligarchs led by Ōkubo Toshimichi who rapidly transformed Japan after 1880. A great achievement in the face of strong traditionalist opposition, it was a remarkable transformation which required the total embrace of western state modernisations and technology. Unlike the diehard Samurai and co-revolutionary, Saigo Takamori, Ōkubo realised that a 'military revolution' (which was the ultimate purpose of the Meiji Restoration 1868 – essentially a revolution – after the Black Ships humiliation 1853) could only co-exist alongside a revolution in state and economic structures. Rebelling against the new regime which he had helped found, then defeated in battle at Shiroyama 1877, Saigo Takamori would commit Seppuku in a small cave. The events of the Satsuma rebellion 1877 are absurdly, though entertainingly portrayed by Tom Cruise 'The last Samurai' (2003). (The cave, cut into the rock on the roadside as it winds up to the upper town, is located near the seafront at Kagoshima opposite Mount Sakurajima Volcano.) In a parallel to Polish lancers' futile efforts against German tanks, Takamori's remaining 500 Samurai with swords charged 30,000 western drilled soldiers armed with Snider-Enfield breach loading rifles backed by modern artillery which fired 7000 shells. Not just a military victory, it represented the triumph of social, economic, and state modernisation. Within a generation Japan had become a militarised nation capable of defeating Russia; within two generations it was a military superpower deploying advanced battleships and aircraft carriers, which sank British and American capital ships.

Japanese seventeenth-century experience tells us that military revolution alone is a stunted child of progress, incapable of development unless there is an associated state modernization and most importantly a strong capitalist, productive, trading, and financial economy. Japan's oligarchy after the Meiji restoration 1868 realised that a military revolution needs total societal and governmental change. In the early seventeenth century, the Swedish economy in harness with the Dutch economy developed the first modern proto-military-industrial states by embracing total change. In the Dutch and English example this was as much driven by bottom-up forces as from the top, whereas Sweden set the future European model for top-down change by absolutist states.

Michael Roberts brough forward his theory of the military revolution; while there were certainly antecedents with fortress and siege guns and especially in the development of naval power, the great take-off in the age of firepower and associated state modernisation was the catalyst effect of the Thirty Years War fought out on a global scale. Its associated and iterative side effect was the acceleration in state modernization as the state tried desperately to catch up with efficiencies already established in Europe's capitalist structures. It was these very structures which enabled the war to last for so long and to spread so widely. States struggled most of all to finance these wars and the associated military revolution; instituting suitable tax structures, state structures and military infrastructures was still work in process by the end of the Thirty Years War in 1648 and the related Treaty of the Pyrenees in 1659. The effects of the miliary revolution in the great European existential struggle for power, territory and primacy were indeed long lasting and are still with us.

Sometimes historians desperately seek to find something new to say but we can often find the better historical truth in the old works which are often too readily cast aside. Ideas can and should develop but they may happily coalesce with what has gone before. Michael Roberts established the idea of the military revolution, and this author can only embellish and develop it at the fringes. The firepower revolution was noticed by none other than JFC Fuller. Writing in 1946 he observed, 'it is not until we come to the Thirty Years War 1618–1648 that in the technique and tactics of Gustavus Adolphus 1594–1632, we find a noticeable advance in armament and firepower'.

Conceived in the conflicts of the late sixteenth and early part of the seventeeth century the age of firepower in the first half of the seventeenth-century detonated the creation of proto-states. Thereafter, state organization for the purpose of delivering firepower became the primary purpose of the state. Having been aroused from their delusional slumber, European states, following Trump's foreign policy démarches in February 2025 have just woken to the fact that national security and firepower still are the main purposes of government.

> Machiavelli: 'A ruler, then, must never stop thinking about war and preparations for war and he must work at it even more in peacetime than in war itself.' (The Prince, Chapter 14)

Notes

Introduction

1. Keith Roberts and Adam Hook, Pike and shot tactics 1590–1660, Osprey 2010, kindle loc 115. Nieuwpoort was an encounter battle; it was not chosen by Maurits and he felt lucky to have won.
2. Nikolaus Gabelmenn Memoires p.45
3. Keith Roberts, Adam Hook, Pike and Shot tactics 1590–1660, Osprey 2010
4. Robert Munro, His Expedition, p.196
5. ed Janos Szabo and Zsolt Schafer, Soldiers of Bethel Gábor, 2017 Mare Temporis Tortenelmi Hagyomanyokert Alpitvany, p.47.
6. JFC Fuller, Armament and History, Eyre and Spottiswoode 1946, p.79
7. Charles Spencer, Prince Rupert, W&N, 2008, p.39, from Warburton, memoirs of Prince Rupert Kessinger 2008

Chapter 1

1. Scots in Sweden quoted above from the Scots attack on Frankfort,
2. Monro, His expeditions, Scots in Sweden, p.197
3. William P. Guthrie, Battles of the Thirty Years War, table p16.
4. John Keegan, Face of battle, Johnathan Cape 1985, p.64
5. CRL Fletcher, Gustavus Adolphus, Capricorn 1963, p.190
6. JFC Fuller, Armament and History, Eyre and Spottiswoode, 1946, p. 98
7. Richard Brzensinski, Lützen 1632, Osprey 2001, Watts, p.71
8. Stephane Thion, French Armies of the Thirty Years War Gramont LRT edition 2008, p.159
9. Ibid,
10. John Keegan, Face of battle, from Marshall, 'Men against fire', Johnathan Cape 1985, p.73
11. Monro. His Expeditions, Praeger 1999, p,135
12. John A Lynn II, Women armies and warfare in Early modern Europe, Cambridge 2008, p.79
13. William P.Guthrie, Later battles of the Thirty Years War, Greenwood press 2003, p.17
14. Thomas Longueville and Francis Lloyd, Turenne, Harford's military discipline 1680, Longman Green 1907-Kessinger press, p.41
15. Ibid,p.42
16. Sir James Turner, Military Effaces of the Ancient Grecian Roman and Modern art of War, Richard chiford, London 1670, Keith Roberts, Adam Hook, Pike and shot tactics 1590–1660, Osprey 2010, kindle loc 154
17. John A. Lynn, Giant of the Grand Siècle, the French army 1610–1715, Cambridge 1998, p.330, Stephane Thion, French Armies of the Thirty Years War, LRT editions 2008, p.70
18. Christopher Duffy, Siege warfare: In the Early Modern World, Routledge 1979, p. 124
19. Peter Young, Marston Moore 1644, Roundwood p.264

20. David Parrott, Business of War, Cambridge 2012, p.100
21. From Zeng Gongliang 曾公亮, *Complete Essentials for the Military Classics Preceding Volume* (*Wujing Zongyao qian ji* 武經總要前集),
22. Willian H McNeil, The Pursuit of Power, Univ of Chicago 1984, p.130
23. Keith Roberts, Adam Hook, Pike and Shot tactics 1590–1660, Osprey 2010, kindle loc 323
24. William P. Guthrie, Later Battles of the Thirty Years War, Greenwood press 2003, p.18
25. de Rohan, Le parfait Capitaine, Geneva 1631
26. Munro, His Expeditions
27. John, Keegan, Face of battle, Johnathan Cape 1985, p. 7,
28. Mate Sepsi Laczko 1521–1624 chronicles, p.50
29. Robert Monro, His Expeditions, p.295
30. Stephane Thion, de Rohan a Turenne website, Henri Campion memoirs
31. Tryntje Helfferich, the Thirty Years War documents, Halleck 2009, Hagendorf, p.290

Chapter 2

1. Prof Michael Howard, War in European History, Oxford, 1993, p.14
2. Louis DiMarco, War horse, Westholme 2008, p.157
3. Bouko de Groot, Nieuwpoort 1600, Osprey, p.75
4. John Stubbs, Reprobates, Viking 2011, p.360
5. Robert Munro, His Expeditions, p.196
6. Peer Wilson, Prof, Lützen, Oxford 2018, p.50/66
7. Prof Peter Wilson, The Thirty Years War Sourcebook, Palgrave Macmillan 2010, Anhalt, p. 67
8. Comte de Bussy-Rabutin, Memoires, Mercure de Fance 2010
9. Paul Krenn, Material Culture and Military History; Test firing early modern small arms, Graz 1995
10. Stephane Thion, French Armies of the Thirty Years War, Count de Grammont LRT edition 2008, p.159
11. Ibid, Turenne LRT edition 2008, p.157
12. Robert Monro, His Expedition, p.193
13. Rerported The Independent, 4th august 2007, evidence of Antje Grothe, chief archaeologist on site
14. Reported 14th April 2007 Scottish Herald, Franz Schopper, direcktor Brandenburg monument preservation and Antje Grothe.
15. Louis DiMarco, War horse, Westholme 2008, p.172
16. Robert Monro, His Expedition, p.193
17. Winston Churchill, My Early Life, Manchester edition, p.279
18. Sydenham Poyntz, a true relation of the Warres in Germanie, Ken Trotman publishing 2005, p.72, f22b
19. Richard Brzezinsky and Richard Hook, Swedish Army in the Thirty Years War, Vol 2 Swedish cavalry, Osprey 2003, p.11
20. Thomas Longueville, and Francis Lloyd, Turenne, Longman Gree 1907-Kessinger, p. 41
21. Tilly battle report from Lutter 1625 to Infanta Isabella in the Netherlands; Stephane Thion blog: de Rohan a Turenne, the Thirty Years War and the art of War in the XVI and XVII centuries
22. Peter young, Marston Moore 1644, Roundwood p.260–261

23. Cruso, John. Militarie instructions for the cavallrie: or Rules and directions for the *service of horse:* Cambridge: Printed by the printers to the Universitie of Cambridge, 1632. This book is said to have influenced Cromwell but only the revised 1644, had moved on past the antiquated caracole tactics to recommend "charging through". So, his tactical ideas probably arose by informal channels and/or by his own methods.
24. Louis DiMarco, War horse, Westholme 2008, p.156
25. John Stubbs, Reprobates, Viking 2011, from Warburton quoting Baker's chronicle, memoirs of Prince Rupert, p.358.
26. Stephane Thion, French Armies of the Thirty Years War, Victome de Montbas, LRT edition 2008, p.92
27. Richard Brzensinski, Lützen 1632, Osprey 2001, Fleetwood, p.52
28. Ibid, Swedish field Chancery diary, p.52
29. Prof Peter Wilson, The Thirty Years War Sourcebook, Palgrave Macmillan 2010, Colonel Dalbier, p.176
30. Peter Young, Edgehill 1642, Roundwood, 1967, p.270
31. John Stubbs, Reprobates, Viking 2011, p.360
32. Golo Mann, Wallenstein, Andre Duetsch 1976, p.671
33. Richard Brzensinski, Lützen 1632, Osprey 2001, p.89/90
34. Thomas M. Barker, Army, Aristocracy, Monarchy, Social Science monographs Columbia 1982, p.119
35. Xenophon, the Persian expedition 401BC
36. Vincent p.29.p.29 Mortimer
37. *Letter of Settlement of the hajdús in Majteny 1611, p.41]*
38. Zoltan Boldog p.40
39. Ed. Zsolt Schafe, *Soldiers of the Age of Bethlen Gabor*, http:Kastonak-Bethlen Gabor Korabol.hu
40. p.15, Memoirs Ferenc Marosvasarhhelyi Nagy Szabo
41. Trynte Hefferich, *The Thirty Years War, a documentary History,* Hackett 2009, Frederick V to his wife Elizabeth
42. recorded István Szamosközi's Historical Remnants
43. Trynte Hefferich, *The Thirty Years War, a documentary History*, Hckett 2009, Count Anhalt to Frederick V Palatine after the battle of White Mountain.
44. Count Barbarino during Bocskai uprising 1605, p.22
45. *ed Janos Szarbo and Zsolt Schafer Soldiers from the age of Gábor Bethlen, Mare Temporis Tortenelmi Hagyomanyokert Alapitvany,* p.50]
46. Janos Kemeny 1658 ed Janos Szarbo and Zsolt Schafer Soldiers from the age of Gábor Bethlen, Mare Temporis Tortenelmi Hagyomanyokert Alapitvany, p.6
47. Zrínyi Miklós, a költő hadvezér és politikus

Chapter 3

1. JF Hayward, The Art of Gun making 2nd ed Barrie and Rockcliff, p.16–17
2. Lisa Jardine, The awful end of Prince William the Silent, Harper Collins 2006, p.79.
3. Gerhard Beneke, Germany in the Thirty Years War, Edward Arnold 1978, p.28, B.Kuske, Koln, Rhein und Reich 1956, p.190–191
4. Suhl Museum, German Hunting Gun Society, History of Gunmaking in Suhl p.1, Website
5. JF Hayward, The Art of Gunmaking 2nd ed Barrie and Rockcliff p.130
6. Ibid p.196
7. Ibid, p.211

Chapter 4

1. B.F Porshnev, Muscovy and Sweden in the Thirty Years War, Cambridge 2012, p.77
2. Major-General JBA Bailey [Royal Artillery], Field artillery and Firepower. Naval Press 2004, p.xvii
3. Harold Peterson, Round Shot and Rammers, Bonanza NY 1948, p.24
4. Goerge Gush, Renaissance Warfare part 4, internet
5. Thomas Carlyle, vol 6 p.188 First Civil War
6. Bi Maokang 畢懋康, *Jun qi tu shuo* 軍器圖說, ca. 1639.
7. Harold Peterson, Round Shot and Rammers, Ranges of Spanish guns in the Early 17th Century, Ufano, Bonanza NY 1948, p.20 and p.24
8. Albert Manucy, Artillery through the Ages, US Dept of the Interior 1949
9. Goerge Gush, Renaissance Warfare part 4, internet
10. Robert Munro, His Expedition, p.196
11. Ibid
12. Fischer, Scots in Sweden p.212
13. Major-General JBA Bailey [Royal Artillery], Field artillery and Firepower, Routledge chapter 3
14. John Stubbs, Reprobates, Viking 2011, Oliver Cromwell to Valentine Walton, p.360
15. Henri Campion Memoires, and Stephane Thion, de Rohan a Turenne website, Henri Campion memoirs.
16. J.I. Israel, Conflicts of Empires: Spain and the low countries and the struggle for world supremacy 1585–1713, Continuum, 1997, p.74
17. Albert Manucy, Artillery through the Ages, US Dept of the Interior 1949
18. Stephanie Thion, La Bataille d' Avins, LRT 2011, Prosegur, p.72
19. Harold Peterson, Round Shot and Rammers, Ranges of Spanish guns in the Early 17th Century, Ufano, Bonanza NY 1948, p.20 and p.24
20. General Wrangel to his father after 2nd Breitenfeld, History of the Swedes, Geijer
21. Stephanie Thion, La Bataille d'Avins 20 Mai 1635, LRT editions 2011, p.72
22. Harold Peterson, Round Shot and Rammers, Bonanza NY 1948, p.26–29
23. Major-General JBA Bailey [Royal Artillery], Field artillery and Firepower, Routledge p.5
24. Ibid
25. Richard Brzezinski, Lützen 1632, Osprey 2001, p.88
26. Stephanie Thion, La Bataille d'Avins 20th Mai 1635, LRT edition 2011, Louis de Pontis, p.70
27. Chris Henry, English Civil War Artillery 1642–51, Osprey 2005, p.35

Chapter 5

1. JFC Fuller, Armament and History, Billings, 1946, p.98
2. Richard Brezininski and Richard Hook, The Army of Gustavus Adolphus, infantry, Sebastian Dehner, German chronicler, Osprey 1996, p.18
3. John A. Lynn, Giant of the Grand Siècle, the French army 1610–1715, Cambridge 1998, p.460
4. William P. Guthrie, The later battles of the Thirty Years War, Greenwood 2003, p.8
5. Richard Brzensinski, Lützen 1632, Osprey 2001, Diodati, p.70
6. Ibid, p.71
7. William P. Guthrie, The later battles of the Thirty Years War, Greenwood 2003, p.8
8. Thomas Longueville and Francis Lloyd, Turenne, Longmans Green 1907-Kessinger, p.42
9. Andreas Klaus, Maximilian I, Styria/Pustet, p.146

10. Sir James Turner, Military Effayes of the Ancient Grecian Roman and Modern art of War, Richard Chiford, London 1670, Keith Roberts, Adam hook, Pike and shot tactics 1590–1660, Osprey 2010, kindle loc 310
11. Keith Roberts, Adam hook, Pike and Shot tactics 1590–1660, Osprey 2010, kindle loc 329
12. John Keegan, Face of Battle, commenting on theories of du Picq, Johnathan Cape 1985, p.71,
13. John Watts de Peyster, Life of Leonard Torstensson, Wrangel, 1st published 1855, Rarebooksclub 2012, p.44
14. Claude Gaier, "L'opinion des chefs de guerre français du XVIe siècle sur les progrès de l'art militaire," *Revue Internationale d'Histoire Militaire* 29 (1970): 723–746; quote from p. 743. See also Frederick J. Baumgartner, «The Final Demise of the Mediaeval Knight in France,» in Jerome Friedman, ed., Regnum, *Religio et Ratio: Essays Presented to Robert M. Kingdon,* Sixteenth Century Essays and Studies, Vol. VIII (Kirksville, MO: Sixteenth Century Journal Publishing, Inc., 1987), 9–17 for a similar judgment.
15. Peter Young, Naseby 1945, Century 1985, p.231
16. Mme de Montpensier, memoires, Internet Archive section
17. Rosie Serdville and John Sadler, the Great siege of Newcastle 1644, p.80
18. Monro: His expedition with the worthy Scots Regiment called Mac-Keys, Praeger1999, p.87
19. Robert Monro, His Expeditions p.250

Chapter 6

1. Fernand Braudel, Civilisation and Capitalism, The Structures of everyday life, Collins p.395
2. Darko Pavolovic, Imperialist Armies of the Thirty Years War, Osprey
3. Braudel, Fernand Braudel, Civilisation and Capitalism15th-18th Century, Structures of everyday life, p.132
4. Geoff Mortimer, Eyewitness accounts of the Thirty Years War, Sir James Turner, Memoirs, His Life and times, Palgrave 2004, p.33
5. Estimates based on assessments by Martin Creveld/Sir James Turner [contemporary] see section on logistics in Part II, Martin Creveld, Supplying War, Cambridge 2005, p.10, Geoff Mortimer, Eyewitness accounts of the Thirty Years War, Sir James Turner, Memoirs, His Life and times, Palgrave 2004, p.33, Geoffrey Parker, Army of Flanders, and the Spanish Road, 2004, p.86, Geoff Mortimer, Eyewitnesses to the Thirty Years War 1618–1648, Palgrave 2004, p.33
6. Salvius 1631 Arkiv II
7. Louis DiMarco, War Horse, Westholme 2008, p.170
8. Ferdinand Braudel, Civilisation and Capitalism 15th – 18th Century, Everyday Structures of life, Collins Vol I, P.192
9. Walter Scott Dunn, The Soviet Economy and the Red Army, 1930–1945, Greenwood Publishing Group 2005, p.226–229
10. Govind P. Sreenivasan, The Peasants of Ottobeuren 1487–1726, Cambridge 2004, p.281
11. John A. Lynn, Giant of the Grand Siècle, the French army 1610–1715, Cambridge 1998, p.129
12. Ibid, p.128
13. Walter Scott Dunn, The Soviet Economy and the Red Army, 1930–1945, Greenwood Publishing Group 2005, p.226–229

14. Richard Brzezinski, Gustavus Adolphus Army [2] cavalry, Osprey,
15. Louis DiMarco, War Horse, Westholme 2008, p.168
16. Ibid, p.319–320, Seaton, Horsemen of the Steppes, p.2002
17. Stephane Thion, LRT French army in the Thirty Years War 2008, p.107
18. Ibid, p.107
19. Brian Sandberg, War, and conflict in the early modern world 1500–1700, polity 2016, p.191, Turenne. Lynn, Giant of the Grand siècle, p,212
20. Martin Creveld, Supplying War, Cambridge 1997, p.80
21. Braudel, Fernand Braudel, Civilisation and Capitalism15th-18th Century, Structures of everyday life, p.132
22. Steven Kaplan, The Famine Plot, Amer Philosophical Society, 1982, p.62–3
23. Martin Creveld, Supplying War, Cambridge 1997, p.80
24. Geoffrey Parker, Global Crisis, Yale 2013, Articulating Grievances kindle loc 21492
25. Olaf van Nimwegen, The Dutch Army, and military Revolutions 1588–1688, Boydell Press 2010, 1588–1688, p. 127
26. Ibid Boydell Press 2010, David Parrott, Business of War, p.129
27. David Parrott, Business of War, Cambridge 2012, p. 176
28. Olaf van Nimwegen, The Dutch Army and the Military Revolutions 1588–1688, Brill 2010, p.222–223
29. Duc de Rohan, *Le Parfait Capitaine*, des vivres, Chapt XVI, Geneva 1631, p.330–333
30. Geoff Mortimer, Eyewitness Accounts- Thirty Years War, Palgrave Macmillan, p.166, 167, 170, 171, Thiele, Plebanus, Sautter, Schleyss's.
31. Munro, His Expedition, Praeger, ed Willian S Brockington, Forward Geoffrey Parker, p.198.
32. Stephanie Thion, The French Army in The Thirty Years War, LRT edition 2008, p.107
33. De Bale, Gazette de France, 21 August 1638
34. Geoffrey Parker, Army of Flanders and the Spanish Road 1557–1659, Cambridge 2nd ed 2004, p.217
35. Geoffrey Parker, Global Crisis, Yale 2013, Articulating Grievances kindle loc 21492
36. Olaf van Nimwegen, The Dutch Army and military Revolutions, Boydell Press 2010, 1588–1688, p. 127
37. Geoff Mortimer, Eyewitnesses of the Thirty Years War 1618–48, Palgrave 2004, p.33
38. Ibid, Palgrave 2004, p.32
39. W.E. Voss, For the Prevention of Even Greater Suffering: The Curse and Blessing of Law in War, in 1648, War and Peace in Europe, ed. K. Bussmann and H. Schilling, vol. 1: Politics, Religion, Law and Society, 275–284. Munster: European Council, 1999, p.276
40. P. Martin, Une Guerre de Trente Ans en Lorraine 1631–1661, Éditions Serpenoise, 2002, p.176
41. Tryntjie Helfferich, The Iron Princess, chapter 6, Kindle loc 2492
42. Dr Robert Reinhold Ergang, The Myth of the All-Destructive Fury of Thirty Years War, Craftsman Pocono Pines Palo alto 1956
43. Govind Sreenivasan, The Peasants of Ottobeuren 1487–1726, Cambridge 2004, p.286
44. Geoff Mort, Eyewitnesses of the Thirty Years War 1618–48, Herbele, Palgrave 2004, p.78
45. Munro; His Expeditions, p.252
46. Munro; His Expedition, p.253,
47. Rene Chartrand, French Musketeers 1622–1775, Osprey 2013, Conditions of service, Kindle loc 376 and John Tincey, Ironsides, Osprey 2010, Campaign Life loc 583, Du Praissac, the Art of War 1625

48. John Tincey, Ironsides, Osprey 2010, Campaign life Kindle loc 575
49. Ibid,583
50. Geoffrey Parker, The Army of Flanders and the Spanish Road, p.80
51. Braudel, Fernand Braudel, Civilization and Capitalism vol II, Fontana 1998
52. David Parrott, Richelieu's Army, Cambridge 2006, p.116, p.147
53. Baron Antoine Henri de Jomini, The Art of War, Greenhill books p.144–5, 1992 first in 1838.
54. Geoff Mortimer, Eyewitnesses to the Thirty Years War 1618–1648, Palgrave 2004, p.33
55. John A Lynn II, Women armies and warfare in Early modern Europe, Cambridge p. 137
56. John A Lynn II, Women armies and warfare in Early modern Europe, Cambridge 2008, Thomas Mallinger Tagbucher, p.149,
57. Fernand Braudel, *The Structure of Everyday life, 15th to 18th century*, Harper Collins, 1981
58. Martin Creveld, Supplying War, Cambridge 2005, p.8/9/17
59. ed Janos Szarbo and Zsolt Schafer Soldiers from the age of Gábor Bethlen, Mare Temporis Tortenelmi Hagyomanyokert Alapitvany, p.23
60. Geoff Mortimer, Eyewitness accounts of the Thirty Years War, Palgrave Macmillan 2004, Burster, p.33
61. Francis Watson, Wallenstein, Soldier under Saturn, Appleton 1938-Kessinger, p.178
62. Martin Creveld, Supplying War, Cambridge 2005, p.10
63. Olaf Asbach and Peter Schroder, ed, Ashgate companion to the Thirty Years War, Prof P. Wilson, Ashgate 2014
64. Monro, His Expeditions II 49
65. Prof Peter Wilson, The Thirty Years War Sourcebook, Palgrave Macmillan 2010, Anhalt, p.63
66. Erik Swart, Qualifications, knowledge, and courage: Dutch military Engineers, c.1550–1660, p.63
67. Baron Antoine Henri de Jomini, The Art of War, Greeenhill 1992, p.226–7
68. Christopher Duff, Siege Warfare, Fortresses in the early Modern world, p. 179, Generalstaben, 1936–8, IV, 257
69. Niccolo Machiavelli, The Art of War, 1st published 1521, amazon fulfilment, Poland sp.Wroclaw, chapt 3, p.91
70 Ibid, p.85
71 Ibid, p.89-93
72 Ibid, p.89-91
73 Ibid, p.91

Chapter 7

1. John A Lynn II, women, armies and Warfare in early modern Europe, Cambridge 2008, p.77
2. John A Lynn II, women, armies, and Warfare in early modern Europe, Wallhausen Defenso Patrie 1621, in Haberling, Cambridge 2008, p.64
3. Sir James Turner, memoirs
4. Richard Bonney, The Thirty Years War, James Turner, p.7
5. Sonke Neitzel and Harald Wetzler, Soldaten, Simon and Schuster, 2013, p.165
6. Ibid,, p.165
7. Goffrey Parker, Global Crisis, Yale 2013, chapter 2, The Century of Soldiers, kindle 1403
8. Geoff Mortimer, Eyewitness accounts of the Thirty Years War 1618–48, Palgrave 2004, Gerlach, p.170

9. Ibid, Sautter, p.170
10. Ibid, Hellgemayr's, p.170
11. Prof Peter Wilson, The Thirty Years War, Sourcebook, Palgrave Macmillan 2010, Friedrich Friese, p.157–164
12. Jayne E Boys, London Press, and the Thirty Years War,
13. John A. Lynn, Giant of the Grand Siècle, the French army 1610–1715, Cambridge 1998, p.192
14. Drexel Father Reitzler p.156–7, Laurence Spring, the Battle of the White Mountain, p.64
15. Veit Hoser Kriegsbuch, p.145 and p.26 Anker Fischer –Kettner, World of Sieges, p.93
16. Prof Peter Wilson, The Thirty Years War a sourcebook, Palgrave Macmillan 2010, p.54
17. Rudyard Kipling, A Father's Advice to his son
18. Hans Medick and Benjamin Marschke experiencing Thirty Years War, Bedford
19. Goffrey Parker, Global Crisis, Yale 2013, Chapter 2, The Century of Soldiers, kindle loc 1394
20. Geoff Mortimer, Eyewitness accounts of the Thirty Years War 1618–48, Palgrave 2004, p.35
21. Geoff Mortimer, Eyewitness accounts of the Thirty Years War 1618–1648, Palgrave 2004, p.84
22. Rabutin de Bussy-Rabutin comte memoires mercure de france 2010, comte de Bussy-Rabutin.p. 49–53
23. Sydenham Poyntz, A True relation of These German Warres 1624–1626, memoirs, Ken Trotman publishing 2005, p 128, f 62
24. Prof Peter Wilson, The Thirty Years War Sourcebook, Palgrave 2010, Sister Maria Anna Junius, p.260
25. Experiencing the Thirty Years War, Hans Medick and Benjamin Marschke experiencing Thirty Years War, Bedford, p.87–90

Chapter 8

1. Sir James Turner, memoirs, p.6
2. Geoff Mortimer, Eyewitness of the Thirty Years War 1618–48, Palgrave Macmillan 2004, p.44
3. Geoff Mortimer, Eyewitness of the Thirty Years War 1618–48, Palgrave Macmillan 2004, p.42
4. Monro, His Expeditions, Praeger, p.310
5. Sir James Turner, memoirs p.7
6. Golo Mann, Wallenstein, Andre Deutsche 1976, p.311
7. Geoff Mortimer, Eyewitness Accounts of the Thirty Years War, Raymond, Palgrave Macmillan 2004, p.33
8. David Parrott Business of War, Cambridge 2012, Hartzfeld, p. 158
9. Trintje Helferrich, Iron Princess, Harvard 2013, chapter 7, Kindle loc 2858
10. Olaf van Nimwegen, Dutch Armies and Military Revolutions, Boydell 2010, p. 121
11. David Parrott, Richelieu's Army, Cambridge 2006, p.164–222
12. Geoffrey Parker, Infante a Isabella 1627, Cardinal Infante 1634, The Army of Flanders, Cambridge 2004 2nd ed, p.180
13. Prof Peter Wilson, Europe's Tragedy, Allen Lane 2009, p.790
14. Olaf van Niimegen the Dutch Army and the military Revolution 1588–1688, Boydell 2010, p.245
15. Tryntke Helfferich, The Thirty Years War, a documentary history, Hackett 2009, p.124–127

16. John A. Lynn II, Women, armies, and Warfare in early modern Europe, Cambridge 2008, p.71
17. Robert Monro, His Expeditions, Praeger. p.174
18. Monro, His Expeditions
19. Francis Watson, Wallenstein, Soldier under Saturn, Appleton 1938-Kessinger, p.161
20. Golo Mann, Wallenstein, Andre Duetsch 1976, p.305
21. Ibid
22. Sonke Neitzel and Harald Weltzer, Soldaten, Simon Schuster 2013, p.53
23. Ibid,, p.89
24. John A Lynn II women, Armies and Warfare in Early Modern Europe, Cambridge 2008, p.153
25. Prof Peter Wilson, The Thirty Years War, documents, Palgrave 2010, p.254
26. Tryntje Helfferich, The Thirty Years War, Halleck 2009, Robert Munro, p.115
27. Prof Peter Wilson, Europe's Tragedy, John Christian Ludwig, 1723, Leipzig, corpus iuris militaris, 2 vols, Allen Lane 2009, p.234–7
28. Prof Peter Wilson, Europe's Tragedy, Johnan Christian Ludwig, 2 vols Leipzig 1723, Allen Lane 2009, p.236/237
29. Reported, The Independent, 4th august 2007, evidence of Antje Grothe, chief archaeologist on site
30. Reported 14th April 2007 Scottish Herald, Franz Schopper, direcktor Brandenburg monument preservation and Antje Grothe.
31. Peter Wilson, Lützen, Oxford 2018
32. Sydenham Poyntz, a True relation of the warres in Germanie, Ken Trotman publishing 2005, p.112
33. Geoff Mortimer, Eyewitness accounts of the Thirty Years War, Palgrave Macmillan 2004, 1618–48, p.40
34. Tryntje Helfferich, The Thirty Years War, Hackett 2009, p.289
35. Geoff Mortimer, Eyewitness accounts of the Thirty Years War 1618–48, p.41
36. Sir James Turner, Memoirs of his own life and times
37. Tryntje Helfferich, The Thirty Years War 1618–48, Hackett 2009, Hagendorf p.280
38. Ibid, p. 280
39. Munro, his Expeditions, ed Willian S Brockington, Praeger 1999, p.160
40. Gyorgy Krauss: plundering at Segesvar 1601. Description of all military and other things that happened between 1599 and 1606 in Ederly.
41. Parrott, Business of War, Cambridge 2012, Kordula Kasper p.163
42. Parrott, Richelieu's Army, Cambridge, 2001
43. Matthew Glozier, Marshall Schomberg 1615–90, Sussex Acadmic Press 2005, p.28/29
44. Gerhard Beneke, Germany in the Thirty Years War, documents, Arnold 1968, p.79
45. ed Hew Strachan, Holger Afflerbach, How the fighting stops; a History of surrender, Oxford 2012, Lynn TYW, p.148
46. Robert Monro, his Expeditions, Mo II 114, Geoff Mortimer, Eyewitnesses of the Thirty Years War 1618–48, Palgrave 2004, p.41
47. Swedish Intelligencer journal 1632
48. Scots in Sweden, p. 210
49. David Parrott, Business of War, Cambridge 2012, p. 253
50. Andreas Klaus, Maximilian I, Styria/Pustet, p.146
51. Sir James Turner, Memoirs His Life and Times p.4
52. Sydenham Poyntz, A True Relation of These German Warres, memoires of Sydenham Poyntz, Ken Totman publishing 2005, f 1a, p.45

53. Geoff Mortimer, Eyewitness accounts of the Thirty Years War 1618–48, Grutzmann,174
54. Geoff Mortimer, Eyewitness accounts of the Thirty Years War 1618–48, Maul, p.89
55. Ibid48, Freund, p.85
56. Robert Munro, His Expeditions, Praeger 1999, p.102
57. Geoff Mortimer, Wallenstein, Palgrave Macmillan 2009, p.3
58. Frances Watson, Wallenstein, soldier under Saturn, Appleton 1938, p.409

Chapter 9

1. John A. Lynn, Giant of the Grand Siècle, the French army 1610–1715, Cambridge 1998, p.330, Stephane Thion, French Armies of the Thirty Years War, LRT editions 2008, p.70
2. Christopher Duffy, siege Warfare, Fortresses of the Early modern Europe, Routledge 1996,
3. Stephane Thion, French Army of the Thirty Years War, LRT editions 2008, p.70,
4. Ibid,, p.82
5. de Motville memoires
6. John A. Lynn, Giant of the Grand Siècle, the French army 1610–1715, Cambridge 1998, p.324
7. Stephane Thion, French Armies of the Thirty Years War, LRT editions, 2008, p.106.
8. John A. Lynn, Giant of the Grand Siècle, the French army 1610–1715, Cambridge 1998, p.326
9. Ibid,, quoting Corvisier, p.324/325
10. Stephane Thion, French Armies of the Thirty Years War, LRT editions 2008, p.84
11. Henri de Campion, Memoires, Truttel & Wurtz,1807 p.73
12. Rene Chartrand, French Musketeer 1622–1775, Osprey 2013, Kindle loc 253
13. Stephane Thion, French Armies of the Thirty Years War, LRT editions 2008, p.50
14. Ibid,, p.50
15. J.H Eliot, Olivarez, Yale 1986, p.78
16. Andreas Kraus, Maximilian I, Styria/Pustet, p.146
17. Ibid, p.147
18. David Parrott, Business of War, Cambridge 2012, p.129
19. Golo Mann, Wallenstein, Andre Deutsch 1976, p. 273
20. Martin Creveldt, Supplying War, Cambridge 2005
21. David Parrott, Business of War, Cambridge 2012, p.128
22. Robert Munro, His expeditions, Praeger 1999, p.209
23. Prof Wilson, Europe's Tragedy, Allen Lane 2009, p.403
24. Francis Watson, Wallenstein: A soldier under Saturn, Appleton 1938-Kessinger, p.112
25. Francis Watson, Wallenstein: A soldier under Saturn, Appleton 1938-Kessinger, p.105
26. Trintje Helferrich, Iron Princess, Harvard 2013, chapter 7, loc 2830
27. David Parrott, Business of War, Cambridge 2012, p.102
28. Prof Wilson, Europe's Tragedy, Allen Lane 2009, p.403
29. Olaf Van Nimwegen, The Dutch Army, and the military Revolutions 1588–1688, Boydell 2010, p.119
30. Brzezinski, The Army of Gustavus Adolphus 2, Osprey 2003, p.9
31. Charles Carlton, Going to the Wars. BCA Routledge 1992, p.22
32. Graham Long (Cambridge) PhD work on the early modern English army
33. Robert Monro, His expeditions, Praeger 2019, p.180
34. Sydenham Poyntz, True Relation of these German Warres, memoirs 1625–36, Ken Trotman 2005, p.46, f.2

35. John Stubbs, Reprobates, John Donne, Viking 2011, p.104,
36. Richard Brzezinski, The Army of Gustavus Adolphus, infantry, Osprey 2000, p. 23
37. Billy Boyle, Uniforms of the Thirty Years War, internet, 2001, p.6
38. Theodore Dodge, Gustavus Adolphus, Tales end Press 2012, chapter X The Polish War continues 1625–27
39. Richard Brzezinski, The Army of Gustavus Adolphus, infantry, John George of Saxony, Osprey 2000, p. 2
40. Ibid, p. 2
41. Ibid, p. 2
42. Geoff Mortimer, Eyewitness accounts of the Thirty Years War 1618–48, Palgrave Macmillan 2004, p. 32
43. Gerhard Beneke, Germany in The Thirty Years War, documents, Arnold 1978, p.66
44. Billy Boyle, Uniforms of the Thirty Years War, internet, 2001.p.7
45. Richard Brzensinski, Lützen 1632, Osprey 2001, Diodati, p.70
46. Pierre Picouet, Les Tercio Espagnols, LRT editions 2010, p.26
47. Vladimir Branardic, Imperial Armies of 30 Years War(I), Osprey 2009, p.17
48. Ibid, p.17
49. Ibid, p.42
50. Ibid, p.11
51. Peter Young, Edgehill 1642, Roundwood 1967, p.298
52. Ibid, p.285

Chapter 10

1. Geoff Mortimer, Eyewitness Accounts of the Thirty Years War 1618–48, Fritsch, Palgrave Macmillan 2004, p.149
2. Von Clausewitz, On War Vol II, Routledge and Kegan, NY 1968, p.196
3. Erik Swart, qualifications, knowledge and courage, Dutch military engineers c 1550-c1660., Lazarus von Schwendi. Der erst, deutsche Verkunder der allgemeinem.... (Hamburg 1939) 92–287, 192
4. Carl von Clausewitz, On War, Routledge and Kegan, NY 1968, p.198–203
5. Henri duc de Rohan, Le parfait capitaine, cologne 1642 posthumously, LRT
6. Christopher Duffy, Siege Warfare, Fortresses in the early Modern World, Routledge 1996, p. 122
7. Parrott, Richelieu's Army, Cambridge 2001
8. Sydenham Poyntz, True Relation of these German Warres, memoirs 1625–36, Ken Trotman 2005, p.46, f.2
9. Robert Munro, His Expeditions, Praeger 1999, p.244,
10. Olaf van Nimwegen, The Dutch Army, and the Military Revolutions 1588–1688, Boydell 2010, p.135
11. Christopher Duffy, Siege Warfare, The Fortress in Early Modern Europe, Routledge 1996, p.101
12. Ibid, p.100
13. officier anonyme, biblio National de France Ms fr 3712 f244r-f293v. Traille ou journal de ce qui s'est observe du siege de Montauban, Dénes Harai (éd.) : Journal d'un officier de Louis XIII sur le siège de Montauban (1621) - Dans l'enfer de la Seconde Rochelle, Paris, Éditions L›Harmattan, 2012
14. Peter, Wenham, The great and close Siege of Yorke, 1644, Roundwood 1970, p.40
15. Des Ekin The Last Armada, siege of 100 days Kinsale 1601, O'Brien p. 133, 2014.

16. Ibid, p. 154
17. Olaf van Nimwegen, Frederick, The Dutch Army and the Military Revolutions 1588–1688, Boydell 2010, p.271
18. Robert Monro, His Expeditions
19. Ibid, p. 165
20. Robert Monro 1637, 211–12, Christopher Duffy, Siege Warfare, Routledge p.185
21. Tryntje Helfferich, The Thirty Years, documents, Hagendorf, Siege of Straubing near Munich in 1632, Hallek 2009, p.287
22. Olaf van Nimwegen, The Dutch Army, and the Military Revolutions 1588–1688, Boydell 2010, p.137
23. Robert Munro, His Expeditions, Praeger 1999, p.244,
24. Des Ekin The Last Armada, siege of 100 days Kinsale 1601, O'Brien p.201, 2014.
25. Comte de Bussy-Rabutin, memoires, Mercure de France, p.99
26. Ibid, p.102
27. Rochefoucauld. Comte de, chapter II
28. Ibid, p.166 and 169
29. Sir James Turner, Memoirs His Life and Times, p.6
30. Geoffry Parker the Army of Flanders and the Spanish Road, Campan Bergues sur le soom assiegee, Cambridge 2004, p.181
31. Geoff Mortimer, Eyewitness Accounts of the Thirty Years War 1618–48, Fritsch, Palgrave Macmillan 2004, p.147
32. Tryntje Helfferich, The Thirty Years War, documents, Hagendorf, Hackett 2009, p.282
33. Geoff Mortimer, Eyewitness Accounts of the Thirty Years War 1618–48, Fritsch, Palgrave Macmillan 2004, p.148
34. Munro; His Expeditions, Praeger 1999, p.280
35. Ibid p.280
36. Comte de Bussy-Rabutin, memoires, Mercure de France, p.110
37. Ibid, p.99–101
38. Cornelis Matelieff, Journals Memorials and Letters, ed Borschberg, NUS 2015, p181
39. Wendham Mace, The Great and Close Siege of York 1644, Roundwood 1970, p. 70
40. Des Ekin The Last Armada, siege of 100 days Kinsale 1601, O'Brien p. 181, 2014.
41. Cornelis Matelieff, Journals Memorials and Letters, ed Borschberg, NUS 2015, p181
42. Maarten Prak, The Dutch Republic in the Golden Age), Cambridge p.68
43. Des Ekin The Last Armada, siege of 100 days Kinsale 1601, O'Brien p. 181, 2014.
44. Geoff Mortimer, Eyewitness of the Thirty Years War 1618–48, Palgrave Macmillan 2004, Ernst, p.61
45. Prof Peter Wilson, The Thirty Years War, Sourcebook, Palgrave Macmillan 2010, Juegen Ackermann, p.67 Mortimer, Eyewitness, p.67
46. David Charmier, journal de son voyage a la cour de Henry IV 1558–1621.
47. Henri de Campion, memoires, Truttel & Wurtz 1807 p.145
48. Geoff Mortimer, Eyewitness Accounts of the Thirty Years War 1618–48, Palgrave Macmillan 2004, p.147
49. Prof Michael Waltzer, Just War, Basic books-Perseus 2000, p.135, Victoria
50. Geoff Mortimer, Eyewitness Accounts of the Thirty Years War 1618–48 Palgrave Macmillan 2004, p.40
51. Robert Munro, His Expeditions, Praeger 1999, p.161
52. CV Wedgewood, Col Henry Bowen, King's War 1641–47, Collins 1967, p.487
53. Olaf Van Nimwegen, Dutch Armies and Military Revolutions, Boydell 2008, p.246

54. Christopher Duffy, siege Warfare; Fortresses in Early modern Europe, Routledge 2004, p.123
55. Prof Peter Wilson, The Thirty Years War, Sourcebook, Palgrave Macmillan 2010, Friedrich Friese, p.157–164
56. Ibid, Akerman, p.166
57. Henri de Campion, Memoires, p.96
58. Ibid, p.98
59. Tryntje Helffereich, The Thirty Years War, documents, Halleck 2009, Hagendorf, p.283
60. Prof Peter Wilson Thirty Years War Source Book, Friedrich Freise p.163
61. Michael Walzer, Just War, Basic books-Perseus 2000, Machiavelli, Art of War, p.164
62. Holger Afflerbach, Hew Strachan, How the fighting end: A History of surrender, Oxford 2012, John Lynn, The Thirty Years War, p.150.
63. Christopher Duffy, Siege Warfare, Fortresses in Early modern world 1494–1660, Routledge 1996, p.130, d'aumerle 1886–96
64. John A Lynn II, Women Armies and Warfare in Early Modern Europe, Cambridge 2008, p.159
65. Umberto Eco, the 'Island of the Day Before' an historical novel set during the Thirty Years War, Secker and Warburg 1995, p.142
66. Robert Monro, His Expeditions, p.262
67. Ibid. p.165
68. Yılmazer 2003, p. 436
69. Gunhan Borekci, A contribution to the Military revolution debate-the Janissaries use of volley fire during the Long Ottoman War of 1593–1606 and the problem of origins, Yilmazar 2003, p.436, Ohio state uni, Acta Orientala, acadamiae Scientiarum vol 59 (4) p. 407–43, p.414
70. David Parrott, Research paper abstract, The Utility of Fortifications in Early Modern Europe: Italian Princes and Their Citadels, 1540–1640 First Published April 1, 2000
71. Prado Museum, Madrid
72. Jean-Denis LePage, Vauban and the French military under Louis XIV, MacFarland 2010, p.90–115
73. Comte de Bussy-Rabutin, memoires, Mercure de france 2010, p.97
74. Réné Chartrand, The Spanish Main 1494–1800, Osprey 2006, p.4
75. Ibid, p.31
76. Jon Latimer, Buccaneers of the Caribbean, how piracy forged an empire 1607–1697, 2009, p.92
77. Geoffrey Parker, Empire War and Faith in early modern Europe, Allen Lane 2002, p.205
78. Geoffrey Parker, Empire War and Faith I early modern Europe, Allen Lane 2002, p. 203
79. Jose Manuel Garcia, Cidades e Fortelezas Estado da India, Quidnovi, 2009, introduction page
80. Ibid, p.18
81. Ibid, 2009, p.32

Chapter 11

1. ed Geza David and Pal Fodor Ottomans, Hungarians, and Habsburgs in Central Europe. Geza Palffy, The origins of the border Defense system against the Ottoman Empire in Hungary, Brill 2000, p. 42
2. Geoffrey Parker, The military revolution, Cambridge 1996, p.13
3. Olaf Van Nimwegen, Dutch Army Military Revolutions 1588–1688, Boydel1995, p.227

4. Ibid, p.229
5. Marc van der Hoeven ed, Exercise of Arms, Warfare in the Netherlands 1566–1648, Brill 2012
6. Ronald Cohn, Jesse Russell, Battle of the Slaak, 2010, and paperback 2012.
7. John Stubbs, Reprobates, Viking 2011, p.106
8. Olaf van Nimwegen, The Dutch army and military revolutions 1588–1688, Boydell 2010, p. 221
9. John Stubbs, Reprobates, Hexham, Viking 2011, p.107
10. Ibid, p.107
11. Robert Nisbet Bain, Slavonic Europe; Apolitical history of Poland and Russia 1447–1796, p.124
12. Brian Davies, Warfare State and Society in the Black Sea Steppe, Routledge, 2007, p.20.
13. Konstantin Nossov, Russian Fortresses 1480–1682, Osprey Kindle loc 705/714–747
14. Ibid
15. Ibid
16. Ibid
17. Ibid
18. Ibid

Chapter 12

1. Tryntje Helfferich, The Thirty Years, documents, Hagendorf, Hallek 2009, p.285
2. Robert Monro, His Experditions p.250
3. Robert Monro, His Expeditions
4. Robert Monro 1637, 211 12, Christopher Duffy, Siege Warfare, Routledge p.185
5. Geoffrey Mortimer, Eyewitnesses of the Thirty Years War 1618–48, Hellgenayer, Palgrave Macmillan 2004, p. 82
6. Prof Peter Wilson, The Thirty Years War, documents, Palgrave 2010, p.255
7. Geoffrey Mortimer, Eyewitnesses of the Thirty Years War, Palgrave 2004, 1618–48, p.78, Preis 120–1.
8. Geoffrey Parker, The Thirty Years War, Military Heritage Press 1987, p.291
9. Ed A V Hatman and B Heuser, War, Peace and World Orders in European History, Routledge 2002, p.176, Albrecht, Maximilian I p.824–6,
10. Albrecht, Maximilian I p.859–61
11. Geoff Mort, Eyewitnesses of the Thirty Years War 1618–48, Herbele, Palgrave 2004, p.78
12. Munro; His Expeditions, p.252
13. Ibid, p.253,
14. Peter Young, Naseby 1645, Century Publishing, p.208–209
15. Ibid, p.223
16. Robert Hodkinson, local Historian, Siege of Leicester pt 1, Sealed Knot Society, Lord Grey's regiment of foot, 2021
17. C.V Wedgewood, The trial of Charles I, the Reprint Society 1964, p.149
18. Geoffrey Robertson KC, The Tyrannicide brief, Pantheon, 2005, p.15
19. Peter Young,, Naseby 1645, Century Publishing, p.232
20. David Parrott, Richelieu's Army, Cambridge, 2001
21. John A. Lynn, Giant of the Grand Siècle, the French army 1610–1715, Cambridge 1998, p.125
22. B.F.Porshnev, Muscovy and Sweden in the Thirty Years War 1630–1635, Cambridge 1995, p.77

23. Droysen Achives for Saxon history, volume 7, p. 391–392
24. Robert Munro, His Expeditions, p.196
25. Keith Roberts, Adam Hook, Pike and Shot tactics 1590–1660, Osprey 2010, kindle loc 273
26. Ibid, loc 201
27. Sir James Turner, Military Effayes of the Ancient Grecian Roman and Modern art of War, Richard Chiford, London 1670, Keith Roberts, Adam Hook, Pike and shot tactics 1590–1660, Osprey 2010, kindle loc 254

Chapter 13

1. Richard Bonney, The Thirty Years War, Osprey 2003, p.79
2. Jayne EE Boys, London News Press, and the Thirty Years War, Boydell Press 2011, p.3
3. Ibid, p.9
4. A.L. Hinton R.J Lifton Why did they kill? University of California 2005, p.243
5. Prof Michel Nassiet, la France au XVII siècle, Belin 2006, p.109
6. Ibid, Belin 2006, p.109
7. Hervé Drévillon, Les Roi Absolu, 1629–1715, Belin 2011, p.118
8. Ibid, Belin 2011, p.11
9. Carl Goldstein, Print culture in Early Modern France, Cambridge, 2012, chapter 1 Kindle Loc 453
10. Ibid,chapter 1 Kindle Loc

Chapter 14

1. Brian M Downing, 'The military revolution and political change' Princeton 1992, p.3
2. Jan Gete, War and State in Early Modern Europe, Routledge 2002, p.41
3. Rosa Luxemburg, The Accumulation of Capital, Yale 1951, Section 3 XXXII kindle loc 6871
4. Sir James Turner, Military Effayes of the Ancient Grecian Roman and Modern art of War, Richard Chiford, London 1670, Keith Roberts, Adam Hook, Pike and shot tactics 1590–1660, Osprey 2010, kindle loc 154
5. Robert Monro, His Expedition, p.193
6. Geoffrey Parker, The army of Flanders and the Spanish Road 1567–1659, Cambridge, 2004

Chapter 15

1. Richard Brzezinski, Polish Armies 1569–1696 1, Osprey 1987, p.19
2. A.Pawinski, ed Batory pod Gdanskiem [Batory at Danzig 1576–77], Warsaw 1877, p.54
3. Richard Brzezinski, Polish Winged Hussar 1576–1775, Osprey 2006, p.21
4. Ibid, Osprey 2006, p.7
5. Ibid, Polish Winged Hussar 1576–1775, Osprey 2006, p.4
6. Richard Brzezinski, Polish armies 1569–1696 1, Ospery 1987, p.13
7. Ibid, p.14
8. Richard Brzezinski, Polish Winged Hussar 1576–1775, Osprey 2006 p.44
9. Ibid, Giorgio Basta 1612 cavalry manual.p.44/5
10. Ibid, p.26
11. Jayne EE Boys
12. Gyorgy Krauss: plundering at Segesvar 1601. Description of all military and other things that happened between 1599 and 1606 in Ederly.
13. Letter of Settlement of the hajdús in Majteny 1611, p.41

14. Zoltan Boldog p.40
15. Memoirs Ferenc Marosvasarhhelyi Nagy Szabo, p.15
16. Prof Peter Wilson, The Thirty Years War Sourcebook, Palgrave Macmillan 2010, Anhalt, p.66
17. ed Janos Szarbo and Zsolt Schafer Soldiers from the age of Gábor Bethlen, Mare Temporis Tortenelmi Hagyomanyokert Alapitvany, p.50
18. Count Barbarino during Bocskai uprising 1605, p.22
19. Janos Kemeny 1658 ed Janos Szarbo and Zsolt Schafer Soldiers from the age of Gábor Bethlen, Mare Temporis Tortenelmi Hagyomanyokert Alapitvany, p.6
20. Istvan Imreh, Agrarian bylaws, History of Early modern Transylvania, Atlantic Research and Publications 2011, p.226
21. Ibid, p.226
22. Veronika Dein, The Comitatus of his eminence, ed Kovac Kiss, Studies in Early modern Transylvania, RSM 2011p.45–47
23. , p.27
24. Simon Winder, Danubia; a personal history of Habsburg Europe, Pan Mcmillan
25. Fernand Braudel, Civilization and Capitalism vol II, Fontana 1981, p.193
26. Istvan Imrech, Agrarian bylaws, History of Early modern Transylvania, Atlantic Research and Publications 2011, p.228
27. Halef Verioglu, Relationi di constntinopoli del Bailo, Swedish envoy Paul Strassburg's diplomatic mission to Istanbul 1932–33 Guney-Dogu, Avrupa Arastirmalari Dergisi Yil 2014-Sati 2651 1–50, p. 24
28. Strassburg, Relatio de Byzabntino Itinere ac Negotiis, p.25
29. Godfrey Goodwin, Janissaries, Baham 1994
30. Ibid
31. Ibid
32. Ekram Bugra Eking, Daily Sabah September 2015
33. Anthony Reid, Charting the Shape of Early modern SEA, letter to EIC, calendar of state papers 1625–29, 368, Silkworm 1999 p. 144,
34. Professor Eric Jones, Crossroads lecture, 21st Nov 2003
35. Victor Lieberman, Strange Parallels, Cambridge 2003, p.852
36. Anthony Reid, Southeast Asia in the age of commerce, Silkworm books vol II, p.229
37. AR Disney English agent, letter received III p.150–1, A. Reid Charting the shape of early modern SEA, Silkworm 1999, p.121
38. Geoffrey Parker, Empire War and Faith in early modern Europe, Penguin 2003, p. 213
39. Anthony Reid, Charting the Shape of Early modern SEA, Silkworm 1999, English agent Cockayne to Jourdain p.136
40. Victor Lieberman, Strange Parallels, Cambridge 2003, p.854
41. Anthony Reid, ed Tarling, Cambridge history of South East Asia, p.140, Anthony Reid, Charting the Shape of Early modern SEA, Silkworm 1999, English agent Cockayne to Jourdain p.135
42. Samson, vol III a History of Japan 1615–1867, Standford 1963, p. 37–38
43. Prof Sarah Lyons Watts, Department of History, Wake Forest University Winston-Salem, North Carolina, translated doc, internet
44. Ibid,
45. Sushaku Endo, novel 'Silence', historical fiction 1966, winner of the Tanizaki prize
46. Dr Barry Coward Cromwellian Association AGM lecture 2003 p.7–10

47. de Vries and Tertius Chandler Four Thousand Years of Urban Growth St Davids University Press, 1987
48. de Vries, European Urbanisation 1500–1700, Methuen 1984, p.348
49. Rosa Luxemburg, The Accumulation of Capital, Yale 1951, Section 3 XXXII kindle loc 6871
50. Benno Teschke, The Myth of 1648, Verso 2003, p.219
51. Ibid, p.217

Abbreviated Bibliography

General books the Empire and the wars of the early 17th Century
Acton, Lord, Cambridge History, *The Thirty Years War*, (Cambridge 1902)
Asch Roland, *The Thirty Years War. The Holy Roman Empire and Europe, 1618–1648*, (Palgrave 1997)
Anderson, Alison D, *On the Verge of War: International Relations and the Jülich-Kleve Crises, 1609–1614.* (Studies in Central European Histories series. Boston, Massachusetts: Humanities Press, 1999)
Asbach Olaf and Peter Schroder ed, *Ashgate companion to the Thirty Years War*, (Ashgate 2014)
Bonney Richard, *The European dynastic States 1494–1660*, (Oxford University Press 1999)
Braudel Ferdinand, *The Wheels of Commerce 15th-18th Century*, (Collins 1988)
Cameron Euan Ed, *Early Modern Europe*, (Oxford 1999)
Ceasar Julius, *The Gallic Wars*
Chaline, Olivier, *The Battle of White Mountain (8 November 1620)*, (In *Politics, Religion, Law and Society.* Volume I, *1648: War and Peace in Europe.* Ed Klaus Bussmann and Heinz Schilling. Münster/Osnabrück, Germany: Westfälisches Landesmuseum, 1998)
Cooper J.P ed, *The New Cambridge History IV, The Decline of Spain and The Thirty Years War*, (Cambridge)
Gutmann, Myron P. *The Origins of the Thirty Years War*, (Journal of Interdisciplinary History 18,1988: 749–70)
Kamen Henry, European Society 1500–1700, (Hutchinson 1984)
Koenigsberger H.G, *The Habsburgs and Europe 1500–1789*, (Longman 1997)
Koenigsberger H.G. *The European Civil War.* Chapter 3 in *Habsburgs and Europe, 1516–1660.* (Ithaca: Cornell University Press, 1971)
Ogg David, *Europe in the 17th Century*, (A&C Black)
Pages G., *The Thirty Years War 1618–1648*, (1970)
Parker Geoffrey, *Europe in Crisis 1598–1648 2nd ed*, (Blackwell 2001)
Parker Geoffrey, *General Crisis of the Seventeenth Century*, (Routledge 1997)
Petráň, Josef, *The Beginnings of the War in Bohemia.* (In *Politics, Religion, Law and Society.* Volume I in *1648: War and Peace in Europe.* (Ed. Klaus Bussmann and Heinz Schilling. Münster/Osnabrück, German 1998)
Polišenský J.V *The Thirty Years War and the Crises and Revolutions of Seventeenth-Century Europe.* (Past and Present No. 39 (April 1968))
Sturdy David, Fractured Europe, 1600–1721, (Wily Blackwell, 2002)
Theibault, John. *The Demography of the Thirty Years War Re-visited: Gunther Franz and His Critics*, (*German History* 15 January 1997 1- 21)
Wilson, Peter H, *The Thirty Years War: A Sourcebook.* (New York: Palgrave Macmillan, 2010)
Wilson, Peter H, *Who Won the Thirty Years War?* (History Today 59 (August 2009): 12–19)
Wedgewood C.V, *The Thirty Years War*, (Pimlico 1997)
Wilson Peter H, *Europe's Tragedy, A History of The Thirty Years War*, (Allen Lane 2009)
Wilson Peter H, *Absolutism in Central Europe*, (Routledge, 2000)

Czech History
Brazant Jan, *The Czech Reader, history, culture, Politics*, (Duke, 2010)
Demetz, *Prague in Black and Gold*, (Penguin 1997)

ELK ed, *The Czech contribution to Peace and War in Europe*, (ELK 2002)
Hojda, Zdenek, *The Battle of Prague in 1648 and the End of the Thirty Years War*, (In Politics, Religion, Law and Society. Volume I in 1648: War and Peace in Europe.
Ed. Klaus Bussmann and Heinz Schilling, Westfälisches Landesmuseum, 1998)
Panek Jaroslav, Tuma Olkdrich and Alii Et, *A History of the Czech Lands*, (Charles university, Prague 2011)
Polisensky J.V, *Britain and Czechoslovakia*, (Orbis 1947)
Polisensky J.V, *The History of Czechoslovakia in Outline*, (Sfinx Pragur 1947)

Germany and the Empire
Albrecht, Dieter, *Maximilian I von Bayer 1573–1651,* (R. Oldenbourg Verlag, Munchen 1998)
Altmann Dr Ruth, *Wallenstein, Feldher die Driessigjahrekrieg*, (Bohlau, 1997)
Asbach Olaf and Peter Schroder, ed, *Ashgate companion to the Thirty Years War,* (Ashgate 2014)
Barker, Thomas, *Army, Aristocracy, Monarchy, Piccolomin,* (East European Monographs 1982)
Barusdio Gunter, *Germany in the Thirty Years War,* (S. Fischer 1985))
Beneke Gerhard, *Germany in the Thirty Years War*, (Edward Arnold 197)
Berning Benita, *die Bohemisshen Konigskromungen*, (Bolhau, 2008)
Berthier Kathrin, *Die Politik Maximilians I von Bayer und seiner verbundeten 1618–1651, Zeiter teil, Zehtner Band Der Prager Frieden 1635, 1 Teilband*, (R.Oldenourg verlag, Munchen wien1997)
Boehn Max von, Wallenstein, (Verlag (1992)
Croxton Derek, *Peacemaking in early modern Europe, Cardinal Mazarin and the Congress of Westphalia*, (Susquehanna 1999
Diwald Helmut, *Wallenstein*, (Bechtle 1968)
Dixon Scott C., *The Reformation in Germany*, (Blackwell, 2002)
Englund Peter Dier, *Verwustung Deutchlands, eine Geschicte des Dreisigjahren Krieges translated from Swedish*, (Kletstutt Gartt-Cotta 1998)
Evans R, *The makings of the Habsburg monarchy*, (Oxford 1979)
Fichtner Paula, *The Habsburg Monarchy 1618–1815*, (Cambridge, 2000)
Forster Marc, *The Counter-Reformation in the villages of the Bishopric of Speyer*, (Cornell 1992
Franz Gunther, *War and the German People*, Verlag Fischer.1949, Jena, -1st published 1943
Gantet Claire, *La Paix de Westphalie* (1648, Belin)
Greyerz, Kaspar von, *Switzerland during the Thirty Years War*, (In *Politics, Religion, Law and Society.* Volume I in *1648: War and Peace in Europe.* Edited by Klaus Bussmann and Heinz Schilling. Münster/Osnabrück, Germany: Westfälisches Landesmuseum, 1998)
Glozier Matthew, *Marshal Schomberg 1615–1690*, (Sussex, 2005)
Helfferich Tryntje, *The Iron Princess, Amelia Elisabeth and the Thirty Years War*, (Harvard, 2013)
Klaus Andreas, *Maximilian I*, (Styria/Pustet, 1990)
Koenigsberger H.G, *The Habsburgs and Europe 1516–1660*, (Cornell, 1971)
Krussman Walter von, *Ernst von Mansfeld 1580–1626*, (Dunker and Humbolt, 2007)
Lindquist, Thea L, *The Politics of Diplomacy: The Palatinate and Anglo-Imperial Relations in the Thirty Years War*, (Ph.D, Wisconsin, 2001)
Macchardy Karin, *War, Religion, and Court patronage in Habsburg Austria*, (Palsgrave 2003)
Mann, *Wallenstein*, (Andre Deutsch, 1976)
Mortimer Geoff, *Wallenstein-Enigma of the Thirty Years War*, (Palgrave 2010)
Parrott, David, *The Peace of Westphalia*, (Journal of Early Modern History 8 (2004):, 153–590)
Darko Pavolovic, *Imperialist Armies of the Thirty Years War*, (Osprey)
Phelps, Dominic, *Reich, Religion and Dynasty: The Formation of Saxon Policy, 1555–1619* (Ph.D, London, 2005)
Polisensky J. V, *Wallenstein Feldherr des dreisigahrigen Kriege*, (Bolhau Verlag Weimar Wein, 1997)
Polišensky̌, J. V. *The Tragic Triangle: The Netherlands, Spain and Bohemia, 1617–1621.* Prague, Czech Republic: Charles University, 1991.

Portner Regina, *The counter Reformation in Central Europe*, (Clarendon Press, 2001)
Pursell, Brennan C, *The Winter King: Frederick V of the Palatinate and the Coming of the Thirty Years War.* (Ashgate, 2003)
Ranke Leopold von, *Wallenstein und Seine Zeit*, (Verlag die Heimbu Churei Berlin, 1942)
Teschke Benno, *The Myth of 1648*, (Verro 2003)
Henry Sigfrid Steinberg, *The Thirty Years War, A New interpretation*, (Norton and co 1967)
Volcelka Karl, *Rudolf II und seine Zeit*, (Hermann Bolhaus Nachf, 1985)
Wandruszka Adam, *Reichspatriotismus und Reichpolitik zue Zeit des Prager Friedens von 1635*, (Hermann bolhaus Nache, 1995)
Weatcroft Andrew, *The Habsburg*, (BCA, 1995)
Whaley Joachim, *Germany and the Holy Roman Empire*, (Oxford. 2012)
Wilson Peter H, *The Holy Roman Empire*, (Allen Lane 2009)
Wilson Prof P.H, *Iron and Blood*, (Allen Lane 2022)
Wolf Peter Philipp/von Breyer Carl Wilhelm Freidrich, *Gesichte Maximilian I und Seimer Zeit vol 1–4 1597–1651*, (Nabu Press, 2011)

Spain

Allen, Paul C. *Philip III and the Pax Hispanica, 1598–1621: The Failure of Grand Strategy.* (Yale University 2000)
Allen, Paul C. *The Strategy of Peace: Spanish Foreign Policy and the Pax Hispanica, 1598–1609.* (Ph.D. Yale1995)
Black Christopher, *Early modern Italy*, (Routledge, 2002)
Blanning Tim, The Pursuit of glory Europe 1648–1815, (Penguin 2007)
Brightwell, Peter, Spain and Bohemia: The Decision to Intervene, 1619, (European Studies Review 12 April 1982: 117–41)
Brightwell, Peter, *Spain and the Origins of the Thirty Years War*, (Ph.D, Cambridge, 1967)
Brightwell, Peter *Spain, Bohemia and Europe, 1619–1621*, (European Studies Review 12 October 1982: 371–99) Brightwell, *Peter The Spanish Origins of the Thirty Years War*, (European Studies Review 9,1979: 409–31)
Brightwell, Peter *The Spanish System and the Twelve Years Truce* (*The English Historical Review* 89,1974 270–92) Casey James, *Early modern Spain. A Social History*, (Routledge 1999)
Carter, Charles H, *Belgian 'Autonomy' under the Archdukes, 1598- 1621*, (The Journal of Modern History 36, 1964: 245–59)
Carter, Charles H, Gondomar, *Ambassador to James I*, (The Historical Journal 7, June 1964: 189–208)Carter, Charles H, *The Secret History of the Habsburgs, 1598–1625.* (Columbia, 1964)
Duerloo, Luc, Dynasty and Piety: Archduke Albert (1598–1621) and Habsburg Political Culture in an Age of Religious Wars, (Ashgate, 2012)
Domingues, Mario, *A Revolucao De 1640*, (Edicao Romano Torres, 1970)
Elliott J.H, *Imperial Spain*, (Arnold, 1963)
Elliott J.H, *The Revolt of the Catalans*, (Cambridge University Press, 1963)
Elliott J.H, *Richelieu and Olivarez*, (Cambridge-Canto, 1991)
Elliott J.H, *Spain and its world 1500–1700*, (Yale, 1989)
Elliott J.H. *Review Article: A Question of Reputation? Spanish Foreign Policy in the Seventeenth Century.* (*The Journal of Modern History* 55, 1983): 475–83; reprinted in *Spain and Its World, 1500–1700: Selected Essays.* Yale 1989)
Elliott J.H, Foreign Policy and Domestic Crisis: Spain, 1598–1659, In *Krieg und Politik 1618–1648: Europäische Probleme und Perspektiven.* Edited by K. Repgen. Munich, Germany: R. Oldenbourg Verlag, 1988; reprinted in *Spain and Its World, 1500–1700: Selected Essays.* New Haven: Yale University Press, 1989.
Elliott J.H, *Managing Decline: Olivares and the Grand Strategy of Imperial Spain*, (In *Grand Strategies in War and Peace.* Edited by Paul M. Kennedy. New Haven: Yale University Press, 1991)

Elliott J.H, *Power and Propaganda in the Spain of Philip IV*, (In *Rights of Power: Symbolism, Ritual and Politics since the Middle Ages.*

Elliott J.H, *Richelieu and Olivares.* Cambridge Studies in Early Modern History series. Cambridge: Cambridge University Press, 1984. Elliott J.H, Self-Perception and Decline in Early Seventeenth Century Spain, (*Past and Present* No. 74, 1977): 41–61; reprinted in *Spain and Its World, 1500–1700: Selected Essays.* Princeton, 1989)

Elliott J.H, *The Count-Duke of Olivares: The Statesman in the Age of Decline.* (Yale, 1986)

Elliott J.H, *The Decline of Spain.* (In Crisis in Europe, 1469–1660: Essays from Past and Present. Ed Trevor Henry Aston. Routledge and Kegan Paul, 1965; reprinted Spain and Its World, 1500–1700: Yale 1989)

Elliott J.H, *The Revolt of the Catalans: A Study in the Decline of Spain.* (Cambridge, 1963)

Elliott J.H, *The Spanish Monarchy and the Kingdom of Portugal, 1580- 1640* (In *Conquest and Coalescence: The Shaping of the State in Early Modern Europe.* Edited by Mark Greengrass. London: Edward Arnold, 1991)

Elliott J.H, *The Statecraft of Olivares. In The Diversity of History: Essays in Honour of Sir Herbert Butterfield.* Edited by John Huxtable Elliott and Helmut Georg Koenigsberger. Ithaca: Cornell, 1970.

Feros, Antonio. *Kingship and Favoritism in the Spain of Philip III, 1598–1621.* (Cambridge University Press, 2000)

Goodman David, *Spanish Naval Power 1589–1665*, (Cambridge 1997)

González de León, Fernando. *The Road to Rocroi: Class, Culture and Command in the Spanish Army of Flanders, 1567–1659.* (History in Warfare series. Leiden, The Netherlands: Brill, 2009)

Israel, Jonathan Irvine, *Olivares and the Government of the Spanish Netherlands, 1621–1643,* (In *Empires and Entrepots: The Dutch, the Spanish Monarchy, and the Jews, 1585–1713.* Hambledon Press, 1990)

Israel, Jonathan Irvine, *The Dutch-Spanish War and the Holy Roman Empire (1568- 1648),* (In *Politics, Religion, Law and Society.* Volume I in *1648: War and Peace in Europe.* Ed. Klaus Bussmann and Heinz Schilling. Westfälisches Landesmuseum, 1998)

Kagan Richard, *Clio and the clown: The politics of History in mediaeval and early modern Spain*, (2013)

Kamen Henry, *Spain 1469–1714*, (A society of conflict, Longman, 1983)

Kirk Thomas Allen, *Genoa and the sea: Policy power in an early modern republic 1559–1684.* (John Hopkins, 2012)

Koenigsberger H.G, *Politicians and Virtuosi-essays in modern History*, (Hambledon Press, 1986)

Konstam Angus, *Spanish Galleon*, (Osprey, 2004)

Lynch John, *Spain under the Habsburgs*, (Basil Blackwell 1969)

Lynch John, *Spain 1516–1598: From Modern State to World Empire*, (Wiley-Blackwell, 1994)

Lynch John, *Hispanic world in Crisis and change*, (Wiley-Blackwell, 1994)

Mckay Ruth, *The Limits of Royal authority, Resistance and Obedience in 17th Century Castile*, (Cambridge 1999)

Maltby William, *The Rise and the Fall of the Spanish Empire*, (Palgrave Macmillan, 2009)

Mauro Frederico, *Portugal o Brasil e o atlantico, 1570–1670,* Editorial Estampa vol II 1997

Parker Geoffrey, *Emperor, a New Life of Charles* (V, Yale 2019)

Parker Geoffrey, *the Grand Strategy of Philip II*, (Yale, 1998)

Parry J.H, *The Spanish Seaborne Empire*, (Hutchinson, 1966)

Pendrill Colin, *Spain 1474–1700*, (Heinemann, 2002)

Rawlings Henry, *Church, religion and society in Early Modern Spain*, (Palgrave Macmillan, 2002)

Redworth Glyn, *The Prince and the Infanta*, (Yale 2003)

Lesaffer, Randall, *Defensive Warfare, Prevention and Hegemony: The Justifications for the Franco-Spanish War of 1635.* (Journal of the History of International Law 8, 2006: 91–123, 141–179)

Lynch, John. *The Hispanic World in Crisis and Change 1598–1700.* (Oxford: Blackwell, 1992)

Picouet Pierre, *Les Tercio Espagnols*, (LRT editions 2010)

Wilentz Sean, ed Philadelphia: University of Pennsylvania Press, 1985; reprinted in *Spain and Its World, 1500–1700: Selected Essays,* Yale University, 1989)

Williams, Patrick, *The Great Favourite: The Duke of Lerma and the Court and Government of Philip III of Spain, 1598–1621,* (Manchester, 2007)

Tortella Gabriella and Franscisco Comin, Fiscal and monetary institutions in Spain 1600–1900, ed Michael Condé and Roberto Cortez-Condé, Tranferring wealth and power from the Old World to the New World,(Cambridge)

Sánchez-Marcos, Fernando. "The Struggle for Freedom in Catalonia and Portugal." In *Politics, Religion, Law and Society.* Volume I in *1648: War and Peace in Europe.* (Ed. Klaus Bussmann and Heinz Schilling. Münster/Osnabrück, Germany: Westfälisches Landesmuseum, 1998)

Stradling, Robert A. *Europe and the Decline of Spain: A Study of the Spanish System, 1580–1720.* (George Allen and Unwin, 1981.)

Stradling, Robert A. *Olivares and the Origins of the Franco-Spanish War, 1627- 1635*, (The English Historical Review 101, 1986, 68–94; Spains Struggle for Europe, 1598–1668, Hambledon Press, 1994)

Stradling, Robert A, *Philip IV and the Government of Spain, 1621–1665,* (Cambridge, 1988)

Stradling R.A, *Spain's struggle for Europe 1598–1668*, (Hambledon Press 1994)

Stradling R.A, *The Armada of Flanders*, (Cambridge, 1992)

Vermeir, René. *Power Elites and Royal Government in the Spanish Netherlands during the Last Phase of the Eighty Years War (1621- 1648)*, (In *Religion and Political Change in Europe: Past and Present)*

Vasconcelos, Jose Frazao de, *Os Portugueses no Oriente,* Lisboa Academia Portuguesa MCMXCIII

France

Alan James, *The Navy and Government in Early Modern France*, (Royal History Society, 2004)

Beik William, *Absolutism and Society in Seventeenth Century France in the Languedoc*, (Cambridge 1995)

Beik William, *A Social and Cultural History of Early Modern France*, (Cambridge 2009)

Bertiere Simone, *Condé Le Heros forvoye*, (Edition de Fallois, 2011)

Bertiere Simone, *Mazarin Le Maite du Jeu*, (Editions de Fallois, 2007)

Bergin, Joseph and Laurence Brockliss, ed. *Richelieu and His Age.* (Oxford, England: Clarendon Press, 1992)

Berenger Jean, *Turenne*, (Fayard 1970)

Bonney Richard, *Political Life in France under Richelieu and Mazarin 1564–1661*, (Oxford, 2006)

Bouyer Christian, *Louis XII*, (Tallendier, 2006)

Bonney Richard, *Politics and life in France under Richelieu and Mazarin, 1624–1661* (Oxford, 1978)

Bonney Richard, *The French Civil War, 1649–1653*, (European Studies Review 8 (January 1978): 71–100)

Bonney Richard, *The Paradox of Mazarin,* (History Today 32 (February 1982): 18–24)

Briggs Robin, *Early Modern France*, (Opus, 1998)

Buisseret David, *Sully*, (E&S, 1968)

Bussmann, Klaus and Heinz Schilling, editors. *1648: War and Peace in Europe.* (3 volumes. Münster/Osnabrück, Germany:

Burckhardt Carl J, *Richelieu his Rise to Power*, (George Allen and Unwin Ltd, 1940)

Burckhardt Carl J, *Richelieu and his Age*, (George Allen and Unwin, 1971)

Buisseret, David. *Henry IV.* London: George Allen and Unwin, 1984. Buisseret, David. *Sully and the Growth of Centralized Government in France, 1598- 1610.* (Eyre and Spottiswoode, 1968. 22)

Capefigue, *Richelieu and Mazarin La fronde vol I&II*, (Ulan, 2012)

Carel Pierre, *La Revolte Des Nu-Pieds*, (Edition Ditmar, 2006)
Chevallier Pierre, *Louis XIII*, (Fayard, 1979)
Church William, *Impact of Absolutism in France under Richelieu and Mazarin and Louis XIV*, (Wiley&Sons, 1969)
Church, William Farr. *Richelieu and Reason of State.* (Princeton 1972)
Collins James B., *The State in Early modern France*, (Cambridge)
Comite pour L'Histoire economique et financiere de La France, *De L'Estime au Cadastre en Europe L'époque modern,* (Ministre de L'Economie, 2003)
Cousin Victor, *French Government under Richelieu and Mazarin or the Life and times of mme de Chevreuse*, (Delissier & Proctor, 1895)
Croxton, Derek, *Territorial Imperative? The Military Revolution, Strategy, and Peacemaking in the Thirty Years War*, (War in History 5 (July 1998): 253–79)
Croxton Derek, *The Prosperity of Arms is Never Continual*: Military Intelligence, Surprise, and Diplomacy in 1640s Germany. (The Journal of Military History 64 (October 2000): 981–1004)
Devillon Herve, *Les Rois absolu 1629–1715*, (Belin, 2011)
Deakin, Quentin. *Expansion, War* Hayden, James Michael *and Rebellion: Europe, 1598–1661.* (Cambridge Perspectives in History series. Cambridge: Cambridge University Press, 2000)
Dethan, Georges. *The Young Mazarin.* (Men in Office series. London: Thames and Hudson, 1977)
Duccini Helene, *Guerre et Paix, Abel servien: diplomatie et serviteur de l'etat 1593–1659,* (Champ Vallon 2012)
Elliott J.H, *Richelieu and Olivarez*, (Canto, 1991)
Elliott, J.H. *War and Peace in Europe, 1618–1648.* In *Politics, Religion, Law and Society.* Volume I in *1648: War and Peace in Europe.* (Edited by Klaus Bussmann and Heinz Schilling. Münster/Osnabrück, Germany: Westfälisches Landesmuseum, 1998)
Ekberg, Carl J.Abel Servien, Cardinal Mazarin, and the Formulation of French Foreign Policy, 1653–1659." *The International History Review* 3 (July 1981): 317–29.
Erlanger Philippe, *Richelieu*, (Perin1985)
Faure Marie-Noelle, *La guerre de Trente Ans*, (Ellipses, 2019)
Goldstein Carl, *Print culture in Early Modern France Adan Bosse and the Purposes of Print*, (Cambridge 2012)
Goubert Pierre, *Mazarin*, (Fayard, 1990)
Guth Paul, *Mazarin*, (Flammar 1972)
Hassall, Arthur. *Mazarin.* (Macmillan, 1903; reprint, Nabu Press, 2010)
——, *Continuity in the France of Henry IV and Louis XIII: French Foreign Policy,* 1598–1615. (The Journal of Modern History 45 (March 1973): 1–23).
Hayden, James Michael. *France and the Estates General of 1614.* (Cambridge Studies in Early Modern History series. Cambridge 1974)
Helie Jerome, *Les Relation Internationals dans L'europe modern 1453–1789*, (Armad Colin 2008)
Henri de Campion, Menoires
Hildensheimer Francoise, *La double mort du roi Louis XIII*, (Flammar 2007)
Hildensheimer Francoise, *Richelieu*, (Flammar 2004)
Holt Mack P, *Renaissance and reformation France*, (Oxford, 2002)
Inglis-Jones, J.J, *The Grand Condé: Power Politics in France, Spain, and the Spanish Netherlands, 1652–1659,* (Ph.D, University of Oxford, 1994)
Knecht Robert J, *The French wars of religion*, (Osprey 2002)
Knecht, Robert Jean. *Richelieu.* (Longman, 1991)
Kleinman, Ruth. *Anne of Austria, Queen of France.* (Columbus: Ohio State University Press, 1985.)
Le Roux Nicolas, *Les guerres de religion 1559–1629*, (Belin 2009)
Lee, Stephen J, *French Foreign Policy in the Seventeenth Century*, (Chapter 23 in *Aspects of European History 1494–1789.* Second edition. Abingdon, England: Routledge, 1984)

Livet, Georges, *International Relations and the Role of France, 1648–1660.* (In *The Decline of Spain and the Thirty Years War, 1609–48/59.* Volume 4 in *The New Cambridge Modern History.* Ed. John Phillips Cooper. Cambridge: Cambridge University Press, 1970)

Lodge, Richard. *Richelieu.* (Macmillan, 1896; reprint: BiblioBazaar, 2010)

Lough John, *France Observed in the Seventeenth Century by British Travellers,* (Oriel Press 1985)

Marvick Elizabeth, *Louis XIII, the making of a king,* (Yale, 1986)

Malettke, Klaus. "France's Imperial Policy during the Thirty Years War and the Peace of Westphalia." In *Politics, Religion, Law and Society.* Volume I in *1648: War and Peace in Europe.* Edited by Klaus Bussmann and Heinz Schilling. Münster/Osnabrück, Germany: Westfälisches Landesmuseum, 1998.

Moote, A. Lloyd. *Louis XIII the Just.* (Berkeley and Los Angeles: University of California Press, 1989.) Mousnier, Roland. *The Assassination of Henry IV: The Tyrannicide Problem and the Consolidation of the French Absolute Monarchy in the Early Seventeenth Century.* (London: Faber and Faber, 1973.)

Mironneau Paul, *Henri IV,* (Edition Gisserot, 2005)

Moote Lloyd A, *Louis XIII,* (California 1989)

Montpensier Mme de, memoires,

Nassiet Michel, *La France au XVIIe,* (Belin, 2006)

O'Connell D.P, *Richelieu,* (Weidenfeld and Nicolson, 1968)

O'Brien, Dennis H. Mazarin's Diplomatic Corps, 1648–1661. *North Dakota Quarterly* (Winter 1977): 31–42.

O'Connell, Daniel P. *Richelieu.* Cleveland: World Publishing Co., 1968.

ParkerDavid, *TheMakingofFrenchAbsolutism,* (EdwardArnold,1983)

Parrott, David, A *prince souverain* and the French Crown: Charles de Nevers, 1580–1637. In *Royal and Republican Sovereignty in Early Modern Europe: Essays in Memory of Ragnhild Hatton.* (Edited by Robert Oresko, Graham C. Gibbs, and Hamish M. Scott. Cambridge: Cambridge University Press, 1997.)

Parrott, David, *The Causes of the Franco-Spanish War of 1635–1659.* (In *The Origins of War in Early Modern Europe.* Edited by Jeremy Black. Edinburgh, Scotland: John Donald, 1987)

Parrott, David, *The Mantuan Succession, 1627–1631: A Sovereignty Dispute in Early Modern Europe.* (The English Historical Review 112, February 1997, 20–65)

Petefils Jean-Christian, *Louis XIII,* (Perrin, 2008)

Pitts, Vincent J. *Henri VI of France, His Reign and Age.* (Baltimore, Johns Hopkins University Press, 2008)

Ripert, Pierre, *Richelieu, Mazarin: Le Temps des Cardinaux,* (Privat 2008)

Ranum, Orest, *Richelieu and the Councillors of Louis XIII: A Study of the Secretaries of State and Superintendents of Finance in the Ministry of Richelieu, 1635–1642.* (Clarendon Press, 1963)

Sonnino Paul, *Mazarin's quest,* (Harvard, 2008)

Stuart Carroll, *Blood and violence in early modern France,* (Oxford 2006)

Sturdy David J, *Richelieu and Mazarin,* (Palgrave 2003)

Tapié, Victor Lucien, *France in the Age of Louis XIII and Richelieu.* (Praeger, 1974; reprinted, Cambridge, 1984)

Thion Stephanie, *French armies of the Thirty Years War,* (LRT Edition 2008)

Thion Stephanie, *Rocroi 1643,* (Histoire & Collections 2013)

Treasure Geoffrey, *The crisis of absolutism in France,* (Routledge 2012)

Treasure, Geoffrey, *Cardinal Richelieu and the Development of Absolutism.* (Adam and Charles Black, 1972)

Treasure, Geoffrey, *Mazarin: The Crisis of Absolutism in France.* (London: Routledge, 1995.)

Treasure, Geoffrey, *Richelieu and Mazarin.* (Routledge, 1998)

Weber, Hermann, *Une Bonne Paix': Richelieu's Foreign Policy and the Peace of Christendom,* (In *Richelieu and His Age.* Ed. Joseph Bergin and Laurence W.B Brockliss. Clarendon Press, 1992)

Wedgwood, C. V, *Richelieu and the French Monarchy.* (English Universities Press, 1949)

Weyland, Max. *Turenne: Marshal of France.* London: George G. Harrap, 1930.
Wilkinson Richard, *France and the Cardinals*, (Hodder and Staunton, 1999)
Williams Noel, *A fair conspirator, Marie de Rohan Duchess de Chevreuse*, (Charles Schribner 1913)
Rabutin comte de Bussy, *Memoires*, (Mercure de France)
Rochefoucauld. Comte de, *Memoires*, (Vermillon 1993)
Richelieu, *Testament Politique*, (Perrin 2011)

Polish and East European History
Butterwick, *The Polish Lithuanian Monarchy in the European context c1500–1795*, (Palgrave Macmillan 2001)
Brezezinski Richard, *Polish armies 1596–1696*, (Osprey 1996)
Davies, Brian L. Guliai-Gorod, Wagenburg, and Tabor Tactics in Sixteenth and Seventeenth Century Muscovy and Eastern Europe. In *Warfare in Eastern Europe, 1500–1800. History of Warfare series. Edited by Brian L. Davies. Leiden, The Netherlands:* (Brill, 2012.)
Dukes, Paul, New Perspectives: *Alexander Leslie and the Smolensk War, 1632–1634*, (In *Scotland and the Thirty Years War, 1618–1648.* (History of Warfare series. Ed. Steve Murdoch, Brill, 2001)
Freidrich Karin, *The Other Prussia, Royal Prussia, Poland and Liberty 1569–1772* (Cambridge 2000)
Frost, Robert, *New Beginnings. Chapter 6 in The Northern Wars: War, State, and Society in Northeastern Europe, 1558–1721.* (Longman, 2000) .
Geza David and Pal Fodor *Ottomanns, Hungarians, and Habsburgs in Central Europe. Geza Palffy, The origins of the border Defense system against the Ottoman Empire in Hungary,* (Brill 2000, p. 42)
Ludowsksi Jerzy and Zwadzki Hubert, *A concise history of Poland*, (Palgrave Macmillan 2011)
Murdoch, *The Thirty Years War, the Smolensk War and the Modernization of International Relations in Europe*, (In *Modernizing Muscovy: Reform and Social Change in Seventeenth-Century Muscovy.* (Ed. Jarmo Kotilaine and Marshall Poe. Routledge/Curzon, 2004)
Nozdrin, Oleg, *The Flodorf Project: Russia in the International Mercenary Market in the Early Seventeenth Century*, (In *Warfare in Eastern Europe, 1500–1800.* (History of Warfare series. Edited by Brian L. Davies. Leiden, The Netherlands: Brill, 2012)
Nisbet Bain Robert, *Slavonic Europe; A political history of Poland and Russia 1447–1796*,
Porshnev, Boris Fedorovich. *Muscovy and Sweden in the Thirty Years War, 1630–1635.* (Ed. Paul Dukes. Translated by Brian Pearce. Cambridge: Cambridge University Press, 1995)
Stone Daniel, *The Polish Lithuanian state 1386–1795*, (Univ of Washington 2001)

The Dutch Republic
Boxer, CR, *The Dutch Seaborn Empire*, (Pelican 1988)
Gelderblom, Oscar, *The political economy of the Dutch Republic*, (Ashgat)
Geyl Pieter, *The revolt of the Netherlands 1555–1609*, (Ernest Benn, 1970
Geyl, Pieter *The Netherlands in the Seventeenth Century: Part I, 1609–1648.* (Second Edition, Ernest Benn, 1961) Groenveld, Simon, *The House of Orange and the House of Stuart, 1639-1650: A Revision*, (*The Historical Journal* 34 (December 1991): 955–72)
Israel, Jonathan Irvine, *A Conflict of Empires: Spain and the Netherlands, 1618–1648*, (*Past and Present* No. 76 (August 1977): 34–74
Israel, Jonathan Irvine, *Frederick Henry and the Dutch Political Factions, 1625–1642.* (The English Historical Review 98 (January 1983): 1–27)
Israel, Jonathan Irvine *The Dutch Republic and the Hispanic World, 1606–1661.* (Clarendon Press, 1982)
Jones, James Rees, *The Dutch Navy and National Survival in the Seventeenth Century*, (The International History Review 10 1988: 18–320)
Limm Peter, *The Dutch Revolt*, (Pearson Education 1989)

Nimwegen Olaf van, *The Dutch armies and military Revolutions 1588–1688*, (Boydell Press, 2010)
Parker Geoffrey, *The Dutch Revolt*, (Yale 2000)
Silva da Filipa Roberto, *The Dutch and Portuguese in West Africa, European merchants and the Atlantic system 1580–1674*
Vries Jan de, *The first modern economy 1500–1815*,
Vogel, H.Ph, *Arms Production and Exports in the Dutch Republic, 1600- 1650*, (In *Exercise of Arms: Warfare in the Netherlands (1568–1648).*

Sweden, Denmark and the Baltic
Ahnlund, Nils. *Gustavus Adolphus the Great.* (Translated by Michael Roberts. Princeton: Princeton University Press, 1940; reprinted, New York: History Book Club, 1999)
Bain Nisbet Robert, Scandanavia, *A political history of Denmark, Norway, and Sweden 1513–1900*, (Elibron Classics, 2006)
Bellamy Martin, *Christian IV and his navy: history of the Danish Navy 1596–1648*, (Brill 2006)
Bellamy, Martin, *Christian IV and His Navy: A Political and Administrative History of the Danish Navy, 1596–1648.* (The Northern World series. Leiden, The Netherlands: Brill, 2006)
Buckley Veronica, *Queen of Sweden, 4th estate*, (2004)
Chemix French, *Gustavus Adolphus in Germany and other lectures on the Thirty Years War*, (1997)
Erik, *Muscovy and Sweden in the Thirty Years War 1630–1635*, (Cambridge 2005)
Essen, Michael Friedholm von, *The lion from the North, The Swedish army during the Thirty Years War, vol I 618–32* (Helion and co 2020)
Findesein Jorg-Peter, *Axel Oxenstierna*, (Casimir Katz Verlag, 2007)
Fletcher CRC, *Gustavus Adolphus and the struggle for Protestant existence*, (2005)
Frost Robert I, *The northern wars 1558–1721*, (Longman 2000)
Hein, Jørgen, *The 'Danish War' and Denmark's Further Role in Conflict*, In *Politics, Religion, Law and Society.* Volume I in *1648: War and Peace in Europe.* Edited by Klaus Bussmann and Heinz Schilling. Münster/Osnabrück, Germany: Westfälisches Landesmuseum, 1998.
Jespersen Prof Knud, *History of Denmark*, (Palgrave 2011)
Kent Neal, *A concise History of Sweden, (*Cambridge *2008)*
Kirkby D, *Northern Europe in the early modern period: Baltic world 1492–1772*, (Longman 1990)
Langer, Herbert, *The Royal Swedish War in Germany,* (In Politics, Religion, Law and Society. Volume I in 1648: War and Peace in Europe. Ed Klaus Bussmann and Heinz Schilling, (Westfälisches Landesmuseum, 1998)
Lewis Paul, *Queen of Caprice biography of Kristina of Sweden*, (Holt Reinhart and Winston New York, 1962)
Lisk, *The struggle for supremacy in the Baltic 1600–1725,* (University of London, 1971)
Lockhart Paul Douglas, *Denmark 1513–1660, The Rise and decline of a renaissance monarchy*, (Oxford, 2007)
Lockhart, Paul Douglas, *Denmark and the Empire: A Reassessment of Danish Foreign Policy under King Christian IV.* (Scandinavian Studies 64 (Summer 1992): 390–416)
Lockhart, Paul Douglas, *Denmark, 1513–1660: The Rise and Decline of a Renaissance Monarchy.* (Oxford, 2007) Lockhart, Paul Douglas. *Denmark in the Thirty Years War, 1618–1648: King Christian IV and the Decline of the Oldenburg State.* (Selinsgrove, Pennsylvania: Susquehanna University Press, 1996)
Masson Georgina, *Queen Christina*, (Cardinal, 1974))
Oxenstierna Axel, *Oxenstierna Kansleren correspondence*, (2012)
Ortala, Count, *Life of Lennart Torstenson*, (1855)
Paul Douglas Lockhart, *Sweden in the 17th Century*, (Palgrave 2004)
Petersen Garry Dean, *Warrior Kings of Sweden: the rise of an empire in the sixteenth and seventeenth-century*, (Mcfarland 2007)
John Watts de Peyster, *Life of Leonard Torstensson, Wrangel,* (1st published 1855, Rarebooksclub 2012)

Ringmar, Erik. *Identity, Interest and Action: A Cultural Explanation of Sweden's Intervention in the Thirty Years War.* (Cambridge 1996)
Roberts Michael, *The Swedish imperial Experience 1560–1718*, (Cambridge)
Robert Michael, *Gustavus Adolphus* (2nd ed, Longman, 1992)
Roberts Michael, *Sweden as a Great Power 1611–1697*, (Svenska riksddets protokoll Viii, 329, Arnold 1968)
Roberts, Michael. *Gustavus Adolphus: A History of Sweden, 1611–1632. Vol I&II* (Longmans, Green and Co., 1953–1958)
Roberts, Michael, *Gustavus Adolphus and the Rise of Sweden.* (Longman, 1992)
Roberts, Michael, *Oxenstierna in Germany, 1633–1636*, (Scandia: Tidskrift för Historisk Forskning 48 (1982): 61–105)
Roberts, Michael, *Queen Christina and the General Crisis of the Seventeenth Century, Past and Present,* (No. 22 (July1962): 36–59)
Roberts, Michael, *The Political Objectives of Gustavus Adolphus in Germany, 1630–1632*, (Transactions of the Royal Historical Society, Fifth series 7 (1957): 19–46)
Stiles Andriana, *Sweden and the Baltic 1623–1721*, (Hodder and Stoughton 1992)
Thorkild Kjaegaard/Huhnen David, *The Danish Revolution 1500–1800*, (Cambridge 2006

Turkey and Transylvania

Goodwin Godrey, *the Janissaries,* (Saqui Essentials, p.164)
Goffman Daniel, *the Ottoman Empire and Early modern Europe*, (Cambridge 2002
Buzogany, Dezso, *The Transylvanian Reformation, Studies in the History of Transylvania,* (Atlantic Research and Publications 2011)
Davies Brian, Warfare, State and Society on the Black Sea Steppe, 2007, 1500–1700
Istvan Imreh, *Agrarian bylaws, History of Early modern Transylvania*, (Atlantic Research and Publications 2011)
Fisher Alan, *The Crimean Tatars,* (Hoover Press 1987)
Gábor Agoston, *Ottoman Warfare in Europe 1453~1826*
Gábor Karman & Lovro Kuncevic, *The European Tribute States of the Ottoman Empire in the 16th and 17th centuries* (Brill 2013)
Kiss Gyorgy, *Studies in the history of Early Modern Transylvania, (*East European Monographs 2102)
Kiss Gyorgy, *The Transylvanian Reformation, Studies in the History of Transylvania,* (Atlantic Research and Publications 2011)
Stevens Samuel, *Hungarian Borderlands and the crisis in the Ottoman Empire, 2019*
Szabo, Janos, ed Gábor Karman and Lovro Kuncevic, *The European Tributary states of the Ottoman Empire in the sixteenth and seventeenth centuries,*

Empires and Global Conflict

Ames, Glen, *Renascent Empire, the House of Braganza*, (Amsterdam University Press 2000)
Aldenburgk, Johannes Gegorius, Relação da conquista e perda da cidade do Salvador pelos Holandeses em 1624–1625 *xlvii* Carlos Ziller Camenietzki; Gianriccardo Grassia Pastore Topoi vol.2 no.se Rio de Janeiro 2006, 1625, fire and ink
Bailey W. Diffie and Winius George ed *Foundations of the Portuguese Empire*, (Univ Minnesota, 1977)
Bassett, DK *The Amboina Massacre, 1623*, (Journal of South East Asia, 1960 vol I issue 2)
Bethencourt Curto, *Portuguese Oceanic empire*, (Cambridge 2007)
ed Bethencourt Francis and Diogo Curto, *Portuguese Overseas Empire 1400–1800*, A.J.R Russell-Wood
Blackburn, *The making of New world slavery, from the Baroque to the modern 1492–1800*, (Verso, 1998)
Biggar Nigel, *Colonialism, A Moral Reckoning, William Collins*, 2023
Boxer C.R, *the Portuguese Seaborn Empire*,

Boxer C.R, *The Great Ship from Amacon*, (Instituto cultural de Macau 1988)

Boxer C.R, *The Dutch Seaborne Empire*, (Pelican 1988)

Boxer C.R, *Salvador da Sa and the Struggle for Brazil and Angola*, 1602–1686 (1952)

Boxer C.R, *The Dutch in Brazil* (1957)

Boxer C.R, *European rivalry in the Indian Seas 1600–1700*, (Mariners Mirror vol xiv no 1 Jan 1928 p.13–15)

Boxer C.R, *The Swan song of the Portuguese in Japan 1635–39*, (Transactions of the Japan society, vol xxvii p.4–11)

Boxer C.R *An introduction to Joao riberio's Historical Tragedy of the Island of Ceylon 1685*, (Ceylon historical Journa *Ribeiro and his History of Ceylon 1622–1693*, (Journal of the Royal Asiatic Society parts 1–2 april 1955, p.1–12)

Boxer C.R *The Carriera da India (Ships, me, carges, Voyages)*, (O Centro de Estudis Historicos Ultramarinse as Comemoracoes Henriquinas Lisbon 1961, p.33–82)

Boxer C.R, *The Sailing-Orders for the Manila Galleons of 1635–36*, (Terrae Incognitae, The annals of the Society for the History of discoveries, Amsterdam vol iv, 1972, p.7–17)

Boxer C.R *Opera Minora vol I-III, (Fundacao Oriente*, 2002)

Boxer C.R *Estudios Para a Historia de Macau, seculos XVI a XVIII*, (Fundacao Oriente, 1991)

Borao, Prof Jose Eugenio, *An overview of the Spaniards in Taiwan 1626–1642, (* National University of Taiwan, May 2007)

Borschberg Peter, *Singapore and Malaka straits, Violence, security, and diplomacy in the 17th Century*, (Brill 2010)

Borschberg Peter, *Hugo Grotius, the Portuguese and free trade in the East Indies* (Brill 2011)

Borschberg, Peter, *Maritime intra-Asian trade and the Estado da India, ed Blom Property, Piracy and punishment; Grotius and war booty*, (Brill 2005)

Borshberg, Peter ed, *the Memoirs and memorials of Jacques de Coutre, Security, Trade and society in the 16th and 17th century, Sothcast Asia*, (NUS Press SG, 2014)

Borschberg Peter ed, *Journal Memorials and letters of Cornelis Matelieff de Jonge, Security, diplomacy and commerce in 17th century south east Asia*, (NUS Press SG, 2015)

Bowin H, *Trade in Indian cotton and textiles in the early modern period*, (Routledge 2010 online)

Boyajian James C, *Portuguese trade in Asia under the Habsburgs 1580–1640*, (John Hopkins, 2008)

Brown, Stephen R, *Merchant Kings, When companies ruled the world 1600–1900*, (Douglas Mcintyre, D&M Quebec 2009)

Candido M, *An African slaving port and the Atlantic world: Benguela and its hinterland*, (Cambridge 2013)

Chandler Prof David, *A history of Cambodia*, (Silkworm, 1993)

Chartrand Rene, *The Spanish Main 1492–1800*, (Osprey 2006)

Chaudry Sushil, Michel Morineau, *Merchants, companies, trade, Europe and Asia in the early modern era*, (Cambridge 2007)

Clements, Jonathan, Coxinga, and the fall of the Mings, (The History Press 2005)

Collins following John Hughen van Linshoten 1563–1611 *The travels of Father Sebastian Manrique, Augustian missionary,, Voyage to the East Indies.* (published 1649)

Disney A.R. *A history of Portugal and the Portuguese Empire Vol II*, (Cambridge, 2009)

Donkin, Robin A. *Between east and west, the Moluccas and the traffic in spices until the arrival of Europeans*, (American Philosophical Society 2004)

Ellis D, *The rise of African slavery in the Americas*, (Cambridge)

Floor Willem, *The Persian gulf, a political and economic history of five port cities 1500–1730*, (Mage, 2006)

Fonseca Jose Nicolau da, *Histrorical Archeological Sketch of the City of Goa*, (Ulan Press, 2012)

Foster, Sir William *England's Quest of Eastern Trade.* (A & C. Black 1933)

Frey, James *The India Saltpetre Trade, (*The Historian vol.71)

Garrett Richard, *The defences of Macau*, (Hong Kong Univ, 2010)

Goslier, *Ankor and Cambodia in the 16th Century*, (Orchid press 2006)

Grotius Hugo *De Indis*, (1604)
Hao, Zhidong, *History of Macao*, (Hong Kong University Press 2011)
Israel, Jonathan Irvine *The Dutch Republic and the Hispanic World, 1606–1661.* (Clarendon Press, 1982)
Israel, Jonathan Irvine, *A Conflict of Empires: Spain and the Netherlands, 1618–1648*, (*Past and Present* No. 76 (August 1977): 34–74
Kraan Alfons Van der, *Murder mayhem in seventeenth-century Cambodia*, (Silkworm Books, 2009)
Kraan, Alfons van der, *Anthony van Diemen*, (The journal of the Australian association for Maritime History, vol 26, no2)
Kupperman, Karen Ordahl. *Errand to the Indies: Puritan Colonization from Providence Island through the Western Design.* (*William and Mary Quarterly*,Thirdseries(January1988):70–99)
Heywood Linda, *Central, African atlantic creoles and the founding of the Americas 1585–1660*, (Cambridge 2007)
Holt, John, *Sri Lanka Reader-history, culture and politics*, (Duke 2011)
Lach, D and E.Vakley, *Asia in the making of Europe vol III*, (1993 Univ Chicago)
Latimer Jon, *Buccaneers of the Caribbean*, (W&N, 2009)
Liberman Victor, *Strange Parallels, Southeast Asiain global context c.800–1830*, (Cambridge 2010)
Linshoten, W. Lodwycksz *Der Erste schipvaart der Nederlanders naar Oost-Indie onder cornelis de Hautman*, (Silkworm 1999)
Lorge Peter, *The Asian Military Revolution*, (Cambridge, 2008)
Malekandathil Pius, *The Indian Ocean and the Making of Early modern India.* (Manohar 2016)
Milton Giles, *Nathaniel's Nutmeg*, (Sceptre 2005)
Monteiro, Armando da Silva Saturnino. *The Decline and Fall of Portuguese Seapower, 1583–1663.* (The Journal of Military History 65 (January 2001), 9–20)
Morga Sanchez Garay, Antonio de, *Sucesos de Las Islas Filipina* (1609 Edited and annotated by Emma Helen Blair and James Alexander Robertson, History of the Philippines 1493–1898, Volume IX, 1593–1597, and additional notes by Edward Gaylord Bourne.)
de Narbona y Zuñinga, Eugenio, *Historia de la Recuperación del Brasil hecha por las armas de España y Portugal el año de 1623 Carlos Ziller Camenietzki;* (Gianriccardo Grassia Pastore Topoi vol.2 no.se Rio de Janeiro 2006, 1625, fire and ink: battle of Salvador in accounts of the war)
Newitt Malyn, *The Portuguese in West Africa 1415–1670*, (Cambridge 2010)
Newitt Malyn, *A history of the Portuguese Overseas expansion 1400—1668*, (Routledge 2009)
Neville David, *The Portuguese in the age of discovery, 1300–1580*, (Osprey 2012)
Oliveira e Costa, Joao Paulo, *A route under pressure; communication between Nagasaki and Macao*, (New University of Lisbon 2000)
Osborne Milton, *Phnom Penh, A cultural history* (Signal 2008)
Ortega, Friar Fray Francisco, *Report concerning the Filipinas Islands and other papers 1594*, (letter to Philip I)
Prestage, Edgar. *The Diplomatic Relations of Portugal with France, England, and Holland from 1640 to 1668.* (Watford: Voss and Michael, 1925)
Pedreira, Jorge, *Costs and financial trends in the Portuguese Empire p 1415–1822* (Cambridge 2007)
Pinto, *Paulo Jorge de souse, Portugueses e Malaaios, 1575–1619*, (Lisboa 1997)
Papal Bull, *Translation of Papal Bull Inter Caetera, Alexander VI, 4th May 1493*, (Nativeweb)
Quiroga da San Antonio, *A brief and truthful realtion of events in the kingdoms of Cambodia*, (White Lotus, 1998)
Rahn Phillips, *Carla Six Galleons for the King of Spain*, (John Hopkins 1992)
Reid, *Charting the shape of early modern Asia, silkworm books*, (1999)
Report of WIC *to estates general of Dutch republic 1623, 27th Oct 1623*, (Netherlands national archive states general 5751)
Ribeiro, Joao, Fatalide historica da Iiha de Ceilao, (Boxer 1985)

Ribeiro da Silva Filipa, *Dutch and Portuguese in western Africa 1580–1674*, (Brill, 2011)
Ricklef M.C, *History of Indonesia from 1300*, (Standford 2008)
de Ronquillo Tello, Governor Juan Edited and annotated by Emma Helen Blair and James Alexander Robertson *History of the Philippines*
1493–1898, (Volume IX, 1593–1597, with historical introduction and additional notes by Edward Gaylord Bou)
Roy Tirthanka, *An Economic History of Early Modern India*, (Routledge 2013).
Russell-Wood AJR, *The Portuguese Empire 1415–1808*, (John Hopkins, 1998)
Sánchez-Marcos, Fernando, *The Struggle for Freedom in Catalonia and Portugal, In Politics, Religion, Law and Society.* (Volume I in 1648: War and Peace in Europe). (Ed. Klaus Bussmann and Heinz Schilling. Münster/Osnabrück: Westfälisches Landesmuseum, 1998)
Sansom, *History of Japan 3 vols*, (Folkstone 1978)
Silva de K.M, *A history of Sri Lanka*, (Vijitha Yapa 2005
Subrahahmanyan Sanjay, *The Portuguese Empire in Asia 1500–1700*, (Wiley Blackwell, 2012)
Tarling Nicholas, *The Cambridge history of southeast Asia, vol I part II*, Vol II Part II(Cambridge 1992 and 1999)
Tracy Jones, *The rise of the merchant empires in early modern Asia*, (Cambridge 2012)
ed Tarling, N, Anthony Reid ANU, *Cambridge history of South East Asia*,, (Cambridge 2007)
Waley-Cohen, J. *The Sextants of Beijing*, (Norton 2000)
Ward, Kerry, *Networks of Empire, Forced migration in the Dutch East India Company*, (Cambridge 2009)
Hanna Willard, and Des Alawi, *Turbulent times past in Ternate and Tidore*, (Yasan Warisan Banda Naira 1990)
Hanna Willard, *Indonesia Banda, Colonialism and its aftermath in the nutmeg islands* (date and publisher not given. Available in Banda Neira)
Burma and the Bay of Bengal
Wil.O.Dijk, *17th Century Burma and the Dutch East Indies Company* 1634–1680, (2006 NUS
Suthachai Yumoprasert, *Portugeuse in the Arakan in the sixteenth and seventeenth centuries*, Chilalonykorn University Bangkok, Downloaded W. H. Moreland (Brill.com12/24/2019 (tr. and ed). 1934.)
Peter Floris: *His Voyage to East Indies in the Globe, 1611–1615*, (London: The Hakluyt Society Publications, second serialno.bociv)
Caytano j Socarras, *The Portugeuse in lower Burma: Filipe de Brito de Nicote,* (Lso-Brazilian Review, wint 1966, p.3–24 univ Wisconsin)
Suthachai Yumoprasert, *Portugeuse in the Arakan in the sixteenth and seventeenth centuries*, (Chilalonykorn University Bangkok, Brill.com12/24/2019)
Caytano j Socarras, The Portugeuse in lower Burma: Filipe de Brito de Nicote,(Lso-Brazilian Review, wint1966, p.3–24 univ Wisconsin)
G.E. Harvey, *History of Burma,* (Frank Cass and company 1925, 1613 Feria y Sousa III, p.187)
Wil.O.Dijk, *17th Century Burma and the Dutch East Indies Company* 1634–1680,(2006 NUS)
Deeprashee Dutta, *Portugal in Bengal,* (Jadavpur Uni Kolkata Aug 2019, Tomas Pirez, 'the Suma Orientale of Tome Pirez' 91).
Deeprashee Dutta, *Portugal in Bengal*,(Jadavpur Uni Kolkata Aug 2019, letter of fr Boves to the General of the society of Jesus 1599)
Father Cabral, *A history of the Portugeuse in Asia* (unknown*)*
Suthachai Yimprasert, *The Portuguese in the Arakan in the sixteenth and seventeenth centuries*,(Brill downlaid 24th dec 2019)
Deeprashee Dutta, *Portugal in Bengal, Aug 2019, letter to the Jesuit General from fr Pimenta*, 54 (History of Hooghly Chapt II, Jadavpur Uni Kolkata p. 115)

Religion

Bireley, Robert, *The Jesuits and the Thirty Years War*, Cambridge 2003
Collinson Patrick, *The reformation*, Modern Library Chronicles, 2004

Cameron Euan, *The European Reformation*, (Oxford 1999)
Carbonnier-Burkhard Marianne, *Jean Calvin Une Vie*, (Desclee de Brouwer, 2009)
The counter reformation in central Europe, Oxford 2001
Eulop-Muller, *The Jesuits and the Thirty Years War*, 2006
Elton Geoffrey, *The reformation Europe: 1517–1559*, Wiley Blackwell 1999
Machardy Karin J, *Wars of religion and court patronage in Habsburg Austria, The Social and Cultural Dimensions of Political Interaction, 1521–1622*, (Palgrave 2002)
MacCulloch Diarmaid *The Reformation: A History*
Mullet M, *Calvin*, Routledge 2011
Perrens Francois Tommy, *L'eglise at L'etat en France*, (Megariotis Reprints, 1872)
Portner Regina, *the Counter reformation in central Europe*, Oxford, 2001
MacHardy Karin J, *War, Religion and Court Patronage in Habsburg Austria:*, Palgrave 2002

Literature
Brecht Berthol, *Mother Courage*
Eco Umberto, *The island of the day before*, (Secker and Warburg, 1994)
Endo Shusaku, *Silence*, (Taplinger 1980)
Grimmelhausen John, *Simplicissimus*, (Dedalus, 1999, (1668))
Hermann Loens, *The Warwolf*, (Westholme, 2006, (1910))
Jan Komensky, (Comenius), *To our oppressors*, (Cauly 1995)
Schiller, *Wallenstein*, (DC Heath Boston, 1902)
Schiller, *The robbers and Wallenstein* (Penguin classics 1979)

Selection of source compendiums
Benecke Gerhard, *Germany in the Thirty Years War, documents*, (Arnold 1978)
Barros, de, Joao, *India da decades*
Mazarin, Cousin V, *Des carnets autographes du cardinal Mazarin conservés à la Bibliothèque impériale, dans le Journal des savants, août à décembre 1854, janvier à novembre 1855, janvier et février 1856.* — (A. Chéruel, Les carnets Mazarin pendant la Fronde, dans la Revue historique, IV, mai-août 1877)
Struck Walter, *John Georg, and Oxenstierna, von den tod Gustav Adolp nov 1632 bis zum schluss des Ersten Frankfurtewr konferez herbst 1635. Ein Beitrag zur Gesichte des Driessjahrenkriegs*, (British Library History ed prints 2011)
Motville de, *memoires*, internet
Gardner Samuel Rawlinson, *Letters and other documents illustrating the relations between England and Germany at the commencement of The Thirty Years War [1865]*, (Kessubger Legacy reprint 1865)
Helfferich Tryntje, *The Thirty Years War, discussions*, (Hackett 2009)
Medick Hans and Marschke Benjamin, *Experiencing the Thirty Years War*, (Bedford cultural Editions, 2013)
Munro Robert, *His expeditions with the worthy Scots Regiments called Mac-keys*, (London W. Jones, 1637)
De Marmy Alexandre Charles *Oxenstierna et Richelieu a Compiegne Traite de 1635*, (N de Vier 1878)
Morga Sanchez Garay, Antonio de, *Sucesos de Las Islas Filipina* (1609 Edited and annotated by Emma Helen Blair and James Alexander Robertson History of the Philippines 1493–1898, Volume IX, 1593–1597, and additional notes by Edward Gaylord Bourne.)
Mundy, Peter
Poyntz Sydenham, *A true relation of these German warres 1624–1636. The Thirty Years War memoirs Sydenham Poyntz*, (Ken Trotman Publishing, 2005)
Pires Thomas, *Memoires of his travels is Asia 1513–1515*, (Hakluyt Society 1944)
Richelieu, *Testament Politique*, (Richelieu 1620–1640)

Spence Sir James: *letters from Sir James Spens and Jan Rutgers 2007 (works and corresp.Axel Oxenstierna)* (Royal academy of letters, history, and antiquities 2013)
Turner Sir James, *Memoirs*
Torick Ali Ameer, *Memoirs of Sir Andrew Melville and the wars of the 17th century*, (Trotman 2003)
Wilson Peter H, *The Thirty Years War, a sourcebook*, (Palgrave Mcmillan 2010)
Coonie J, *Spain and the Early Stuarts*, (Palgrave 2010)
Cowans, *Early modern Spain : a documentary History*, (2013)

Italy

Hanlon, Gregory, Early modern Italy (Palgrave MacMillan 2000)
Kleinman, Ruth, *Charles-Emanuel I of Savoy and the Bohemian Election of 1619*, (European Studies Review 5 (January 1975): 3–29)
Mason, Norman David, *The War of Candia, 1645–1669*. (Ph.D. dissertation, Louisiana State University, 1972)
Maine J, *Early modern Italy*, (Oxford)
Oresko, Robert and David Parrott, Reichsitalien and the Thirty Years War, (In *Politics, Religion, Law and Society*. Volume I in *1648: War and Peace in Europe*. Ed. Klaus Bussmann and Heinz Schilling, Westfälisches Landesmuseum, 1998.
Osborne, Toby, Abbot Scaglia, *The Duke of Buckingham and Anglo- Savoyard Relations during the 1620s*, (European History Quarterly 30 (January 2000): 5–32)
Osborne, Toby *Dynasty and Diplomacy in the Court of Savoy: Political Culture and the Thirty Years War*. (Cambridge Studies in Italian History and Culture series. Cambridge: Cambridge University Press, 2002.)
Osborne, Toby, *Van Dyke, Alessandro Scaglia and the Caroline Court: Friendship, Collecting, and Diplomacy in the Early Seventeenth Century*. (The Seventeenth Century 22 (Spring 2007), 24–41)
Roeck, Bernd, *The Role of Venice in the War and during the Peace Negotiations*. (In *Politics, Religion, Law and Society*. Volume I in *1648: War and Peace in Europe*. (Ed. Klaus Bussmann and Heinz Schilling. Westfälisches Landesmuseum, 1998)
Wilson P.H, *War of the Mantuan succession (1628–1631* (Wiley online 13th Nov 2011)

Military-Tactics, armies, strategy

*Sample list of books on war and strategy including classics and important military books from other eras that inform on strategy and tactics in war. Military issues are most universal across through times so any period is relevant to war studies. Other relevant books are listed under countries, eg Roberts, Gustavus in two volumes under Sweden. There are innumerable relevant articles from, papers etc some of whch are refenced in the footnotes of the book.

Afflerbach
Acemoglu & Robinson, *Why nations fail*, (Profile 2013)
Adair John *Cheriton 1944*, (Roundwood, 1973)
Adair John, *Roundhead General*, The Campaigns of Sir William Waller, (Sutton 1997)
Anderson, MS, *War and Society in Europe of the Old Regime 1618–1789*, (Sutton, 1998
Armitage David, *Civil war, A History of Ideas*, (Yale, 2018)
Bagnall, *The Punic War*, (Pimlico 1990)
Beringer, Hattaway, Jones, Still, *Why the south Lost the Civil War*, University of Georgia Press 1986
Black, Jeremy, *Warfare in Europe, 1600–1680* (Chapter 4, The Cambridge Illustrated Atlas of Warfare: Renaissance to Revolution, 1492–1792. Cambridge 1996)
Black Jeremy, *War past present and future*, (Sutton 2000)

Black Jeremy *Rethinking Military Strategy*, (Routledge, 2004)
Black Jeremy, *Military strategy A Global History*, (Yale, 2020)
Blaise de Monluc,ed Peter Young/Ian Roy, *Blaise de Monluc military memoirs, Longman, !971*
Boxer Charles, *The siege of Macau*
Brotton Jerry, *A History of the World in Twelve Maps*, (Allen Lane 2012)
Burn & Young, *The Great Civil War*, (Eyre & Spottiswoode 1959)
Burbank Jane, Cooper Frederick, (Empires in World History, Princeton 2010)
Brezezinski Richard, *The Army of Gustavus Adolphus*, (Osprey 2000)
Brown, Cote, Lynn-Jones. Miller, *Theories of War and Peace*, (The MIT Press 1998)
Bryant Anthony, Sekigahara 1600, (Osprey, 2003)
Brnardic Vladimir, *Imperial Armies of the Thirty Years War, Cavalry*, (2010)
Callwell CE Colonel, *Small Wars*, Greenhill Books, Small Wars, (Greenhill books)
Cooper JP, Cambridge modern history, *Decline of Spain and the Thirty Years War*, (1609–48/59.Cambridge 1970)
Ceasar Julius, *The Gallic Wars and Civil Wars*
Carlton Charles, Going to the War, BCA Routledge, (1992)
Chandler David, *Marlborough as Military commander*, (Spellmount 2003)
Chandler David, *The Art of War in the time of Marlborough*,
Chandler David, *A guide to the Battlefields of Europe*, (1989)
Chandler David, *The Campaigns of Napoleon*, (Weidenfeld & Nicholson 1993)
Chartrand Rene, Donato Spedalier, *The Spanish Main 1492- 1800*, (Osprey 2006)
Clausewitz, von Otto, *On War*
Colley Prof, *The Gun the ship and the Pen*, (Princeton, 2021)
Cowan Roman, *Battle Tactics*, (Osprey, 2007,)
Cunningham and Grell, *The Four Horsemen of the Apocalypse*, (Cambridge 2002)
Cramer Kevin, *The Thirty Years War &Germany Memory in the 19th Century*, (Nebraska University Press, 2007)
Creveld, van, *Supplying war logistics from Wallenstein to Patton*, (Cambridge, 2010),
Debr, Hans, *The Dawn of Modern Warfare*, (Univ Nebraska 1990)
Downing B, *The military revolution and political change*, (Princeton, 1992)
Duccini Helene, *Guerre et Paix Dans La France du Grand Siecle*, (Belin 2011)
Duffy Christopher, *Siege Warfare, 1494–1660*, (Routledge 1979)
Dunthorne, Hugh. *Scots in the Wars of the Low Countries, 1572–1648*.In *Scotland and the Low Countries, 1124–1994*. (Ed. Grant Simpson, Tuckwell Press, 1996)
Drevillon Herve, *Histoire de France*, (Belin 2011)
Embleton Gerry, *Auldearn, Montrose campaign*, (Osprey 2003)
Ericson, Lars, *The Swedish Army and Navy during the Thirty Years War: From a National to a Multinational Force*. In *Politics, Religion, Law and Society*.
Klaus Bussmann and Heinz Schilling. (Münster/Osnabrück, Germany: Westfälisches Landesmuseum, 1998, Volume I in 1648: War and Peace in Europe.)
Evans Martin, *Naseby* 1645, (Osprey, 2007)
Fallon, James, *Scottish Mercenaries in the Service of Denmark and Sweden, 1626–1632* (University of Glasgow, 1972)
Fuller JFC, *The other side of the hill*, (Pan 1970)
Fuller JFC, *Generalship*, (Pentagon Press)
Fuller JFC, *Julius Ceasar*, (Eyre & Spottiswoode 1965)
Fuler JFC, *The Foundation of the Science of War*, (Hutchinson, 2012)
Fuller JFC, *Armament and History*, (Eyre & Spottiswood, 1946)
Fuller JFC, *The Generalship of Ulysses s Grant*, (Da Capo1958)
Fuller JFC *Grant & Lee*, 1933. SPA1992
Fuller JFC *The Generalship of Alexander the Great*, (Eyre & Spottiswood 1958)
Fuller JFC Decisive battles in history,

Franz Gunther, *War and the German People*, Verlag Fischer.1949, Jena, -1st published 1943
Freedman Lawrence, *Strategy, a History*, (Oxford, 2013)
Freedman Lawrence, *Kennedy's Wars*, (Oxford, 2000)
Ferguson Niall, *The war of the World*, (Penguin 2006)
Gaunt Peter, *The English Civil War*, (Blackwell, 2000)
Gaddis John Lewis, *On Grand Strategy*, (Penguin Press 2018)
Gajecky, George and Oleksander Baran, *The Cossacks in the Thirty Years War.* (2 volumes. Analecta OSBM series. Rome, Italy: P.P. Basiliani, 1969–83)
Gat Azar, *The Origins of Military Thought from the Enlightenment to Clausewitz* (1989)
Gat Azar, *Fascist and Liberal Visions of War: Fuller, Liddell Hart, Douhet, and Other Modernists* (1998)
Gat Azar, *The Development of Military Thought: The Nineteenth Century* (1992)
Gat Azar, *War in Human Civilization,* (Oxford 2006)
Gat Azar, *The Causes of War and the Spread of Peace: But Will War Rebound?*
Gat Azar, *Victorious and Vulnerable: Why Democracy Won in the 20th Century and How it is still Imperiled?* (2010)
Gete Jan, *Warfare at Sea 1500–1650*, (Routledge 2002)
Gete Jan, *War and the State in Early modern Europe*, (Routledge, 2002)
Giap. General Ngyen Vo, *Dien Bien Phu*, (Gioi Hanoi 2008)
Goodwin Godfrey, *The Janissaries,* (Saqi essentials, 1994)
Godley, E.C. *The Great Condé: A Life of Louis II de Bourbon, Prince of Condé.* (John Murray, 1915; reprint, Biblio Bazaar, 2011)
Guthrie William P, *Battles of the Thirty Years War*, (Greenwood Press, 2001)
Guthrie William P, *Later battles of the Thirty Years War*, (Greenwood 2003)
Guthrie William P, *Naval actions of the Thirty Years War*, (Mariners Mirror 87)
Griffith Paddy, *Battle Tactics of the Civil War*, (Yale 1989)
Groot, Bouko de. *Nieuwpoort*, (Osprey, 2019)
Grant, Ulysses s General, *The Memoires of Ulysses S Grant* (Da capo 1958)
Green Peter, *Greco-Persian Wars*, (University of California Press, 1998)
Grosjean, Alexia, *An Unofficial Alliance: Scotland and Sweden, 1569–1654.* (The Northern World series. Leiden, The Netherlands: Brill, 2003.)
Haldon John, *The Byzantine Wars*, (Tempus 2001)
Hanlon, Gregory, *The Twilight of a Military Tradition: Italian Aristocrats and European Conflicts, 1560–1800.* (New York: Holmes and Meier, 1998)
Hastings Max, *Armageddon*, (McMillan 2004)
Haude, Sigrun, *Coping with Life during the Thirty Years War, (1618–1648),* (Brill, 2021)
Helfferich Tryntje, *The Thirty Years War*, (Hakkett 2009)
Healey Mark, *Cannae 216 BC*, (Osprey 1994)
Hoeven, Marco van der, editor. *Exercise of Arms: Warfare in the Netherlands (1568–1648).* (History of Warfare series. Leiden, The Netherlands: Brill, 1997)
Holt Mack, *The French Wars of Religion, 1562–1629*, (Cambridge 2005)
Howard Michael Prof, *The Franco Prussian War,* (Rupert Hart Davis 1961)
Howard Michael Prof, *War in European History*, (Oxford 2009)
Hunt, Tristram, *The English civil War*, (Weidenfeld & Nicholson, 2002)
James, Alan, *The Navy and Government in Early Modern France, 1572–1661.* (Royal Historical Society Studies in History series. Woodbridge, England: Boydell Press, 2004)
Jomini Antoine Baron de, *The Art of War*, (Greenhill 1992)
Jones, James Rees, *The Dutch Navy and National Survival in the Seventeenth Century*. (The International History Review 10 (February 1988): 18–32)
Kagan Donald, *The Pelopennesian War*, (Harper Collins 2003)
Kaiser Wolfgang, *L'Europe en Conflict, Presses*, (Universites de Rennes, 2008)
Keegan John, *Warfare in the Seventeenth Century*, (John Childs, 2001)

Keegan John, *The face of battle*, Jonathan (Cape, 1976)
Keegan John *A History of Warfare*, (Hutchinson, Random House, 1993)
Kissinger Henry, *World Order*, (Penguin 2014)
Kissinger Henry, *Diplomacy*, (1994)
Konstam Angus, *Lepanto 1571,* (2009)
Lawrence, Co, *The Seven Pillars of Wisdom*
Liddel-Hart Basil, *strategy,* Meridian 1991
Lliddell Hart Basil, *Strategy of the Indirect approach*, (Faber and Faber)
Lliddell Hart Basil, *Julius Ceasar*,
Lliddel-Hart Basil, *The Sword and the Pen,* 1998 Book (Club Associates, 1998)
Lliddel-Hart Basil, *History of the First world War/History of the Second world War*,
Lockyer Roger, (Buckingham, Longman 1991)
Long Graham, *English army and recruitment in the Thirty Years War,* (Cambridge PHD)
Lorge Peter, *The Asian military Revolution*, (Cambridge, 2008)
Lynn John A II, *The Thirty Years War*,
Lynn John A II, *Women, Armies, and Warfare in Early modern Europe,* (Cambridge 2008)
Machiavelli, *The Art of War,*
McNeil William, *Pursuit of Power*, Chicago, University of Chicago, 1982
Mahan, Alfred Thayer Admiral, *The Influence of Sea Power Upon History, 1660–1783* (1890)
Marley David, *Wars of the Americas*, (ABC:CLIO, 2008)
Marshall Tim, *Prisoners of Geography*, (Elliott& Thompson, 2015)
Marshal Tim, The Power of Geogaphy, (Elliot and Thompson 2021)
Michalski Milena & Gow James, *War, Image, and Legitimacy*, (Routledge 2007)
Monro, Robert, *Monro: His Expedition with the Worthy Scots Regiment Called Mac-Keys.* (Ed. William S. Brockington. Praeger, 1999. Orig. 1637)
Monteiro, Armando da Silva Saturnino, The Decline and Fall of Portuguese Seapower, 1583–1663.(The Journal of Military History 65 January 2001): 9–20
Mortimer Geoff, *War by Contract, Credit and Contribution: The Thirty Years War.*" In *Early Modern Military History, 1450–1815.* Edited by
Mortimer Geoff, *Eyewitness Accounts of the Thirty Years War 1618–48*,(Palgrave 2002,)
Murdoch, Steve, editor. *Scotland and the Thirty Years War, 1618–1648.* History of Warfare series. Brill, 2001. Moore-Coyler R.J *Horse supply for the British army.* (Journal of Historical Research)
Mortimer Geoff, Eyewitness accounts of the Thirty Years War, Palgrave Macmillan 2004
Nimwegen Olaf van, *The Dutch armies and military Revolutions 1588–1688*, (Boydell Press, 2010)
Noailles Amblard Narue Raymond, *Bernard de Saxe-Weimar, 1604–1639,* (Perrin 1908, and Kessinger reprint)
Notario Lopez, *Ignacio &Ivan*, The Spanish Tercios, 1536–1704
O'Dowd Edward, *Chinese Military Strategy*, (Routledge 2009)
Oman Sir Charles, *A History of the Art of War in the Middle Ages, Vol. II: A.D. 1278–1485* (1898; 2nd ed. 1924)
Oman Sir Charles, *A History of the Art of War in the Sixteenth Century* (1937)
Palmer Gregory, *The McNamara Strategy and the Vietnam War,* (Greenwood, 1978)
Parker Geoffrey, *the Military revolution,* (Cambridge 1996)
Parker, Geoffrey, *The Army of Flanders*, (Cambridge)
Parker Geoffrey, *The Military Revolution*, (Cambridge 1990)
Parrott David, *Richelieu's Army*, (Cambridge, 2006)
Parrott David, *the Business of War,* (Cambridge 2012)
Philips Rahn Carla, *Six galleons for the King*, (John Hopkins, 1986)
Ralston David, *Importing the European army*, (Chicago, 1996, 1990)
Reid Stuart *The Campaigns of Montrose*, (Mercat 1990)

Roberts, Keith, *Cromwell's War Machine*, (Pen & Sword, 2009)
Roberts Michael, *The Military Revolution, 1560–1660*: (An Inaugural Lecture Delivered Before the Queen's University of Belfast, 1956)
Spencer Charles, *Prince Rupert*, (Weidenfeld & Nicholson 2007)
Rohan, duc de, *Le Parfait Capitaine*, (1631)
Roux Nicholas, *Les Guerre de Religion, 1559–1629*, (Belin, 2009)
Sherman William Tecunseh General, *Memoirs of General Sherman*, (Library of America, 1990)
Sabin, Wees, Whitby, *Greek and Roman Warfare*, (Cambridge, 2007)
Slim General, *Defeat into victory*
Sun Tzu, *The Art of War*
Sronek & Hausenblasova, *Gloria & Miseria, Prague during the Thirty Years War*, (Gallery 1998)
Stone Norman, *A short History of WWI*, (2007)
Strachan Hew, *How the fighting end:A History of surrender,* (Oxford 2012)
Sweetman, John, *Tannenberg, 1914*, (Cassel 2002)
Roberts Keith, *Pike and Shot Tactics*, (Osprey 2010)
Robinson Charles M III, *The Spanish Invasion of Mexico*, (1519–1521, (Osprey 2004)
Simms Brendan, *Europe, The Struggle for Supremacy, 1453-present*, (Allen Lane 2013)
Spring Laurence, *The Battle of the White Mountain 1620*, (Helion 2018)
Stradling R.A, *Prelude to disaster, Precipitation of the War of the Mantuan succession*, (History Journal 1990, vol 33, issue 4)
Stradling RA, *The Armarda of Flanders*, (Cambridge 1992)
Taite& Bertrand, *War, Identities in conflict, ed*, (Sutton 1998)
Tenenti Alberto, *Piracy & The Decline of Venice 1580–1615,* (Longman 1967)
Tibble Dr Stephen, *Crusader Strategy*, (Yale 2020)
Tibble Dr Stephen, *Crusader Armies*, (Yale, 2010)
Thion Stephane, *French Armies of the Thirty Years War* (Turenne LRT edition 2008)
Thion Stephane, *Rocroi 1643*, (Histoire and collections 2103)
Thion Stephanie *Rocroi*, *Histoire and collections,* (LRT)
Trotsky Leo, *History of the Russian Revolution*
Thucydides, *The Peloponnesian War*
Walter and Snyder, *Civil wars, Insecurity and Intervention*, (Colòmbia, 1999)
Wanklyn & Jones, *A Military History of the English civil war*, (Pearson 2005)
Wenham, Peter, *The Great Siege of York*, (Roundwood, 1970)
Wijn, Jan Willem, *Military Forces and Warfare, 1610–1648,* (In *The Decline of Spain and the Thirty Years War, 1609–48/59*. Volume 4 in *The New Cambridge Modern History*. Ed John Phillips Cooper. (Cambridge: Cambridge University Press, 1970.)
Wilson Peter Prof, Lützen, *Oxford*, 2018
Wilson Peter Prof, *Blood and Iron,* (2022)
Wilson Peter Prof, Europe's Tragedy, *history of the Thirty Years War*, (2010
Young Brigadier Peter, *Naseby*, Century 1985
Young Brigadier Peter, *Cavalier army*, Allen & Unwin 1974
Young Brigadier Peter, *Marston Moor*, Roundwood, 1970
Young Brigadier Peter, *Edgehill*, Roundwood 1977
Young, Brigadier Peter, *Copredy Bridge*, Roundwood, 1970

Index